THE TRANSLATIONS AND ADAPTATIONS OF LADY GREGORY AND HER COLLABORATIONS WITH DOUGLAS HYDE AND W. B. YEATS BEING THE FOURTH VOLUME OF THE COLLECTED PLAYS

edited and with a foreword by
Ann Saddlemyer

COLIN SMYTHE
GERRARDS CROSS
1979

Copyright © 1971 The Lady Gregory Estate
Foreword Copyright © 1971 Colin Smythe Ltd.

First published in one volume on 1 March 1971
by Colin Smythe Ltd, Gerrards Cross, Buckinghamshire
as the eighth volume of the Coole Edition
ISBN 0–900675–32–2

First published in paperback format in 1979

British Library Cataloguing in Publication Data

Gregory, Isabella Augusta, *Lady*
    The collected plays
    4: The translations and adaptations of
    Lady Gregory and her collaborations with
    Douglas Hyde and W. B. Yeats – Coole ed.
    I. Title   II. Saddlemyer, Ann
    822′.9′12   PR4728.G5A19

    ISBN 0–86140–019–4

Printed in Great Britain

ACKNOWLEDGEMENTS

Teja is reproduced in this volume by permission of the heirs of the Estate of Hermann Sudermann. All enquiries regarding performance to The International Copyright Bureau Ltd., 26 Charing Cross Road, London, W.C.2.

The Poorhouse is reproduced by permission of the Dr. Douglas Hyde Trust.

The Unicorn from the Stars is reproduced by kind permission of Michael Yeats, Miss Anne Yeats and Macmillan & Co. Ltd.

Heads or Harps is reproduced by kind permission of Mr. Michael Yeats and Miss Anne Yeats.

ACKNOWLEDGEMENT

Acknowledgement is made to The Henry W. and Albert A. Berg Collection of The New York Library, Astor, Lenox and Tilden Foundations, for its kind permission to reproduce Lady Gregory's translation of Sudermann's *Teja*, and *Heads or Harps* by W. B. Yeats and Lady Gregory, as it holds the only surviving manuscripts of these plays.

FOREWORD

*"I did feel proud and satisfied—a Theatre of our own, Irish plays,
such a fine one by our countryman—company playing it so splen-
didly, all our own—something to have lived to see!"*

(*Lady Gregory's Journals*, 12 May 1927)

"I sometimes think my life has been a series of enthusiasms,"
Lady Gregory once commented in her diary. Certainly the most
lasting and satisfying enthusiasm was her care for the theatre
which was for her the most important single vehicle in bringing
back to Ireland its ancient dignity. For close to thirty years Lady
Gregory was the conscience of the Abbey Theatre, chastising and
prodding when necessary, encouraging and supporting at all times.
She began as a fund-raiser (a position never abandoned in those
early pre-subsidy years), soon become a collaborator and adviser,
then a practising dramatist, and finally resident translator; she
directed, designed costumes and scenery, taught playwriting, and
on one memorable occasion acted the role of Kathleen ni Houlihan.
Despite her genuine concern for Yeats's verse plays, it is evident
from her own notes and memoirs that the activity which gave her
greatest satisfaction was the challenging one of providing plays for
actors and audience. "One has to go on with experiment or interest
in creation fades, at least so it is with me", she rationalizes in her
chapter on play-writing, and many years later adds in her journals:
"the balance of weight, the minute calculating of it in advance, (as
they say, the dome of St. Paul's was built on a sheet of paper,) comes
into the building of a play, as does 'music'—the balanced delight of
sentences—of words."
  She never really considered translations to be "creative work";
instead, as she explains in *Our Irish Theatre*, they were simply part
of her responsibility to the Abbey:
  "We wanted to put on some of Molière's plays. They seemed
akin to our own. But when one translation after another was tried,
it did not seem to carry, to 'go across the footlights.' So I tried putting one into our own Kiltartan dialect, *The Doctor in Spite of
Himself*, and it went very well. I went on, therefore, and translated
Scapin and *The Miser*. Our players give them with great spirit;

vii

the chief parts—Scapin, Harpagon, and Frosine—could hardly be bettered in any theatre. I confess their genius does not suit so well the sentimental and artificial young lovers."

Seventeen years later one of the players (Barry Fitzgerald, whose first big part had been as the sleepy King in *The Dragon*), returned from a visit to Paris and suggested she put *Le Bourgeois Gentilhomme* into English for the Abbey. Once more she set to work, producing a working script of *The Would-Be Gentleman* within several months.

She also translated Sudermann's *Teja* (published here for the first time), Goldoni's *Mirandolina*, had a hand in Maeterlinck's *Interior* (probably with Synge), and was in her last years, at Yeats's suggestion, contemplating a Kiltartan Theocritus for the Cuala Press. But her chief work of this kind, and to many her most successful, was the introduction of Molière to the Abbey audiences. This is not surprising when one considers the strengths in her own comedies; Bernard Shaw once remarked, "she writes about the Irish as Molière wrote about the French, having a talent curiously like Molière."[1] Certainly she too had a natural gift for writing dialogue (as Shaw has elsewhere commented), and the sharp contrapuntal exchange of speeches, the quick series of successive encounters between different pairs of characters, the choric commentaries of her minor characters, are all familiar devices in the comedy of character and manners. So also her approach to the follies and tricks of mankind bears a close resemblance to the seventeenth century French master's; Hyacinth Halvey's predicament when he builds his own "character" and the effect of greed on young Simon and Damer are not restricted to the post office square of Cloon. Her natural delight in songs, fantastic but simple costumes, and choreographic staging blended well with the original spirit of the plays; when the Abbey company produced their Kiltartan Molière, they scrupulously followed the stage business of the Comédie Française prompt-scripts.

"Don Quixote cannot be put on the stage: its action cannot be represented there," Bernard Shaw warned her. But she had long wished to re-tell Cervante's story of the greatest dreamer of all time; perhaps because in the narrative of the romantic idealist and his follower she recognized also the dual nature of her own "fool-driven" land. "They see in us one part boastful quarrelsome adventurer, one part vulgar rollicking buffoon," she wrote of England's false half-vision of Ireland. "Poetry and pathos may be granted to us, but when we claim dignity, those who see only the sham fights

viii

of Westminster shake their heads. But here, in real Ireland, dignity can live side by side with the strongest political feeling."[2] There is an additional irony in the decision to face at last the challenge of her favourite narrative, for here we have not only the prototype to cranky Conan of *Aristotle's Bellows* ("Yes, tyrants and enchanters. If they are not among us yet, where does all the oppression come from and all the misery?") but the greatest most tenacious Image-maker of them all ("The business is that without seeing, you believe and confess, affirm and maintain it!") And so, alongside the morality play *Dave, Sancho's Master* is re-born; these two last plays are a fitting benediction of both the folk and the unknown dream. The final messages are for her nation as well as for her art: "Freedom is best. It is one of the biggest gifts heaven has bestowed upon men. The treasures that the earth encloses or the sea covers are not to be compared with it. Life may and ought to be risked for liberty as well as for honour."

Yeats wrote to Synge in 1906 from Coole concerning the staging of his own play:

"The great difficulty is that it is impossible to have *Deirdre* so late in the month, as Robert Gregory who is doing the scenery must be there to supervise it and he can't at that time of the year, furthermore Lady Gregory has helped me very much with the scenario and it is necessary to have the play performed at a season when she can see it."[3]

To the writers, actors and designers of the Abbey Theatre, all art was indeed a collaboration, and nowhere does one see the benefit of this more clearly than in Lady Gregory's own contributions. She had of course begun as a contributor, diffidently providing scenarios for Douglas Hyde's little folk plays, *The Nativity* (with Yeats), *The Marriage* and *The Poorhouse*. As always, she wrote out of her own experience: "As to *The Poorhouse*, the idea came from a visit to Gort Workhouse one day when I heard that the wife of an old man, who had been long there, maimed by something, a knife I think, that she had thrown at him in a quarrel, had herself now been brought into the hospital. I wondered how they would meet, as enemies or as friends, and I thought it likely they would be glad to end their days together for old sake's sake." When Douglas Hyde wrote the play, he departed very little from that first scenario as she quotes it in *Our Irish Theatre*. Later, too, she was to give help to—and receive it from—her two fellow directors, and provide untold advice to aspiring younger dramatists.

But the most significant collaboration occurred with her closest friend, W. B. Yeats. Apart from her own comments in *Our Irish Theatre* and Yeats's open acknowledgment in the frequent editions of his plays during his lifetime, we are provided with very little help in determining the extent of that co-operation. Some letters exist, and many memoirs speculate, including Oliver St. John Gogarty's malicious claim that Yeats wrote all her plays, but "did not want the comic to interfere with his fame as an outstanding poet."[4] However, if we take Yeats's word alone it is clear that very few of his plays were written without her advice and actual contribution, beginning with *Cathleen ni Houlihan*. ("We turned my dream into a little play . . ."[5]) and ending in 1928 with his translation of *King Oedipus* ("Lady Gregory went through it all, altering every sentence . . .").

Her greatest contribution seems to have been in dialogue, and she first helped him with *The Stories of Red Hanrahan* before moving on to the plays.[6] "I have sometimes asked her help because I could not write dialect", he writes in his preface to *Plays in Prose and Verse* (1922), "and sometimes because my construction had fallen into confusion." In his notes to *The Pot of Broth* in the same volume he goes on, "I hardly know how much of the play is my work, for Lady Gregory helped me as she has helped in every play of mine where there is dialect, and sometimes where there is not. In those first years of the theatre we all helped one another with plots, ideas, and dialogue, but certainly I was the most indebted as I had no mastery of speech that purported to be of real life. This play may be more Lady Gregory's than mine, for I remember once urging her to include it in her own work, and her refusing to do so." [7] Of the ten plays in that volume, he is indebted to her for help with eight: *Cathleen ni Houlihan, The Pot of Broth, The Hour-Glass, The King's Threshold, On Baile's Strand,* acting version of *The Shadowy Waters, Deirdre, The Unicorn from the Stars.*[8] The strange story of *Diarmuid and Grania*, which involved not only Yeats and George Moore but at least Lady Gregory and possibly both Edward Martyn and George Russell by the time it was completed, provokes further entertaining speculation on the extent of early collaboration.

The situation with *Where There is Nothing* and *The Unicorn from the Stars*, however, is somewhat special. The original version, as Yeats explains in his preface, was written in great haste by Yeats, Lady Gregory and Douglas Hyde to save the plot from their one-time colleague, George Moore; it appeared as a supplement to the *United Irishman*, November 1, 1902, with little to recommend it but the Irishman's joy of a good battle well fought. "I knew that my first version was hurried and oratorical," Yeats confesses, "with events cast into the plot because they seemed lively or amusing in themselves, and not because they grew out of the characters and the plot." The American editions contained a dedication to Lady Gregory beginning, "I offer you a book which is in part your own," which she proudly reproduced in *Our Irish Theatre*; but the play was not a success. Out of that rash early endeavour, however, came *The Unicorn from the Stars* five years later. Again collaboration was so close that neither could with any certainty isolate his contribution, but this time Lady Gregory agreed to sign her name to the work; it is only since Yeats's own death that the publishers have neglected to acknowledge the weight of Lady Gregory's share in this strange, fantastic play that reflects so completely the power of their lifelong collaboration. And at the Abbey Theatre production, first-nighter Joseph Holloway complained, "Yeats and Gregory are too violent when taken in one draught, however palatable either may be when taken neat."[9]

It is tempting to speculate on the circumstances surrounding *Heads or Harps*, the only example we have of joint political satire. Two typescript drafts exist, and in a note on the longer one Lady Gregory has written, "WBY and I made up this—but never put it on. It was chiefly his." But neither draft is dated and, wisely, the two friends refrained from further dramatic chastisement of their enemies. That role remained the poet's own.

When Yeats was awarded the Nobel Prize Lady Gregory wrote in her diary, "I am proud and glad of this triumph for I believed in him always and was glad he 'never made a poorer song that he might have a heavier purse'. In these twenty-six years our friendship has never been broken." Yeats in his turn has paid a graceful tribute not only to her but to the spirit she did so much to foster: "What I have done is but a form and colour in an elaborate composion, where they [my fellow-workers] have painted the other forms and colours. The extravagance, the joyous irony, the far-flying phantasy, the aristocratic gaiety, the resounding and rushing words of the comedy of the countryside, of the folk as we say, is akin to the elevation of poetry, which can but shrink even to the world's edge from the harsh, cunning, traditionless humour of the towns. I write of the tragic stories told over the fire by people who are in the comedies of my friends, and I never see my work played with theirs that I do not feel that my tragedy heightens their comedy and tragicomedy, and grows itself more moving and intelligible from being mixed into the circumstance of the world by the circumstantial art of comedy. Nor is it only the stories and the country mind that have made us one school, for we have talked over one another's work so many times, that when a play of mine comes into my memory I cannot always tell how much even of the radical structure I may not owe to the writer of 'The Lost Saint', or of 'The Shadow of the Glen', or more than all, to the writer of 'Hyacinth Halvey'; or that I would have written at all in so heady a mood if I did not know that one or the other were at hand to throw a bushel of laughter into the common basket." [10]

The history of the Abbey Theatre rightly serves as a record of the strength and direction of that friendship. And, despite the blurring with time of the acknowledgement of that bond and the emphasis inevitably placed on the great genius of her two colleagues, the significance of Lady Gregory's contribution to Ireland's dramatic movement cannot, and should not be ignored.

Ann Saddlemyer

[1] In an "interview" for the New York *Evening Sun* written by Shaw himself, quoted in an Appendix to *Our Irish Theatre*.

[2] "Ireland, Real and Ideal," *Nineteenth Century*, November 1898, pp. 769–82.

[3] Letter dated 3 October 1906 in the possession of Trinity College Dublin by whose permission and that of Michael Yeats it is here reproduced.

[4] *It Isn't This Time of Year at All* (London: McGibbon and Kee, 1954), p. 216.

[5] See *Joseph Holloway's Abbey Theatre*, ed. Robert Hogan and Michael J. O'Neill (Carbondale: Southern Illinois University Press, 1967), p. 278n2.

[6] See Note to *Early Poems and Stories* (London: Macmillan, 1925), p. 528.

[7] *Plays in Prose and Verse* (London: Macmillan, 1922), Preface and p. 421. See also his Preface to *The Collected Plays of W. B. Yeats* (London: Macmillan, 1934).

[8] A letter written to Lady Gregory, 14 January 1905, in the possession of the Yeats estate reads, "I cannot do the new 'Baile Strand' without your help with the opening conversation"; see also *Letters on Poetry from W. B. Yeats to Dorothy Wellesley* (London: Oxford University Press, 1964), p. 46: "Lady Gregory wrote the end of my 'Deirdre' on my fundamental mass".

[9] *Joseph Holloway's Abbey Theatre*, p. 96.

[10] Preface to *Poems 1899–1905* (Dublin: Maunsel, 1906).

THE PLAYS OF LADY GREGORY
HISTORY OF FIRST PRODUCTIONS BY THE ABBEY
THEATRE COMPANY AND PUBLICATION DATES

Colman and Guaire [1901]. Not produced. Published under title *My First Play* (London: Elkin Mathews and Marrot, 1930).

A Losing Game. Not produced. Published only in *The Gael* (New York), December 1902.

Twenty-Five [*A Losing Game* revised]. Produced 14 March 1903. Never published.

The Poorhouse (with Douglas Hyde). Produced 3 April 1907. Published in *Samhain*, September 1903; with *Spreading the News* and *The Rising of the Moon* as Vol. IX of Abbey Theatre Series (First Series) (Dublin: Maunsel, 1906).

The Rising of the Moon. Produced 9 March 1907. Published in *Samhain*, December 1904; with *Spreading the News* and *The Poorhouse* as Vol. IX of Abbey Theatre Series (First Series) (Dublin: Maunsel, 1906); and included in *Seven Short Plays* (Dublin: Maunsel, 1909).

Spreading the News. Produced 27 December 1904. Published in *Samhain*, November 1905; with *The Rising of the Moon* and *The Poorhouse* as Vol. IX of Abbey Theatre Series (First Series) (Dublin: Maunsel, 1906); and included in *Seven Short Plays* (Dublin: Maunsel, 1909).

Kincora. First version produced 25 March 1905; revised version 11 February 1909. Published as Vol. II of Abbey Theatre Series (First Series) (Dublin: The Abbey Theatre, 1905); revised form in *Irish Folk-History Plays First Series* (New York and London: Putnam, 1912).

The White Cockade. Produced 9 December 1905. Published as Vol. VIII of Abbey Theatre Series (First Series) (Dublin:

xiii

Maunsel, 1906); included in *Irish Folk-History Plays Second Series* New York and London (Putnam, 1912).

Hyacinth Halvey. Produced 19 February 1906. Published in *Samhain*, December 1906; and included in *Seven Short Plays* (Dublin: Maunsel, 1909).

The Doctor in Spite of Himself (from Molière). Produced 16 April 1906. Published in *The Kiltartan Molière* (Dublin: Maunsel, 1910).

The Gaol Gate. Produced 20 October 1906. Published in *Seven Short Plays* (Dublin: Maunsel, 1909).

The Canavans. Produced 8 December 1906; revised version produced 31 October 1907. Published in *Irish Folk-History Plays Second Series* (New York and London: Putnam, 1912).

The Jackdaw. Produced 23 February 1907. Published in *Seven Short Plays* (Dublin: Maunsel, 1909).

Dervorgilla. Produced 31 October 1907. Published in *Samhain*, November 1908; included in *Irish Folk-History Plays First Series* (New York and London: Putnam, 1912).

The Unicorn from the Stars (with W. B. Yeats [a re-working of *Where There is Nothing* written by Yeats in 1912 with the help of Lady Gregory and Douglas Hyde]. Produced 21 November 1907. Published in *The Unicorn from the Stars and Other Plays* (New York: Macmillan, 1908) and included in the Third Volume of *The Collected Works of William Butler Yeats* (Stratford-on-Avon: Shakespeare Head Press, 1908).

Teja (from Sudermann). Produced 19 March 1908. Never published.

The Rogueries of Scapin (from Molière). Produced 4 April 1908. Published in *The Kiltartan Molière* (Dublin: Maunsel, 1910).

The Workhouse Ward [*The Poorhouse* revised]. Produced 20 April 1908. Published in *Seven Short Plays* (Dublin: Maunsel, 1909).

The Travelling Man. Produced 2 March 1910. Published in *Seven Short Plays* (Dublin: Maunsel, 1909).

The Miser (from Molière). Produced 21 January 1909. Published in *The Kiltartan Molière* (Dublin: Maunsel, 1910).

The Image. Produced 11 November 1909. Published as Vol. I of Abbey Theatre Series (Second Series) Dublin: Maunsel, 1910).

Mirandolina (from Goldoni). Produced 24 February 1910. Published separately (London and New York: Putnam, 1924).

The Full Moon. Produced 10 November 1910. Published by the Author at the Abbey Theatre, 1911; included in *New Comedies* (New York and London: Putnam, 1913).

Coats. Produced 1 December 1910. Published in *New Comedies* (New York and London: Putnam, 1913).

The Deliverer. Produced 12 January 1911. Published in *Irish Folk-History Plays Second Series* (New York and London: Putnam, 1912).

Grania. Not produced. Published in *Irish Folk-History Plays First Series* (New York and London: Putnam, 1912).

McDonough's Wife. Produced 11 January 1912. Published in *New Comedies* (New York and London: Putnam, 1913).

The Bogie Men. Produced 4 July 1912 at the Court Theatre, London. Published in *New Comedies* (New York and London: Putnam, 1913). Later revised.

Damer's Gold. Produced 21 November 1912. Published in *New Comedies* (New York and London: Putnam, 1913).

The Wrens. Produced 1 June 1914 at the Court Theatre, London. Published in *The Image and Other Plays* (London: Putnam, 1922).

Shanwalla. Produced 8 April 1915. Published in *The Image and Other Plays* (London: Putnam, 1922). Later revised.

The Golden Apple. Produced 6 January 1920. Published separately (London: John Murray, 1916).

The Dragon. Produced 21 April 1919. Published separately (Dublin: Talbot Press, 1920); included in *Three Wonder Plays* (London: Putnam: 1923).

Hanrahan's Oath. Produced 29 January 1918. Published in *The Image and Other Plays* (London: Putnam, 1922).

The Jester. Not produced professionally. Published in *Three Wonder Plays* (London: Putnam, 1923).

Aristotle's Bellows. Produced 17 March 1921. Published in *Three Wonder Plays* (London: Putnam, 1923).

The Old Woman Remembers. Produced 31 December 1923. Published in *The Irish Statesman,* 22 March 1924; included in *A Little Anthology of Modern Irish Verse,* selected by Lennox Robinson (Dublin: Cuala Press, 1928).

The Story Brought By Brigit. Produced 15 April 1924. Published separately (London and New York: Putnam, 1924).

On the Racecourse [a re-writing of *Twenty-Five*]. Not produced. Published separately (London and New York: Putnam, 1926).

The Would-Be Gentleman (from Molière). Produced 4 January 1926. Published in *Three Last Plays* (London and New York: Putnam, 1928).

Sancho's Master. Produced 14 March 1927. Published in *Three Last Plays* (London and New York: Putnam, 1928).

Dave. Produced 9 May 1927. Published in *Three Last Plays* (London and New York: Putnam, 1928).

PLAYS UNPUBLISHED AND UNPRODUCED

Michelin
The Meadow Gate
The Dispensary
The Shoelace
The Lighted Window
Heads or Harps (with W. B. Yeats)

CONTENTS

Acknowledgements   v

Foreword by Ann Saddlemyer   vii

Complete list of plays   xiii

Translations and Adaptations

Teja   3

The Doctor in Spite of Himself   25

The Rogueries of Scapin   51

The Miser   89

The Would-Be Gentleman   141

Mirandolina   193

Sancho's Master   235

Collaborations

The Poorhouse   293

The Unicorn from the Stars   303

Heads or Harps   341

Notes and Music   351

First Performances at the Abbey Theatre and their
     Casts   371

Appendix: Heads or Harps (incomplete version)   365

Translations and Adaptations

TEJA
BY HERMANN SUDERMANN

TEJA

PERSONS

TEJA. *King of the Goths.*
BALTHILDA. *His newly wedded wife.*
AMALABERGA. *Her mother.*
BISHOP AGILA.
THEODEMIR ⎫
EURICH ⎬ *Great men of the Gothic Kingdom.*
ILDEBAD. *The King's spear-bearer.*
WATCHMAN.
TWO GUARDS.
TWO CHOIRBOYS.
LORDS, COUNCILLORS AND SOLDIERS.

*The scene represents the King's tent. The hangings in the back-
ground are open, and beyond the Gothic army is seen a glimpse of
Vesuvius, and of the sea, which is shining in the setting sun. To the
left the King's Throne. In the middle a table surrounded with seats.
To the right the King's couch, made of piled up skins, over it a
stand with arms of various sorts. Rings for torches right and left.
Two soldiers are standing on guard.*

1ST GUARD. Hey, are you asleep?
2ND GUARD. Why should I be asleep?
1ST GUARD. You are doubled up over your spearshaft, as crooked
as a hunnish bow.
2ND GUARD. I double myself up to keep the hunger from giving
me the gripes.
1ST GUARD. That's no use. It does no more good than tightening
your belt. It's all the harder to stand straight again.
2ND GUARD. How long will this go on?
1ST GUARD. Till the ships come—that is plain enough.
2ND GUARD. Yes, but when will the ships come?
1ST GUARD. How can I know that? Look up there at the height,
there up on the hill where the watchmen are. They can see five

5

miles out to sea. It is from behind the headland of Messina they will come.

2ND GUARD (*at door*). They will, if the Byzantine lets them through.

1ST GUARD. The Byzantine has no ships.

2ND GUARD. The Byzantine has so many ships that he can hedge in the whole of Italy with them, as close as the Byzantine Eunuch has hedged us in these seven weeks.

1ST GUARD. Is it only seven weeks?

2ND GUARD. Do you know what I got for my dinner today? The same old bacon rind I broke my teeth on a week ago. I knew it by the three crosses I had made on it with my knife. That was a meeting! A great holiday dish for a king's wedding! (*Walks up and down.*)

1ST GUARD. Do you suppose the king had more?

2ND GUARD. Do you suppose we would let ourselves be killed, riddled, spitted and starved for him if he had more than ourselves? Do you suppose we would stop and watch here like chained hounds if we did not know that he owns nothing worth the watching?

1ST GUARD (*to chest R.C.*). There is gold stored here.

2ND GUARD. Gold! Where's the use of gold? I have gold enough myself! I have a treasure buried in my cellar at Camusiam. Ah! I tell you the wives there beyond in the Wagenburg, will get meat . . . yes and wine they will get along with it.

1ST GUARD. Yes, the wives are there safe enough . . . but you have no wife?

2ND GUARD. A Greek dishonoured her, and I struck her dead! (*A pause.*) Well there *will* be meat for the women, meat and wine. But how long will it be till it comes? (*Sounds and clashing of arms coming near.*) The wedding must be over.

1ST GUARD. Be quiet. Here comes old Ildebad with the king's shield. (*They both stand erect, R.C. and L.C.*).

ILDEBAD (*hanging the shield in its place over throne and clearing away the weapons that are lying about*). Has any messenger come?

1ST GUARD. None!

ILDEBAD. Are you hungry?

2ND GUARD. I am indeed.

ILDEBAD. Hunger is for women, give heed to that, and don't be showing such a gloomy face to your young queen. That is not fitting for a wedding day.

(*Parts curtain.* TEJA *and* BALTHILDA *appear before the tent, surrounded by shouting people. They come in led by*

6

BISHOP AGILA, *two choir boys swinging censers before them. After them* AMALABERGA, EURICH, THEODEMIR *and others, nobles and leaders of armies. The tent curtains are let down. The two guards go out.* THE BISHOP *lets go the hands of the newly wedded pair and turns back to* AMALABERGA. TEJA *stands gloomily thinking.* BALTHILDA *casts a shy beseeching glance around. A painful silence.* TEJA *goes to throne left.)*

ILDEBAD (*in low voice*). You must say some word now King, to welcome your young wife.

TEJA (*in a low voice*). Must I? (*taking one of the choir boys by the shoulder.*) Not so forward boy, the smoke is getting into our nostrils. What do you do when you are not swinging censers?

BOY. I swing my sword King.

TEJA. That is right. But hurry on with your sword-swinging or you may be too late. (*Aside.*) Ildebad, is nothing to be seen of the ships?

ILDEBAD. Nothing, King. But you should say something now to your young wife.

TEJA. Yes, I have a wife now Bishop?

BISHOP. Your wife is standing here King, waiting for you to speak a word.

TEJA. Forgive me queen if I cannot find that word. I have grown up in battles and I have known no other lodging. You will hardly care to share it with me.

BALTHILDA. King ... my mother ... taught me ... (*stops.*)

TEJA (*more gently*). And what did your mother teach you?

AMALABERGA. That a wife belongs to her husband—above all in the hour of need. I taught her that King.

TEJA. That may be right and true for you women ... if only the man belonged to the wife in the hour of need. And another thing, Amalaberga, I have been told that this morning fowl were heard cackling up in the Wagenburg, in you women's quarters. The soldiers have had no meat these three weeks past. I recommend you to give up those fowl to them. (AMALABERGA *does not answer*).

BISHOP. Oh my king!

TEJA. Ha? You preached very well just now before your field altar Bishop ... Do you want to give us another sermon?

BISHOP. I will speak, because bitterness is destroying your soul.

TEJA. Is that so? You think that? Very well, I am listening.

BISHOP. Young man, you are standing among us like the spirit of the wrath of God. It is not your years that people count, but your doings. The old men submit themselves willingly to you a young man. Upon Theodoric's golden throne where justice and mercy sat together, where Totilas gave out his pardons with a smile, your harsh words have been heard. But misfortune is with us like a poisoned wound. We are shut in here under the fiery mouth of Vesuvius, and Byzantium hold us in its grip.

TEJA. That it does indeed. Ha! ha! Not a mouse can get through.

BISHOP. We look over the sea and pray for it is from there God has promised us bread.

TEJA (aside). Nothing has been heard of the ships?

ILDEBAD. Nothing.

BISHOP. Before we made ready for another red battle, we free men resolved, according to the old law, to choose a queen for you, that the king himself may know in his own body the reason that the Goth loves death.

TEJA. Do you find that your king loves life too much?

BISHOP. My king!

TEJA. No you do not think that . . . And even if the old law commanded it, why must you smelt me together with a young life that trembles before me and hides in the mother's dress? And this on such a fitting day, when hunger makes our wedding feast . . . Look at me Queen . . . I must call you already by our title of half an hour, for, by God, I hardly know your name. I pray you look at me. Do you know me?

BALTHILDA. Sir, you are the king.

TEJA. Yes. But for you I must be a man and not a king . . . and do you know what sort of man is before you? . . . Look! These arms have up to this been steeped in smoking blood . . . not blood of men spilled in the fight with men—I am not speaking of that, men hold that in honour. Blood of white helpless children, of (shudders) . . . You will feel great joy when I put these arms about you . . . Do you hear me? Is it not true I have a pleasant voice, a sweet voice? It is only a little hoarse, it has shouted itself tired giving out death orders . . . It will give you a special pleasure when you hear tender words in this gentle hoarseness. Am I not as if made to be a lover? These wise men knew that; they knew my calling . . . Or did you think it was your duty to amuse, to divert your king in the dullness of the camp life, as the great Justinian is amused in Byzantium while he sends his eunuchs out to kill the Goths! Ha, ha, ha!

BISHOP. My king, do not let anger get a hold of you.

8

TEJA. I thank you friend. But it is nothing. It is but my wedding humour. But now I will talk with you in earnest. (*Steps on to the throne.*)

On Theodoric's golden throne, where mercy and justice sat together, I cannot alas! take a place, for it was hacked into firewood in Byzantium . . . And neither can I give out smiling pardons like Totilas, for no one covets our forgiveness now. The shining nation of the Goths has become a pack of starving wolves. That is why it makes use of a wolf for its king. You, Bishop, called me the spirit of the wrath of God. I am not that, I am only the spirit of your desperate despair. As one who has hoped nothing and wished for nothing through his lifetime, so you see me standing here, and so you will see me fall. You knew that, and knowing that you did wrong, nursing a secret reproach against me. Do not contradict me! I can read it clearly through your frowning faces. Because things go badly with us, do not make a scapegoat of me. I give you that advice!

THEODEMIR. King, you need not reproach us. The last drop of blood belongs to you. Do not throw us in the one pot with that old man!

EURICH. If we are old men, we fight as well and we love you lad, as well as these.

TEJA. Then make an end of this. Your queen will learn soon enough how friends can quarrel with one another when bad luck comes. And if you are going through the camp tell the soldiers the only thing that vexes the king on his wedding day—on this joyful day, is that right? is, that he cannot bid them to a worthy wedding feast . . . or perhaps . . . Ildebad . . .

ILDEBAD (*who has been speaking aside with a sentinel who has come in and is upset*). Yes, master.

TEJA. What have we still in our larder, old man?

ILDEBAD (*mastering his emotion*). You have given away nearly all your rations King.

TEJA. I ask you what is left?

ILDEBAD. A jug of sour milk and a couple of stale crusts.

TEJA. Ha, ha, ha, ha! You see now queen what sort of a poor man you have come to! But when the ships are here, tell the people this, I will entertain them all as a king should. But no, do not tell them that . . . it would drive them out of their wits with joy. But whenever the trumpets are heard sounding, then meat and wine shall be set out on a long table . . . as much . . . (*to* ILDEBAD *who has crossed the stage to him with signs of disturbance.*) What is it?

ILDEBAD (*aside*). The watchman has come back. The ships are lost.

TEJA (*with no change of countenance*). Lost! How? Through what?

ILDEBAD. Through treachery!

TEJA. Just so. Yes, meat and wine, as much as everyone wants, on long white tables. I will divide it all, fruits of Sicily for the women, and sweet things from Messilia. (*He sinks reeling to the throne and looks absently in the distance.*)

ALL. What is wrong with the king? Look to the king!

BALTHILDA. It must be hunger Mother. (*She comes to him, all making way for her.*) My king!

TEJA. Who are you woman? What do you want?

BALTHILDA. Can I help you sir?

TEJA. Ah, it is the queen! Forgive me . . . and you also my people forgive me. (*Stands up*).

BISHOP. King, you must take care of your strength.

THEODEMIR. Yes king, for all our sakes.

ALL. For all our sakes!

TEJA. That is a right warning. I pray you women, go back to your own quarters . . . we have a council to hold. You Bishop take charge of them.

AMALABERGA (*aside*). Make your curtsey, child!

BALTHILDA (*aside*). Mother, will he say nothing more to me?

AMALABERGA. Make your curtsey. (BALTHILDA *does so*.)

TEJA. Farewell!

(BALTHILDA, AMALABERGA *and* BISHOP *go. They are received outside with applause.*)

TEJA. I have sent away the women and the priest, for the business we have now is only for soldiers. Where is the watchman? Come forward.

ALL (*murmuring*). The watchman from the hill! The watchman!

TEJA. You must hear his news now men. The ships are lost!

(*Tumult. Cries of horror.* "Lost! lost! the ships are lost! ")

TEJA. Quiet, friends, quiet . . . You are called Haribelt?

WATCHMAN. Yes, master.

TEJA. How long were you at your post?

WATCHMAN. Since early yesterday, master.

TEJA. Where are your companions.

WATCHMAN. They have stopped up there, as you ordered them, master.

TEJA. Good. Now, what was it you saw?

WATCHMAN. The smoke of Vesuvius, master, was hiding the

headland and the sea. By reason of that, we saw nothing until the sixth hour of this evening. Then of a sudden the ships came in sight, five in all quite near to the shore, there where as they say the Roman city lies buried. One of us was just going to hurry back here to tell you ... but ...

TEJA. Stop! What sign did the ships carry?

WATCHMAN. The foresail tied up crossways ... and ...

TEJA. And?

WATCHMAN. A bunch of palm leaves at the helm.

TEJA. You saw the palm leaves?

WATCHMAN. As plain as I see yourself, master.

TEJA. Good. Go on.

WATCHMAN. Then we saw the little fishing boats the Byzantines make use of to get their meals come swarming around the ships, very close, and then ...

TEJA. What then?

WATCHMAN. Yes master, then they all steered together, quite friendly, to where the enemy has his camp. And there they were unloaded.

(*The men cover their heads in silence.*)

TEJA (*looking smilingly from one to another*). That is well. That is our call! (*to* WATCHMAN.) Say nothing outside. I will tell it myself. (WATCHMAN *goes out.*) Now what is your advice?

THEODEMIR. Sir, we have none to give.

TEJA. And you Eurich, with all your wisdom?

EURICH. Sir, I served under Theodoric the great. And neither would he have known now what to advise.

TEJA. But I know it. It is short and quite easy to understand. To die! ... Why do you look at me so suspiciously? Do you not understand me? Do you think I want you to cover your heads with your cloaks, like cowardly Greeks, and beg your neighbour to give you a blow from behind? Be easy, I will at least save you from insult, even if I may never lead you again to any honour. Our camp cannot be taken as long as thirty among us can hold our spears. But the hour will come, and it is not far off, when the last hunger wasted arm can no longer be raised to beg mercy from the enemies breaking in.

THEODEMIR. No man of the Goth does that King!

TEJA. As to that, you can answer for what you are but not for what you may become. And so I advise you and command you, to prepare yourselves this night for the last battle. At the first grey of morning we will break out of the camp, and attack the Byzantines in the open field.

ALL. Sir, that is impossible.

THEODEMIR. Remember king we are one against a hundred.

TEJA. What do you say Eurich?

EURICH. Master, you are leading us to destruction.

TEJA. That is so. Did I say anything else? Do you believe I am so unpractised in war business that I did not know that? Why then are you so unready? When Totilas led us we were more than a hundred thousand . . . now we are but five. All the rest understood what death is . . . have we the poor remnant forgotten it?

ALL. No king, no!

EURICH. King, give us time to grow accustomed to this dread!

TEJA. This dread! What is it seems terrible to you? I am not speaking to Romans, who live reeling from the Mass into Lupanar and from Lupanar to the Mass! Is there any one of you whose breast is not as scored with scars as a weather beaten rock? You have played with death these twenty years, and now the play turns to earnest, men of the Goths speak of dread! . . . What is it you want? Will you lie down and starve? Will you gnaw one another like rats? . . . Very good . . . But I will not do it with you! Not I! Tomorrow I will take my spear and my shield, I will go to rob with my own hand that something, death, that I have craved and coveted like a thief ever since I made myself leader of your lost cause! . . . You at least Ildebad, old comrade, will come with me, ha?

ILDEBAD. I thank you master. I will come!

ALL. We also King, all of us, all!

THEODEMIR. We must thank you King, for you have found the good way for us. Do not look down on us because we were not quick to follow you. Your high thought is clear to us now. Out of quarrels and troubles and despair we are going up, not going down, to our death. Each one will step laughing on the body of another, that he may die laughing as he died . . . A flame will go out from us over the wide world . . . Ah! it will be like drinking a draught from a golden cup . . . it will be a drunkenness, a merry shout! My king, I thank you. I have often grudged you your crown. I will never do so again!

TEJA. We have certainly a good portion as you have shown it Theodemir. I am glad there is so much of ecstacy still left in the Goths.

EURICH. Give me a word too King, for I once saw the golden time . . . You are not only the bravest, you are the wisest of all . . . If we held back just now, it was that we were not prepared for the stroke of death . . . it was not only of ourselves we thought, but the sick, and the children, and the women.

TEJA. Ah yes, the women. I had not thought of them at all.

EURICH. But tomorrow, and the next day, and the third day, if the fight lasts so long, we will spread wonder and fright among the Byzantine army and all the hunnish rabble it drags after it. We cannot destroy it, but we can tire it out, and clog it with our blood. And when no one among them can hold spear or bow any more, the time will come when the Eunuchs will say "Go home in peace" . . . any that are living still . . . not many I am afraid . . .

TEJA (*laughing out*). Certainly not many of us!

ALL (*with a loud laugh*). No, not many of us!

EURICH. We will put the women and children in our midst, and hold up our heads and draw our swords going through the Byzantine camp to Neapolis to buy a bit of bread for them. I tell you there will be such terror before us not a dog will dare to bark at us! That is the way that at least wife and child can be saved.

TEJA. Wife and child! Wife and child! What have we to do with that?

EURICH. King, you despise the dearest thing we own.

TEJA. Maybe so. All I know is that a great many useless mouths were here every morning at the giving out of food. But for them, perhaps we might have held on. And I say this, and I will say it again to the men outside, not a word must be said to the women of what we are going to do! I will not have even one man turned weak through a woman's cries and tears!

EURICH. Sir, it would be an unmanly thing to take no leave of our wives.

TEJA. Take leave of them then, but be dumb in doing it! Let whoever here has wife or child go to the women's quarters, let him get food and drink there, it is likely the women may have kept some remnant between their fingers. Share what you get with the wifeless men, and be merry while you can.

EURICH. What reason can we give the women for going to them? You had given strong orders against it.

TEJA. Say it is because of my wedding . . . or that the ships have come in, if that seems a more likely reason. Say whatever you like.

THEODEMIR. And you yourself King, you will not see your young wife?

TEJA. I? No . . . I do not feel the least inclination. Now I am going to speak to the people. I wish I had your tongue Theodemir. This going out to them sours me, for I must say big words without

feeling them. . . . Come! (ALL *go out,* ILDEBAD *a long way behind.
One hears the king's voice which is received with acclamation.
Then after some seconds, subdued lamentations.* ILDEBAD *comes
back, and sits crouching for a minute on a log in the background.
Then he lights two torches that are in the rings, and makes ready
the king's arms. Outside there is a jubilant shout which dies away
again.* BISHOP AGILA *reels in, exhausted and bewildered.*)

ILDEBAD. Will you take a seat, reverend sir?

BISHOP. You have not gone out to hear what the king is saying?

ILDEBAD. That is not needful reverend sir. The king and I are
fellow tradesmen this long time.

BISHOP (*looking out*). He is standing there like death's angel.

ILDEBAD. Angel or devil, it is all one to me. (*The cries of ecstasy
are raised anew, and come nearer the tent. The* KING *comes in,
white but tranquil, his eyes flaming.*)

TEJA. Are the arms in order? . . . Ah, Bishop, is it you?

BISHOP (*striking his face with his hands*). King, my king!

TEJA. Yes, you must look for another flock now Bishop. If you
have a mind to give me a blessing, give it quickly. I want Theodemir here. (ILDEBAD *goes out.*)

BISHOP. You feel yourself free, my son, from the quaking of all
dying creatures.

TEJA. Bishop, I have been a good servant to your Church. I did
not consecrate your temple as Totilas did, I had not knowledge
enough for that—but for your benefit, I have killed all there was
to kill. Shall I deliver any orders to the holy Arius?

BISHOP. My son, I do not understand you.

TEJA. I am sorry for that, Father.

BISHOP. Have you said your farewell?

TEJA. To whom should I say it? I would rather say welcome . . .
but even then there is nobody there.

BISHOP (*angrily*). I meant your wife, sir.

TEJA. I have only had to do with men up to this, I know nothing
of women. Good-bye!

(THEODEMIR *and* ILDEBAD *come in.*)

BISHOP. Farewell, and God be merciful to your soul!

TEJA. I thank you, Bishop. Ah there you are, Theodemir . . .
(BISHOP *goes.* ILDEBAD *shoves curtains aside for* BISHOP, *then
busied in the background with the king's weapons goes to and fro
noiselessly.*) What are the soldiers doing?

THEODEMIR. Those who have wives have gone to the Wagenburg . . . they will eat and drink there, and play with their children.

TEJA. Your wife is there?

THEODEMIR. Yes, sir.

TEJA. And your children?

THEODEMIR. Two boys, sir.

TEJA. And you have not gone?

THEODEMIR. I was waiting for your call, sir.

TEJA. What hour is it?

THEODEMIR. The ninth, sir.

TEJA. And what are those doing who have no belongings? The bachelors and those whose wives are not here?

THEODEMIR. They are lying beside the fire, they are saying no word.

(ILDEBAD *goes out.*)

TEJA. See that they are brought something to eat. I ordered it. Does anyone want to sleep?

THEODEMIR. No one will sleep.

TEJA. Come and fetch me at midnight.

THEODEMIR. I will, sir. (*Is going.*)

TEJA (*troubled*). Theodemir! Stay! You have always been against me.

THEODEMIR. I was, sir, but not for a long time past.

TEJA (*opens his arms*). Come! (*He holds him embraced, then they clasp hands.*) I would keep you here, but you must go to your wife. (ILDEBAD *comes in again.*) And do not forget to send food to those who are staring in the fire. They will have work to do. Thinking does no good at such a time.

THEODEMIR. I will see to it, sir. (*Goes out.*)

TEJA (*to* ILDEBAD). Now old man, we have nothing more to do on this earth. Will you stop and talk with me?

ILDEBAD. Master! Might I dare to ask something of you?

TEJA. Have I still something to give? I believe you want to flatter me!

ILDEBAD. Master, I am old. My arm will get tired carrying the spear sooner than is good for your life. And it must not be through my fault that you die. Though no one else is sleeping, do not think bad of me, but let me sleep for a couple of hours.

TEJA (*with a shiver of trouble*). Do not go far away!

ILDEBAD. Master, I have always slept as your hound before your tent. I will make no change on this last night . . . Have you any orders, sir?

TEJA. Good night! (ILDEBAD *goes.*)

(TEJA *remaining alone throws himself upon the couch with a bitter tired laugh, and gazes before him.* BALTHILDA *comes in timidly. She carries a basket in her hand in which are bread, meat and fruit, in the other a golden vessel with wine. She makes several steps towards the table.*)

TEJA (*rouses himself*). Who are you?

BALTHILDA (*low and timidly*). Do you not know me King?

TEJA (*standing up from the couch*). The torches burn dimly . . . I have heard your voice before . . . What do you want from me?

BALTHILDA. I am your wife, King.

TEJA (*after a silence*). And what do you want from me?

BALTHILDA. My mother sent me . . . I have brought you food and wine . . . the others are eating and drinking, and my mother said . . . (*she stops.*)

TEJA. How did you get in here? Did not the guards forbid you to come in?

BALTHILDA (*standing straight*). I, sir, am the queen!

TEJA. Yes indeed. And Ildebad, what did he say?

BALTHILDA. Your old spearbearer was lying asleep. I stepped over him. (*She offers food.*)

TEJA. I thank you, Balthilda. I am not hungry. I thank you (*A silence.* BALTHILDA *stands and looks imploring at him.*) I see you still want something of me.

BALTHILDA. My king . . . if I should turn back with the basket still untouched . . . I would be a mockery to all the women . . . and the men would say . . .

TEJA (*smiling*). Well, what would the men say?

BALTHILDA. He thinks her so unworthy that . . . he would not even for once take food from her hand.

TEJA (*laughing*). I give you my word Balthilda that men have some other thing to think of . . . yet, perhaps . . . You shall not be thought little of through me . . . Put down your basket here . . . Have you still much of this left?

BALTHILDA. Sir, my mother and I and the women who are with us, we have been laying aside what was best in our portions these two weeks past, meal and fruit . . . and we did not kill the fowls until today.

TEJA. You must have been pinched with hunger, you women?

BALTHILDA. Ah we did not mind that sir. It was all for the wedding feast.

TEJA. Is that so? You believed we would hold a feast today?

BALTHILDA. And . . . is it not a feast sir?

TEJA (*is silent and bites his under lip, looking closely at her aside*). Will you not sit down Balthilda? . . . Indeed I dare not let you go home yet. That would be a shame would it not?

(BALTHILDA *is silent and looks down*.)

TEJA. And if I ask you would you be willing to stay?

BALTHILDA. Why not sir? Does not a wife stay willingly with her husband?

TEJA. Do you feel then in your heart . . . that I am your husband?

BALTHILDA. And what else sir? The Bishop has joined us together.

TEJA. And are you glad he has done that?

BALTHILDA. Yes, no . . . it does not make me glad.

TEJA. Why not?

BALTHILDA (*with shining eyes*). Perhaps . . . because . . . because . . . I was, I was anxious . . . I prayed . . .

TEJA. What did you pray?

BALTHILDA. That God would lend strength to me, an unworthy girl, to bring you the happiness you deserved, and that you looked for in me.

TEJA. That I looked for! . . . That is what you prayed?

BALTHILDA. Sir, may I not offer you this food and wine?

TEJA. No, no . . . Listen Balthilda, there are soldiers out there by the fires . . . they are hungry. I am not hungry.

BALTHILDA. Sir, give them what you will. Give them all.

TEJA. I thank you Balthilda. (*Lifting up the curtain.*) Hey there! Guard! Come in . . . but take care . . . do not wake the old man. (*A* GUARD *comes in.*) Here, take this basket of food and this wine and divide it honestly . . . Say that your queen has sent it.

GUARD. May I dare to thank the queen sir?

(TEJA *nods.* GUARD *shakes her hand heartily and goes out.*)

TEJA. That is all right. And now, give me something to eat.

BALTHILDA (*troubled*). Sir . . . why are you jesting with me ?

TEJA. Do you not understand me? If you will be my wife, what belongs to me must satisfy you, not what belongs to you.

BALTHILDA. Is not all I have yours sir?

TEJA. Hm! (*A silence. They clasp hands.*) Do not call me sir, and do not call me King. Do you not know my name?

BALTHILDA. You are called Teja.

TEJA. Say it again.

BALTHILDA (*low, turning away*). Teja!

TEJA. Is the name so strange to you? (BALTHILDA *shakes her head.*) Why are you so slow then?

BALTHILDA. Not because it is strange sir. Since I knew I was to

17

serve you as your wife, I often said that name by day and by night, only I never said it out aloud . . .

TEJA. And before you knew that, what did you think about it?

BALTHILDA. Sir, why do you ask me? Sir, when I heard of the orders you were giving to kill and not to spare and the like, I was troubled . . . for I often thought, how unhappy he surely is, being forced to such deeds through the hard necessity of the Goths!

TEJA. You thought that? You thought . . .

BALTHILDA. Was I doing wrong thinking it?

TEJA. You had never seen my face, and you understood me? And all who were with me here, the counsellors, the men wise in war, they did not understand me . . . Who are you woman? Who has taught you to read my heart? You, only you among all?

BALTHILDA. Sir . . . I . . .

TEJA. They all shuddered at me . . . they slunk away in corners grumbling against me . . . and they did not see the way, the one way, they might still save themselves, with the butcher's knife already at their throat. They told themselves fables, that all was going well. Then the cunning Greeks came and got round them, and murdered them one by one . . . and thus the hundred thousand wore away. And I wrapped myself up in grief and fury . . . I threw off hope as a wornout rag . . . I scoffed and laughed as I leaped into battle gaps . . . I spread horror about me when my own heart was working with horror of myself . . . I was never drunk with blood, I killed, killed, knowing all the while it was no use . . . no use . . . (*he sinks down overcome with trouble, on a seat, and stares before him.*)

BALTHILDA (*with a bashful effort at a caress*). My king! My king!

TEJA (*raises his head and looks at her puzzled*). Why am I telling you all this? You must not despise me for being such a prattler! . . . and you must not think it is any new thing that has forced me to such an outbreak . . . Maybe I feel sorry for the slaughtered . . . for those I kill . . . but the knowledge I do right stands high over all that! . . . much higher than my poor Gothic throne . . . Look at me now . . . it is something in your eyes that has compelled me to bring out my innermost thoughts for you . . . Who has given you this power over me? Go home . . . no stay . . . stay . . . I will tell you something before you go, quite as a secret . . . I dare not say it out loud, the guard might hear it . . . Bend down your ear to me. I have never owned it to any one, I did not think it possible I should ever confess it . . . I am jealous, there is a jealousy in me that has been gnawing me for a long time. Do you know who I am

18

jealous of? Of Totilas! Yes, of Totilas in his grave . . . They called him "sunny Totilas" and he is still their desire . . . their eyes still shine at the very thought of him.

BALTHILDA. Ah sir, how you are tormenting yourself!

TEJA (*full of trouble*). Did you ever see him?

BALTHILDA. Never.

TEJA. Thank God for that! For if you had seen him, as I saw him on the morning of the battle where he died, . . . in golden armour . . . his white horse prancing under him . . . his fair hair about him like sunshine . . . He laughed the enemy in the face . . . laughed like a child . . . Ah! To die laughing like him!

BALTHILDA. Sir, it was easy for him. He passed away from here, but he left you the inheritance of the half ruined kingdom. How should you be able to laugh?

TEJA (*eagerly*). That is true . . . Is that not true? (*stretching himself*). Ah you have done me good!

BALTHILDA. How proud you are making me sir!

TEJA. But if you had seen him, and compared me with him, you would fling me away!

BALTHILDA (*full of fervour*). I would not have seen anyone but you, my dear, dear lord!

(TEJA *looks at her sideways shyly and distrustfully, then goes silently to the left, sinks down on step and hiding his face on the throne weeps bitterly.*)

BALTHILDA (*follows him shyly and kneels down beside him*). Teja, dear, if I have vexed you forgive me!

TEJA (*lifts himself and seizes her arm*). Tell no one.

BALTHILDA. What must I not tell?

TEJA. That you saw me cry. Swear it!

BALTHILDA. It was said to me that I am now as a part of your body, . . . and also a part of your soul! Why should I swear?

TEJA. If you are a part of myself, come nearer to me that you may not see my tears.

BALTHILDA. Let me dry them! See . . . that is what I am here for.

TEJA. Ah, it is well with me . . . but indeed I should hide myself for ever, for no one has ever seen a man of the Goths cry. Even when we were laying Totilas in the grave we shed no tears . . . But I am not ashamed. If I could only know why everything is so well with me! Balthilda, I will tell you something . . . but you must not laugh at me . . .

BALTHILDA. Why should I laugh at you my dear?

TEJA. I am hungry.

BALTHILDA (*getting up troubled*). Ah, me! You have given all you had away!

TEJA. Oh, not at all! Go over there . . . (*she goes*) behind my couch . . . do you see the hearth?

BALTHILDA. Here where the ashes are lying? Yes?

TEJA. There is a chest there is there not?

BALTHILDA. Yes.

TEJA. Can you take the lid off?

BALTHILDA. Ah, it is heavy!

TEJA. Now try in it . . . deep, deep . . . the same as Ildebad, the old niggard . . . well?

BALTHILDA (*disappointed*). A couple of old crusts; is that all sir?

TEJA. It is not likely there is anything more.

BALTHILDA. May I hurry back to the women . . . perhaps there is something still . . .

TEJA. Oh no they want all they have. Bring it here . . . we will share it like two brothers . . . Ha? then it will be enough for us both. Will you?

BALTHILDA. Yes (*sits on throne step*).

TEJA. That is right, give it here. Ah, that tastes good! Does it not taste good? Ah, but you must eat also.

BALTHILDA. I am afraid there is not enough for you.

TEJA. No, that is against the bargain. There . . . Is it not true that it tastes good?

BALTHILDA. I have never tasted anything so good.

TEJA. Come nearer to me . . . I will gather up the crumbs of your crust . . . That is it . . . What has hunger to do with us here? See now, we are making our wedding feast.

BALTHILDA. And we are better off than those outside with their meat and wine. Are we not?

TEJA. There, now, did I not tell you so? But you have a bad place to sit.

BALTHILDA. No, it is a very good place.

TEJA. Come, stand up . . . will you not stand up?

BALTHILDA. And now?

TEJA. Sit yourself up there.

BALTHILDA (*startled*). On the throne? My God! How dare I?

TEJA. Are you not then the queen?

BALTHILDA (*resolutely*). If I must sit there it will be in earnest but as a jest . . . no!

TEJA. Ah, the stupid bit of wood! (*He throws down the throne.*)

Now at all events it will be of some use . . . There, lean against it . . .

BALTHILDA (*pleadingly*). Teja, are you doing right?

TEJA. No! (*He put up the throne again in its former place and sets her with her head against the seat.*) There now you are well placed . . . yes . . . And we are not sinning against this timber . . . If the bishop had heard that! Ha, ha, ha, ha! Wait I will eat some more.

BALTHILDA. Take it then.

TEJA. Quiet, don't move, I can help myself quite well! (*He kneels on the Podium beside her.*) Now I am on my knees before you . . . Ah! one does not know everything! You are beautiful! . . . I never knew my mother.

BALTHILDA. Never knew her?

TEJA. And I never had a sister . . . no one . . . I never played in my life . . . I am learning that now at the very last!

BALTHILDA. Why do you say at the very last?

TEJA. Do not ask! No? Ah, you . . . you . . . ha, ha, ha . . . eat I pray you . . . take a bite from mine then . . . Obedience . . . you know what the Bishop said?

BATHILDA (*bites it, then springs up*). But will you not drink also?

TEJA. Ah yes . . . Bring me the jug of milk . . . You know what Ildebad told us?

BALTHILDA (*who has gone across*). Is this it?

TEJA (*standing up*). That should be it. But you must drink too.

BALTHILDA. Must I?

TEJA. Yes, it is befitting.

BALTHILDA. Well then . . . (*She drinks and shudders laughingly.*) Ah, that has no good taste.

TEJA. Give it here! (*He drinks in large gulps.*) There! (*he drinks again.*) There! What sort of a wastrel are you . . . What are you altogether? And how do you come here? And what do you really want with me?

BALTHILDA. I want your love.

TEJA. You . . . my wife . . . You . . . (*They go into one another's arms.*) And will you kiss me?

(BALTHILDA *shakes her head bashfully.*)

TEJA. Why not?

(*She shakes her head again.*)

TEJA. Tell me then, why not?

BALTHILDA. I will say it in your ear.

TEJA. Now!

BALTHILDA. You have milk upon your lips!

TEJA (*wipes his mouth horrified and then in mock anger*). How dare you tell your king that he . . . say it once more and see what I will do!

BALTHILDA (*laughing*). You have milk upon your beard.

TEJA (*laughing*). Wait now! (ILDEBAD *comes in.*)

ILDEBAD Did you call master? (*He starts, stands still with surprise and is going back silently.*)

> (TEJA *suddenly composes himself. His look, his bearing turn back again to the gloomy energy that has possessed him before.*)

TEJA. Stay! Stop here. What is happening outside?

ILDEBAD. The soldiers are coming back from the Wagenburg. Most of the women are coming with them.

TEJA. Are the leaders together?

ILDEBAD. Yes master.

TEJA. They can wait a moment. For I also have a wife.

ILDEBAD. Very well, master. (*Goes.*)

BALTHILDA. Teja, my dear, what is happening?

TEJA (*standing before her takes her head in his hands.*) It seems to me as if we had in this last hour wandered hand in hand through a whole world of joy and of grief. It is sinking away, all is sinking away. I am again . . . what I was . . . No, I am not that. But you will lift yourself high above all women, you the Queen . . . Will you?

BALTHILDA. Sir, what do you ask of me?

TEJA. You will not plead and you will not cry out?

BALTHILDA. No my lord.

TEJA. The day is coming near. Death is before us.

BALTHILDA. I do not understand . . . no one can attack us here. The ships are coming . . .

TEJA. The ships are not coming!

> (BALTHILDA *strikes her face and then stands still.*)

TEJA. But we men are going out to fight.

BALTHILDA. You cannot do that. It is impossible.

TEJA. We must. You are the Queen, and you do not see that we must?

BALTHILDA. Yes . . . I . . . see . . . it.

TEJA. The king fights in the first line. We shall never see one another living again . . . Do you know that?

BALTHILDA. Yes, I know it.

(*A silence. They look at each other.*)

TEJA. I will ask for your blessing on my path. (*He sinks down before her on his knees, she lays her hands on his hair, bends trembling and kisses him on the forehead.*)

TEJA (*springs up and tears back the curtain*). Come in, whoever is waiting there!

(AMALABERGA, EURICH, AGILA, THEODEMIR *and other leaders come in.*)

AMALABERGA. King, I sent my child to you. I know what you men have to do. Give her back to me!

TEJA. Here is your child. (BALTHILDA *and her mother go out.*)

TEJA (*looks after them, then composes himself and sees the* BISHOP). Bishop, I spoke to you scoffingly this evening. Forgive me and take my thanks, for now I also know why the Goths love death. (*Takes up his sword.*) Now are you ready? Are the partings over?

THEODEMIR. Sir, we did not hold to your orders. What the women guessed or what we told them need not be said. It is enough to say they all know.

TEJA. And did they cry out woe and alas?

THEODEMIR. Sir, they gave us in silence the blessing before death and kissed us on the forehead.

TEJA (*startled, half to himself*). They also! Surely we are a nation of kings. It is a pity for us. Come!

Curtain.

THE DOCTOR IN SPITE OF HIMSELF

AFTER
JEAN BAPTISTE MOLIÈRE

THE DOCTOR IN SPITE OF HIMSELF

PERSONS

    SGANARELLE. *A Woodcutter.*
    MARTHA. *His Wife.*
    ROBERT. *His Neighbour.*
    VALERE. *Servant of Geronte.*
    LUCAS. *The same.*
    GERONTE. *Father of Lucy.*
    JACQUELINE. *Nurse at Geronte's, and Wife of Lucas.*
    LUCY. *Daughter of Geronte.*
    LEANDRE. *In Love with Lucy.*

ACT I

SCENE: *A cottage.* SGANARELLE *and* MARTHA *come in quarrelling.*

SGANARELLE. I tell you I will not do it or any other thing. It is I myself will give out orders, I tell you, and will have the upper hand.

MARTHA. And I tell you it is I myself will be uppermost! I made no promise the day I married you to put up with your pranks and your tricks.

SGANARELLE. Well now, isn't a wife the great torment! Aristotle was surely right the time he said a woman to be worse in the house than the devil!

MARTHA. Will you look now at this great scholar with his fool talk of an Aristotle!

SGANARELLE. So I am, too, a great scholar. Where now would you find any other cutter of scollops that has as much knowledge as myself? I that served a high-up doctor through the length of six years, and that knew the rudiments and I a young boy.

MARTHA. Bad 'cess to you. Sure you havn't the sense of an ass!

SGANARELLE. Bad 'cess to yourself!

MARTHA. It was a bad day and hour for me that brought me into your house!

SGANARELLE. A bad end indeed to them that made the match!

MARTHA. You look well making that complaint! It is thanking

God every minute of your life you should be for getting the like of myself for a wife. It is little you deserved it!

SGANARELLE. Oh, to be sure, I didn't deserve such a great honour at all! I have my own story to tell of the way you behaved from then until now! Believe me, it was well for you to get me.

MARTHA. Well for me to get you, is it? A man that is bringing me to the poorhouse. A schemer, a traitor, that is eating up all I have!

SGANARELLE. That is a lie you are telling. I drink some of it.

MARTHA. Selling, bit by bit, everything that is in the house.

SGANARELLE. Sure that is living on one's property.

MARTHA. That has taken my bed from under me!

SGANARELLE. You will get up the earlier.

MARTHA. That has made away with the furniture——

SGANARELLE. We have the more room in the house.

MARTHA. That is drinking and card playing night and morning——

SGANARELLE. To keep myself from fretting.

MARTHA. And what now would you have me do with the children?

SGANARELLE. Please yourself in that.

MARTHA. The weight of four little one-eens on my shoulders!

SGANARELLE. Leave them down on the floor!

MARTHA. And they crying to me for food——

SGANARELLE. Give them a taste of the stick!

MARTHA. Is it this way you will be going on for ever, you sot?

SGANARELLE. Be easy now, if you please.

MARTHA. Am I to put up with your abuse and your scattering?

SGANARELLE. Don't now be letting us get into a passion!

MARTHA. What way at all can I make you behave yourself?

SGANARELLE. Mind what you say! If my temper is not good my arm is good!

MARTHA. I am not in dread of your threats.

SGANARELLE. Oh, my sky-woman, you are wanting to coax something out of me!

MARTHA. Do you think I give heed to what you're saying?

SGANARELLE. My Helen, my Venus, I'll pull your ears for you.

MARTHA. You drunken vagabond!

SGANARELLE. I'll give you a welting.

MARTHA. You sneaking tippler!

SGANARELLE. A good thrashing——

MARTHA. You ruffian you!

28

THE DOCTOR IN SPITE OF HIMSELF

SGANARELLE. Let me at you!

MARTHA. You good for nothing villain! You traitor, you thief, you coward, you scoundrel, you rascal, you cheat, you whelp, you informer, you backbiter, you rogue of ill-luck!

SGANARELLE (*taking up a stick and beating her*). If you have your mind set on it, here it is for you!

MARTHA. Oh, oh, oh, oh!

(ROBERT, *a man of the neighbours, comes in.*)

ROBERT. Hallo, hallo, hallo! What is this? For shame, for shame. Misfortune on the man that is mistreating his wife!

MARTHA (*flies at* ROBERT, *drives him round the stage and at last gives him a box on the ear*). I say he is welcome to beat me!

ROBERT. Let him do it so, and I'm satisfied.

MARTHA. What call have you to come meddling here?

ROBERT. I wish I didn't come.

MARTHA. What business is it of yours?

ROBERT. None at all.

MARTHA. Look at him now, the impudent meddler, trying to hinder a husband from beating his own wife!

ROBERT. I'll hinder him no more.

MARTHA. What have you to say now?

ROBERT. Nothing at all.

MARTHA. Why would you be thrusting in your face?

ROBERT. You may say so.

MARTHA. Mind your own business.

ROBERT. I'll say no more.

MARTHA. It's my own wish to be beaten.

ROBERT. I'm not against it.

MARTHA. It is not you will pay for it.

ROBERT. That is so.

MARTHA. It is a fool that comes meddling where he is not wanted.

ROBERT (*to* SGANARELLE). I ask your pardon, neighbour, for interfering. Go on, thrash your wife. If you wish it I will give you a hand.

SGANARELLE. I don't want your help.

ROBERT. All right so.

SGANARELLE. I'll beat her when I have a mind, and when I have a mind I'll let her alone.

ROBERT. Very well, very well.

SGANARELLE. She is my wife and not yours.

ROBERT. That's the truth.

SGANARELLE. It's not for you to be giving me orders.

ROBERT. I suppose not.

SGANARELLE. I can do without your help.

ROBERT. I'm satisfied so.

SGANARELLE. What impudence you have with your interfering! It is what Cicero says: "Do not thrust in your finger between the tree and the bark." (*He attacks* ROBERT *with his stick and drives him out.*) (*To* MARTHA.) Here now, we'll make it up.

MARTHA. I will not make it up after the way you treated me.

SGANARELLE. That's nothing at all. Come here now.

MARTHA. I will not.

SGANARELLE. Aye?

MARTHA. I won't.

SGANARELLE. Come on now, there's the good woman.

MARTHA. I tell you I will not.

SGANARELLE. Do now as I ask you.

MARTHA. I will not.

SGANARELLE. Come on now, come.

MARTHA. I am rightly vexed this time.

SGANARELLE. Sure it was nothing at all.

MARTHA. Let me alone.

SGANARELLE. Give me the hand now.

MARTHA. I will not after the way you treated me.

SGANARELLE. Well, sure I ask your pardon. Give me the hand.

MARTHA. Well, I forgive. (*Aside.*) But I'll make you pay for it!

SGANARELLE. You would be foolish now to be giving heed to a thing of the sort. Sure there are no friends but have a falling out some time. There is nothing can serve friendship like a few blows of a stick. Well, I'll be going to the wood. Wait till you see all the scollops I will cut on this day. (*He goes out.*)

MARTHA (*alone*). My joy go with you! It is long before I'll forget to you the way you are after beating me, although I may let on to forget it. It is no common punishment I will be satisfied to put on him this time, but a punishment he will remember the longest day he lives.

(*Enter* VALERE *and* LUCAS.)

LUCAS (*to* VALERE, *without seeing* MARTHA). In my opinion it is a queer sort of a search we are sent on, and it is little profit we are likely to get of it.

VALERE. What can we do? Sure we must obey our master. And if that wasn't so itself, we must be sorry to see the poor young lady the way she is—— for till she gets well there can be no wedding, and that wedding should bring in something to ourselves. It is likely

Horace will be the husband, and he is known to be a generous man. There are some say she had her mind set on one Leandre, but the master never would be willing to take *him* for a son-in-law.

MARTHA. Whatever happens I will pay him out. Those blows are sticking in me, I feel them yet. (*Stumbling against* VALERE *and* LUCAS.) I ask your pardon, gentlemen. I did not take notice of you. I had my mind taken up with something that was annoying me.

VALERE. There is no one but has trouble in this world. We ourselves are going about looking for a thing we would be glad to meet with.

MARTHA. Maybe it is something I could help you to find?

VALERE. Maybe so. It is what we are in search of, some good doctor, some skilful man, that might give relief to our master's daughter that has lost the talk with some sickness that has come upon her. Doctors and doctors she has had, but they could do nothing at all for her. Now there are men to be found sometimes that can do great cures with some secret remedy of their own. That is the sort of a man we are seeking out.

MARTHA (*to herself*). The Lord has sent me a way to get my revenge on that rascal of mine! (*To them.*) You could never have found anyone better than myself to put you into the way of getting the thing you want. There is a doctor in this place is the best hand in the world at curing the worst of diseases.

VALERE. Is that so? But where can we find him?

MARTHA. You will find him in that little wood there beyond, amusing himself. He is cutting scollops.

LUCAS. A doctor to be cutting scollops?

VALERE. I suppose you mean he is gathering herbs.

MARTHA. Not at all. He is a queer sort of a man, he takes his amusement that way. Full of cranks and fancies he is——you would never take him to be a doctor at all, by his dress or by his ways. Sometimes he will let on to be ignorant, the way you would think he was in dread to use his gift and his knowledge, and they so great as they are.

VALERE. It is a strange thing indeed the way the greatest of men will have some grain of folly mixed up with all their learning.

MARTHA. You never met so contrary a man as this one. It sometimes happens he will let himself be beaten before he will own to being a doctor at all. It is likely you will have to take a stick to him before he will own to it. That is what we ourselves are used to do when we have occasion for him.

VALERE. That is great foolishness in him indeed.

31

MARTHA. If it is, it's true. But when you have him well beaten he will do wonders.

VALERE. What now is his name?

MARTHA. Sganarelle his name is. You will know him easy enough, a black beard he has, and a frilled collar and a green and yellow coat.

LUCAS. A green and yellow coat! It is a parrot doctor he has a right to be.

VALERE. But tell me now, is it surely true he is as clever as what you say.

MARTHA. I tell you he is a man that does wonders. It is not six months since there was a woman that was given over by all the other doctors. Dead they thought her to be through the length of six hours. Stretched out for her burying she was. Well this doctor we are speaking of was brought in, and when he saw her he put a little drop out of a bottle into her mouth, and she rose up from her bed on the moment and went about the room as if nothing had happened.

LUCAS. Do you tell me so!

VALERE. That drop he gave her was surely worth gold.

MARTHA. About three weeks ago there was a little lad fell down from the top of a tower. All broken and destroyed he was, his head and his arms and his legs. They brought this man we are speaking of to him then, and he rubbed the whole of his body with an ointment he has the secret of, and with that the little lad stood up on his two feet, and away with him to play pitch and toss.

LUCAS. Is that a fact now?

VALERE. This man must have a cure for everything.

MARTHA. So he has, too.

LUCAS. That is the sort of a man we are in search of. Let us go now and find him.

VALERE. We are thankful to you, ma'am, for what you have done for us.

MARTHA. Don't forget now the advice I gave you.

LUCAS. We will not. If it is but a few blows of a stick he is wanting, we are sure of him.

VALERE (*to* LUCAS). We had great luck in meeting with this woman. I have good hopes now our journey will not go for nothing.

SCENE II: *A Wood*. VALERE *and* LUCAS. SGANARELLE *heard singing.*

32

VALERE. I hear some person singing——and cutting wood.

SGANARELLE (*comes in without seeing them. Has a bottle in his hand*). La——la——la——Faith I have worked hard enough. It is well I have earned a drop. (*Drinks.*) It is very dry work to be cutting timber. (*Sings.*)

> O little bottle of my heart,
>   Apple of every eye!
> All the world would envy me
>   If you were never dry!
> There's many a lad and lass is dead,
>   I'll cry them bye and bye.
> Its little I need think of them
>   Until the bottle's dry!

Well there's no use in fretting.

VALERE. That is the man himself.

LUCAS. It is likely it is. We had luck to chance upon him.

VALERE. Wait till we take a nearer view of him.

SGANARELLE (*hugs his bottle, then seeing them watching him, lowers his voice*). Ah! my little rogue of a comrade, it is yourself is my treasure!

> All the world would envy me
>   If you were never dry!

(*Seeing them look closer at him.*) What the mischief are these wanting?

VALERE. It is himself surely.

LUCAS. He answers to what she told us, anyway.

> (SGANARELLE *puts down bottle on the ground.* VALERE *bows to salute him, and he thinking it is with a design to take it away puts it on the other side.* LUCAS *also bowing,* SGANARELLE *takes it up again and holds it close to his body, which makes "un jeu de theatre."*)

SGANARELLE. They are whispering with one another, they are looking very hard at myself. What plan are they making up, I wonder?

VALERE. Is it you now, sir, that is called Sganarelle?

SGANARELLE. Aye? What's that?

VALERE. I am asking is your name Sganarelle.

SGANARELLE (*turning towards* VALERE, *then towards* LUCAS). It is and it is not, according to what you want with him.

VALERE. All we want is to show him all the civility we can.

SGANARELLE. If that is so, my name is Sganarelle.

VALERE. It is well pleased we are to see you, sir. We were sent looking for you to ask your help about a thing we are in need of.

SGANARELLE. If it is anything that belongs to my little business I will give it, and welcome.

VALERE. You are too good to us, indeed. Put on your hat if you please. The sun might be too strong for you.

LUCAS. Do so, sir, cover your head.

SGANARELLE (aside). What great manners they have!

VALERE. Do not be wondering now we two have come to you. People that are gifted are always in demand, and we heard a great account of you.

SGANARELLE. So you might too. I am the best man in the world at cutting scollops.

VALERE. Ah now, sir!

SGANARELLE. I don't spare myself at all. Cutting and sorting them, the way no one can find any fault.

VALERE. That is not what we are talking about.

SGANARELLE. But I sell them at no less than fivepence the hundred.

VALERE. Don't be talking of that now, if you please.

SGANARELLE. I tell you I cannot give them for less.

VALERE. We know all about that, sir.

SGANARELLE. Then if you know all about it you know I get that much for them.

VALERE. It is joking you are, sir——but——

SGANARELLE. It is not joking I am, I will take no less.

VALERE. Leave talking this way now if you please.

SGANARELLE. You might get them cheaper from some other one. There are scollops and scollops, but for those that I cut——

VALERE. Let us leave talking of scollops.

SGANARELLE. I give you my word you won't get them for one farthing under what I say.

VALERE. Be ashamed now.

SGANARELLE. Upon my word you will pay that much. It is the truth I am speaking. I am not one to be asking what is not fair.

VALERE. Look now, sir, is it right for a man like yourself to be playing tricks and to be letting himself down with this sort of talk. Is it right for a man of learning and a great doctor like yourself to be hiding himself away from the world with all his skill and his knowledge.

SGANARELLE (aside). The man is surely cracked.

34

VALERE. Don't be humbugging us now, if you please.

SGANARELLE. What are you talking about?

VALERE. All this is but letting on. I know more than what you think.

SGANARELLE. What is it you know? Who is it you are taking me for?

VALERE. For what you are, and that is a great doctor.

SGANARELLE. Doctor yourself! I am not one, and I never was one.

VALERE (*aside*). This is the foolishness he puts on. (*To him.*) Do not be denying the truth, sir, it would be a pity were we to be forced to do a thing which would be displeasing to you.

SGANARELLE. What thing is that?

VALERE. A thing we would be sorry to do.

SGANARELLE. What do I care what you may do? I am no doctor, and I don't understand what you are saying.

VALERE (*aside*). We must try the cure on him. (*To him.*) Look-at here, sir, I will give you another chance to own to be what you are.

LUCAS. Do not be humbugging any more, but confess straight and fair that you are a doctor.

SGANARELLE. I am getting vexed.

VALERE. Where is the use of hiding what we know?

LUCAS. Why would you be making pretences? What good will it do you?

SGANARELLE. Look here now, one word is as good as ten thousand. I tell you I am no doctor.

VALERE. You are no doctor?

SGANARELLE. I am not.

LUCAS. You are not you say?

SGANARELLE. No, I tell you.

VALERE. Since you will have it, we must do as we can.

(*Each takes a big stick and they beat him.*)

SGANARELLE. Ah, ah, ah! I am anything you like!

VALERE. Why did you force us to this, sir?

LUCAS. Why did you give us the trouble of beating you?

VALERE. Believe me, I was loth to do it.

LUCAS. Faith I was sorry myself, and very sorry.

SGANARELLE. What the devil are you saying? Is it joking you are, or is it mad you both are, that you will have me to be a doctor?

VALERE. Will you not give in yet? Are you denying yet that you are a doctor?

SGANARELLE. May the devil take me if I am.

35

LUCAS. It is not true so that you understand physic?

SGANARELLE. That I may die if I do! (*They begin to beat him.*) Stop, stop! O yes, if you will have it so I am a doctor, a doctor I say, and an apothecary if you wish it along with that. I would sooner agree to anything than be clouted on the head.

VALERE. That is right now. I am well pleased to see you listen to reason.

LUCAS. I am well satisfied now when you talk like that.

VALERE. I ask your pardon from the bottom of my soul.

LUCAS. Will you forgive me, sir, for making so free?

SGANARELLE (*aside*). Is it true it is? Was I deceiving myself? Was I turned into a doctor and never knowing it till now?

VALERE. Believe me you will never repent of confessing to the truth. You will be well satisfied that you did it.

SGANARELLE. But tell me now, isn't it you yourselves might be under a mistake? Is it quite sure I am doctor?

LUCAS. Sure and certain.

SGANARELLE. Is that so?

VALERE. No doubt at all of it.

SGANARELLE. And I without knowing it!

VALERE. What are you talking about? You are the greatest doctor in the world.

SGANARELLE. Am I, indeed?

LUCAS. A doctor that has cured a great deal of sick people.

SGANARELLE. The Lord save us!

VALERE. A woman was thought to be dead for six hours. They were ready to bury her, when with one drop of a cure you brought her to life again and set her walking about the room.

SGANARELLE. The deuce I did!

LUCAS. A little lad of twelve years that fell from the top of a tower you cured. With an ointment you did it, putting it on his head and his legs and his arms that were broken, till he rose up on his feet and went playing pitch and toss.

SGANARELLE. I did that too!

VALERE. So you may as well be content to go with us. You will get great gains if you will come where we will bring you.

SGANARELLE. Great gains is it?

VALERE. That is what I said.

SGANARELLE. Then I am a doctor and no mistake. I had forgotten it for a while, but I remember it now. What is the matter? Where must I go?

VALERE. We will bring you there. You have to see a young lady that has lost her talk.

SGANARELLE. Faith I have not found it!

VALERE (*aside*). He likes to be funning. Come on now, sir.

SGANARELLE. Without a doctor's suit?

VALERE. We will get you one.

SGANARELLE (*offering his bottle to* VALERE). You may carry that. It is in that bottle I keep my physic. Now, march, walk on, by the doctor's orders!

LUCAS. A very pleasant man. It is my opinion he will do the job.

Curtain.

ACT II

SCENE I: *A Room in* GERONTE'S *House*. GERONTE, VALERE, LUCAS.

VALERE. Believe me, sir, you will be satisfied and well satisfied. The doctor we have brought you is the best on the whole ridge of the world.

LUCAS. You may say that! All the rest put together are not fit to clean his boots for him.

VALERE. A man he is that has done wonderful cures.

LUCAS. He has brought back to life some that were dead.

VALERE. Some queer ways he has, as I was telling you. There are times when his wits would seem to be gone from him, the way you would never believe him to be the thing that he is.

LUCAS. Playing he does be at foolishness, that anyone nearly would take him to be cracked.

VALERE. And he having great knowledge all the time. Very high talk he does be giving out now and again.

LUCAS. So he does too, for all the world as if he was saying it out of a book.

VALERE. He has a great name in every place. There are people coming to him from far and near.

GERONTE. I am longing to see him. Bring him here at once.

VALERE. I will go call him.

(*Enter* JACQUELINE.)

37

JACQUELINE. It is my belief, sir, this doctor will do no more than the rest of them, no worse and no better. In my opinion the best doctor you can give Miss Lucy is a good handsome husband that is to her liking.

GERONTE. Be quiet, nurse. You are too fond of meddling.

LUCAS. Hold your tongue now, wife Jacqueline. Let you not come pushing yourself here.

JACQUELINE. I tell you, Lucas, and I tell the two of you, that all these doctors will do her no more good than a drink of water. It is something more than rhubarb and senna the child wants. Believe me, a good husband is the best cure for any young girl.

GERONTE. Who would take charge of her in the state she is in now? And when I wanted her to marry she would not listen to me.

JACQUELINE. That is so. But you were wanting her to marry a man she had no liking for. Why didn't you let her marry that young Mr. Leandre that she had her heart fixed on? I'll engage she'd have obeyed you that time quick enough. I'll tell you more again, she would take him now if she did but get the chance.

GERONTE. Leandre is no match for her. He is not well off like the other.

JACQUELINE. He has an uncle that is well off. It is he will be the heir.

GERONTE. These tales of riches to come are all on the breeze. Those who are waiting for a funeral feast may have plenty of time to go hungry.

JACQUELINE. It is what I often heard said, that in marriage, as in many another thing, contentment is better than riches. Fathers and mothers have a bad habit, asking always "How much has he got?" "How much has she got?" Look at the way old Peter went marrying his daughter to that Thomas, just because he had a couple of acres more of a garden than the boy she had set her mind on; and the poor thing is not the better of it now, but is turned as yellow as yellow. What do you say to that, sir? Everyone must have their own pleasure at one time or another. I'd sooner give a girl her choice man than all the money that is in the bank.

GERONTE. That will do, nurse, give your tongue a rest, or you will talk yourself into trouble.

LUCAS (*striking her on the shoulder at every sentence*). Come now——be easy——It is too free you are making with the master. Let you go rock the cradle, and let him take his own way. Sure the master will do what is best for her——isn't she his own? (*pushes her away.*)

GERONTE. Gently, gently.

LUCAS (*again striking her on the shoulder*). It is some sort of a lesson I must give her, sir. I must teach her the way to behave herself before you.

GERONTE. Yes, yes, but you need not go quite so far.

VALERE (*coming in*). Here he is coming, sir. Here is our doctor.
(*Enter* SGANARELLE.)

GERONTE. I am very happy, sir, to see you at my house. We were very much in need of you.

SGANARELLE. Hippocrates says: "Let us both be covered."

GERONTE. Does Hippocrates say that?

SGANARELLE. He does.

GERONTE. In what chapter may I ask?

SGANARELLE. In his chapter——upon hats.

GERONTE. Since Hippocrates says it, it must be done.

SGANARELLE. Well, doctor, having heard of the wonderful things——

GERONTE. To whom are you speaking if you please?

SGANARELLE. To yourself.

GERONTE. But I am not a doctor.

SGANARELLE. What is that? You are not a doctor?

GERONTE. No indeed.

SGANARELLE (*taking a stick and beating* GERONTE *as he had been beaten*). Do you mean that?

GERONTE. I do mean it. Ah, ah, ah!

SGANARELLE. You are a doctor now. That is all the licence I myself got.

GERONTE. What devil of a man have you brought me?

VALERE. I told you, sir, he was apt to be humbugging.

GERONTE. I will send him about his business with his humbugging!

LUCAS. O don't give heed to it, sir. It was only a sort of a joke.

GERONTE. I do not like this sort of joking.

SGANARELLE. I ask pardon, sir, for the liberty I have taken.

GERONTE. Do not mention it, sir.

SGANARELLE. I am sorry.

GERONTE. O, it is nothing at all.

SGANARELLE. For the blows——

GERONTE. There is no harm done.

SGANARELLE. That I have had the honour to give you.

GERONTE. You need not waste time talking of that. I have a daughter who is suffering from a very strange disease.

SGANARELLE. I am well pleased, sir, to think your daughter has occasion for me. Indeed I wish that you yourself and your whole family had occasion for me along with her, till I would show the desire I have to serve you.

GERONTE. I am much obliged for your good wishes.

SGANARELLE. Believe me, it is in earnest I am.

GERONTE. You do me too much honour.

SGANARELLE. What now is your daughter's name?

GERONTE. Lucy.

SGANARELLE. Lucy! That now is a very nice name for a patient to have.

GERONTE. I will go and see what she is doing.

SGANARELLE. Who is that fine young woman there?

GERONTE. She is nurse to a young child of mine. (*Goes out.*)

LUCAS. She is, and she is wife to myself.

SGANARELLE. Ah! that is a very nice looking woman now to have in the house (*takes her hand*). If there is anything at all I can do for you, tell me at any time and I will do it.

LUCAS. Now, doctor, if you please, leave talking to my wife.

SGANARELLE. Oh, she is your wife, is she?

LUCAS. She is so.

SGANARELLE. Well, I wish her joy of so good a man, and I wish yourself joy of so handsome a wife, so sensible, so well shaped——

LUCAS. That will do you, doctor. I have no great mind for those sort of compliments.

(GERONTE *brings in* LUCY.)

SGANARELLE. Is this the patient?

GERONTE. Here she is. I have no other daughter, doctor, and if anything should happen to her it would break my heart.

SGANARELLE. Nothing will happen her. She cannot die, you know, without a prescription from the doctor.

GERONTE. A chair here.

SGANARELLE (*sitting between* LUCY *and* GERONTE). Here is a patient that is no way disagreeable to be looking at. I think a man having good sense would be very well pleased with her.

GERONTE. You have made her laugh, sir.

SGANARELLE. That is right. When a doctor can make his patient laugh it is the best sign in the world. Now let us hear the case. What is it ails you? Have you a pain in any place?

LUCY (*putting her hands to her mouth, her head, and under her chin*). Han, hi, hon, han.

SGANARELLE. What is that?

40

LUCY (*with the same gestures*). Han, hi, hon, han, hi, hon.

SGANARELLE. What is it?

LUCY. Han, hi, hon.

SGANARELLE. Han, hi, hon, han, ha. I can't understand what you are saying. What sort of a language at all is this?

GERONTE. That is what is wrong with her. She has lost her speech, and we cannot tell why or wherefore. We have had to put off her marriage on account of it.

SGANARELLE. Why so?

GERONTE. The gentleman she is engaged to wants to see her cured before making his settlements.

SGANARELLE. What a fool he must be! I wish to God my wife had the same disease. It would be long before I would want to cure her.

GERONTE. And so, sir, we are looking to you to give her some relief.

SGANARELLE. O, you need not put yourself out about it. Tell me this now, does it lie very heavy on her?

GERONTE. It does indeed.

SGANARELLE. So much the better. Does she feel much pain?

GERONTE. A great deal.

SGANARELLE (*turning to patient*). Give me your wrist. Here now, this pulse tells me that your daughter is dumb.

GERONTE. Yes, but I would be glad if you would tell me how it came about.

SGANARELLE. Easy enough. It came about because she lost her speech.

GERONTE. Yes, yes, but how was it she lost her speech?

SGANARELLE. All our best writers will tell you that loss of speech comes from an impediment in the action of the tongue.

GERONTE. Yes, yes, but tell me your theory as to this impediment.

SGANARELLE. Aristotle says——some very fine things about it.

GERONTE. That is likely enough.

SGANARELLE. That now was a great man!

GERONTE. No doubt, no doubt.

SGANARELLE. A very great man (*holding up his arm from the elbow*). He was greater than myself by the length of that. Stop now till we go back to our discourse. It is what I hold to that this impediment to the action of the tongue is caused by certain humours that are called by scholars peccant humours—peccant you know ——peccant humours; the same as the clouds that are caused by the exhalation of influences that rise up in the region of diseases ——coming as you may say to——I suppose you understand Latin?

GERONTE. Not a word.

SGANARELLE (*getting up, brusquely*). You don't know Latin!

GERONTE. Not a word.

SGANARELLE (*with enthusiasm*). Cabricias arci thuram, catalamus, singularite nominative, haec musa, the muse, bonus, bona, bonum. Deus sanctus, est-ne oratio latinas? Etiam, yes. Quare? Quia substantive adjectivum concordate in generi, numerum et casus.

GERONTE. O, why did I never study Latin!

JACQULINE. Well, now, hasn't he great learning!

LUCAS. So he has. It is that great I can't make head or tail of it.

SGANARELLE. These vapours now, as I was telling you, in passing from the left side where the liver is to the right side where the heart is, find that the lungs, that we call in Latin, *Armyan*, having communication with the brain, that we call in Greek, *Nasmus*, by means of the hollow vein that we call in Hebrew, *Cubile*, meets in its way the said vapours that fill the ventricles of the omoplate—— and because the said vapours——listen well now till you understand this——have a certain malignity——pay attention now I tell you.

GERONTE. Yes, yes.

SGANARELLE. Have a certain malignity that is caused by the acrimony of the humours engendered by the concavity of the diaphragm, it happens that these vapours——ossabandus, niqueis, nequer potarinum, quipsa milus, that now is the very thing that has brought dumbness on your daughter.

JACQUELINE. Well that is great talk, and no mistake.

LUCAS. I wish I could twist my tongue the like of that.

GERONTE. No doubt about it, no one could have reasoned a thing out better. But there is just one thing that puzzled me——and that is the position of the liver and of the heart. It seems to me you put them out of their proper places. Is not the heart on the left side, and the liver on the right?

SGANARELLE. That is the way they used to be, but we have changed all that. We practise medicine in quite a different manner in these days.

GERONTE. That is what I did not know. You must forgive my ignorance.

SGANARELLE. To be sure, to be sure. You are not expected to be as learned as what we doctors are.

GERONTE. No, indeed. But tell me now, what should be done to cure her?

SGANARELLE. What do I think should be done?

GERONTE. Just so.

SGANARELLE. It is my opinion she should be sent to her bed, and the cure I would recommend her would be a good share of bread that has been soaked in wine.

GERONTE. What effect could that have on her?

SGANARELLE. Sure there is some virtue in bread and wine that acts upon the speech. Isn't it what they give to parrots, and don't they learn to speak?

GERONTE. That is true. What a clever man he is! Hurry, hurry, bring in plenty of bread and wine!

SGANARELLE. I will come back in the evening to see what way is she going on.

GERONTE. Stop, stop a moment!

SGANARELLE. What should I stop for?

GERONTE. Well, sir, I should like to offer you a fee.

SGANARELLE. I will not take it (*putting his hands behind his back, while* GERONTE *opens his purse*).

GERONTE. Sir!

SGANARELLE. No, no!

GERONTE. Wait one minute.

SGANARELLE. I will not.

GERONTE. I beg of you.

SGANARELLE. You are making a mistake.

GERONTE. No, no, it is all right.

SGANARELLE. I won't take it!

GERONTE. Why not?

SGANARELLE. I don't care to be doing cures for money.

GERONTE. I can quite believe that.

SGANARELLE (*having taken the money*). Is this now good money?

GERONTE. O, yes it is.

SGANARELLE. I am not a doctor that cares for profit!

GERONTE. I am sure of that.

SGANARELLE. It is not of gain I am thinking.

GERONTE. Such a thing never entered my head.

SGANARELLE (*alone, looking at the money*). Faith I haven't done so badly after all.

(LEANDRE *comes in cautiously by opposite door to that by which* GERONTE *has gone out. He comes close to* SGANA-RELLE *and speaks in a low voice.*)

LEANDRE. I have been waiting on the chance of seeing you, doctor. I have come to ask for your help.

SGANARELLE (*feeling his pulse*). A very bad pulse, very bad indeed.

LEANDRE. There is nothing wrong with my health, sir——that is not what has brought me.

SGANARELLE. If there is nothing ails you, why the mischief couldn't you say so?

LEANDRE. I will tell you the whole story in two words. My name is Leandre. I am in love with the young lady you have come to prescribe for. Her father is against me and won't let me see her, and I want you to help me in a plan I have thought out. My life and my happiness depend on my getting a chance of saying a few words to her.

SGANARELLE. What do you take me to be? What are you saying? How dare you come asking me to help to make your match! It is a right thing to ask of a doctor?

LEANDRE. Don't speak so loud, sir.

SGANARELLE (*pushing him away*). I will do as I like. What impudence you have!

LEANDRE. O, be quiet, sir!

SGANARELLE. Ah! even a fool should have more sense than that.

LEANDRE. I beg of you, sir——

SGANARELLE. I will show you I am not that sort of a man. Great impertinence indeed!

LEANDRE (*taking out a purse and giving it to him*). Sir——

SGANARELLE. Thinking to make use of me——(*taking the purse*) ——I am not speaking of you at all, sir, you are a real gentleman. Anything I can do for you, I will be well pleased to do it. Thinking I was of some that should know better——impudent chaps that would not give a man credit for being what he is——no wonder for me to be put out, thinking of them.

LEANDRE. I beg your pardon, sir, for taking such a liberty——

SGANARELLE. You are joking now——but tell what is it you are wanting?

LEANDRE. Well, sir, I should tell you, this dumbness you have been called in to cure is not a real disease at all. The doctors have given their opinions on it, they were bound to do that; one says it comes from the brain, one from the stomach, one from the spleen, one from the liver. But I can tell you the real truth, love is the only cause of it. Lucy is only pretending to be dumb that she may escape from a marriage they are trying to force her into.——Just come with me——they might see us here——and I will tell you what my plan is.

SGANARELLE. Come on then, sir. It is a wonder now what an interest you have given me in your match. Believe me, the young lady will either die, or she will be married to you, as sure as I'm a doctor!

Curtain.

ACT III

SCENE. *Same as last.* SGANARELLE, LEANDRE.

LEANDRE. There now, I think I should pass very well for an apothecary. Her father hardly knows me by sight, he will never recognise me in those clothes and this wig.

SGANARELLE. No fear at all of it.

LEANDRE. All I want now is a few good medical terms to bring out when I am speaking, that will give me an air of learning.

SGANARELLE. Never mind that. The clothes are sufficient. Sure I know no more of medicine than yourself.

LEANDRE. What!

SGANARELLE. Devil mend me if I know anything at all about it! You are a gentleman, and I will tell you no lie, as you told me no lie.

LEANDRE. You are not really a doctor!

SGANARELLE. I am not. I tell you they made me a doctor in spite of myself. I never had tried for such great learning as that. All I could do never rose me from the bottom of the school. What it was first put the notion in their heads I don't know, but so soon as I found they had set their minds on making me a doctor by force, I made up my own mind I would be one at the expense of whoever would meet with me. You would hardly believe now the way the mistake has spread itself, everyone believing me to be a very skilful man. They are coming to consult me from all parts, and if things go on the way they are doing, it is as well for me to stick to doctoring to the end of my life. It seems to me it is the best trade of all, for whether we kill or cure, we must be paid for the job. Bad work is never sent back on our hands, and we have leave to cut the stuff we are working on to our own liking. If a shoemaker, now, should spoil a piece of leather, he must be at the loss of it, but whatever injury we may do to a man, it costs us nothing at all. It is not on us the fault is laid, the fault is with the man that died. Another great advantage there is in our profession, the dead always keep a civil tongue, they are very decent indeed, you will never hear them make a complaint against the doctor that killed them.

LEANDRE. That is true. The dead keep a very honourable silence upon that point.

(GERONTE *comes in.*)

GERONTE. O, doctor! I was just looking for you.

SGANARELLE. How is the young lady getting on?

GERONTE. Rather worse since your prescription.

SGANARELLE. That is a good sign. It shows it is working.

GERONTE. Yes, but I am afraid that in its working it will choke her.

SGANARELLE. Don't be uneasy. I have certain cures against everything, but I delay giving them till the very last.

GERONTE. Who is that with you?

SGANARELLE (*making signs with his hands that it is an apothecary*). He is——

GERONTE. What?

SGANARELLE. He is——

GERONTE. Aye?

SGANARELLE. A man who——

GERONTE. I understand you.

SGANARELLE. Your daughter will be in need of him.

JACQUELINE (*bringing in* LUCY). Here is Miss Lucy, sir. She has taken a fancy to walk about for a while.

SGANARELLE. That will serve her. Go now, apothecary, and feel her pulse. I will be consulting you bye and bye about her complaint. (*He takes* GERONTE *into a corner and puts his arm round his shoulders to prevent him from turning his head towards* LEANDRE *and* LUCY.) It is a great question now among doctors, is it easier to cure a woman or a man. Listen to me now if you please. Some say it is, and more say it is not; but for my part I say it is, and it is not. Because, inasmuch as the incongruity of the opaque humours that meet in the natural temper of women, cause the animal part to gain the mastery of the feelings, we see that the difference in their opinions follows on the sideway motion of the circle of the moon; and as the sun that darts its rays on the concavity of the earth finds——

LUCY. You may be quite sure that I can never change my mind.

GERONTE. My daughter is speaking! O, what great power there was in that cure! What a wonderful doctor! You can't think how grateful I am! What can I ever do to repay you?

SGANARELLE (*walking about the stage and fanning himself with his hat*). I have had a great deal of trouble over this illness!

LUCY. Yes father, I have recovered my speech, but I have recovered it to tell you that I will have no other husband than Leandre. It is no use your trying to force anyone else upon me.

GERONTE. But——

LUCY. Nothing can make me change my mind.

GERONTE. What?

LUCY. There is no use in wasting argument upon me.

GERONTE. If——

GERONTE. I——

LUCY. Nothing you can say will make any difference.

LUCY. I have made up my mind.

GERONTE. But——

LUCY. All the fathers in the world could not make me marry against my will.

GERONTE. I have——

LUCY. You may save yourself the trouble.

GERONTE. If——

LUCY. My heart will not give in to tyranny.

GERONTE. Then——

LUCY. I would rather go into a convent than marry a man I don't care for.

GERONTE. But——

LUCY (*speaking in a very loud voice*). No, no——by no means ——not at all. You are wasting time. I will not do it. I have made up my mind!

GERONTE. What a rush of words! There is no stopping her. I must ask you, doctor, to make her dumb again.

SGANARELLE. That now is more than I can do. All I can do for you, if you wish it, is to make yourself deaf!

GERONTE. I am much obliged to you. (*To* LUCY) Do you think then——

LUCY. No, no. I don't care for any of your reasons!

GERONTE. You shall marry the man I have chosen this very day.

LUCY. No, I would sooner marry death!

SGANARELLE. Be quiet, be quiet, and let me prescribe——I know the cure for whatever is wrong with her.

GERONTE. Can you cure the mind as well as the body?

SGANARELLE. Leave me alone! I have cures for everything, and the apothecary will be able to give me a hand this time. (*To* LEANDRE) Here I have a word to say. You see that the liking she has for this young man is quite against her father's wish. There is no time to lose, the symptoms are very acrimonious. It is needful to find some cure for this disease before it gets worse with delay. Now the only cure I can see is a dose of runaway oil, which you will mix as is right with two drachms of matrimonial pills. It is likely she may make some objection to taking this dose, but as you are a skilful man in your business you will bring her to it, and make her swallow it as well as you can. Go now and take a walk in the garden with her, while I stop talking here with her father. Mind above all that you lose no time, give her the dose and make no delay.

(LUCY *and* LEANDRE *go out.*)

GERONTE. What drugs, doctor, were those you were speaking of? I don't remember having heard of them before.

SGANARELLE. Drugs they are that are used in very severe cases.

GERONTE. Did you ever hear such insolence as she gave me!

SGANARELLE. Young girls are apt to be a bit headstrong.

GERONTE. You would not believe how she is set on this fellow Leandre.

SGANARELLE. The heat of the blood puts youngsters above themselves.

GERONTE. Ever since I found it out I have kept her under my eye.

SGANARELLE. You showed good sense doing that.

GERONTE. I have taken good care never to let them write to one another.

SGANARELLE. You did well.

GERONTE. If I had let them see one another, some folly might have come of it.

SGANARELLE. So there might, too.

GERONTE. I believe she would have run away with him.

SGANARELLE. She would sure enough.

GERONTE. I am told he has done his best to get a chance of seeing her.

SGANARELLE. Great folly, indeed.

GERONTE. He is only losing his time.

SGANARELLE. Ha, ha!

GERONTE. I will take good care he doesn't see her.

SGANARELLE. Ah, it is no fool he has to deal with! It's likely you know tricks he never heard of. Believe me, any person that knows more than what you know is a wise man.

LUCAS (*coming in*). What will you say at all, sir! Did ever any-one hear the like! Miss Lucy is gone away with Mr. Leandre! It was he was the apothecary! And who was it managed the whole trick but that doctor!

GERONTE. What are you saying! What a terrible blow! Go and call the constables! Don't let him escape; O, you rascal, I will give you up to the law!

LUCAS. Ah, ha, doctor, do you hear that! It's hanged you will be! Stop where you are!

(MARTHA *comes in.*)

MARTHA. God help us! All the trouble I had making out this house. What news have you for me now of the doctor I recom-mended you?

LUCAS. There he is before you, and he just going to be hanged.

MARTHA. What are you saying? My man going to be hanged! And what is he after doing to deserve that?

LUCAS. It is what he did, he got our master's daughter to be run away with.

MARTHA. My grief, my dear comrade, is it hanged you are to be?

SGANARELLE. You see the way I am. Ah——

MARTHA. And brought to your death with all the crowds looking at you?

SGANARELLE. Sure what can I do?

MARTHA. If you had cut all the scollops you had to cut itself, that would be some comfort.

SGANARELLE. Go away out of that! You are breaking my heart!

MARTHA. I will not. I will stop here to hold up your courage until you die! I will not leave you till such time as I have seen you hanged.

SGANARELLE. Ah!

(*Enter* GERONTE.)

GERONTE. The constables will be here in a minute. They will put you in a place where you will be well minded!

SGANARELLE (*on his knees*). Oh, oh, couldn't you be satisfied with a few blows of a stick!

GERONTE. No, no! I must give you up to justice——But what do I see here?

49

(*Enter* LEANDRE *and* LUCY.)

LEANDRE. Here, sir, I have brought myself before you, and I have brought Lucy back to you. We had intended to go and be married without your leave, but we think it better to act openly. I don't want to steal her from you, I want you to give her to me. What I have to say is, that letters have just come telling me of the death of my uncle, and that I have come into possession of all he had.

GERONTE. You are a worthy man, sir, and I give you my daughter with the greatest pleasure.

SGANARELLE (*aside*). Faith, the doctor has come well out of this scrape after all.

MARTHA. So as you are not to be hanged, you should be thankful to me for being as you are a doctor. It was I did that much for you.

SGANARELLE. You did; and you got me a great beating with a stick!

LEANDRE. You can afford to forget that now, all has turned out so well.

SGANARELLE. Very well, so; I will let it pass this time. I will forgive you the chastising I got in consideration of the trade you have started me in. But mind yourself from this out. Let you remember there is no worse thing to face in the whole world than a doctor's ill-will.

Curtain.

THE ROGUERIES OF SCAPIN
AFTER
JEAN BAPTISTE MOLIÈRE

THE ROGUERIES OF SCAPIN

CHARACTERS

ARGANTE. *Father of Octave and Zerbinette.*
GERONTE. *Father of Leandre and Hyacinth.*
OCTAVE. *Married to Hyacinth.*
LEANDRE. *In love with Zerbinette.*
ZERBINETTE. *Thought to be a gipsy.*
HYACINTH. *Wife of Octave.*
SCAPIN. *Valet to Leandre.*
SILVESTER. *Valet to Octave.*
NERINE. *Hyacinth's nurse.*
CARLE. *A cheat.*
TWO PORTERS.

ACT I

SCENE. *A Street at Naples.*

OCTAVE. Oh! What news for a lover! What a fix I am in. You say, Silvester, you have just heard at the port that my father has landed from his voyage?

SILVESTER. Just so.

OCTAVE. And that he is on the point of coming to the house.

SILVESTER. Just so.

OCTAVE. And that he has made up a match for me?

SILVESTER. That's it.

OCTAVE. A daughter of Geronte's?

SILVESTER. Of Mr. Geronte's.

OCTAVE. That they are bringing her from Tarentum?

SILVESTER. That's what I said.

OCTAVE. And you've this news from my uncle?

SILVESTER. From your uncle.

OCTAVE. And my uncle knows all our affairs?

SILVESTER. All our affairs.

OCTAVE. Look here now. (*Threatens* SILVESTER.) Speak or don't speak, but don't go this way, making me drag the words out of your mouth.

53

SILVESTER. What have I to say? You are not forgetting anything. You are telling it all out just as you heard it.

OCTAVE. You might give me some word of advice. Can't you tell me what to do in this crisis?

SILVESTER. I am badly off myself. I wish I could find some person to advise me.

OCTAVE. Bad luck to my father's homecoming. What a nuisance it is.

SILVESTER. So it is to myself.

OCTAVE. When he finds out what has happened I'll never hear the end of it.

SILVESTER. I wish *I* could get off with no more than abuse. It's worse than that I'm looking out for.

OCTAVE. Good heavens! How am I to get out of this tangle?

SILVESTER. You had a right to have thought of that before you got into it.

OCTAVE. Don't worry me to death with your preachings.

SILVESTER. You are a worse worry to me with your fooleries.

OCTAVE. What am I to do? What can I do? How can I help myself?

(SCAPIN *comes in.*)

SCAPIN. Well, Master Octave. What's the matter with you? What ails you, you would seem to be some way upset.

OCTAVE. Oh, my good Scapin, I am done for. I am the unluckiest chap in the world.

SCAPIN. How is that now?

OCTAVE. Haven't you heard the news?

SCAPIN. I have not.

OCTAVE. My father is come home this morning, and Geronte with him, and they want to make up a match for me.

SCAPIN. Well, what is there so terrible in that?

OCTAVE. You don't know then why it upsets me so much?

SCAPIN (*close to* OCTAVE). It's your own fault if I have to go so long without knowing. I am a good comforter. I am always ready to give attention to young gentlemen that are in trouble.

OCTAVE. Oh, Scapin, if you could but think of any plot or plan to get me out of this fix I would owe you my life and all.

SCAPIN. I can tell you there are few things I can't succeed in if once I put my hand to them. No doubt at all it is from beyond the world I got the intellect and the wit to do all these feats the ignorant people are apt to call rogueries. I am telling no lie saying there never was any man better than myself for doing jobs of the sort, or that had his name more up for it. But it's little thanks one gets in these hard times, and I've given all up since a little misfortune that happened me.

OCTAVE. What was that?

SCAPIN. Just a little falling out I had with the law.

OCTAVE. With the law?

SCAPIN. A little disagreement I had with it. Badly treated I was; and the times being so ungrateful I said I would do no more to help anyone. (OCTAVE *and* SILVESTER *start back, disappointed.*) No matter, tell me out your story.

OCTAVE (*coming back quickly to* SCAPIN). You know, Scapin, that my father and his friend Geronte set out a couple of months ago to see after some business they both have an interest in?

SCAPIN. I know that much.

OCTAVE. And that I was left under Silvester's care, and Leandre under yours?

SCAPIN. Ay, and well minded he has been.

OCTAVE. Soon after that Leandre met with a young girl among the gipsies, and fell in love with her.

SCAPIN. I know that too.

OCTAVE. We being friends he told me about it, and took me to see the girl, who I thought good-looking enough, but not so handsome as he would have liked me to think her. He talked about her all day long, and he was ready to quarrel with me for not taking it all more seriously.

SCAPIN. I don't know yet what this is leading to.

OCTAVE (*puts his hand on* SCAPIN'S *shoulder*). One day I was going to see her with him, and we heard a great sobbing and crying in a little house we were passing. We asked what it was, and we were told there were some strangers there in a very bad way, and that no on could help pitying them.

SCAPIN. But what are we coming to, I wonder.

OCTAVE. We looked in and saw an old woman at the point of death, a nurse attending on her, and a girl, the greatest beauty you ever saw, crying her heart out.

SCAPIN. Ah, ah!

OCTAVE. Anyone else in her place would have looked an object, for she was dressed in a shabby little skirt and jacket, and with untidy hair. But nothing was able to spoil her beauty.

SCAPIN. I see we are coming to the point.

OCTAVE. If you had seen her, Scapin, as I did, you would have admired her as I did.

SCAPIN. I'll engage I would. And so I do without seeing her.

OCTAVE. Her tears were not those horrid blobby ones. She had a most engaging way of crying.

SCAPIN. I understand.

OCTAVE. It was heart-breaking to see the way she clung to the poor woman she was calling mother.

SCAPIN. Very pretty, indeed. It is easily seen you fell in love with this good daughter.

OCTAVE. Oh, Scapin, a savage would have fallen in love with her.

SCAPIN. To be sure he would. What way could he help it?

OCTAVE. When we left the house I asked Leandre what he thought of her, and he said, quite coolly, "Rather pretty." Of course, after that I didn't tell him what I thought of her.

SILVESTER (*coming between them*). If you don't shorten this story we'll be here till to-morrow. I'll make a finish of it in two words. (*To* SCAPIN.) The girl was honest, there was nothing for it but marriage, and he has been married to her these three days.

SCAPIN. I understand.

SILVESTER (*counting on his fingers*). Now put to that his father coming home before his time, his uncle finding out the secret of his marriage, and the match they have made up for him with Geronte's daughter by his second wife, her that was of Tarentum.

OCTAVE. And add to all that my not having a penny in the world to support a wife on.

SCAPIN. Is that all? That's a very small thing to be upsetting you. You should be ashamed to be at a loss for a trifle of that sort. What the mischief! You to be as big as father and mother and not to be able to make some plan in your head, some little trick to straighten things for yourself. I wish I had got the chance at your age to have these old heroes to play my game on. I'm the boy that could have done it. I wasn't that height when I could beat the world for tricks.

SILVESTER. I'm not gifted in the same way at all. I haven't the wit like you to have got into the grip of the law.

OCTAVE. Here comes my wife, my dear Hyacinth.

(HYACINTH *comes in*.)

HYACINTH. Oh, Octave, is it true what I hear, that your father has come back and has made a match for you?

OCTAVE. True, indeed, dear Hyacinth. The news was a great upset to me, but there is a man (*pointing to* SCAPIN) who could if he likes be the greatest help to us.

SCAPIN (*coming to* OCTAVE). I have taken my oath often enough to have nothing more to do with the business of this world——but if both of you begged me very hard maybe——.

OCTAVE. Oh, if it's a question of begging you, I beg you with all my heart to take the rudder of our boat.

SCAPIN. And have you no word to say to me?

HYACINTH. I beg and pray you in the name of whatever is dearest to you to help us.

SCAPIN. I suppose I must give in so, and show you some kindness. Well, I'll do my best for you.

OCTAVE. You may be sure——.

SCAPIN. That'll do (*to* HYACINTH.) You may go now, and make yourself easy.

(OCTAVE *gives his hand to* HYACINTH *and leads her to door.*)

SCAPIN (*to* OCTAVE). You must embolden yourself now before you will meet your father.

OCTAVE. The very thought of meeting him makes me shiver. I am nervous by nature, and I can't get over it.

SCAPIN. You must speak up to him at the first meeting, or he will think you a child yet for him to be leading by the hand. Learn now a little courage the same as you would learn a lesson. Settle out what way you will give an answer to anything he may say.

OCTAVE. I will do the best I can.

SCAPIN. Come now, till I practise you. Speak out your part till we'll see do you say it well. Here now——a hardy look——the head up—a straight carriage.

OCTAVE. This way?

SCAPIN. That'll do, now let on to yourself that I'm your father, and give me out answers as you would to himself. (*He goes up room, turns round to* OCTAVE.) What's that? You fool, you dog-boy! You ill-conditioned idiot! Would you dare come before me after your behaviour, after the dirty trick you played and my back turned? Is that the harvest I get for caring for you, you hound? Is that the respect you show me, the respect that is due to me? You have the impudence, you rascal, to go engage yourself without my consent, to make an underhand marriage. Answer me, you villain. Answer me, I say? Let me hear now your grand excuses——Oh, the deuce take it, have you nothing to say?

OCTAVE. Because I keep thinking it is my father who is speaking.

SCAPIN. Just so. And that is the reason you must behave like an innocent!

OCTAVE. I will be all right; you will see how well I will answer.

57

SCAPIN. You are sure of that?

OCTAVE. Quite sure.

SILVESTER. Here's your father coming.

OCTAVE. Oh, I say. I am done for. (*Runs out.*)

SCAPIN. (*runs after him*). Hallo, Octave. Stop here, Octave. (*Comes back.*) What a poor creature of a man! We'll stop here now for the master of the house.

SILVESTER. What am I to say to him?

SCAPIN. Let me speak, and let you do nothing but back me up.
    (ARGANTE *comes in.*)

ARGANTE (*believing himself alone*). Did anyone ever hear of such a thing.

SCAPIN (*to* SILVESTER). He is after hearing of it. He can't but talk of it, and he alone.

ARGANTE. Such confounded daring.

SCAPIN (*to* SILVESTER). Listen to him.

ARGANTE. I would like to know what they will say to me about this accursed marriage.

SCAPIN. That is what we are thinking ourselves.

ARGANTE. Will they try to deny it?

SCAPIN. No, we won't do that.

ARGANTE. Will they try to make excuses?

SCAPIN. That might be a thing to do.

ARGANTE. Will they put me off with fairy tales?

SCAPIN. They may.

ARGANTE. All their talk won't help them.

SCAPIN. We'll see about that.
    (SCAPIN *advances a little towards* ARGANTE. SILVESTER *goes behind* ARGANTE.)

ARGANTE. They can't take *me* in.

SCAPIN. I wouldn't swear to it.

ARGANTE. I will shut up that ass of a son of mine in some safe place.

SCAPIN. We'll see about that.

ARGANTE. As for that rascal Silvester, I will flog the skin off him.

SILVESTER. It would be a wonder if he forgot me.

ARGANTE (*seeing* SILVESTER). Ah, ha, there you are, my good trusty man. A good guide you are for the young! (*Lifts his cane to strike him.* SCAPIN *catches* ARGANTE'S *arm with his left hand.*)

SCAPIN. I'm well pleased to see you coming home, sir.

ARGANTE. How are you, Scapin? (*To* SILVESTER.) You have

carried out my orders properly. My son has behaved very well while I was away!

SCAPIN. I'm glad, and very glad to see you look so well.

ARGANTE. I'm well enough. (*To* SILVESTER.) You are not saying a word, you brute.

SCAPIN. Did your honour get a good journey?

ARGANTE. Good enough——Can't you leave me to quarrel in peace?

SCAPIN. You are wishful to quarrel?

ARGANTE. Yes I am.

SCAPIN. And with who now?

ARGANTE. This blackguard here.

SCAPIN. Why is that now?

ARGANTE. You haven't heard what has been going on while I was away?

SCAPIN. I heard talk of some little thing.

ARGANTE. Some little thing! A thing of that sort.

SCAPIN. You are maybe right.

ARGANTE. Such a daring thing as that!

SCAPIN. True for you.

ARGANTE. A son to marry without his father's consent!

SCAPIN. Well, there's something in that. But I'd recommend you, sir, not to be making too much noise about it.

ARGANTE. That's not my opinion. I'll make as much noise as I choose. What? Don't you think I've good cause to be angry?

SCAPIN. That's so. I was mad out and out myself when I got word of it. I took your side. I went so far as to give your son my opinion. Ask himself what abuse I gave him, and the way I spoke of the disrespect he showed to his father in place of kissing the print of his footstep the way he ought to be. Your honour's self could not have said more than what I did. But where's the use of it? Maybe he didn't behave as badly as you think.

ARGANTE. What are you saying? He didn't behave badly in marrying a girl no one knows anything about?

SCAPIN. Sure what can you do? What must happen will happen!

ARGANTE. That's a good reason to give. One may commit all the crimes in the world—kill, cheat, rob, and say as an excuse that what must happen will happen!

SCAPIN. Ah! now you are going too deep into things. All I meant to say is, he got into this business and couldn't get out of it.

ARGANTE. Why should he have got into it?

SCAPIN. Well, now would you wish him to be as sensible as yourself? Youngsters are youngsters, and don't always keep on the straight road. Look at our Leandre now, in spite of all my warnings, all my preachings. He has done worse again than your son. Weren't you yourself young one time, and didn't you play your little pranks the same as the others? (ARGANTE *smiles*.) I heard it said you used to be a terror among the ladies——Well able to coax them you were.

> (ARGANTE *roars with laughter. While he is laughing* SCAPIN *and* SILVESTER *both go to back.*)

ARGANTE. That may be so, but I never went so far.

SCAPIN (*coming to* ARGANTE). What would you have him to do? He sees a young girl that fancies him, for he takes after you, in all the women running after him. He is taken with her, makes love to her; she is no way unwilling. Her people make an outcry and force him to marry her?

ARGANTE (*going to* SILVESTER). He was forced to marry her?

SILVESTER. He was, sir.

SCAPIN. Is it I to have told you a lie?

ARGANTE. He should have prosecuted them for intimidation.

SCAPIN. That is what he would not do.

ARGANTE. That would have made it easier for me to break the marriage.

SCAPIN. To break it?

ARGANTE. Certainly.

SCAPIN. You will not break it.

ARGANTE. I won't break it?

SCAPIN. You will not.

ARGANTE. Haven't I the rights of a father on my side, and the threats they used to my son?

SCAPIN. That is a thing he will never agree to.

ARGANTE. He won't agree to?

SCAPIN. He will not.

ARGANTE. My son?

SCAPIN. Your son. Would you have him confess he was in dread, and that they used compulsion and force? He will never own to that. It would put a disgrace on him, and leave him unworthy of belonging to you.

ARGANTE. I care nothing for that.

SCAPIN. For his own sake and for your sake he has to say it was of his own free will he married her.

ARGANTE. For my sake and for his own sake I'll make him say the contrary.

SCAPIN. I'm sure he'll not say that.
ARGANTE. I'll force him to say it.
SCAPIN. I tell you he will not.
ARGANTE. If he doesn't, I'll disinherit him.
SCAPIN. You will?
ARGANTE. I will.
SCAPIN. Very good.
ARGANTE. How very good?
SCAPIN. You will not disinherit him.
ARGANTE. Not disinherit him?
SCAPIN. No.
ARGANTE. No?
SCAPIN. No.
ARGANTE (*getting angry*). That's a good joke. I'll not disinherit my son?
SCAPIN. I say you will not.
ARGANTE. Who will hinder me?
SCAPIN. Yourself.
ARGANTE. Myself?
SCAPIN. That's it. You will not have the heart to do it.
ARGANTE. I will have the heart.
SCAPIN. You are making fun now.
ARGANTE. I am not making fun.
SCAPIN. Fatherly tenderness will gain the day.
ARGANTE. It will do no such thing.
SCAPIN. It will, it will.
ARGANTE. I tell you it shall be done.
SCAPIN. Good-morrow to you.
ARGANTE. You must not say "good-morrow to you."
SCAPIN. Sure I know you well. You are kind by nature.
ARGANTE (*furiously, going towards* SCAPIN, *who backs from him*). I am not kind. I am wicked when I have a mind. Have done, you are vexing me with your talk. (*Crosses to* SILVESTER.) Go, you good-for-nothing. Look for that oaf of mine. I am going to tell Geronte of my misfortune.

(SILVESTER *goes behind* ARGANTE *and* SCAPIN.)

SCAPIN. If I can be helpful to you in any way, sir, you have but to give me orders.

ARGANTE. Thanks (*aside.*) It is a hard thing to have one son only. If I had not lost my poor daughter, she would have been my heiress now. (*Goes out.*)

SILVESTER. You are a great man, surely, and the work is going well, but we must have money to go on with for all that. There are creditors in full cry after us on every side.

SCAPIN. Leave me alone. I have made my plan. I am searching my mind for some one I can have trust in to personate a man I want to bring in. Wait a minute——Pull your hat over your eyes like a sort of bully—Rest upon one leg——Clap your hand to your side——Walk like a king you would see in a theatre. (SILVESTER *marches about.*) That's it. Come with me, I'll make you that your barber wouldn't know you, I know all the ways of disguising the face and the voice.

(SILVESTER *goes out, followed by* SCAPIN.)

Curtain.

ACT II

SCENE: *Same as before.*

(ARGANTE *and* GERONTE *come in, leaning on their canes.*)

GERONTE. Our people will be here to-day with this fine weather. A sailor just come from Tarentum tells me he saw my man on the point of starting. But when my daughter does come she will find everything upside down. That folly of your son's has upset all our plans.

ARGANTE. Don't worry yourself about that. I'll engage to do away with that difficulty. I am going to set about it now. (*He makes a movement towards door.* GERONTE *stops him by speaking.*)

GERONTE. Faith, Mr. Argante, do you know what I think? The right bringing up of children takes a great deal of pains.

ARGANTE (*coming near to* GERONTE). No doubt about it. But what do you mean by saying that?

GERONTE. I say that the bad behaviour of youngsters generally comes from the bad education their fathers have given them.

ARGANTE. That is so sometimes. But what are you driving at?

GERONTE. What am I driving at?

ARGANTE. Yes.

GERONTE. If you had brought up your son as a good father should, he would not have played you this trick.

ARGANTE. Very well. And you have brought up your own son better?

GERONTE. Of course I have. I should be sorry to see him doing anything of the sort.

ARGANTE. And suppose this son of yours that you have reared so well had done something worse again than mine?

GERONTE. What?

ARGANTE. What?

GERONTE. What are you talking about?

ARGANTE. I am saying it is a pity to be so ready to run down other peoples doings. And that those who live in glass houses shouldn't throw stones.

GERONTE. I don't understand your riddles.

ARGANTE. You will learn to understand them.

GERONTE. Is it that you've heard something about my son?

ARGANTE. Maybe.

GERONTE. And what is it I ask you?

ARGANTE. Your Scapin gave me a hint of it when he saw me so put out. He or someone else can tell you all about it. I give you my compliments for the way you have brought up your son. (*Makes a sweeping bow.*) As for myself, I am going to consult a lawyer to know what I had best do; I'll be back again. (*Goes off.*)

GERONTE. What can he have done? Worse, he said, than the other. I don't see how it could be worse. I think to marry without your father's consent is about the worst crime that can be committed. (LEANDRE *comes in.*) Ah, there you are!

LEANDRE (*running up to embrace* GERONTE). Oh, papa, I'm so glad to see you safe at home.

GERONTE (*refusing to embrace him*). Gently. Wait till we have had a few words on business.

LEANDRE. Let me welcome you, and then——.

GERONTE (*pushing him back*). Gently, I say. There is a certain matter must be cleared up between us.

LEANDRE. What is it?

GERONTE. Let me have a look at you.

LEANDRE. What?

GERONTE. Look me straight in the face.

LEANDRE. Well?

GERONTE. What has happened here?

LEANDRE. What has happened?

GERONTE. Yes. What have you been doing while I was away?

LEANDRE. What did you want me to do?

GERONTE. I am not saying I wanted anything done. I am asking what you have done.

LEANDRE. I. Nothing for you to complain of.
GERONTE. Nothing?
LEANDRE. No.
GERONTE. You are quite sure?
LEANDRE. I am sure I have done nothing wrong.
GERONTE. For all that I have heard news of you from Scapin.
LEANDRE. Scapin?
GERONTE. Ah, ah! That name makes you start.
LEANDRE. He has told you something about me?
GERONTE. This is not the proper place to look into it. We'll talk about it elsewhere. Go back to the house. I will be there immediately. (*Going to* LEANDRE, *who retreats*.) If you have disgraced me I will give you up altogether, and you may as well leave the country. (*Goes out.*)
LEANDRE. To betray me like this. A rascal who ought for every reason to be the last to tell my secrets, to be the first to betray them to my father. By heaven he must not escape without punishment. (OCTAVE *and* SCAPIN *come in.*)
OCTAVE. My dear Scapin, what a lot I owe you. What a splendid man you are. Fortune was good sending you to my help.
LEANDRE (*goes to* SCAPIN). Ah, there you are, I am glad to have met you, you rascal.
SCAPIN. Thank you, sir. You are too kind.
LEANDRE (*drawing his sword*). You are pretending to play the fool. I'll give you a lesson.
SCAPIN (*passing to front of* OCTAVE, *falling on his knees*). Sir!
OCTAVE (*coming between them to keep* LEANDRE *from striking* SCAPIN). Oh, Leandre!
LEANDRE. No, Octave, don't hold me off.
SCAPIN (*to* LEANDRE). Oh, sir.
OCTAVE (*holding* LEANDRE). I beg you.
LEANDRE (*wanting to strike* SCAPIN). Let me get at him!
OCTAVE. In the name of friendship don't touch him.
SCAPIN. What have I done, sir?
LEANDRE (*as before*). What have you done, traitor?
    (SCAPIN *falls on his face, groaning*.)
OCTAVE (*still holding him back*). Gently now.
LEANDRE. No, Octave. I must make him confess his treachery to me. Yes, rascal. I know the trick you have played me. I have heard of it. You thought, I suppose, I wouldn't find it out. But I'll have the confession from your own mouth, or I will run this sword through your body.

64

SCAPIN (*raising his head*). Oh, sir, you wouldn't have the heart to do it.

LEANDRE. Own up, then.

SCAPIN. Have I done anything at all, sir?

LEANDRE. You have, and your conscience knows well what it is.

SCAPIN. I declare I don't know in the world what it is.

LEANDRE (*advancing to strike him*). You don't know? (SCAPIN *falls down.*)

OCTAVE (*holding him*). Leandre!

SCAPIN (*lifting his head and pretending to weep*). Very well, sir, if you will have it. I confess it was I drank with my friends that little cask of sherry was sent you the other day. It was I made a hole in the cork and wet it round about, the way you'd think the wine had run out.

LEANDRE. It was you, gaol bird, who drank my cask of wine, and made me scold the maid, thinking she had taken it?

SCAPIN. That was so. I ask your pardon for it.

LEANDRE. I am very glad to have found that out. But that is not the question just now.

SCAPIN. It was not that, sir?

LEANDRE. It is something that touches me nearer, and I will make you tell it.

SCAPIN. I don't remember, sir, doing any other thing.

LEANDRE (*trying to strike him*). You won't tell?

SCAPIN (*falls again*). Sir.

OCTAVE (*holding* SCAPIN). Quiet yourself.

SCAPIN (*raising head as before*). I will, sir. That day you sent me three weeks ago to bring a little watch to that gipsy of yours, I came back to the house, my clothes covered with mud, my face bloody, and I told you I had met with thieves that had beaten me and taken the watch from me. It was I myself, sir, that kept it.

LEANDRE. It was you stole my watch?

SCAPIN. It was, sir, to be able to know what the time was.

LEANDRE. Well, I am learning a good deal. I have an honest servant, surely; but that is not the story I want.

SCAPIN (*very astonished*). It's not that?

LEANDRE. No, I tell you. It's another thing you have to confess.

SCAPIN (*aside*). Bad luck to it.

LEANDRE. Speak up, I'm in a hurry.

SCAPIN. That is all I ever did.

LEANDRE (*striking at him*). Is that all?

OCTAVE (*putting himself before him*). Ay?

65

SCAPIN (*falling down again*). If you will have it. Are you remembering, sir, that wicked ghost you met with six months ago in the night time, that gave you a beating and near made you break your neck falling into a cellar as you ran?

LEANDRE. Well?

SCAPIN. It was myself, sir, was that ghost.

LEANDRE. You dressed up to frighten me? You scoundrel!

SCAPIN. If I did give you a fright, it was to get you out of that habit you had of wanting me to go out with you in the night.

LEANDRE. I will remind you at the right time of all you have told me. (*Coming to him.*) But just now what I want you to confess is what you have been telling my father.

SCAPIN. Telling your father, is it?

LEANDRE. Yes, you villain. My father.

SCAPIN. I give you my word I didn't so much as see him since he came back.

LEANDRE. You haven't seen him?

SCAPIN. I have not.

SCAPIN. You are sure of that?

SCAPIN. He will tell you the same himself.

LEANDRE. But I heard it from his own lips——

SCAPIN. Begging your pardon, he's a liar——. He was not telling the truth. (CARLE *comes in.*)

CARLE. I am come with bad news to you, sir.

LEANDRE (*goes to* CARLE). What is that?

CARLE. Your gipsies are on the point of carrying away Zerbinette from you. It is she herself sent me to you, and the tears standing in her eyes. She bade me tell you that if you fail to bring them the money they are asking for her, within two hours she is lost to you for ever.

LEANDRE. Within two hours?

CARLE. That's it, two hours.

(CARLE *goes out; a pause, during which* LEANDRE *looks at* OCTAVE, *who points to* SCAPIN. SCAPIN *is still on his knees.*)

LEANDRE. Oh, my good Scapin, will you give me your help?

SCAPIN. (*still kneeling*). "Oh, my good Scapin!" I am "my good Scapin" now that you are in need of me.

LEANDRE. I will forgive you all that you told me, and worse again if you have it to tell.

SCAPIN (*rising, and walking up and down, followed by* LEANDRE).

Not at all. Don't forgive me anything. Thrust your sword out through my body, I would be well pleased you to kill me.

LEANDRE. No, no, you must keep me alive by helping my love affair.

SCAPIN (*still walking up and down*). Not at all. It's best for you kill me.

LEANDRE. You are too valuable. I want that cleverness of yours that brings everything to victory.

SCAPIN. No, no! Make an end of me.

LEANDRE. Ah, give over thinking of that. Set your mind to helping me, I ask you.

OCTAVE (*stopping* SCAPIN). Look here, Scapin, you must do something for him.

SCAPIN. Is it after the insult he put upon me?

LEANDRE. Now do forget what I said, and come to my help.

SCAPIN. That insult is preying on my heart.

OCTAVE. You must try to forget it.

LEANDRE. Would you desert me, Scapin, when I am at my wits end?

SCAPIN. To have wronged me the way you did without any warning.

LEANDRE. I was in the wrong, I confess it.

SCAPIN. Wanting to thrust your sword through my body.

LEANDRE. I beg your pardon if I did. If you want me to go on my knees I'll do it. (*Kneels.*) Only don't give me up.

OCTAVE. Hang it all, Scapin, you must give in to that. (SCAPIN *turns his back on* LEANDRE, *and wraps his cloak about him. Then turns and looks at* LEANDRE.) Get up so. But you must not be so hasty another time.

LEANDRE (*getting up*). You promise to work for me?

SCAPIN. I will think about it.

LEANDRE. But there is no time to lose.

SCAPIN. Don't be troubling yourself. How much is it you want?

LEANDRE. Five hundred crowns.

SCAPIN. And you?

OCTAVE. Two hundred pounds.

SCAPIN. It is from your own two fathers I will draw the money. (*To* OCTAVE.) As for yours, I have the machinery settled already. (*To* LEANDRE.) As for your father, though he is the worst miser in the place, I will have less trouble again with him, for the Lord be praised he has no great provision of sense. I take him to be a man you could make believe anything you would choose. Don't be taking offence now, there's no sort of resemblance at all between himself and yourself. Sure there are many that say he was never your father at all.

LEANDRE. Drop that, Scapin.

SCAPIN. Very good, very good. There are some do not like to hear a thing like that. Is it humbugging you are——Hush. I see Octave's father coming towards us. We'll begin with him so as he puts himself forward. Go away the two of you. (*To* OCTAVE.) Go tell your Silvester it is time for him to come play his part.

(OCTAVE *passes behind* SCAPIN, *and goes out left with* LEANDRE. ARGANTE *comes in from right*.)

SCAPIN. Meditating he is.

ARGANTE (*believing himself alone*). To have so little sense and so little behaviour, to run himself into an engagement like this. Ah, ah, the folly of youngsters.

SCAPIN (*behind* ARGANTE). I beg your pardon, sir.

ARGANTE. Is that you, Scapin?

SCAPIN. You are thinking over this business of your son's?

ARGANTE. I confess it makes me very angry.

SCAPIN. Life is full of crosses; it is well to be always prepared for them. There was a thing I heard said by an old man long ago, I have always kept in my mind.

ARGANTE. What was that?

SCAPIN. It is what he used to be saying, that no matter how short the time the father of a family to be leaving home, he should run through in his mind all the misfortunes might meet him at his return. He should lay out to himself he would find his house burned down, his wife buried, his son be-crippled, his daughter on the streets. And none of these things to happen, he should put it to the good luck he has. As for myself, I strive always to exercise myself in this little philosophy, indeed I never come back to the house without expecting to meet with the ill temper of my masters, with scoldings, kickings, hits, raps and cuts. And if all that fails to happen me, I give thanks to my good fortune. (*Makes an elaborate bow with his hat off.*)

ARGANTE. That is right enough. But this silly marriage that upsets the one I wanted him to make is a thing I can't put up with. I have just been consulting my lawyer about breaking it.

SCAPIN. If you'll mind me, sir, you'll take some other way of settling the business. You know what sort a lawsuit is in this country. Before long you'll find yourself gripped in a briar bush.

68

ARGANTE. You are right, I know that well enough. But what else is there to do?

SCAPIN (*putting his hat on*). I think I have lit on a plan. I was that sorry seeing your trouble that I went searching my mind for some means to ease you. It's a thing I hate to see—good fathers vexed by their children. And I always had a great wish for yourself, sir.

ARGANTE (*shaking* SCAPIN'S *hand*). I'm obliged to you.

SCAPIN. So I went looking for the brother of this girl he's after marrying. He is a bullying sort of chap, one of those that has always his hand upon his sword, that talks of nothing but strokes and slashes, and would think no more of killing a man than of drinking a glass of spirits. I led him to talk of the marriage, I showed him how easy broken it would be on the head of the threats used. I made much of your rights as a father and of the support your means and your friends would get you in the Court. At last I had worked the matter so well that he offered to take it in hand and break the marriage himself in consideration of you giving him a certain sum of money.

ARGANTE. How much did he ask?

SCAPIN. Oh, at first, the world and all.

ARGANTE. And then?

SCAPIN. Something beyond all bounds.

ARGANTE. But now?

SCAPIN. He talks of no less than five or six hundred pounds.

ARGANTE. Five or six hundred pains take hold of him. Is he making a butt of us?

SCAPIN. That is what I said to him myself. I wouldn't listen to such a proposal at all. I made him understand well you were no fool, that he would be asking you five or six hundred pounds. At last after a great deal of talk this is what came of our bargaining. (SCAPIN *puts on a big voice.*) "The time has come" said he, "when I have to go join the army. I'm after buying an outfit, and the need I have of money is the only thing would make me consent to your offer." (*He roars.*) "I have to find a horse for myself," says he, "and I couldn't get one would be any good at all for less than sixty pounds."

ARGANTE. Well, as far as sixty pounds, I consent to that.

SCAPIN. Saddle and bridle he'll need, and arms. That will mount to twenty pounds more.

ARGANTE. Twenty and sixty, that makes eighty.

SCAPIN. So it does.

69

ARGANTE. That is a great deal. But never mind. I'll go as far as that.

SCAPIN (*still in a loud voice*). "I must have a mount for my servant too," said he, "and that will be thirty pounds more."

ARGANTE. What the deuce! Let him walk. He will get nothing at all.

SCAPIN. Sir?

ARGANTE. Nothing. Such impudence.

SCAPIN. Would you wish his man to travel after him walking?

ARGANTE. Let him travel as he likes, and his master with him.

SCAPIN. Ah, now sir, don't be breaking off for so small a trifle as that. Don't be going to law now. Better to give all than get into the hands of justice.

ARGANTE (*coming to* SCAPIN). Well, well, I give in, I give in to the extra thirty pounds.

SCAPIN. "I must have along with that," said he, "a mule to carry the luggage."

ARGANTE. Let him go to the devil with his mule. That is too much. I will go into Court.

SCAPIN. Oh, if you please, sir.

ARGANTE. I'll give him nothing.

SCAPIN. A *little* mule, sir.

ARGANTE. I wouldn't give him as much as an ass.

SCAPIN. Think now.

ARGANTE. I would rather go to law.

SCAPIN. Ah, sir, what are you saying? What is it you are making up your mind to? Throw your eye on the windings of justice. Look how many appeals there are, and degrees of jurisdiction. Look at all the troublesome proceedings of it, look at all the beasts of prey will be sticking their claws in you. Sergeants, attorneys, King's counsels, registrars, substitutes, reporters, judges and their clerks. There is not one of the whole flock but is ready to upset the best case in the world for the least little thing. A sergeant will issue false writs that will lose you the case before you know it. Your attorney will have an understanding with the other side, and will sell you for gold. Your counsel, bought in the same way, is not to be found when your case comes on, or he will give out arguments that lead to nothing at all. The registrar will be serving sentences and arrests on you. The reporter's clerk will be stealing your papers, or the reporter will give no clear account. And at the last, when with the greatest work in the world you have got through all that, you will wonder to find the judges set against you by religion or by their

70

wives. If you will mind me you'll keep yourself out of that hell upon earth. To be in a lawsuit is the same as to be in hell before your time. The very thought of such a thing would send me running as far as the blacks of India.

ARGANTE (*to* SCAPIN). How much would the mule come to?

SCAPIN. He was saying, for the mule, and the horse, and his servant's horse, and the saddle and arms, and some little thing he owed his landlady, he is asking in all two hundred pounds.

ARGANTE (*with a jump*). Two hundred pounds!

SCAPIN. Just that.

ARGANTE (*furiously, walking up and down*). No, no, we'll have the case tried.

SCAPIN. Think it over.

ARGANTE. I'll go to law.

SCAPIN. Don't be throwing yourself——.

ARGANTE. I will go to law.

SCAPIN. But to try the case, money will be needful, money for the registration, money for the attorney's letters, money for putting in an appearance, for counsel, for the witnesses and the solicitor's time. Along with that you must pay for consultation, for counsel's pleadings, for getting back your papers, for engrossing the documents. Money you will want for reports, for judges' fees, for the enrolment of the registrar, the form of the decree, sentences, arrests, controls, signatures, and duplicate copies. Add to that all the presents you must make. But give the money to this man, and you are clear of it all.

ARGANTE (*to* SCAPIN). What are you saying? Two hundred pounds?

SCAPIN. You'll gain by it. I am after doing up a little sum myself of the expenses of the case, and as I bring it out, by giving this man two hundred pounds you will save at the least a hundred and fifty, without reckoning the cares, the troubles, the vexations you will spare yourself. If it was for nothing at all but to be safe from all the impudent things those lawyers will be saying out before the world, I would sooner give three hundred pounds than go into the Courts.

ARGANTE. I don't care for that. I defy the lawyers to say anything against me.

SCAPIN. Well, you must do as pleases you. But if I was in your place I would keep free of the lawsuit.

ARGANTE. I will not give two hundred pounds.

(*A voice heard off.*)

SCAPIN. Here is now the very man we were talking about.

(*Enter* SILVESTER *disguised as a bully.*)

SILVESTER (*speaks in a big voice*). Here, Scapin, let me see this rogue that is Octave's father.

SCAPIN. Why so, Sir?

SILVESTER. I have just heard he is going to take an action against me and to break my sister's marriage.

SCAPIN. I don't know has he any thought of that. But he won't consent to give the two hundred pounds you are seeking. He says it is too much.

SILVESTER (*stamping his foot*). By all the holies! If I get a hold of him, I'll slaughter him if I'm hanged for it.

SCAPIN. Octave's father is a courageous man, sir, he will not be afraid of you.

SILVESTER. Ha, ha. By this and by that if I had him I'd spit him on my sword. (*Seeing* ARGANTE.) Who is that fellow?

SCAPIN. It isn't him at all, it isn't him.

SILVESTER. Maybe it's one of his friends.

SCAPIN. Not at all. So far from that it's his bitter enemy.

SILVESTER (*jumps in the air and comes down heavily*). His bitter enemy?

SCAPIN. That's what I said.

SILVESTER (*passes before* SCAPIN). I am well pleased to hear that. (*To* ARGANTE, *hitting him playfully in the stomach.*) You are an enemy to this wretched Argante?

SCAPIN. Didn't I tell you he is?

SILVESTER (*shaking* ARGANTE'S *hand, roughly*). Shake hands, shake hands. I give you my word, and I swear to you on my honour and on my sword that before the day is out I will have rid you of that scum of the world, that rogue Argante. You may trust my word.

SCAPIN (*to* SILVESTER). There are laws against violence in this country.

SILVESTER. What do I care. I have nothing to lose.

SCAPIN. He will be on his guard against you. Relations he has, and servants, and friends for his protection.

SILVESTER. That will suit me well. That is what I ask. (*Draws his sword.*) Blood and thunder! Why can't I meet him at this minute with all his help? Why doesn't he come before me, and thirty with him? Let them come make an attack on me with their swords. (*He jumps in the air, brandishing his sword.* ARGANTE *and* SCAPIN *fall on their faces,* SILVESTER *goes up and down, then mak-*

ing passes with his sword in every direction.) Ha, ha, rascals, you are daring to come at me? Come on now. No quarter (*striking right and left.*) Lay on. Drive home. Eye straight. Foot sure. Ah, you ruffians you. I'll give you what you want. Stand to it. Come on. Have at you——and you——and you, what. You're giving way? Stand your ground, I tell you stand your ground.

SCAPIN. He, he, he——Oh, sir! we have nothing to do with him.

(SILVESTER *comes to* SCAPIN *and pinches his leg;* SCAPIN *gives him his left hand without rising; they shake hands.* ARGANTE *is going to rise.* SILVESTER *hits him on the back with the flat of his sword; he falls down again.*)

SILVESTER (*wipes his sword on his sleeve*). I'll show what it is to dare play with me. (*Goes out.*)

(ARGANTE *and* SCAPIN *rise slowly to their knees, face to face.*)

SCAPIN. All right. You see how many people will be killed for the sake of two hundred pounds. That'll do. I wish you good luck.

ARGANTE (*trembling*). Scapin.

SCAPIN. What is it?

ARGANTE. I have decided to give him the two hundred pounds.

SCAPIN. I'm glad to hear it for your own sake.

ARGANTE (*standing up*). Let us go after him. I have them in my pocket.

SCAPIN. You have but to give them to me. Sure you wouldn't like to go before him after passing yourself off here as some other person? And I'm in dread that knowing you, he would ask for more money again.

ARGANTE. Yes, but I should have liked to see him get the money.

SCAPIN. Is it that you are mistrusting me?

ARGANTE. Oh, no——but——.

SCAPIN. Look here now, I am a rogue or I am an honest man, one or the other I am. Is it that I'm wanting to deceive you? Have I any interest outside yourself and my master? If it is suspecting me you are I will meddle no more, and you can find some other one to settle your business. (*Walks away from him.*)

ARGANTE (*following* SCAPIN). Take it then.

SCAPIN. No, don't be trusting me with your money at all. I would be well pleased you to make use of some other one.

ARGANTE. Oh, take it, take it.

SCAPIN. No, I tell you, don't be trusting me at all. How do you know but I might be wanting to make off with your money?

ARGANTE (*giving purse*). Take it, I say. That's enough of arguing. But mind you get a receipt from him.

SCAPIN. Leave me alone. It is no fool he has to deal with.

ARGANTE. I will go and wait for you in the house.

SCAPIN. I won't fail you there. (ARGANTE *goes out.*) One bird caught. I have but to look for the other. (*Looks out of door.*) Well, if he isn't coming this way! It's like as if heaven itself was sending them one by one into my net. (GERONTE *comes in.*)

SCAPIN (*running about stage, pretending not to see* GERONTE). What'll he do——What'll he do? Ah, the poor father. Oh, poor Geronte. What'll he do at all at all.

GERONTE (*aside*). What is he saying about me? Something must have happened.

SCAPIN. Can anyone tell me where at all is Mr. Geronte?

GERONTE. What is it, Scapin?

SCAPIN (*running here and there*). Where can I find him to tell him this great misfortune?

GERONTE. Tell me what is the matter?

SCAPIN. I am running there and hither looking for him.

GERONTE. Here I am.

SCAPIN. He must be hid in some place no one would think of.

GERONTE (*stopping him*). Here, are you blind that you don't see me?

SCAPIN. Oh, sir, it is hard indeed to meet with you.

GERONTE. I have been here before you for the last hour. What is all this about?

SCAPIN. Oh, sir.

GERONTE. What is it?

SCAPIN. Your son, sir.

GERONTE. Well, my son?

SCAPIN. The queerest misfortune in the world has happened him.

GERONTE. What is that?

SCAPIN. I found him a while ago greatly put out at something you said to him, and that you had a right not to have mixed my name in at all. I brought him walking down by the docks striving to take the load off his mind. Looking we were at one thing and another, and we cast our eyes on a Turkish galley——a grand one it was——and a very nice-looking young Turk invited us to go on board, and to see it nearer. We did that, and he gave us the best of good treatment—fruit of all sorts and wine the best in the world.

GERONTE. I see no cause for complaint in all that.

SCAPIN (*coming to* GERONTE). Wait a while, we are coming to it. While we were eating and drinking it's what he did——he got out the galley to sea. When we were clear of the harbour he put me out in a boat and sent me back with a message that if you do not send him by my hand five hundred crowns he will carry off your son to Algiers.

GERONTE. What the mischief. Five hundred crowns!

SCAPIN. Five hundred. And what is worse he has given me but two hours to get them.

GERONTE. Oh, the robber. To destroy me like this!

SCAPIN. Let you make your mind up now what way will you save your darling son from slavery.

GERONTE. But what the devil brought him into that galley?

SCAPIN. He never thought of what would happen.

GERONTE (*coming to* SCAPIN). Go and tell this Turk I will bring him to justice.

SCAPIN. In the open sea. Is it making a fool of me you are?

GERONTE. What the devil did he want going into that galley?

SCAPIN. It is often some bad chance will lead a man astray.

GERONTE. Scapin, you must do now what a faithful servant should do.

SCAPIN. What is that, now?

GERONTE. Go and tell this Turk that he must send back my son, and that he may keep you in place of him until I have gathered the ransom he wants.

SCAPIN. Ah, what are you talking about. Do you think the Turk has so little sense as to take a poor creature like myself in the place of a gentleman like your son?

GERONTE (*going a little to left*). What the devil brought him into that galley?

SCAPIN. Sure he never guessed what would happen. Think now I was given but two hours——.

GERONTE (*coming to* SCAPIN). You say he is asking——

SCAPIN. Five hundred crowns.

GERONTE. Has he no conscience?

SCAPIN. He has indeed, the conscience of a Turk.

GERONTE. Does he know what five hundred crowns means?

SCAPIN. He does, he knows they are a hundred and twenty-five pounds.

GERONTE. Does he think a hundred and twenty-five pounds are to be picked up on the ground?

SCAPIN. There are people that don't understand reasons.

GERONTE. But what the devil did he want going into that galley?

SCAPIN. That is true, but it's hard to foresee all. Hurry on, sir, if you please.

GERONTE. Well, well here's the key of my press.

SCAPIN. All right.

GERONTE. You can open it.

SCAPIN. I will do that.

GERONTE. You will find a large key on the left side, the key of my lumber room.

SCAPIN. Right.

GERONTE. You will take all the clothes you will find in the big hamper there, and sell them to a dealer to redeem my son.

SCAPIN. Are you dreaming? (GERONTE *is about to go, but* SCAPIN *catches him and gives him back key.*) I wouldn't get a hundred francs for all that's in it. Besides that you know how little I have been given.

GERONTE. What the devil brought him into that galley?

SCAPIN. Ah, what a lot of words to be spending. Have done talking of that galley and remember that time is passing, and you in danger of losing your son. (*Rocks himself, wringing his hands.*) My grief, my poor master. It is likely I will never see you again, maybe at this minute they are bringing you away as a slave to Algiers. But the Lord knows I have done all I could for you. If you fail of being ransomed all you have to lay the blame on is the unkindness of your own father.

GERONTE (*going towards door*). Wait, Scapin, I will go and look for the money.

SCAPIN. Hurry on, then, I'm in dread of the hour going by.

GERONTE (*coming back to* SCAPIN). Isn't it four hundred crowns you said?

SCAPIN. No, but five hundred.

GERONTE. Five hundred crowns.

SCAPIN. You have it now.

GERONTE. What the devil brought him into that galley?

SCAPIN. What indeed. But hurry on.

GERONTE. Was there no other place to take a walk in?

SCAPIN. There might be——but don't delay.

GERONTE. That accursed galley.

SCAPIN. That galley is sticking in his gizzard.

GERONTE (*taking purse from pocket*). Here, Scapin, I have just remembered, I had received a little while ago the very sum of gold, but I never thought it would be swept away from me so soon. (*Holds out purse.*) Take it and ransom my son.

SCAPIN. I will, sir.

GERONTE (*still keeping purse*). But tell this Turk he is a villain.

SCAPIN (*holding out hand*). So I will.

GERONTE. A wretch.

SCAPIN. I will.

GERONTE. A traitor. A thief.

SCAPIN. Let me alone.

GERONTE. That he is dragging this money out of me against all right.

SCAPIN. I'll tell him that.

GERONTE. That I don't give it of my own free will.

SCAPIN. All right.

GERONTE. That if ever I take him I'll make him pay for it.

SCAPIN. That's it.

GERONTE (*puting purse in his pocket and going out*). Go at once and bring back my son.

SCAPIN. Hallo, hallo.

GERONTE. What is it?

SCAPIN. Where's the money?

GERONTE (*coming back to* SCAPIN). Didn't I give it to you?

SCAPIN. Not at all. You put it in your pocket.

GERONTE. Ah, it is the grief that has confused my mind. (*Searching his left pocket.*)

SCAPIN. No, the other. (*Pointing to his right pocket.*)

GERONTE (*giving purse*). What the devil did he want in that galley. My curse upon that galley. The devil take that robber of a Turk!

(*He goes out.*)

SCAPIN (*at back*). He can't get over this, that I have got it out of him. But I have not done with him. I'll make him pay in some other coin for the way he slandered me to my master.

(OCTAVE *and* LEANDRE *come in.*)

OCTAVE (*coming to* SCAPIN, *right side*). Well, Scapin, what success for me have you had?

LEANDRE (*coming to* SCAPIN, *left side*). Have you done anything to help my case?

SCAPIN (*to* OCTAVE). Here are two hundred pounds I have got out of your father.

OCTAVE. Oh, that is splendid.

SCAPIN (*to* LEANDRE). I was able to do nothing for you.

LEANDRE (*turning to go*). Then I have nothing to do but to die. I have nothing to live for if Zerbinette is taken away from me.

SCAPIN. Wait a minute. What a hurry you are in.

LEANDRE (*coming back*). What is there for me to do here?

SCAPIN. Here now. I have got what you want.

LEANDRE. Ah, you have brought me back to life.

SCAPIN. But I make one condition. You must give me leave to take some little vengeance on your father for the trick he played on me.

LEANDRE. Do it, and welcome.

SCAPIN. You give me that leave before a witness?

LEANDRE. Yes, of course.

SCAPIN. Here then are your five hundred crowns.

LEANDRE. Now let's be off and make sure of Zerbinette.

Curtain.

ACT III

(*Enter* ZERBINETTE *and* HYACINTH, *holding hands, followed by* SCAPIN *and* SILVESTER.)

SILVESTER. It is what our masters have settled that the two of you should be put to keep one another company. We have obeyed now the order they gave us.

HYACINTH. That is an order that pleases me very well. I hope Zerbinette, the friendship between my Octave and your Leandre will lead to a friendship between you and me?

ZERBINETTE. I hope so indeed. I never refuse a chance of friendship.

SCAPIN. And have you the same welcome now for love?

ZERBINETTE. Ah, that's another thing. That's not quite so safe. Tell us now, Scapin, the story of how you got the money out of your old miser. You know telling a story to me is not lost time. I love a good story.

SCAPIN. Here is Silvester—he will tell it better than myself. I have a little revenge to go do now, that I am well pleased to think of.

SILVESTER. I think you are cracked running yourself into risks of the sort.

SCAPIN. I like well to be playing an odd game that has some taste of danger in it.

SILVESTER. If you'd mind me you'd give up that game you have in hand.

78

SCAPIN. I would, but it's myself I mind.

SILVESTER. What the mischief do you want with tricks of the kind?

SCAPIN. What the mischief are you bothering about?

SILVESTER. I see you are going to bring down a rod on your back when there is no need for it.

SCAPIN. If I am it's on my own back it'll fall and not on yours.

SILVESTER. To be sure you are master of your own skin, do what you like with it so.

(*Goes out.*)

SCAPIN. It's not a fear of that sort would ever stop me. I hate those sort of timorous persons that will never go into anything fearing some harm might come of it.

ZERBINETTE. But, Scapin, we have not done with you yet.

SCAPIN. I'll be back with you immediately.

(*They go into the house followed by* SILVESTER.)

SCAPIN. It must never be said that I let myself be slandered, accused of betraying my master's secret, and that slanderer got off free. He will not get off free. I'm the one that will punish him. (*Goes to right, and puts down his sack and stick.*)

(GERONTE *enters left.*)

GERONTE (*crosses to* SCAPIN). Well, Scapin, what about my son?

SCAPIN. He is safe enough, sir. But it is you yourself is in the greatest danger. I would give all I have in the world you to be safe in your own house.

GERONTE. What is it?

SCAPIN. At this very minute there are some searching for you in every place to make an end of you.

GERONTE. Of me?

SCAPIN. Of yourself.

GERONTE. But who are they?

SCAPIN. The brother of that girl Octave has married it is. He thinks it is by reason of you wanting your daughter put in his sister's place that the marriage is to be broke. It is on you his anger has fallen, and he is calling out that he will have your life. All his friends, terrible men like himself, are tracking you up and down and asking news of you, questioning every person they meet. I saw them myself setting a picket on every path leading to your house, the way you can't go home or take a step right or left without falling into their hands.

GERONTE. Oh, my poor Scapin, what can I do?

SCAPIN. That is what I don't know——it is a very unlooked for

thing to have happened. It is trembling I am from head to foot——
Wait a minute. (*Gives a cry and runs to right.*)

GERONTE (*trembling*). Ah!

SCAPIN (*comes back*). No, no, it's nothing.

GERONTE. Can't you think of some way of saving me from this danger?

SCAPIN. There is a way I thought of, but I'd be in danger myself of getting my brains knocked out.

GERONTE. Oh, Scapin, that's no matter, show me what a faithful servant you can be. Don't forsake me.

SCAPIN. Well, I'm willing to try it. I have such a great leaning to you, I'd be loth to leave you without help.

GERONTE. You will get a good reward I promise you, I'll give you this coat when I have had a little more wear out of it.

SCAPIN. Wait now, this is what I'm thinking is the handiest way to save you. First of all you have got to get into this sack. (*Brings sack over.*)

GERONTE (*thinking he sees someone*). Ah!

SCAPIN. No, no, no, no, it's no one at all. I tell you, you must get into it, and you must keep yourself from stirring. I will put you up on my back like a sack of——anything at all, till I'll carry you through your enemies as far as your house. Once there we can barricade ourselves and send looking for help.

(GERONTE *has been getting into the sack during* SCAPIN'S *speech.*)

GERONTE. That is not a bad plan.

SCAPIN. It is the best in the world. Wait till you see. (*Aside*) I'll make you pay for that defamation of character!

GERONTE. Eh?

SCAPIN. I was saying your enemies will be well tricked. Get down well into the bottom, and be sure above all not to show yourself, or to make a stir whatever may happen. (*Closes sack over* GERONTE.)

GERONTE. Let me alone, I know how to mind myself.

SCAPIN. Hide, hide, here comes a bully of them in search of you. (*Takes hold of stick, changing his voice.*) "What's that? Amn't I to get a chance of killing that Geronte? Is there no one for charity's sake will tell me where to find him?" (*To* GERONTE *in his usual voice*) Don't show yourself. (*As before*) "By gob, I'll find him if he is hiding in the depths of the earth. Here, you fellow with the sack——" Sir?——"I'll give you a guinea if you will tell me where this Geronte can be." You are looking for that gentleman? "Believe me I am"—And for what, sir?——"For what?——" Yes, sir——"For to thrash him well with this thorn stick." Oh, sir, you wouldn't strike a gentleman of that sort. It isn't for a man of his sort to be treated that way. "Who, that cur of a Geronte? That knave, that ruffian, that rascal——" He is not a knave, sir, or a rascal, or a ruffian, and you should not, if you please, be speaking that way. "Is it impudence you are giving me?" I am but defending as I should, an honourable gentleman that is abused——"You are, maybe, one of his friends?——" I am, sir——"You are, are you?" That's right. (*Striking the sack several times*) "There I give you that for him" (*Crying out as if the blows were falling on him*) Ah, ah, ah, sir. Oh, sir, gently. That's enough. Oh, oh, oh. "Be off. Give him that from me." Oh, the devil take the Northerner, oh!

(SCAPIN *moves away and throws down stick.*)

GERONTE (*putting his head out of sack*). Oh, Scapin, I can't bear any more.

SCAPIN. Oh, I'm pounded to death. My shoulders are destroyed.

GERONTE. How is that? It was my back the blows fell on.

SCAPIN. Not at all, sir, it was my own.

GERONTE. What do you mean? I felt the blows, and I feel them still.

SCAPIN. I tell you it was but the end of the stick that reached you.

GERONTE. You should have moved a little further off to have spared me.

SCAPIN (*pushing his head into the sack*). Take care——here is some other one coming that has the look of a stranger——(*Changes voice.*) "Look at me running through the day like a greyhound, and not able to find that rat of a Geronte." Hide yourself well——"Tell me now if you please do you know where is this Geronte we are looking for?"——I do not, sir. I know nothing of him——"Tell me if you can. I have no great cruelty to show him, just a dozen or so strokes of my cane and three or four prods of my sword?"—— Indeed, sir, I don't know where he is——"I think I see something moving in the sack"——Not at all, sir——"There is something going on"——Not at all, sir——"I have a mind to run my sword through that sack"——Oh, sir, don't do that——"Show me then what is in it"——Gently, sir——"Why gently?"——It's no business of yours what I have in it——"I say I will look"——You will not look——"Stuff and nonsense"——There are clothes that belong to myself——"Show them to me I say"——I will not—— "You won't?"——No——"Then you'll feel my stick on your back"——I don't care—— "Ah, you don't care, don't you?" (*Hitting sack*) Ah, ah, ah, oh, sir, oh, oh, oh——"Good-bye to you now, that's just a little lesson to teach you manners"——a bad end to the blackguard. Oh! ——

GERONTE (*putting his head out of sack*). Oh, I'm destroyed.

SCAPIN. Oh, I'm killed altogether.

GERONTE. Why the deuce should they assault me?

SCAPIN (*pushing his head into sack*). Have a care. Here are half a dozen of them all together. (*Mimicking the voices of several people.*) "Come along——we must make out this Geronte, we must seek him out. Don't spare yourselves. Ransack the town. Forget no corner. Try every hole. Rummage on every side. Where will we go? Turn this way——no, but that way——to the left, to the right"——Hide yourself well——"Ah, cowards, look at his servant. Ha, rascal, we'll teach you who is your master." (SCAPIN *falls on his knees, with his back to* GERONTE.) Oh, gentlemen, don't be ill-treating me——"Come on tell us where he is. Speak up, no delay." Don't show yourself. (GERONTE *puts his head out of the sack and perceives* SCAPIN'S *trick.*) "If we don't find your master at once it's a hail storm of blows will be falling on you"——I would suffer all sooner than betray my master——"We'll knock your brains out"——Do as pleases you——"It's a thrashing you want, here is a taste of it." (*He turns to strike sack, sees* GERONTE, *and flies out right, throws stick in the air.*)

GERONTE (*throwing sack after* SCAPIN). You scoundrel. You hound. You villain. This is the way you are bringing me to my death.

(ZERBINETTE *comes in, laughing, doesn't see* GERONTE.)

ZERBINETTE. Ha, ha, ha. What a joke. What a silly old man.

GERONTE (*coming forward*). There is nothing at all amusing in it for you to laugh at.

ZERBINETTE. What, what are you saying, sir?

GERONTE. I say you have no business to laugh at me.

ZERBINETTE. At you?

GERONTE. Yes.

ZERBINETTE. But who thought of laughing at you?

GERONTE. Why, you are, laughing at me to my face.

ZERBINETTE. I wasn't laughing at you, I was laughing at a story I have just been told, the funniest I have ever heard. Perhaps it's because I'm concerned in it myself, but I never in my life heard anything so funny as a trick played on a father by his son to get money out of him.

GERONTE. A trick played on a father to get money out of him?

ZERBINETTE. Yes. I'll tell it to you if you like. I'm dying to tell it to someone.

GERONTE. Tell it to me if you please.

ZERBINETTE. I will——it doesn't matter for it can't be long hidden anyhow——I must tell you that I had been carried from place to place by a troop of gipsies, and a young gentleman of this town saw me and fell in love with me, and wanted to marry me. But the gipsies wouldn't give up without a sum of money, and he has none. His father though has plenty, but he is a dreadful miser, the stingiest wretch in the world——Wait, I can't think of his name ——can you help me? Tell me the name of someone who is well known here as the most niggardly person in the town?

GERONTE. I don't know him.

ZERBINETTE. There is a ron in his name——ron—ronte—— Oronte? No. G——Geronte. That's it, that's the old wretch. I have him, that's the miser I'm telling of. Well, my gipsies were going to carry me off from this, but for the cleverness of a servant he has, I know his name well, Scapin—a wonderful man. He deserves all the praise we can give him.

GERONTE. The scoundrel!

ZERBINETTE. Here is the trick he played, ha, ha, ha——I can't think of it without laughing myself sick. He went to this dreadful old man and told him that in walking on the quays with his son—— He, he! ——They had seen a Turkish galley——had been invited on board——that a young Turk had entertained them——ha, ha, ha——That while they were eating, the galley had put out to sea, and that the Turk had sent him back alone in a boat with a threat to the father that if he didn't send five hundred crowns within an hour his son would be a slave in Algiers. Ha, ha, ha! You may fancy the old niggard torn in two between his feeling for his son and his stinginess. The five hundred crowns he asked were like five hundred stabs of a dagger to him, ha, ha, ha! He couldn't make up his mind to disgorge such a sum, and he kept thinking of a hundred other ways of getting back his son, ha, ha, ha! He wanted to serve a writ on the Turk in his galley. He wanted Scapin to be made a slave in his son's place——he wanted him to go and sell a few suits of old clothes to make up the ransom——ha, ha, ha—— And every time Scapin told him he must send the full sum he made a lament: "But what the devil brought him into that galley"—— But my story doesn't seem to amuse you. What do you think of it?

GERONTE. I think that the young man is a rascal, an insolent puppy, who will be well punished by his father for the trick he played him. As to the gipsy, she is an ill-bred piece of impudence to tell such things to an honourable man who will teach her to come here leading gentlemen's sons astray. I say Scapin is a criminal who shall be sent to the gallows by me myself before morning. (*Goes out.*)

SILVESTER (*coming in*). Who is that running away from you? Do you know that you have been talking to Leandre's father?

ZERBINETTE. So it seems. Only think I had been telling him his own story.

SILVESTER. His own story?

ZERBINETTE. Yes, I was so full of it I was dying to tell it to someone. What does it matter? So much the worse for him. I don't see it will make things either better or worse for us.

SILVESTER. You were in a great hurry to go chattering. People that cannot keep in their own affairs have too long a tongue.

ZERBINETTE. Oh, he would have heard it from someone else.

ARGANTE (*heard in the distance*). Hallo, Silvester.

SILVESTER (*to* ZERBINETTE). Go back into the house, here is my master calling me.

(*She goes into house;* SILVESTER *goes to meet* ARGANTE, *who threatens him with his stick.*)

ARGANTE. You have put your minds together to cheat me, you and Scapin and my son. You have joined to rob me and you think I will put up with it?

SILVESTER (*falls on his knees*). Ah, sir, if Scapin has wronged you I have done with him. I will have nothing more to do with it at all.

ARGANTE. We'll see into this, you good-for-nothing, we'll see into this, I am not a man to let myself be cheated.

GERONTE (*coming in as* SILVESTER *rises*). Ah, my friend——

ARGANTE. You see me overwhelmed with misfortunes.

GERONTE. And you see me in the same way. (SILVESTER *goes behind them and picks up* SCAPIN'S *stick.*) That gaol-bird, Scapin, has got five hundred crowns out of me by his roguery.

ARGANTE. That same gaol-bird, Scapin, has robbed me of two hundred pounds.

GERONTE. He was not content with plundering me, he has treated me in a way I am really ashamed to tell you. But he'll pay for it.

ARGANTE. I'll make him pay too for the trick he played me.

GERONTE. I'll make an example of him.

SILVESTER (*aside*). I hope I won't be made another example of.

GERONTE. But that's not all, and one misfortune is followed by another. I was looking forward to-day to seeing my daughter, all my hopes of happiness were in her. But I have just got word she left Tarentum a long while ago, and it is believed she was lost with the ship.

ARGANTE. And why did you leave her all her life at Tarentum?

GERONTE. I had to keep my second marriage a secret till now ——But who is that I see? (*Enter* NERINE.) Is that you, nurse?

NERINE. Ah, Signor Pandolfe.

GERONTE. Call me Geronte, don't use that name any more. I have no reason now for hiding my name as I did at Tarentum.

NERINE. Oh, and all the trials and troubles we were put to through that wrong name, trying to find you here.

GERONTE. Where are my daughter and her mother?

NERINE. Your daughter is not far off, sir, but before you see her I ask your forgiveness for letting her get married. It was because of the state we were in and not being able to find you.

GERONTE. My daughter married?

NERINE. Yes, sir.

GERONTE. And to whom?

NERINE. A young gentleman called Octave, son of a certain Argante.

GERONTE. Good heavens!

ARGANTE. What a chance.

GERONTE. Take me to her at once, at once.

NERINE. You have only to go into this house.

GERONTE. Go on. Follow me, follow me, Argante. (*They go into the house.*)

SILVESTER. That now is a very strange thing to have happened.

SCAPIN (*coming in*). Well, Silvester, what are our people doing?

SILVESTER (*giving him stick*). I have two bits of news for you. The first is, Octave's business is settled. Who does this Hyacinth turn out to be but old Geronte's daughter. Chance has done what the fathers were working for. The other is that the two fathers are making terrible threats against you, more especially Geronte.

SCAPIN. That's nothing. Threats do no great injury. Clouds above in the sky they are.

SILVESTER. You'd best mind yourself. The sons will make up with their fathers, and you yourself will be left out in the cold.

SCAPIN. Leave me alone, I'll find some way to take the sting out of them.

SILVESTER. Quit this, they are coming out.

85

(SCAPIN *runs out. Enter* GERONTE, ARGANTE, HYACINTH, ZERBINETTE, NERINE.)

GERONTE. Come, my girl, come home with me. I should have nothing left to wish for if your poor mother were but with you.

ARGANTE (*looks out and sees* OCTAVE). Here is Octave in the nick of time. (OCTAVE *comes in.*) Come, my son, till we congratulate you on the happy prospect of your marriage.

OCTAVE. No, father, all your proposals of marrying me go for nothing. I won't deceive you. You have been told of my engagement?

ARGANTE. Yes, but you don't know——

OCTAVE. I know all I need know.

ARGANTE. I tell you Geronte's daughter——

OCTAVE. Geronte's daughter will never be anything to me.

GERONTE. It is she——

OCTAVE. No, you must excuse me, I have made up my mind.

SILVESTER (*to* OCTAVE). Listen.

OCTAVE. Hold your tongue, I will listen to nothing.

ARGANTE. Your wife——

OCTAVE. No, I tell you. I would rather die than give up my sweet Hyacinth. (*Comes over and stands beside her.*) It's no use. My faith is pledged to her, I will love her all my life and I don't want any other woman.

ARGANTE. Well, we are giving her to you. What an obstinate chap he is, sticking to his own way.

HYACINTH (*pointing to* GERONTE). Yes, Octave, that is my father. I have found him. No more troubles now.

GERONTE. Come to my house, we can settle things better over there. (LEANDRE *comes in from right.*)

HYACINTH (*pointing to* ZERBINETTE). Oh, father, please don't separate me from that dear girl, I know you will take a liking to her when you know her.

GERONTE. Would you have me bring home the girl your brother is in love with, and that told me just now to my face, all the spiteful things that are said against me?

ZERBINETTE. Please forgive me, sir. I would never have spoken like that had I known it was you——and I only knew you by report.

GERONTE. What, by report?

HYACINTH. My brother is set on marrying her, and she is a very good girl.

GERONTE. This is too much. Wanting me to marry my son to a girl no one knows, that goes about as a stroller.

LEANDRE (*coming in between* ARGANTE *and* GERONTE). Don't say now that I am marrying a girl of no birth. The people I bought her from have just told me she belongs to this town and to a good family. They stole her away when she was four years old. They have given me this bracelet to help to identify her.

ARGANTE (*takes bracelet*). Heavens! If this is her bracelet, she is the daughter I lost at that age.

GERONTE. Your daughter?

ARGANTE. Yes, yes, and I see a likeness in her that makes me sure of it. Oh, my dear daughter.

(ZERBINETTE *goes to him, throws herself into his arms*.)

HYACINTH. What wonderful things are happening?

CARLE (*comes in*). Oh, gentlemen, there has been a terrible accident.

GERONTE. Anyone hurt?

CARLE. That poor Scapin!

GERONTE. That rascal I want to see hanged.

CARLE. Oh, sir, you needn't go to that trouble. It is passing by a new building he was, and the stone-cutters hammer chanced to fall upon his head and shattered it. Dying he is, and all he asked was to be brought back here to speak with you before his death meets him.

(SCAPIN *is carried in, his head bandaged*.)

SCAPIN. Ah, ah, ah——Oh, gentlemen, you see the way I am, you see me indeed in a very strange case, ah——I was loth to die before I would come to ask pardon of all I might have wronged in any way. And above all of their honours Mr. Argante and Mr. Geronte. Ah, ah——

ARGANTE. As for me, I forgive you, go die in peace.

SCAPIN (*to* GERONTE). It is you, sir, I offended the most with those blows that——

GERONTE. Say no more. I also forgive you.

SCAPIN. It was very bold of me giving those blows——

GERONTE. Leave talking of that.

SCAPIN. It breaks my heart, and I dying, to think of those blows——

GERONTE. Will you hold your tongue.

SCAPIN. Those unlucky blows that I gave——

GERONTE. Be quiet, I forgot all about them.

SCAPIN. Oh, what great goodness. But are you in earnest saying you will forgive me those blows?

GERONTE. Oh, yes, no more about it, I forgive all. That is done with.

SCAPIN. That word now is the greatest comfort to me.

(*He snatches bandage off his head and waves it in the air.*)

GERONTE. But I only forgive you on condition that you die.

SCAPIN. What is that, sir?

GERONTE. I take back my pardon if you recover.

SCAPIN (*putting bandage on his head again*). Oh, oh! Look at my weakness that is coming on me again.

ARGANTE. I think, Geronte, you ought to forgive him without any conditions in honour of our own good luck.

GERONTE. Well, I will if you wish it.

ARGANTE. Come, we'll have supper together to celebrate this happy day.

SCAPIN. Let you carry me to the lower end of the table while I am waiting for my death!

Curtain.

THE MISER
AFTER
JEAN BAPTISTE MOLIÈRE

THE MISER

PERSONS
    HARPAGON. *Father of Cleante and Elise.*
    CLEANTE. *Harpagon's son, in love with Marian.*
    ELISE. *Harpagon's daughter, in love with Valere.*
    VALERE. *Anselme's son, in love with Elise.*
    MARIAN. *In love with Cleante.*
    FROSINE. *A matchmaking woman.*
    SIMON. *A moneylender.*
    JACQUES. *Cook and coachman to Harpagon.*
    LA FLECHE. *Valet to Cleante.*
    DAME CLAUDE. *Harpagon's housekeeper.*
    BRINDAVOINE ⎫
    LA MERLUCHE ⎬ *Servants to Harpagon.*
    A POLICE OFFICER.

ACT I

SCENE. *A Room in Harpagon's House.*

VALERE. What ails you and what is vexing you, Elise, and you having given me your word you would never break with me. Is it right for you to be fretting at the time I am so well content? Is it that you are sorry now for the good words you said to me? Are you drawing back from the promise I maybe hurried you into, with the strength of my asking and my love?

ELISE. No, Valere, I cannot be sorry for that. I feel myself as if drawn along by some power that is very pleasing to me. I cannot wish things to be different from what they are. But to tell you the truth, everything is going so well that I must feel uneasy. I am afraid I care for you a little more than I should.

VALERE. Ah, what is there for you to be afraid of in that?

ELISE. Oh, I am afraid of a great many things—my father in a rage, my family scolding at me, everybody abusing me. And what I am most afraid of, Valere, is that you yourself will change. That is the way men are, when they know they have won your love they pay you back by not wanting it.

VALERE. Ah, now you are misjudging me, thinking me to be the same as other men! Think any bad thing of me but that I can change. I love you too much to treat you that way, and my love will last through the whole of my lifetime.

ELISE. Ah, Valere, that is the way they all talk! Every man is as loyal as another so far as words go. It is only when it comes to doing we see the difference.

VALERE. Well if you can only judge us by what we do, wait till you see how I will never change, and don't be worrying by expecting the worst that can happen. Don't make an end of me altogether, fixing these suspicions on me. Give me time to prove to you, by thousands and thousands of proofs, that I am in real earnest.

ELISE. It is a pity one can be so easily talked over by any person one cares for. Yes, Valere, I don't think you could deceive me. I believe you love me with a real true love, and that it will never change. I will never doubt you any more! I will be afraid of nothing but the blame that is sure to fall upon me.

VALERE. Why are you so uneasy about that?

ELISE. There would be nothing to be afraid of if everybody could see you with my own eyes. You yourself are the excuse for everything! And heaven knows I must be grateful to you! There is not a minute of the day I do not think of that terrible danger that threw us together! Your wonderful goodness that led you to risk your own life to save me from drowning in the sea! The care you took of me after that! The devotion that led you to pass yourself off to my father as a servant that you might be near me! All that is excuse enough for the promise I have given you. But maybe other people will not look at the matter in the same way.

VALERE. The only thing deserves any return at all from you is my love! Don't worry yourself so much about your father. The way he stints you, and his miserly ways, are an excuse for more than that. Don't be vexed with me for saying it. You know well there is no one at all could stand up for him. But if I can find my own people again, and I am sure to find them, there will not be much trouble in bringing him round. I am looking for news of them, and if it doesn't come soon I will go looking for them myself.

ELISE. Oh, Valere, don't stir from this place! You have nothing to think of now but how to get round my father.

VALERE. Oh, I am getting on very well with him. What a lot of lies I had to tell before I could get into his service! What a humbug I have turned to be. But I am getting on well now, for I find that all I have to do is to agree to all he says, to praise his fooleries, and to make much of all he may do. There is no fear of overdoing it. I need not put on any disguise at all. The smarter a man of his sort thinks himself to be, the easier it is to give him plaster of Paris. There is nothing I couldn't make him swallow. Maybe it is not good for my own honesty, but what can we do? I have to get round him for my own purpose. It is not the man that flatters should be blamed, but the man that asks to be flattered.

ELISE. But why don't you try and get my brother to help you?

VALERE. I have enough to do managing one of them. It would be best for you yourself to manage your brother. He is fond of you, and you will coax him to help us. Here he is coming. I will be off. Speak to him now, but don't tell him more than you think wise.

ELISE. I don't know if I have courage enough to tell him. (VALERE *goes out*.)

CLEANTE (*coming in*). I am glad you are alone Elise. I want to have a talk with you, to tell you a secret.

ELISE. Here I am ready to listen to you. What have you to tell?

CLEANTE. A great many things all in one word. I have fallen in love.

ELISE. In love!

CLEANTE. Just so. But before going on, I should say that I am dependent on my father, that a son should give in to his father, that we ought not to get into engagements without the consent of those we owe our life to; that heaven has made them the masters of our wishes, and we should never make a promise without their consent. I am telling you all this that you may save yourself the trouble of telling it to me. So as I will not listen to anything of the kind you need not start making objections.

ELISE. Have you engaged yourself to the girl you are in love with?

CLEANTE. Not yet, but I am going to engage myself, and you need not begin talking against it.

ELISE. You must have a very strange opinion of me.

CLEANTE. No, but you not being in love yourself, you have no notion what it is. It is your good sense I am afraid of.

ELISE. Oh, don't be talking of my good sense! There is no one it does not fail once in a lifetime. If I tell you the truth you will very likely think me even more of a fool than yourself!

CLEANTE. Not if your sweetheart is anything like mine!

ELISE. Let us make a finish of your business first. Tell me who is she?

CLEANTE. A young girl who has been staying here this while

back. Everyone that sees her falls in love with her. There is not her equal in the whole world. I was done for from the first minute I got a sight of her. Her name is Marian. She is in charge of a good old soul, who is nearly always laid up with something or other. You can't think how fond she is of that old woman. She looks after her, takes care of her, comforts her, with a kindness that would touch your heart. She has the most engaging ways! She is shining with goodness and kindness and modesty, and—— Oh, I wish you had seen her!

ELISE. I see a great deal in what you are telling me. It is enough anyhow to tell me that you care for her.

CLEANTE. I have found out that they are not well off, and that it is all they can do to pay their way. Just fancy what a joy it would be to be able to help the woman you love! And think what a trouble it is to me that I can do nothing at all for her because my father is a miser!

ELISE. I understand how you must feel that.

CLEANTE. Oh, no one would believe what it is to me! Could anything be worse than the way he treats us! His stinginess, the bareness of our way of living! Where is the use of money if it only comes when you are too old to enjoy it? I have to run into debt on every side to keep myself going at all. We have both of us to coax the shopkeepers to let us have so much as clothes to put on. Well, what I am coming to is, I want you to sound our father, and if he will do nothing for me I have made up my mind to go away and to take Marian with me, and trust heaven for the rest. I am looking where I can borrow money to carry out this plan. If your case is anything like mine, you had better run too, and say goodbye to him and his niggardly ways.

ELISE. He makes us feel the loss of our mother more and more every day.

CLEANTE. I hear his voice! Come away till we talk it over. We must make our attack on him together bye and bye.

(*They go out.* HARPAGON *and* LA FLECHE *come in.*)

HARPAGON. Be off out of this on the minute, and don't be answering me! Get out I say! You good for nothing, you carrion!

LA FLECHE (*aside*). I never saw the like of him for wickedness! It is what I think, the devil is in his hide!

HARPAGON. What's that you are mumbling?

LA FLECHE. For what cause are you dismissing me?

HARPAGON. I like your impudence asking my reasons! Be off out of this or you'll get a clout on the head!

LA FLECHE. What at all did I do to you?

HARPAGON. You did this, you have my mind made up to hunt you!

LA FLECHE. Your son, that is my master, bade me to wait here for him.

HARPAGON. Go wait for him in the street so, and don't be stuck in my house, planted at attention the same as a sentinel, to be taking notice of all that goes on, and to make your own profit. I will not have a spy put upon me to be sneaking into my business, squinting into all I do, devouring all I own and ferreting about on every side to see is there anything handy to rob.

LA FLECHE. How the mischief could any man rob you? What way could you be robbed, and you locking up every earthly thing, and watching over it night and day?

HARPAGON. I will lock up what I think well to lock up, and I will watch it whatever way pleases myself. Aren't there enough of spies around me taking notice of all that I do? (*Aside.* I am in dread he has some suspicion about my money.) Aren't you just the sort of a man to be giving out reports I have money hid in my house?

LA FLECHE. You have money hid in your house?

HARPAGON. No you rascal, I said no such thing. (*Aside.* I am getting angry.) I am asking did you, through ill will, give out reports that I had?

LA FLECHE. Ah, what signifies you owning riches or not owning them. It is the one thing to me.

HARPAGON (*lifting his hand to strike him*). Is it that you are arguing? Mind yourself or I'll gag you with a clout on the jaw! I tell you again to get out of that!

LA FLECHE. All right. I'll go.

HARPAGON. Stop! Are you bringing away anything?

LA FLECHE. What would I be bringing away?

HARPAGON. Come here till I see. Show me your hands.

LA FLECHE. There they are.

HARPAGON. Now the others.

LA FLECHE. The others?

HARPAGON. That's what I said.

LA FLECHE (*turning up palms of hands*). There they are.

HARPAGON (*pointing to* LA FLECHE'S *breeches*). Have you anything hid in there?

LA FLECHE. Look for yourself.

HARPAGON (*feeling them*). These big breeches are very answerable for warehouses of stolen goods. Whoever invented them has a right to be hung.

LA FLECHE (*aside*). Ah, a man of that sort deserves all he is in dread of! It is well satisfied I would be to be robbing him!

HARPAGON. Aye?

LA FLECHE. Well?

HARPAGON. What's that you were saying about robbing?

LA FLECHE. I say you are making a great rummaging to see did I rob you.

HARPAGON. That's what I want to do! (*Feels his pockets.*)

LA FLECHE (*aside*). The devil fly away with misers and misery!

HARPAGON. What's that you're saying?

LA FLECHE. What am I saying?

HARPAGON. That's it. What are you saying about misers?

LA FLECHE. I said let the devil take them.

HARPAGON. Who are you talking about?

LA FLECHE. About misers.

HARPAGON. What misers are those?

LA FLECHE. Thieves and villains.

HARPAGON. What do you mean saying that?

LA FLECHE. Why would you want to know?

HARPAGON. Because I have a right to know.

LA FLECHE. Is it what you think it is of yourself I am talking?

HARPAGON. I think what I think. But tell me what you mean saying that, or I will make you tell me.

LA FLECHE. I was talking to my hat.

HARPAGON. I'll hat you!

LA FLECHE. Won't you allow me to put curses on misers?

HARPAGON. I won't let you go on with your impudence and your gab. Hold your tongue!

LA FLECHE. I made no mention of any person's name.

HARPAGON. If you say one word you'll be sorry for it!

LA FLECHE. Whoever the cap fits let him wear it.

HARPAGON. Will you hold your tongue!

LA FLECHE. If I do it is against my will.

HARPAGON. Ah!

LA FLECHE (*showing* HARPAGON *the pocket of his waistcoat*). Look at here another pocket. Are you satisfied now?

HARPAGON. Come on, give up what you have, without me searching you!

LA FLECHE. Give what up?

HARPAGON. What you took from me.

96

LA FLECHE. I took nothing at all from you.

HARPAGON. Are you sure of that?

LA FLECHE. Sure and certain.

HARPAGON. Then go to the devil!

LA FLECHE (*aside*). That's a pleasant sort of a goodbye! (*Goes.*)

HARPAGON. I leave it between you and your soul!—That now is a rogue of a fellow, he put me out greatly. I would sooner not to see such a cur about the house. Indeed and indeed it is no little care it will need, I to be keeping so large a sum of money about the place. It is well for those that can put it out at interest, and keep with them but what is wanting from day to day. There would be no need then to be searching here and there striving to find a hiding place. It is not in a chest I would wish to put it, or a safe that would be rousing suspicions. I would put no trust at all in anything of the sort. Nothing but a bait to tempt thieves it would be, and the very first thing they would make their attack on.

(ELISE *and* CLEANTE *come in talking together and stop at back of stage.*)

HARPAGON (*believing himself alone*). For all that, I don't know did I do right burying in my garden those ten thousand crowns were paid to me yesterday. Ten thousand pounds in gold is a very large sum to be minding. (*Catches sight of them.*) Good jewel! Am I after betraying myself! I'm not sure was I talking aloud in the heat of my anger. (*To* CLEANTE *and* ELISE) What are you wanting?

CLEANTE. Nothing at all, sir.

HARPAGON. It is long you are standing there?

ELISE. We are but just come in.

HARPAGON. Did you hear?

CLEANTE. Did we hear what?

HARPAGON. The thing——

ELISE. What thing?

HARPAGON. The thing I am after saying.

CLEANTE. We did not.

HARPAGON. You did! you did!

ELISE. I beg your pardon, we did not.

HARPAGON. I know well you overheard some words! I was only just saying to myself how hard it is to get money in these days, and what a lucky man it would be that would have in his hand ten thousand crowns.

CLEANTE. We had no notion of coming to listen to you, or of disturbing you at all.

HARPAGON. I am glad you did not, or you might have got it in your head that it is I myself owns ten thousand crowns.

CLEANTE. We have no concern with your business.

HARPAGON. I wish to God I had ten thousand crowns!

CLEANTE. I don't believe——

HARPAGON. That would be a good thing for me.

ELISE. There are things that——

HARPAGON. I would find a good use for them.

CLEANTE. I am thinking——

HARPAGON. They would be answerable to me.

ELISE. You are——

HARPAGON. I would not be complaining the way I am now of the times being so hard.

CLEANTE. Why would you be complaining? Everybody knows you are full of money.

HARPAGON. What are you saying? I am full of money? Whoever is saying that is telling lies! There is no greater lie can be told. Rascals they are that set that story going.

ELISE. Don't be so put out about it.

HARPAGON. It is a queer thing my own children to betray me, and to turn to be my enemies.

CLEANTE. Is it saying you are well off makes me your enemy?

HARPAGON. It is. That sort of talk, and the way you are scattering money, will be the cause one of these days of my throat being cut. There will a notion go about that I am made of money.

CLEANTE. What way am I spending money?

HARPAGON. Do you ask me that? Is there any worse scandal than the dear suits you are wearing about the town? I was faulting your sister yesterday, but you are worse again. It is likely it will call down a judgment from heaven! The price of your clothes from your hat to your shoes would be enough capital to start making a fortune. I have told you twenty times I like none of your ways. You are as if setting up to be a lord, and you must surely be robbing me to go dressed the way you are.

CLEANTE. What way am I robbing you?

HARPAGON. How would I know? What way could you keep up that appearance, and you not robbing me?

CLEANTE. Luck was with me card playing. What I win I put upon my back.

HARPAGON. A great shame for you. What you win you have a right to put out at interest, the way it would come back to you again. Tell me now without going any farther, where is the use of all those ribbons you are tufted with? Wouldn't a half dozen of ties be enough to hold your clothes together? What call have you to go spending on wigs, and having your own hair that would put you to no expense at all? I'll engage there is in your wigs and your ribbons at the least twenty pounds. Twenty pounds bring in every year eighteen shillings, six pence and three farthings, at only common interest.

CLEANTE. That is it.

HARPAGON. Now there is another thing. (*He sees* CLEANTE *and* ELISE *making signals*.) (*Aside.* It is likely they are making signs one to another to make a snap at my purse.) What are you making signs for?

ELISE. We were consulting between ourselves which of us should take the first turn. We have each of us something to tell you.

HARPAGON. And I myself have something to tell to the two of you.

CLEANTE. What we have to speak about is marriage.

HARPAGON. And what I myself have to talk to you about is marriage.

ELISE. Oh, father!

HARPAGON. What do you mean saying Oh, father! Is it the word that affrights you or the thing?

CLEANTE. It is no wonder if we are put in a fright by such a notion. It is likely the choice you might make for us would not satisfy ourselves.

HARPAGON. Never fear. Wait a while. I know very well what is right for the both of you. You will have no occasion to find fault with what I am going to do. And to begin at the beginning. Did you ever see a young girl, Marian her name is, that is lodging not far from this?

CLEANTE. I did see her.

HARPAGON (*to* ELISE). Did you?

ELISE. I heard of her.

HARPAGON. What do you think of her?

CLEANTE. I think well of her.

HARPAGON. Good looking?

CLEANTE. Very bright and pleasing.

HARPAGON. Well mannered?

CLEANTE. She is that.

HARPAGON. Wouldn't you say such a girl as that is worth thinking of?

CLEANTE. I would indeed.

HARPAGON. And that she would be a nice match?

CLEANTE. She would indeed.

HARPAGON. It is likely she would make a good housekeeper?

CLEANTE. I wouldn't doubt it.

HARPAGON. A man would have satisfaction with her?

CLEANTE. He would.

HARPAGON. There is but one small drawback. I am afraid she has not so good a fortune as one would wish.

CLEANTE. Oh, a fortune is no great matter beside marrying the right girl.

HARPAGON. I beg your pardon. But what I have to say is, that if the fortune is not all one could wish, it might be made up for in other ways.

CLEANTE. To be sure it might.

HARPAGON. I am well pleased that you agree with me. Her good looks and her civility have gained my heart entirely, and if I can hear that she has any fortune at all, I have my mind made up to marry her.

CLEANTE. What!

HARPAGON. Well?

CLEANTE. You have made up your mind?

HARPAGON. To marry Marian.

CLEANTE. Who? You——You?

HARPAGON. Yes, I, I, I. What about it?

CLEANTE. It has made my head go round. I will go away for a while.

HARPAGON. That's nothing to signify. Go drink a glass of cold water in the kitchen. Young fellows in these times have not the strength of a chicken. Now Elise, that is what I have settled for myself. As to your brother, I have a widow-woman in my eye for him. There was mention made of her to me this morning; and as to yourself, I will bestow you on Mr. Anselme.

ELISE. Mr. Anselme!

HARPAGON. The same. A sensible settled man up to no more than fifty years, and said to have whips of money.

ELISE. I won't want to be married, please father.

HARPAGON (*imitating her*). But I want you to be married, my little dote of a daughter!

ELISE (*with another curtsey*). But begging Mr. Anselme's pardon (*curtseys*), I have no mind to marry him, with respects to you.

HARPAGON. But begging your pardon (*mimicking curtsey*), you will marry him this very night.

ELISE. To-night!

HARPAGON. To-night.

ELISE (*curtseying*). That will not happen, father.

HARPAGON. It will happen, daughter.

ELISE. It will not.

HARPAGON. I say it will.

ELISE. No, I say.

HARPAGON. Yes, I say.

ELISE. It is a thing you will never force me to.

HARPAGON. It is a thing I will force you to.

ELISE. I would rather kill myself than marry such a husband.

HARPAGON. You will not kill yourself, and you will marry him. What impudence you have! Was there ever heard a daughter to be speaking in that manner to her father!

ELISE. Was there ever known a father marrying his daughter in such a way?

HARPAGON. It is a match there can be nothing said against. I'll engage there is no person at all but will say I have done well.

ELISE. And I'll engage no person with any sense will think well of it.

HARPAGON (*seeing* VALERE *in the distance*). Here is Valere coming. Will you agree to make him the judge between us.

ELISE. I agree to that.

HARPAGON. Will you give in to his judgment?

ELISE. I will go by whatever he will say.

HARPAGON. That's a bargain. (VALERE *comes in.*) Here, Valere, we have agreed on you to judge which of us is in the right, myself or my daughter.

VALERE. It is yourself sir, not a doubt at all about it.

HARPAGON. Do you know what we were talking about?

VALERE. I do not. But I am sure you could not be wrong, you must be in the right.

HARPAGON. It is my intention to give her this very day to a husband that has good means and good sense, and she tells me to my face that she will not have him. What do you say to that?

VALERE. What do I say is it?

HARPAGON. Yes.

VALERE. Aye?

HARPAGON. What is it?

VALERE. I say that in my heart I am in agreement with yourself, and that you cannot but be right. But on the other hand, she is not entirely in the wrong.

HARPAGON. What are you saying? Mr. Anselme is a very good match—well reared, civil, and obliging, and with no child of his first marriage. Could she get anything better than that?

VALERE. That is so. But she might be thinking there is too much hurry, and that she would want a little time to make sure was her mind well satisfied.

HARPAGON. It is a chance she ought not to miss. He will do for me what no other one will do, for he is ready to take her without a fortune.

VALERE. Without a fortune?

HARPAGON. That's it.

VALERE. I have no more to say. (*To* ELISE.) That is a reason no one can go against. You have to give in to that.

HARPAGON. It is a great saving to myself.

VALERE. So it should be too. To be sure your daughter might be saying to you that marriage is a bigger thing than anyone might think; that according as it turns out there will be happiness or there will be misery through the whole of the lifetime; a contract that will last till death is not a thing to be made in a hurry.

HARPAGON. Without a fortune!

VALERE. You are right there. That should settle all. And there are people would be telling you, you should take notice of a girl's own liking. They might be saying the man is too far gone in age, and fixed in his own ways, for such a marriage to turn out well.

HARPAGON. Without a fortune!

VALERE. Sure enough there is no answer to that. Who the mischief could go against it? To be sure there are a great many fathers would sooner give their daughter to a man that would be pleasing to her, than to one with the riches of the world.

HARPAGON. Without a fortune!

VALERE. That is true. It is that shuts my mouth altogether. Without a fortune! There is no one at all would go against such a reason as that.

HARPAGON. (*aside, looking towards the garden*). Whist! It seems to me I hear the barking of a dog. It might be some person in search of my money. (*To* VALERE.) Stop where you are. I will be back on the minute. (*Goes.*)

ELISE. Are you joking, Valere, talking to him as you are?

VALERE. I did it not to vex him, and to gain my way with him in the end. To go against him altogether would be the way to spoil all. Let on that you consent, and you will have some chance of getting your own way.

ELISE. But this marriage!

VALERE. We must find some excuse to stop it.

ELISE. But what excuse can we find between this and evening?

VALERE. You must ask a delay, pretending some illness.

ELISE. But they will find out I am pretending when they bring a doctor.

VALERE. You are joking. What do doctors know about it? Believe me you can have any sickness you may choose, and they will be able to tell you what it was brought it on you.

HARPAGON (*at back of stage*). It was nothing at all, the Lord be praised!

VALERE (*not seeing him*). If the worst comes to the worst we must make a run for it. Will you and love go as far as that? (*See ing* HARPAGON.) It is fitting for a daughter to be obedient to her father. She has a right not to ask what sort the husband is at all. So soon as the great word is said "Without a fortune," she should be satisfied to take him with no more delay!

HARPAGON. That is right talk now.

VALERE. I ask your pardon if I went too far saying what I did.

HARPAGON. I am well satisfied with you. I will give her in charge to you. (*To* ELISE.) You need not be running away, I put it on him to keep a watch over you the same as myself.

VALERE (*to* ELISE). After that you should give in to what I say. (*To* HARPAGON, *as she goes*.) I will follow after her and be giving her good advice.

HARPAGON. Do so and I'll be obliged to you.

VALERE. It is right to keep a tight hand on her.

HARPAGON. That is so. We ought now——

VALERE. Don't be troubling yourself at all. I am well able to make a good job of it.

HARPAGON. Do that, do that. I am going to take a little ramble in the town; I will be coming back within two minutes.

VALERE (*to* ELISE, *going to side where she went out*). There is nothing in the wide world to put beside riches! It is thanking God you should be for giving you so good a father. It is he knows well what way to settle your life for you. When there is an offer made to take a girl without a fortune, there is no other thing to look to. There is no other thing outside of that. A man to be young, handsome, upreared, quiet, steady, what is he at all compared with the man that wants no fortune!

HARPAGON. That's the chat! Troth he is talking like Aristotle! Didn't I have great luck getting a servant the like of him?

ACT II

Cleante, La Fleche.

Cleante. Ah, you traitor you, where did you go hiding? Didn't I give you my orders?

La Fleche. You did sir, and I came here to wait as you bade me, but your tyrant of a father hunted me in spite of myself, and I went near getting a thrashing.

Cleante. What way is our business going? There is more hurry than I thought. Since I saw you I found out that I have a rival in my father, no less!

La Fleche. Your father in love!

Cleante. Just so, and I had the work of the world to hide from him how greatly I was upset by the news.

La Fleche. That one to be meddling with love! What the hell is he thinking about? Is it a joke he is going to put on the world? Is it that love was made for the like of him?

Cleante. It is no less than a judgment on my sins, that fancy having come into his head.

La Fleche. And why did you hide from him that you had some notion of the girl yourself?

Cleante. I gave him no suspicion, the way I would find it easier to upset this plan he has——What answers did they give you?

La Fleche. Troth, sir, those that go borrowing go sorrowing. Any man must put up with strange things, and he getting like yourself into the hands of the moneylenders.

Cleante. You cannot manage to get the loan?

La Fleche. That is not what I said. There is one Mr. Simon, a very smart willing man. has taken a great fancy to you. The very look of you, he was saying, is after gaining his heart.

Cleante. Will he give me the fifteen hundred pounds I am wanting?

La Fleche. He will, but there are a few small conditions you must agree to if you want to carry the business through.

Cleante. Did you see the man that is going to lend me the money?

La Fleche. Ah now, that is not the way this sort of work has to be done. He is more secret about it than yourself, and there is more of mystery than you would think. His name is not to be told whatever happens. He is to be brought to meet you to-day in a house that is loaned him for the purpose, until you will give him information as to your family and your means. It is certain that the name of your father will be enough, with itself only, to carry all through.

CLEANTE. And above all my mother being dead, so that no one can take her fortune from me.

LA FLECHE. Here are a few little clauses he made the broker write out, to be showed you before anything could be done:

"Supposing that the lender sees all the securities, and is satisfied that the borrower is of age, and of a family of good property, safe, solid, and clear of encumbrances, a fair and proper deed shall be executed before an attorney, the most honest that can be found, he to be chosen by the lender, it being of most importance to him that the deed should be rightly drawn up."

CLEANTE. There is nothing to be said against that.

LA FLECHE. "The lender, not willing to put any weight upon his conscience, will ask no more interest than five and a half per cent."

CLEANTE. Five and a half per cent. That is fair enough. There is nothing to object to in that.

LA FLECHE. That is true. "But as the said lender has not by him at present the sum in question, and that to oblige the borrower he is forced to borrow from another at twenty per cent, it is agreed the said borrower should pay this interest without prejudice to the rest, seeing it is only to do the borrower a favour that the said lender engages himself to get this loan."

CLEANTE. What the devil! What sort of a Jew is this, or a bloodsucker! That is more than twenty-five per cent.

LA FLECHE. That is so. That is what I said. You had best think it over a while.

CLEANTE. What would I think over? I must have money, and I must agree to all.

LA FLECHE. The very answer I gave him.

CLEANTE. Is there anything more?

LA FLECHE. Only one little condition. "Of the 1,500 pounds wanted, the lender cannot give more than 1,200 in cash, and as to the rest, the borrower must take it out in wearables, in furniture, and in ornaments, according to the list here following, and that the lender has put down straight and fair at the lowest possible price."

CLEANTE. What does that mean?

LA FLECHE. Listen now to the inventory: "First, one four-post bed, upholstered with Hungary lace, in olive green cloth, with six chairs and a quilt to match, all in good order, and lined with taffeta, shot red and blue.

"Item, a tent bedstead covered with good serge, dead rose colour, with silk fringes and tassels."

CLEANTE. What use does he think I can make of that?

LA FLECHE. Wait a minute. "Item, one set of tapestry hangings, with the loves of Hercules and Venus. Item, one large walnut table, with twelve turned legs like pillars. Can be drawn out at each end, and is furnished with six footstools."

CLEANTE. What is that to me?

LA FLECHE. Wait a minute. "Item, three large muskets, inlaid with mother of pearl, and the rests belonging to them."

"Item, one brick furnace, having two retorts and three receivers, very useful to any person that has a mind to go distilling."

CLEANTE. I am getting vexed!

LA FLECHE. Have patience now. "Item, one Bologna lute, with full set of strings, only a few of them wanting. Item, one bagatelle board and one draught board, with a game of goose, recovered from the Greeks; very suitable for passing the time when a person had nothing to do. Item, one lizard skin, three feet and a half long, stuffed with hay. A very pretty curiosity to hang from the ceiling of a room. The whole of the above being honestly worth more than four hundred and fifty pounds, is reduced by the moderation of the lender."

CLEANTE. That he may be choked with the same moderation! The pickpocket, the blackmailer! Was there ever such robbery heard of! He is not content with the twenty-five per cent. interest without asking me to take his old rubbish heap in the place of three hundred pounds! I won't get five hundred out of the whole loan. And there is nothing to do but to accept his terms, for the brute has his hand upon my throat!

LA FLECHE. Begging your pardon, sir, you would seem to be taking the road Panurge took to his ruin, forestalling your money, buying dear, selling cheap, eating the corn in the ear.

CLEANTE. What can I do? This is what sons are brought to through the miserable meanness of fathers. And then you will hear people wonder if you wish them out of the world!

LA FLECHE. The quietest person on earth would be set raging mad seeing your own father's stinginess. That is sure enough. I have no mind to be hanged more than another. The Lord be praised, I have wits to play my own game and to keep myself free from the rope. But I declare to goodness it would be a right thing to rob that one: in my opinion I would be doing a good action doing that.

CLEANTE. Give me that inventory till I'll take another look at it.

(HARPAGON and SIMON *come in at back of stage.*)

SIMON. Yes, sir, it is a young chap is in want of money; the need is pressing on him, and he will give in to any terms at all.

HARPAGON. But can you be sure there is no danger of any loss? Can you tell me what is his name and his family, and his means?

SIMON. I cannot do that, for it was but by chance I met with him. But he will make all that known to you himself, and his serving man told me anyone would be satisfied when they would hear his account. All I can be certain is, that there is great wealth in his family, that his mother is dead, and that he will promise, if you wish it, that his father will be buried within eight months.

HARPAGON. There is something in that now. Charity tells us, Simon, to oblige any person we can, and it being in our power.

SIMON. So it does too.

LA FLECHE (*aside to* CLEANTE, *recognising* SIMON). What does this mean? Our money-lender, Simon, talking with your father?

CLEANTE. Has somebody told him who I am? Have you yourself betrayed me.

SIMON (*to* CLEANTE *and* LA FLECHE). Ah, ha! you are in a great hurry! Who was it told you this is the house? (*To* HARPAGON.) It was not myself anyway gave them your name and your address. But in my opinion it does no harm at all. They are able to do business, and you can make your own bargain with them.

HARPAGON. What are you saying?

SIMON (*pointing at* CLEANTE). This is the gentleman wants a loan of the fifteen hundred pounds I was talking of.

HARPAGON. What's that you rascal! Is it you that are giving yourself up to such bad practises?

CLEANTE. What's that! It is you, father, are giving yourself up to cheating and extortion!

(SIMON *runs away and* LA FLECHE *hides himself.*)

HARPAGON. Is it to run to ruin you want, by such scandalous borrowing?

CLEANTE. Is it to get riches you are striving by such shameful grabbing?

HARPAGON. How dare you show yourself to me after this!

CLEANTE. How dare you show yourself to any person at all!

HARPAGON. Have you no shame I ask, getting into such bad ways, running into such tremendous expense, for to throw away the property your parents earned for you, sweating it out in their bones!

CLEANTE. Have you no shame, letting yourself down with such a business? Giving up an honourable name for the greed of putting one coin upon another! Charging a higher interest than any extortion that ever was invented by the thirstiest leech of the lot!

HARPAGON. Get out of my sight you scoundrel you! Get out of my sight!

CLEANTE. Is it worse in your opinion for a man to go buy money he is in need of or to steal money he has no use for!

HARPAGON. Get out of that I tell you, and don't be scalding my ears! (*Alone.*) I am no way sorry this has happened. It is a caution to me to keep my eye on him better than before.

(*Enter* FROSINE.)

FROSINE. Sir——

HARPAGON. Wait a minute. I will come back and talk to you. (*Aside.*) It is as well for me to take a look is my money safe. (*Goes out.*)

LA FLECHE (*coming in and not seeing* FROSINE). That now was a very funny thing to happen! The old man must surely have a secondhand warehouse in some place, for we have never seen any of those things he had written in his list.

FROSINE. Is that you my poor La Fleche? What is it brings you here?

LA FLECHE. Ah, ha, that's you, Frosine. What are you doing here?

FROSINE. What I am doing in every place—helping along other peoples business, making myself of use to them, profiting the best way I can by whatever wits I possess. You know that in this world a person has to live by being smart. All the fortune God gave me was a hand to put in every other one's affairs.

LA FLECHE. Are you doing anything for the master of this house?

FROSINE. I am. I have taken a case in hand for him that I hope I will get some reward for.

LA FLECHE. From him is it! You will be clever, and very clever, if you can knock anything out of that one. I tell you money is scarce to find in this place.

FROSINE. There are some services will work wonders.

LA FLECHE. I beg your pardon, you don't know master Harpagon! Of all the men of the whole world, it is he himself is the hardest and the meanest. There is no service anyone could do him would bring his thankfulness so far as to open his pocket. Praises he will give you in plenty, but as to money, not a mite. He shows a very dry sort of gratitude. He wouldn't so much as say "I give you my blessing," like another. "Give" is a word that would seem to scare him.

FROSINE. Let me alone, I know well what way to draw milk from my customers, to open their hearts, to tickle their vanity, till I find out what is their weak side.

LA FLECHE. That will not serve you here. I bet you where it is a question of money you will never get to the soft side of Harpagon. No less than a Turk he is, and beyond any Turk ever came into the world. To burst him in pieces you must, before you would get anything out of him. With him money is before name and fame and behaviour. To see a beggar or a creditor would give him convulsions. To strike at his heart it would, and would give him his death blow. Stop, here he is coming. Good-bye to you!

HARPAGON (*in a low voice*). All is safe, all is safe——Well what is it, Frosine?

FROSINE. Well, its yourself is looking grand out and out!

HARPAGON. Who? Myself is it?

FROSINE. I never saw you so fresh and so airy.

HARPAGON. Do you say so?

FROSINE. It is getting young you are. There are many having but twenty-five years are older than yourself!

HARPAGON. For all that, Frosine, I am up to sixty years.

FROSINE. What signifies sixty years? It is the best time of life that is. You are coming into your bloom.

HARPOGAN. That is so. But twenty years to be taken off, would do no harm at all.

FROSINE. It is funning you are. You have no need of that. Sure the dough you are made of would last through a hundred years.

HARPAGON. You think that?

FROSINE. To be sure I do. You have all the marks of it. Stop a minute. Oh, it is easy seen between your two eyes, the sign of a long life!

HARPAGON. Do you say so?

FROSINE. Not a doubt of it. Show me your hand. Did ever anyone see the like of that for a line of life!

HARPAGON. What is that now?

FROSINE. Can't you see how far that line goes?

HARPAGON. Well, and what may that mean?

FROSINE. Faith I said a hundred years, but you will pass your six score.

HARPAGON. Is that possible?

FROSINE. Nothing would kill you, only to be knocked on the head! You will be burying your children and your children's children.

HARPAGON. That is great. What way is our business going?

FROSINE. You need not ask that. Was I ever known to mix myself with anything I would not bring through? I have great skill in match-making above all. Give me time, and there are no two in the world I could not join. I am sure if I took it in hand I could marry the Grand Turk to the Republic of Venice. To be sure there was no such difficulty in this business, I being acquainted with the girl and her mother. I used to be always talking about you. I told the mother you had your mind made up to marry Marian, through seeing her in the window and walking out in the street.

HARPAGON. What answer did she make?

FROSINE. Believe me she was well pleased. I told her you were wishing her daughter should come this evening to the signing of the marriage contract of your own daughter, and that she could put her in charge of myself.

HARPAGON. It is that I am forced, Frosine, to give a supper for Mr. Anselme, and I would be well pleased she to come to it.

FROSINE. That will do. After dinner she will make acquaintance with your daughter, and then she will go take a view of the fair, and come back here for the supper.

HARPAGON. Very good. They can go together in my carriage to the fair; I will give them the lend of it.

FROSINE. That will suit her well.

HARPAGON. But tell me, Frosine, did you sound the mother as to the fortune she will give her? Did you tell her that she must give her some help, and make some struggle, and go so far as to bleed herself a little on an occasion of this sort. For in the end there is no one would marry a girl unless she would bring something with her.

FROSINE. Ah, that is a girl will bring you in three hundred pounds a year.

HARPAGON. Three hundred pounds a year!

FROSINE. To be sure. First of all, she has been reared up in a very poor way of living; she has been used to live on cabbage and a drop of milk and the like, so she will not be asking grand cooking, or pearl barley, or fancy dishes, as another woman would. And that is no trifle at all, but will save every year fifty pounds at the very least. Besides that, as to dress, all she needs is to be clean; she has no mind for dear stuffs or brooches, or good furniture, that girls the like of her are mostly cracked after. That now is worth more than a hundred pounds in the year. And more again, she is greatly against card playing, and that is not common in these times. I know a lady in our part has lost at Twenty-Five, six hundred pounds in this year. But we will count to her but the quarter of it. A hundred and fifty for play, one hundred for clothes and jewels—that makes two hundred and fifty, and fifty that we put down for diet. There now are your three hundred pounds a year well counted.

HARPAGON. Yes, that is not bad. But the account has nothing solid in it.

FROSINE. I beg your pardon. Is it nothing solid you are getting, and she bringing you great good sense, and great liking for plain dresses, and a great hatred of gambling

HARPAGON. It is only foolishness to be counting up a fortune out of money she will not cause me to spend. I have no intention to give a receipt for what I never handled. And I must get something in my fist.

FROSINE. Never fear, you will get enough. And they were speaking of some property they own in some far place, that you will be the master of.

HARPAGON. I must go look at that. But, Frosine, there is another thing makes me uneasy. The girl is young as you see, and it is the custom for youngsters to like the company of those of their own age, and to be wanting to be always with them. I am in dread a man of my age may not be to her taste, and may bring about some little troubles in the house, and that would not serve me.

FROSINE. Ah, how little you know her! That is another thing about her. I had it in mind to tell you. She has the greatest dislike to young men. It is only for old ones she has any liking at all.

HARPAGON. Is that so?

FROSINE. It is. I wish you could have heard her talking on that point. She cannot bear the sight of any young fellow at all, but she is never better pleased than when she can meet with an old man having a grand long beard. The farther in age they are the more she likes them, and I would advise you not to be giving yourself out younger than what you are. She would wish a man to have sixty years at the least, and it is not four months since she was about to be married, and broke off the match because the bridegroom turned out to be but fifty-six, and wore no spectacles, and he signing the contract.

HARPAGON. For that cause only!

FROSINE. For no other thing. She said fifty-six years would not satisfy her, and that she has no opinion of a man that does not wear spectacles.

HARPAGON. That is news you are giving me.

FROSINE. Oh, she goes farther with it than you would think. There are in her room some pictures, and what are they would you say? Of Adonis, Paris and Apollo? Not at all, but the likeness of Saturn, of King Priam, of old Nestor, of Father Anchisis, and he upon his son's back.

HARPAGON. Very good. I would never now have thought that, and I am well pleased to know that is her taste. Indeed I myself to be a woman, I would have no taste at all for young chaps.

FROSINE. I am sure of that. Queer rubbish they are to be falling in love with. Brats in bibs, pink and white nurselings! No more flavour in them than in the white of an egg.

HARPAGON. I cannot know or understand why it is women should be so fond of them.

FROSINE. Born fools they are. Is there any sense at all in making much of youngsters. Is it men they are at all, those young pups? Is there anyone at all would get fond of them?

HARPAGON. That's what I am always saying. With their voice chirruping the same as a pullet, and their three cats' hairs of a moustache, their waistcoats——their breeches——

FROSINE. They are well built indeed alongside of a man like yourself. There's a man for you! There is something worth looking at! To be shaped the way you are and dressed the way you are— that is the means to awaken love!

HARPAGON. You think me well looking?

FROSINE. Do you ask me that? A lovely man you are, it is drawn in a picture you should be. Turn towards me if you please. There could nothing better be seen. Let me see you walk now. There is a figure for you! Clean and well planned you are, having no blemish at all.

HARPAGON. I have no complaint on me indeed, the Lord be praised, only that the cough comes at me an odd time. (*He coughs.*)

FROSINE. Sure that's nothing. You have a very nice way of coughing that becomes you very well.

HARPAGON. Tell me this now. Did Marian see me yet? Did she take notice of me as I passed?

FROSINE. She did not, but we have talked a great deal about you. I gave her a full account of you, and I was not without putting praises on you, and saying any person would be well off, getting yourself for a husband.

HARPAGON. You did well, and I am obliged to you.

FROSINE. I have one small request to make to you, sir. I am in a lawsuit, and it is going against me for the want of means. (HARPAGON *looks grave*.) It would be easy for you to help me gain it if you have any little friendship for me——You will hardly believe now how glad she will be seeing you——(*He grows lively again*.) It is well pleased she will be with you; that ruff in the ancient fashion will be greatly to her taste. And the tags of twine that join your jacket to your breeches. She will go raving about you. She will be well satisfied having a man with tags.

HARPAGON. I am very glad to hear that.

FROSINE. That lawsuit now is a great weight upon me. (*He grows grave again*.) I am destroyed if I lose it, and some little assistance would give me a good chance.— I would wish you to see her delight hearing me talking of you.—(*He grows cheerful*.) Her eyes were sparkling and I telling her what sort you are. Before I left her she had her heart set on the match being made with no delay.

HARPAGON. I am glad to hear that now, Frosine. I am greatly obliged to you indeed.

FROSINE. You will not refuse me, sir, the little help I am asking of you? (*He grows grave*.) That would straighten things out for me, and I would be thankful to you to the end of life and time.

HARPAGON. Good morrow to you. I have to finish my letters.

FROSINE. You never could help me at any time I would be in more need of it.

HARPAGON. I will give orders for my carriage to bring you out to the fair.

FROSINE. I would not ask it if I was not driven to it.

HARPAGON. I will take care the supper is early, the way it will not disagree with you.

FROSINE. Sure you won't refuse me this little thing I am asking? You cannot think how pleasant——

HARPAGON. I am going. They are calling for me. I will see you again bye and bye. (*Goes out*.)

FROSINE. That the fever may get a grip of you, you ugly cur you! The niggard, to hold out against all my attacks! But I won't give up the business! I have the other side yet to draw my reward from!

ACT III

HARPAGON, CLEANTE, ELISE, VALERE, DAME CLAUDE (*holding a broom*), MASTER JACQUES, LA MERLUCHE, BRINDAVOINE.

HARPAGON. Come here the whole of you, till I'll give you my orders for the evening, and settle everyone's work. Come here, Mrs. Claude, till I'll begin with you. That's right, you are ready armed, let you give the whole place a good cleaning; but take care would you rub the furniture too hard, to be wearing it out. Along with that, I will put you in charge of the bottles while the supper will be going on. If any one of them should be missing, or be broken, it is on you I will lay it, I will stop it out of your wages.

JACQUES (*aside*). That chastising now will not be without profit.

HARPAGON. That will do. (*She goes.*) As to you, Brindavoine, and you, Merluche, what you have to do is to rinse out the glasses and to hand round the wine; but only when people are drouthy, and not like those meddling waiters that go teasing them, putting it in their heads to take drink when they had no thought of it at all. Do not proffer it before they have made a second asking, and don't forget to mix with it a good share of water.

JACQUES (*aside*). That is it. Wine without water is apt to get into the head.

LA MERLUCHE. Will we take off our blouses, sir?

HARPAGON. Do so, the time you see the company coming to the door, and take good care not to spoil your clothes.

BRINDAVOINE. Sure you know one of the flaps of my coat is all stained with a great patch of lamp oil.

LA MERLUCHE. And my own breeches are in holes behind. I'd be ashamed any person to see me.

HARPAGON. Ah, be quiet! Can't you keep your back to the wall, and only show your front to the company? (*To* BRINDAVOINE, *showing him how to hold his hat to hide the oil stain.*) And as to you, let you hold your hat this way when you are attending. (*LA MERLUCHE and* BRINDAVOINE *go out.*) As for you, Elise, you will keep an eye on everything that is taken away, and see there is no waste; that is very suitable work for a young girl. And besides that, make yourself ready to give a welcome to my wife that is to be, that is coming to visit you, and to bring you out with her to the fair. Do you hear what I am saying?

ELISE. Yes, father.

HARPAGON. Yes, you goose. (ELISE *goes*.) (*To* CLEANTE.) And as to you, my young pup of a son, that I was kind enough to forgive that borrowing business, let you not take it in your head to look sour at her.

CLEANTE. I to look sour at her! And why would I look sour?

HARPAGON. Don't I know the way youngsters have, and their father to marry secondly? And the eye they throw on what is called the stepmother. But if you have a mind to make me forget your own bad behaviour, it is what I advise you, to put away all cross looks, and to give her as good a welcome as you can.

CLEANTE. To tell no lie, father, I cannot promise to be satisfied, seeing her my stepmother; but as to giving her a good reception, I promise you I will not fail in doing that.

HARPAGON. Take care would you.

CLEANTE. You will see you will have no reason for complaint on that point.

HARPAGON. You are showing sense. (CLEANTE *goes*.) Now, Valere, I want your help. Come here, Jacques, I have kept you for the last.

JACQUES. Is it to your coachman you are wanting to speak or to your cook?

HARPAGON. I have to speak to the two of them.

JACQUES. Which will you want first?

HARPAGON. The cook.

JACQUES. Wait a minute so, if you please.

(*Takes off his coachman's coat, and appears dressed as a cook.*)

HARPAGON. What the mischief is this for?

JACQUES. You have but to give your orders.

HARPAGON. I have engaged myself to give a supper to-night.

JACQUES (*aside*). That's a great wonder indeed.

HARPAGON. Tell me now, will you do it in style?

JACQUES. I will if you will give me plenty of money?

HARPAGON. What the devil! Always money! It is as if there was no other thing to say. Money! Money! Money! They have but the one word in their mouth, money! Talking always of money! It is as near to them as the five fingers to the hand!

VALERE. I never heard so impudent an answer. That would be a great surprise indeed, to spread out a good meal after going to great expense! That is easy enough. Any fool could do that much. But it needs a clever man to make a great show, and he spending but very little.

JACQUES (*to* VALERE). Faith, Mr. Manager, I'll be obliged to you to tell your secret, or to take my place in the kitchen. It seems as if you are wanting to rule everything in this house.

HARPAGON. Stop your chat. What is it you want.

JACQUES. There is your gentleman of a steward says he will do it cheap for you.

HARPAGON. Hay? I tell you to answer me.

JACQUES. How many will there be at the table?

HARPAGON. Eight or ten we will be——But we need count for but eight. Where there is enough to satisfy eight there is enough for ten.

VALERE. That is true enough.

JACQUES. Well we must have four kinds of soup and five small dishes——Soups——Side dishes.

HARPAGON. What the mischief! Do you want to treat the entire town?

JACQUES. Roast meat——

HARPAGON (*putting his hand on his mouth*). You traitor you, would you devour all my means!

JACQUES. Flank dishes——

HARPAGON (*putting his hand on his mouth again*). Any more?

VALERE (*to* JACQUES). Have you a mind to make all the company burst? Did the master invite his friends for to cram them to death? Go now and read a while the principles of health, and ask the doctors is there any worse danger than over feeding?

HARPAGON. That is it.

VALERE. Let you learn, Master Jacques, yourself and the like of you, that a table spread with too many dishes is no less than a murderer; and that to show yourself the friend of the company that are asked there should be scarcity through the whole of the meal. Wasn't it said in the ancient writings: "We should eat to live and not live to eat."

HARPAGON. Ah! That is a good saying! Draw near till I'll hug you to me for saying that word! That is the best I ever heard in my lifetime. We must live to eat and not eat to live——No, that's not it. What was it you said?

VALERE. We must eat to live and not live to eat.

HARPAGON (*to* JACQUES). That's it. Do you hear? (*To* VALERE.) What great man now was it said that?

VALERE. I disremember his name.

HARPAGON. Don't forget to write out those words for me! I will get them cut in letters of gold on the chimney-piece of my parlour.

VALERE. I will not fail. And as to your supper, you have but to leave it to me; I will regulate it as it should be.

HARPAGON. Do so then, Valere.

JACQUES. All the better. I'll have the less trouble.

HARPAGON (to VALERE). What we want is things people cannot eat much of and that satisfy them very soon. A pie now would be very filling, or a harico of beans that would be greasy.

VALERE. Leave it to me!

HARPAGON. Now, Jacques, let you go wash my carriage.

JACQUES. Wait a minute, it is to the coachman you are speaking (putting on his great coat). You are saying?

HARPAGON. I am bidding you to clean the carriage, and to get ready the horses to bring to the fair.

JACQUES. Your horses is it? Faith, they are not at all in a fitting state to go travel. I will not say they are lying on their litter, that would be a lie, for there is none under them. But you have made them keep so many fast days that they are now but the shadows or the ghosts, or the patterns, of a horse.

HARPAGON. They are very bad! They do not work at all.

JACQUES. If they do nothing, is that a cause they should eat nothing? It would be better the poor beasts to have work and to have food along with it. It is scalding my heart to see them the way they are. I have a wish for my horses, and to see them suffer, it is the same as to suffer myself. It is often I take the bit from my own mouth to give to them. A person would have a very bad nature, showing no pity at all to his neighbour.

HARPAGON. It is no hard work going as far as the fair.

JACQUES. It fails me the courage to bring them. My heart would not allow me give them a cut of the whip. What way could they go drag a carriage, and they not able hardly to drag themselves?

VALERE. I will go ask Picard that is near at hand to come drive them. We will be wanting him anyway to lend a hand with the supper.

JACQUES. You can, and welcome. I would sooner they to die under any person's hand than my own.

VALERE. Master Jacques is very tender-hearted!

HARPAGON. Be quiet!

JACQUES. I tell you, master, I have no liking at all for flattery; I can see all that one does, minding bread, minding wine, sparing salt and candles, is for nothing at all but to be in with you and to

COLLECTED PLAYS: TRANSLATIONS AND ADAPTATIONS

get around you. That must vex me; and another thing, I do not like to hear the way people do be talking of you. For in spite of all I have a wish for you, and after my horses you are nearer to me than any other one.

HARPAGON. And maybe you will tell me, master Jacques, what it is they say of me?

JACQUES. I would sir, if I could but be sure it would not vex you.

HARPAGON. Not at all, but well pleased I would be, knowing what is said about me.

JACQUES. Well, sir, as you wish it, I will tell you, straight and plain, that they do be making fun of you in every place, that they are always humbugging us on your account; they are never better pleased than when they get the better of you. Stories they do be telling about your close ways. There are some say you get an almanac printed for your own use, and the fast days and the days of abstinence doubled in it, the way you will profit, keeping your servants from meat. Others say you always start a quarrel with your workmen about the new year, or the time they will be leaving you, the way you need give them no present. One story lays down that you had a neighbour's cat prosecuted one time, for having ate what was left of a leg of mutton. Another says the coachman that was here before myself caught you one night, and you stealing the oats from your own horses in the darkness, and that he gave you a great thrashing that you never were heard to speak about. Well, if you want more, I may say we can go to no place without hearing you made a mock of. You are the butt and the laughing stock of the whole town. They never speak of you by any other name but the Miser, the money grabber, the niggard, and the bloodsucker.

HARPAGON (*beating* JACQUES). You are a fool, a sot, a rascal, and an impudent villain!

JACQUES. Well now, didn't I make a good guess, only you would not heed me. I told you that you would be vexed, and you hearing the truth.

HARPAGON. Let you learn to mind your tongue! (*Goes.*)

VALERIE (*laughing*). So far as I see, Master Jacques, you got a bad reward for your truth telling.

JACQUES. Begob, Mr. Upstart, you are making a great man of yourself; but this is not your own business. You may go laugh at your own thrashing when you will get it, but you need not come laughing at mine.

VALERE. Ah, now Jacques, don't be getting cross.

JACQUES (*aside*. He is coming down a bit. I'll let on to be a bit

of a bully, and if he is fool enough to be taken in, I'll touch him up.)
Look now, if you are laughing and grinning, I myself am not laugh-
ing, and if you rouse me I will put another sort of a grin on you.
(*He pushes* VALERE *to the back of stage, threatening him.*)

VALERE. Be easy now.

JACQUES. How be easy? It does not please me to be easy.

VALERE. If you please.

JACQUES. You are full of impudence.

VALERE. Mr. Master Jacques!

JACQUES. There is no Mr. Master Jacques at all. If I get a stick
I'll knock the consequence out of you.

VALERE. Is it a stick you are talking about? (VALERE *makes*
JACQUES *go back in his turn.*)

JACQUES. I'm saying nothing about you.

VALERE. Do you know, Mr. Silly, that I am a man to take a
stick to you myself?

JACQUES. I wouldn't doubt it.

VALERE. And that you are nothing but a scum of a cook!

JACQUES. I know it well.

VALERE. And that you don't know me yet.

JACQUES. I ask your pardon.

VALERE. And I have no fancy for your jokes (*giving him some
blows of a stick.*) Let you learn now that you are a bad joker. (*Goes.*)

JACQUES (*alone*). My curse upon truth telling! I give it up from
this out. I say nothing about my master. He has the right to chastise
me. But as to this interloper of a steward, I'll knock satisfaction out
of him yet.

(FROSINE *and* MARIAN *come in.*)

FROSINE. Do you know, Master Jacques, is your master within?

JACQUES. He is, indeed. It is too well I know it.

FROSINE. Tell him, if you please, we are come.

JACQUES. Ah, that's all right. (*Goes.*)

MARIAN. Oh, Frosine, I am greatly upset! To tell the truth I
am in dread of seeing him.

FROSINE. But why would you be so uneasy?

MARIAN. Do you ask me that? Can't you see how affrighted any
person must be coming to see the scaffold they are to suffer on!

FROSINE. I see well that you to choose a death would please you,
it is not Harpagon you would choose for the rope about your neck.
And I know well by the look of you, it is that fair-haired youngster
you were telling me about, is come back into your mind.

MARIAN. That is so. I will tell no lie. I cannot but remember his civility coming to see us as he did.

FROSINE. And you don't know who was he?

MARIAN. I do not. But I know if I had my way, he would be my choice man. And I know it is since I saw him that the thought of the husband you have chosen for me gets uglier every day.

FROSINE. Ah, to be sure, these well-looking lads have a taking way, but the most of them are as poor as rats. It is best for you take an old husband that has a good way of living. To be sure he will not be so pleasing to you, and there will be some drawbacks in a man of the sort, but that will not last for ever. Believe me, the time you bury him you will be left with good means, and you will find a comrade to your liking that will make amends for all.

MARIAN. It is a strange thing, that to be happy we have to wait for some person's death. And death is not always so helpful to our plans as we thought it would be.

FROSINE. Is it humbugging you are? Sure you are only to marry him on the condition he will leave you a widow in a short while. That has a right to be put down in the contract. It would be very unmannerly of him to stay living beyond three months.——Here he is now coming.

MARIAN. Oh, Frosine! What a fright he is!

HARPAGON (*to* MARION). Don't take offence now, my beauty, that I have on my glasses coming to see you. I know well they are no way needed for making out your good looks. But isn't it with glasses we go looking at the stars? And it is what I say, you are yourself a star, and the best of the whole of the stars that are to be found in the country of the stars——Frosine, she is saying no word.——I do not see her to be showing any great joy at the sight of me.

FROSINE. It is that she is strange yet. And besides that, a young girl would always be ashamed to be showing what is in her mind.

HARPAGON (*to* FROSINE). That is so. (*To* MARIAN.) Here, sweetheart, is my daughter come to welcome you. (ELISE *comes in.*)

MARIAN. I should have asked to see you before this.

ELISE. No, but I myself should have called to see you.

HARPAGON. Look at her—how tall she is. There is the quickest growth in the weeds there is no profit in.

MARIAN (*aside to* FROSINE). I do not like him at all.

HARPAGON (*aside to* FROSINE). What does the darling say?

FROSINE. She says she is well pleased with you.

HARPAGON. You are too kind to me my love.

MARIAN (*aside*). The pig!

HARPAGON. I am greatly obliged to you for taking a liking to me.

MARIAN. I can't go on with this.

(CLEANTE, VALERE, *and* BRINDAVOINE *come in.*)

HARPAGON. Here now is my son that is come to salute you.

MARIAN (*aside to* FROSINE). Oh, Frosine, what a meeting! It was of him I was talking to you!

FROSINE (*to* MARIAN). A very strange chance indeed.

HARPAGON. You are wondering to see me with grown-up children. But I will soon be rid of the both of them.

CLEANTE (*to* MARIAN). This is a thing I never expected myself. I was greatly surprised when my father told me of his plans.

MARIAN. I can say the same thing. I am as much amazed as yourself.

CLEANTE. I am sure, ma'am, my father could not have made a better choice——and it is a great delight to me to see you here—— But I will not go so far as to say I will be glad to see you made my stepmother.

HARPAGON. That is great impertinence! That is a strange sort of a compliment.

MARIAN. It is the same way with myself. If you are not craving to have me for a stepmother, neither have I any wish you to be my stepson.

HARPAGON. She is right saying that. Answer a fool according to his foolishness. I ask your pardon, my dear, for his rudeness. He is a young fool doesn't know what he is talking about.

MARIAN. What he said gave me no offence at all. It is best for him tell me his true thoughts. I am better pleased hearing what he said than if he had spoken in any other way.

HARPAGON. It is too good you are, making excuses for him. He will get better sense after a while, and you will see he will change his opinion.

CLEANTE. No I will never change it, and I ask her to believe that.

HARPAGON. This is beyond the beyonds! He is worse again than before.

CLEANTE. Would you wish me to tell a lie?

HARPAGON. At it again! It is best talk of some other thing.

CLEANTE. Very well, as you wish me to make a change, let me put myself in place of my father, and let me tell you I never saw in the world any such a charmer as yourself. Yes, Miss Marian, there could be no good luck so good as to win you. I have set my mind on no other thing. There is nothing I would not do with that before me——the hardest things——

HARPAGON. Go easy now if you please.

CLEANTE. I am just paying her a few compliments on your behalf.

HARPAGON. I have a tongue of my own without wanting an interpreter of your sort. Here, give us those chairs——

FROSINE. No, but it is best go to the fair, the way we can come back sooner and be talking with you.

HARPAGON (*to* BRINDAVOINE). Put the horses to the carriage. (*To* MARIAN) I ask your pardon that I did not think of asking you to take some refreshment before starting.

CLEANTE. But I thought of it, father, and I ordered some China oranges and marmalade and sweet cakes to be brought in. I sent to order them in your name.

HARPAGON (*aside to* VALERE). Valere!

VALERE (*aside to* HARPAGON). He has lost his wits!

CLEANTE. Do you think it is not enough? This lady will be kind enough to excuse it.

MARIAN. It was not needful at all.

CLEANTE. Did you ever see, Miss Marian, a handsomer diamond than the one in my father's ring?

MARIAN. It is very shining indeed.

CLEANTE. You must look at it nearer.

MARIAN. It is beautiful, surely; it would seem to throw out fire.

CLEANTE (*putting himself before* MARIAN, *who is going to give back the diamond*). No, it is on so nice a hand——It is a present my father is giving you.

HARPAGON. Is it me?

CLEANTE. I am sure you would wish her to keep it for your sake.

HARPAGON (*aside to* CLEANTE). What's that?

CLEANTE (*to* MARIAN). He is making signs for you to accept it.

MARIAN. I don't want it.

CLEANTE. You are joking. He would not think of taking it back.

HARPAGON (*aside*). He will drive me mad.

MARIAN. It would be——

CLEANTE (*still preventing her from giving back the diamond*). No, no, I tell you it would offend him.

MARIAN. If you please——

CLEANTE. Not at all.

HARPAGON. My curse——

CLEANTE. See how vexed he is that you refuse it.

HARPAGON (*aside to* CLEANTE). Ah, you traitor!

CLEANTE (*to* MARIAN). You see he is losing patience.

HARPAGON (*aside to* CLEANTE). You villain you!

CLEANTE. It is not my fault, father. I am doing what I can to make her keep it, but she is someway stubborn.

HARPAGON (*aside, threatening* CLEANTE). You scoundrel!

CLEANTE. You are the cause of my father attacking me!

HARPAGON (*aside to* CLEANTE, *with same gesture*). You robber!

CLEANTE (*to* MARIAN). You will bring a fit of sickness on him. Oh do give in, Miss Marian.

FROSINE (*to* MARIAN). Ah, what a fuss you are making! Keep the ring, can't you, and the gentleman wishing it.

MARIAN (*to* HARPAGON). I will keep it now, not to vex you, and I will give it back another time.

BRINDAVOINE (*coming in*). There is a man outside, sir, is wanting to speak with you.

HARPAGON. Tell him I am busy, and to come back another day.

BRINDAVOINE. He says he has brought money for you.

HARPAGON (*to* MARIAN). Excuse me, I will be back in a minute. (BRINDAVOINE *goes*.)

LA MERLUCHE (*running in, and knocking over* HARPAGON). Sir?

HARPAGON. Oh, you have me killed!

CLEANTE. What is it, father. What is the matter?

HARPAGON. The rascal is bribed by my debtors to break my neck.

VALERE (*to* HARPAGON). It won't be much.

LA MERLUCHE (*to* HARPAGON). I beg your pardon, sir, I thought I did well running so fast.

HARPAGON. What was it brought you here, you murderer?

LA MERLUCHE. To tell you your two horses are without shoes!

HARPAGON. Let them be brought to the smith without delay.

CLEANTE. While we are waiting I will entertain the young lady for you, father. I will have the refreshments brought into the garden.

(CLEANTE, MARIAN, FROSINE, LA MERLUCHE *go to garden at back*.)

HARPAGON (*to* VALERE). Valere——here, have an eye to all that ——and save all you can of the sweetcakes till we'll send them back to the shop.

VALERE. That will do. (*Goes*.)

HARPAGON. Oh, the impudence of that son of mine! Has he a mind to bring me to entire ruin?

Curtain.

ACT IV

(CLEANTE, MARIAN, ELISE, FROSINE, *coming in from garden.*)

CLEANTE. Come back here. It is a better place. There is no suspicious person near, and we can say what we like.

ELISE. My brother has told me, Marian, how things are between you. I know what these crosses and vexations are myself, and I can feel for what you are going through.

MARIAN. It is a great comfort to have anyone like you on my side, and I hope you will be my friend always.

FROSINE. It is a great pity for the two of you not to have told me of your troubles before this. I would never have let things go so far as they have gone.

CLEANTE. What could you do? It was through my own back luck it all happened. But, Frosine, good Frosine, couldn't you help us? You may be sure I will be grateful if you can bring it through. And Marian, you should begin by bringing over your mother to our side. Ah, there is a great deal to be done before we can break off this marriage! Try her with every little coaxing way you have, and I am sure she will refuse you nothing.

MARIAN. I will do all I can. I will forget nothing.

HARPAGON (*aside, and not seen*). Ha! my son kissing the hand of his future stepmother! And his future stepmother not forbidding it! Is there some mystery now under this?

ELISE. There is father!

HARPAGON. The carriage is ready. You can set out now when you have a mind.

CLEANTE. As you are not going, father, I will go and take care of them myself.

HARPAGON. You will not. You will stop here. They will get on well enough by themselves, and I am wanting you.

(ELISE, MARIAN, FROSINE *go out.*)

HARPAGON. Well, now, as to the stepmother, what do you think of her?

CLEANTE. What do I think of her?

HARPAGON. Just so; of her carriage and her figure, and her looks and her wit?

CLEANTE. Middling——

HARPAGON. Speak out.

CLEANTE. To say what is true, I did not find her what I had thought her to be. She has a very giddy look; her figure is someway clumsy; she is no great beauty, and has no great sign of wit. You need not think I am saying this to put you against her, for as stepmothers go, I would as soon have her as another.

HARPAGON. But for all that you were saying to her——

CLEANTE. I said some civil things to her in your name, but that was to please yourself.

HARPAGON. And you have no thought of her yourself?

CLEANTE. Is it I? Not at all.

HARPAGON. That is a pity, for it puts an end to a notion had come into my head. Seeing her here, I began thinking on my age, and that I would be blamed for marrying so young a girl. That drove me to give up the intention, but as I have asked her and given my promise, I would have given her to you, if you were not so much against her.

CLEANTE. To me?

HARPAGON. To you.

CLEANTE. In marriage?

HARPAGON. In marriage!

CLEANTE. Listen now. If she is not exactly to my taste itself, I will make up my mind to marry her to oblige you.

HARPAGON. I am not so unreasonable as you may think. I am not for forcing you.

CLEANTE. Oh not at all, but I will force myself for your sake.

HARPAGON. No, no! There can be no happy marriage where there is no liking.

CLEANTE. That is a thing might come after. They say that is what often happens in marriage.

HARPAGON. No, a man must not go to that risk. I will not put you in the way of vexations. If you had felt anyway inclined for her, very good, I would have given you to her in my place. But as you do not, I will go on with my first plan and marry her myself.

CLEANTE. Well, if that is so, I must tell my secret. I have my heart set on her ever since I saw her walking out one day. I was going to ask your consent, and nothing kept me back but hearing what you had in your own mind, and the fear I had of displeasing you.

HARPAGON. Did you go to call on her?

CLEANTE. I did.

HARPAGON. Often?

CLEANTE. Often enough for the shortness of the time.

HARPAGON. Did they give you a good welcome?

CLEANTE. Good enough, but without knowing who I was.

HARPAGON. Did you tell her you wanted to marry her?

CLEANTE. To be sure I did. I went so far as to give some hints to the mother.

HARPAGON. Did she give an ear to them?

CLEANTE. She did; she was very nice.

HARPAGON. Did the daughter return your liking?

CLEANTE. If one can put belief in appearances, I think she has some liking for me.

HARPAGON (*aside*. I am well content to have learned their secret. That is just what I was wanting to know). Now, young fellow, do you know what you have to do? You will set your mind, if you please, to getting rid of your love-thoughts. You will stop your pursuit of a girl that is meant for myself, and you will marry with no delay the person I have laid out for you.

CLEANTE. Is that the way you have been playing on me? Well as things have gone so far, I declare to you that I will not give up Marian; that there is no length I will not go to get her from you; and that if you have her mother on your side, I have maybe some one that is as good upon my own.

HARPAGON. What are you saying? You are daring to cross my path?

CLEANTE. It is you are crossing my own path. I have the first claim.

HARPAGON. Amn't I your father? Do you owe me no respect?

CLEANTE. This is not a case where I can give in to my father! Love cares nothing for fathers!

HARPAGON. I'll make you care for me with a few blows of a stick.

CLEANTE. Your threats are nothing at all to me!

HARPAGON. Will you give her up?

CLEANTE. I will not.

HARPAGON. Let somebody bring me a stick!

(JACQUES *comes in*.)

JACQUES. What is it, gentlemen! What are you thinking about?

CLEANTE. Much I care for your stick!

JACQUES (*to* CLEANTE). Oh, gently, sir!

HARPAGON. To give me such daring talk!

JACQUES (*to* HARPAGON). O, for mercy's sake!

CLEANTE. I won't give in!

JACQUES. What! To your father!

HARPAGON. Leave me alone!

JACQUES (*to* HARPAGON). Is it your own son! Let you stop now!

HARPAGON. I will make yourself judge, Jacques, till you'll see I am in the right.

JACQUES. I am willing. (*To* CLEANTE) Move a little farther off.

HARPAGON. I have taken a fancy to a girl, and I'm going to marry her, and this brat has the impudence to fancy her for himself, and to ask to get her in spite of me refusing.

JACQUES. Oh, he is wrong doing that.

HARPAGON. Isn't it a terrible thing a son to go into competition with his father? Hasn't he a right, through respect, to keep himself from interfering with my wishes?

JACQUES. That is so indeed. Let me speak to him. Stop you where you are.

CLEANTE (*to* JACQUES, *who comes to him*). As he has chosen you for judge, I agree to it. You will do as well as another. I am willing to put our quarrel before you.

JACQUES. That is a great honour for me indeed.

CLEANTE. I want to marry a young lady, and she wants to marry me, and my father comes in to meddle between us, wanting her for himself.

JACQUES. He is wrong doing that.

CLEANTE. Has he no shame, thinking to marry at his age? Is it suitable to him to go courting? Can't he leave that trade to the young?

JACQUES. You are in the right. He is only joking. Wait till I say a couple of words to him. (*To* HARPAGON) Well, sir, your son is not so unreasonable as you might think. He says he knows he owes you respect, and that he was carried away by the heat of his anger. He will not refuse to give in to anything you will say, so long as you will treat him better than what you do, and give him a wife that will be pleasing to him.

HARPAGON. Tell him, so that he may expect good treatment from me, and I will give him leave to make his choice of any woman he will pick out, except Marian.

JACQUES. That will do. (*To* CLEANTE) Well now, your father is not so bad as you make him out. He is after telling me that it was you showing so much temper that put him out. He says he will be content to give you all you wish, so long as you will show such behaviour as a son should do.

CLEANTE. Oh, Jacques, tell him if he will but give up Marian to me he will never have reason to complain of me, and I never will go against him in anything.

JACQUES (*to* HARPAGON). I have that settled. He is satisfied with what you say.

HARPAGON. That is the best news you could bring me.

JACQUES (*to* CLEANTE). There is no more trouble. He is well content with your promises.

CLEANTE. The Lord be praised for that.

JACQUES. The two of you have but to talk the business over together. You are of the one mind now, and you going to quarrel through a mistake a while ago.

CLEANTE. My poor Jacques, I will be thankful to you through the whole of my life-time.

JACQUES. It is nothing at all, sir.

HARPAGON. You have done well, Jacques, and you are deserving of a reward. (*He feels in his pockets.* JACQUES *holds out his hand, but* HARPAGON *pulls out a handkerchief.*) You can go now. I tell you I will not forget it to you.

CLEANTE. I beg your pardon, father, for losing my temper the way I did.

HARPAGON. It doesn't signify.

CLEANTE. I am as sorry as can be.

HARPAGON. And I am as glad as can be, to see you getting sense.

CLEANTE. You are very kind, forgetting my bad behaviour.

HARPAGON. It is easy forgetting it the time you are come back to your duty.

CLEANTE. And you have no bad feeling against me for the flighty things I said?

HARPAGON. Why would I, and you after giving in as you have done.

CLEANTE. I will surely remember your kindness the longest day I live.

HARPAGON. There is surely nothing at all you will not get from me.

CLEANTE. Oh I am not asking that. You have done enough for me, giving me Marian.

HARPAGON. Who is talking about giving you Marian?

CLEANTE. Yourself, father.

HARPAGON. Myself?

CLEANTE. To be sure.

HARPAGON. What do you say? It is yourself promised to give her up!

CLEANTE. I promised to give her up!
HARPAGON. Just so.
CLEANTE. Not at all.
HARPAGON. And you haven't given up thinking of her?
CLEANTE. Not at all. My mind is more set on her than ever.
HARPAGON. Are you at it again, you villain?
CLEANTE. Nothing can change me.
HARPAGON. Let me at you!
CLEANTE. Do what you like.
HARPAGON. I forbid you ever to see her.
CLEANTE. The sooner the better.
HARPAGON. I give you up.
CLEANTE. Do so.
HARPAGON. I cast you out as a son!
CLEANTE. Cast away!
HARPAGON. I disinherit you!
CLEANTE. You can if you like.
HARPAGON. I give you my curse!
CLEANTE. Little I care for your gifts!

(HARPAGON *goes.* LA FLECHE *comes out of garden with a box in his hands.*)

LA FLECHE. Oh, sir, what luck I found you! Follow after me quick!
CLEANTE. What is it?
LA FLECHE. What is it? Follow me, I tell you. It's all right!
CLEANTE. How is that?
LA FLECHE. Here it is for you!
CLEANTE. What is it?
LA FLECHE. I had my eye on this all through the day!
CLEANTE. What is it at all?
LA FLECHE. Your father's treasure that I have brought away.
CLEANTE. How did you do that?
LA FLECHE. I'll tell you. Let us make off! I hear him crying out!

HARPAGON (*crying "stop thief" before he appears, and coming in without his hat*). Stop thief! stop thief! Robbers! Murderers! I ask justice from heaven! I am destroyed! I have met with my death! My throat that is cut! They have brought away my money! Who was it? What happened him? Where is he? Where is he hiding? What way can I catch him? Where should I run? Where should I not run? Is he there beyond? Is he here? Who is he? Stop I say (*seizing his own arm*). Give me back my money! Rascal!——

Ah, it's but myself! My mind is tattered; I don't know where I am, or who I am, or what I am doing! My grief, my poor gold, my money, my dear friend! They have taken you from me. Since you are gone I have lost my support, my comforter, my joy! All is at an end for me, and I have nothing left to do in the world. Without you I cannot go on living, I have done with it all. I can do no more, I am dying, I am dead, I am buried! Is there no one at all to bring me to life, giving me back my darling money, or telling me who has it taken? Aye, what do you say? It's nobody? Whoever it was struck the blow, it is well he chose the hour. The very time when I was talking with my traitor of a son. Let me out! I will go in search of justice! I will have all in the house searched and tortured! The maids, the men, my son, my daughter, and myself! What a crowd! I can't see any one among them that has not a guilty look! Hay? What are you talking about? Are they talking of the thief? What is that noise over there? Is it the robber is there? If you please, if anyone has news of my robber let them tell it out to me! Is it that he's hid there among you? They are all looking at me, they are beginning to laugh. It is easy seen they all have a share in the robbery. Here, police, sergeants, constables, magistrates, judges, gaolers, ropes and hangmen! I will hang the whole world, and if I fail to get back my money, it is myself I will hang at the last!

Curtain.

ACT V

(HARPAGON, OFFICER.)

OFFICER. Let me alone. The Lord be praised I know my trade. It's not to-day I began thief catching. I wish I had a sack of money for every man and woman I have hanged.

HARPAGON. All the police should have an interest in taking this business in hand. If they do not get me back my money I will commit themselves.

OFFICER. We will do all that can be done. How much do you say was in the box?

HARPAGON. Ten thousand crowns in full.

OFFICER. Ten thousand crowns?

HARPAGON. Ten thousand crowns.

OFFICER. It was a serious robbery.

HARPAGON. There is no punishment could be heavy enough for so great a crime. If this thief gets off, it is the churches themselves will be in danger.

OFFICER. In what coin was the money?

HARPAGON. Good gold coin, and full weight.

OFFICER. Who do you suspect of the crime?

HARPAGON. Everyone. I would wish you arrest the whole of the town and the outskirts.

OFFICER. Mind what I say, it is best not to be scaring people too much in the beginning, but to try can you get some proofs on the quiet, the way you can come down on the thief the better in the end. (JACQUES *comes in.*)

JACQUES (*at the back, turning again to the side he entered by*). I'm coming back! Let them cut his throat for me without delay; let them skin his feet, let them scald him in boiling water and hang him up to the ceiling!

HARPAGON (*to* JACQUES). Who are you talking of? The thief that robbed me?

JACQUES. I am talking of a sucking pig your steward is after sending in. I am going to cook it by a recipe of my own.

HARPAGON. It is not a question of sucking pigs! Here is a gentleman you have to talk to about another matter.

OFFICER. Don't be uneasy. I am not a man to scandalise you. Every thing will be done very quiet.

JACQUES. Will this gentleman be at the supper?

OFFICER. Look here, my man, you must hide nothing from your master.

JACQUES. Troth, sir, I'll show what I can do. I will treat you the best way I can.

HARPAGON. That's not it at all.

JACQUES. If I don't treat you as well as I could wish it is the fault of your grand steward, that has my wings cut with the shears of his economies.

HARPAGON. You fool you, we have something to think of besides supper. Give me now some news of my money they have robbed.

JACQUES. They have your money stolen?

HARPAGON. They have, and I will get yourself hanged if you don't get it back.

OFFICER (*to* HARPAGON). Leave him alone. I see by the look of him he is an honest man, and that without sending him to gaol he will find out what you want to know. Yes, my friend, if you will but tell it out there will no harm happen you, and your master will give you a good reward. His money has been stolen from him to-day, and you cannot but know something of the matter.

JACQUES (*aside*). There is the chance I am wanting, to be avenged on Mr. Steward. Since he came into the house he has been the pet, it is his advice is given heed to, and those blows of a rod he gave me are preying on my heart yet.

HARPAGON. What are you mumbling?

OFFICER. Leave him to himself. He is going to do as you wish. I am full sure he is an honest man.

JACQUES. Well, sir, if you force me to speak out, it is my belief it is your pet steward that did it all.

HARPAGON. Valere is it?

JACQUES. That's the man.

HARPAGON. He that seemed so faithful!

JACQUES. Himself. It is what I believe, it was he robbed you.

HARPAGON. Why do you think that?

JACQUES. I think it because I think it.

OFFICER. But you must tell what proofs you have got.

HARPAGON. Did you see him lingering about the place where I had my money hid?

JACQUES. To be sure I did. Where is it it was hid?

HARPAGON. In the garden.

JACQUES. That's it. I saw him rambling in the garden. What was the money in?

HARPAGON. In a box.

JACQUES. That's it, I saw a box with him.

HARPAGON. Tell me what sort of a box was it till I will know was it mine?

JACQUES. What sort was it?

HARPAGON. Yes.

JACQUES. It was like——it was like a box.

OFFICER. I suppose so. But give a better account till we'll know.

JACQUES. It was a large box.

HARPAGON. The box they stole from me is but small.

JACQUES. Oh yes, it is small if you look at it in that way——but I call it large for what is in it.

OFFICER. And what was its colour?

JACQUES. What colour?

OFFICER. Just so.

JACQUES. It was the colour——a sort of a colour, can't you give me a word for it?

HARPAGON. Aye?

JACQUES. Wasn't it red?

HARPAGON. No, but grey.

JACQUES. Oh yes, grey-red——that is what I was striving to say.

HARPAGON. That is it. There is no doubt at all about it. Take it down now, take down his testimony. My good gracious, who at all can I trust? I will swear to nothing from this out. In my opinion, after this happening, it is I myself might go robbing myself.

JACQUES (*to* HARPAGON). Here he is coming in. But mind not to tell him it was I myself found him out!

(VALERE *comes in.*)

HARPAGON. Come here to me and make your confession of the blackest crime, the most horrible villainy that was ever yet committed.

VALERE. What do you mean?

HARPAGON. You traitor! And you not blushing at the thought of your crime!

VALERE. What crime are you talking about?

HARPAGON. What crime am I talking about? As though you did not know it well yourself! There is no use trying to hide it. It is all found out. I have been told all. Is that the way you rewarded my kindness, getting yourself into my house to betray me, and to play me a trick of the sort!

VALERE. As you have found me out, sir, I will not make excuses or deny anything.

JACQUES (*aside*). Ha! Did I guess it and I not knowing!

VALERE. I was intending to speak to you, and I was but waiting for a good chance. But as you know all, I will ask you not to be angry, but to listen to my reasons. It is true I have given you cause of offence, but my fault might be forgiven after all.

HARPAGON. What's that! To forgive it! a trap and a murder of the sort!

VALERE. Don't get into a rage please. When you will listen to me you will find out there is not such great harm done as you make out.

HARPAGON. And you bringing away what is nearer to me than the flesh of my body or my blood!

VALERE. If it is, it is not come into very bad hands. I am well fit to take care of it and to make up for what I have done.

HARPAGON. It is my intention you will do that, and restore to me what you have taken.

VALERE. You will be well satisfied there is no injury to your name.

HARPAGON. There is no question of my good name! But tell me out now what it was led you to it.

VALERE. Oh, sir, can you ask that?

HARPAGON. Indeed I can ask it.

VALEER. It was a little god that brings an excuse for all he causes to be done, and that is Love.

HARPAGON. Love?

.VALERE. Yes.

HARPAGON. That's pretty love indeed! Love of my own gold coin!

VALERE. No sir, it was not your riches tempted me, that is not what I had in my eye. I promise I will ask no more of you if you will but leave me what I have.

HARPAGON. The devil skelp me if I do! I will not leave it with you! Was there ever heard such impudence, asking to keep all you have robbed!

VALERE. Do you call that a theft?

HARPAGON. Do I call it a theft? A great treasure of the sort?

VALERE. Indeed the greatest of all your treasures! But to give it to me is not to lose it. I ask you to do that, on my knees, and it would be right for you to grant me my asking.

HARPAGON. I will do no such thing. What do you mean asking it?

VALERE. We have given one another our word never to let ourselves be parted.

HARPAGON. A very nice promise indeed, and very funny!

VALERE. We have agreed to belong to one another to the end of our life-time.

HARPAGON. You will not, for I will hinder you.

VALERE. Nothing but death can separate us.

HARPAGON. You are very much in love with my money!

VALERE. I told you before it is not covetousness led me to do what I have done.

HARPAGON. It was Christian charity I suppose led you to bring away my gold. But the law will see me righted!

VALERE. You may treat me in any way you will, but you must not put any blame upon your daughter.

HARPAGON. I suppose not indeed! It would be a strange thing my daughter to have mixed herself with a crime. But it is what I want to get back, what you have brought away, and let you confess where is your hiding place.

VALERE. I have brought nothing away.

HARPAGON (*aside*). Oh my dear little box! (*Aloud*) You brought nothing out of the place?

VALERE. Nothing at all.

HARPAGON. You took nothing at all?

VALERE. You are wronging me. I would not have done that no matter how great the flame that was consuming me.

HARPAGON. Consuming him for my money box!

VALERE. The thought of such modesty!

HARPAGON. The modesty of my box!

VALERE. Those beautiful eyes!

HARPAGON (*aside*). My box has beautiful eyes! He is speaking of it like a lover of his sweetheart.

VALERE. Mrs. Claude knows the truth about it all. She can bear witness.

HARPAGON. What! My own housekeeper is an accomplice!

VALERE. She witnessed our engagement. She knew me to be honest, and she gave me her aid, persuading your daughter to consent.

HARPAGON (*aside*). Is it that the fear of the law has set him raving? (*To* VALERE) What are you talking about my daughter?

VALERE. I am saying I had the work of the world to get over her bashfulness.

HARPAGON. Whose bashfulness?

VALERE. Your daughter's. It is only yesterday I brought her so far as to sign a promise of marriage.

HARPAGON. My daughter has signed a promise of marriage?

VALERE. She has, sir, and I myself have signed it with her .

HARPAGON. Good Lord! Another disgrace!

JACQUES (*to* OFFICER). Take it down, sir, take it down!

HARPAGON. Of all the misfortunes! Oh, I am under troubles! (*To* OFFICER) Here now, do according to your office, and write out a warrant against him as a felon and a thief.

JACQUES. A felon and a suborner.

VALERE. Those are not names I deserve. Wait till you know who I am.

(*Enter* MARIAN, ELISE, FROSINE.)

HARPAGON. Ah, you wicked girl, you are not deserving of a father like myself! Is this the way you practice the lessons I have taught you? You let yourself take a liking to a common thief, and you make your promises to him without leave from me! But I'll cure you! (*To* ELISE) It is four strong walls will keep you within bounds! (*To* VALERE) It's a rope and a gallows will punish you for daring me!

VALERE. It is not you being in a rage will make me guilty. I suppose I am to be allowed to speak before I am convicted.

HARPAGON. A gallows did I say? No, but to break you alive on the wheel.

ELISE (*on her knees to* HARPAGON). Oh, father, take the trouble but to cast a look at him! You are not judging him right, and let me tell you that but for him you would have lost me altogether before this, for it was he saved me the time I was nearly drowned.

HARPAGON. That's nothing! It would be better he to have left you to drown than to have done what he has done!

ELISE. Oh, father, if you have any affection for me!

HARPAGON. No, no, I will listen to nothing! The law must take its course.

JACQUES (*aside*). You will be paid out for those blows of a stick.

FROSINE. What at all has happened?

(ANSELME *comes in.*)

ANSELME. What is it, neighbour Harpagon? You seem to be greatly upset.

HARPAGON. Ah, Mr. Anselme, I am the most unfortunate man in the world! There is nothing but trouble and vexation about this contract you are come to sign. They are doing away with my means! They are doing away with my good name! Look there at a traitor, a hound, that has broken all about me, that crept into my house calling himself a serving man, to rob me of my gold and to steal away my daughter's heart! They have given one another a promise of marriage. That is an insult to yourself, Mr. Anselme. It is you should take up the case against him, and prosecute him at your own expense.

ANSELME. It is not my intention to force myself as a husband upon anyone. But I am ready to look on your interest in this matter as the same as my own.

HARPAGON. Here is a very honest officer that is well able, as he tells me, to do his duty. (*To the* OFFICER) Charge him now, as is right, and put down the offence as very criminal.

VALERE. I see nothing very criminal in wishing to marry your daughter. Wait now till you know who I am.

HARPAGON. Little I think of such rubbish. There are plenty of schemers going about in these times, giving themselves out as belonging to the high families.

VALERE. Take notice now that I am not a man to take anything that does not belong to me. As to my family, all Naples can testify to it.

ANSELME. Take care what you are saying. You are speaking before a man that knows all Naples, and that will not be taken in by any story you may make up.

VALERE (*putting on his hat proudly*). I am not a man to be afraid of anything, and if you are acquainted with Naples you should know the name of Don Thomas D'Alburci.

ANSELME. I know it certainly. There are few who know it better than I.

HARPAGON. Little I care for Don Thomas or Don anything else. (*Seeing two candles burning he blows one out.*)

ANSELME. Let him speak if you please. We shall see what he has to say.

VALERE. I have to say he is my father.

ANSELME. He?

VALERE. Yes.

ANSELME. Stop now, you are talking nonsense. Listen to me and I will put you down. The man you are talking of was lost at sea sixteen years ago with his wife and children, that he was bringing away from Naples in the troubled time.

VALERE. And listen till I put you down. There was one son, seven years old, saved along with a servant by a Spanish ship, and that son is myself that is now speaking with you.

ANSELME. But what witnesses have you besides your own word to prove to us that this is not a fable you have built upon a fact?

VALERE. The Spanish Captain for one, and a ruby seal that belonged to my father, an agate bracelet my mother had put upon my arm, and old Pedro, the servant, that was saved with me from the shipwreck.

MARIAN. I myself can bear witness you are not telling a lie, for all that you tell gives me clear proof that you are my brother.

VALERE. You my sister!

ANSELME. Oh! This is a miracle from Heaven! Come here children into the arms of your father!

HARPAGON (*to ANSELME*). Is this your son?

ANSELME. He is!

HARPAGON. I hold you liable, so, to repay me the ten thousand crowns he has stolen from me.

ANSELME. He has stolen from you!

HARPAGON. He himself.

VALERE. Who made that accusation?

HARPAGON. It was Jacques.

VALERE (*to* JACQUES). You said that to him?

JACQUES. I am saying nothing at all.

HARPAGON. He did say it. The Officer has the deposition taken down.

VALERE. Do you think it possible I could do such a thing?

HARPAGON. Possible or not possible, I want back my money.

(CLEANTE *and* LA FLECHE *come in.*)

CLEANTE. Don't be fretting yourself, father, and don't be accusing anyone. I have got news of your money. It will be restored to you if you will give me Marian for my wife.

HARPAGON. Where is it?

CLEANTE. Never mind where it is. I am answerable for it being safe, and all depends on myself. Tell me now, what is your choice? Will you give me Marian, or will you give up your chance of your cash?

HARPAGON. Is there nothing taken from it?

CLEANTE. Nothing at all. Make your mind up now. Her mother leaves her free, will you leave her free?

MARIAN (*to* CLEANTE). There are others to get consent from. God has given me back my brother (*shows* VALERE) and my father (*shows* ANSELME).

ANSELME. It is not to cross you I have been given back to you. You know well, Harpagon, a girl of her age is more likely to incline to the son than the father. If we have to say more, it may be you would not like to hear it. Give now, as I do, your consent to this double marriage.

HARPAGON. I will not till I see my cashbox.

CLEANTE. You will see it, safe and sound.

HARPAGON. I have no fortune to give with either of them.

ANSELME. I have enough for them. That need not trouble you.

HARPAGON. Will you take on yourself the cost of the two weddings?

ANSELME. I will do that. Are you satisfied?

HARPAGON. I am. So long as you will provide me with a new wedding suit.

ANSELME. I agree to that. Come now and we will make the most of this lucky day.

OFFICER. Hallo, gentlemen! Wait a while! Who is going to pay me for making out the warrant?

HARPAGON. We have no use for your warrants.

OFFICER. I having made it out I must be paid.

HARPAGON (*pointing to* JACQUES). There is your payment. Take and hang that one.

JACQUES. It is not easy to know what to do. First they beat me for telling the truth, and now they are going to hang me for telling a lie.

ANSELME. Ah now, you had best let him off.

HARPAGON. Let you pay the Officer so.

ANSELME. I agree to that. Now children, make haste till we go see your mother.

HARPAGON. And I will go see my dear, dear money box!

Curtain.

THE WOULD-BE GENTLEMAN
BY
JEAN BAPTISTE MOLIÈRE

To
Barry Fitzgerald

THE WOULD-BE GENTLEMAN

PERSONS
  MR. JORDAIN.
  MRS. JORDAIN.
  LUCILE. *Their daughter.*
  NICOLA. *A maidservant.*
  CLEONTE. *In love with Lucile.*
  COVIEL. *Servant to Cleonte.*
  DORANTE. *A Count.*
  DORIMENE. *A Marchioness.*
  MUSIC MASTER.
  DANCING MASTER.
  FENCING MASTER.
  PHILOSOPHY MASTER.
  MASTER TAILOR.
  JOURNEYMAN TAILOR.
  FOOTMEN.
  MUSICIANS.
  DANCERS.

SCENE. *A large Hall.*

MUSIC MASTER (*coming in right and speaking from door to his* MUSICIANS). Come on, come in here, you can be resting yourselves until he comes down.

DANCING MASTER (*coming in left and speaking to his* DANCERS). Come in you too, here on the other side.

MUSIC MASTER (*to a* PUPIL). Have you finished it?

PUPIL. Yes, sir, it is here. (*Holds out sheet of music.*)

MUSIC MASTER. Let me see. (*Looks at it.*) Yes, it is good.

DANCING MASTER. Is it something new?

MUSIC MASTER. Yes, it's an air for a serenade that I set him composing, to be ready for our man when he gets up.

DANCING MASTER. May I take a look at it?

MUSIC MASTER. You'll hear it with the words when he comes down. He won't be long now.

DANCING MASTER. You and I have plenty to do these times.

MUSIC MASTER. Mr. Jordain is the very sort of man we want. He's as good as a fortune to us with all the notions of pushing himself into society he's got into his head. It would be well for my music and your dancing if the rest of the world was like him.

DANCING MASTER. I don't know about that. I wish for his own sake he would profit better by the lessons we give him.

MUSIC MASTER. If he doesn't profit by them he pays for them. And that's the best encouragement to our trade.

DANCING MASTER. Well, as for myself I would wish to be appreciated. It is torture for an artist to have to show off his art to those who know nothing about it, and to have it judged by them. Don't talk to me! There is no satisfaction but in working for people who can understand the difficulties and delicacies of one's art. I'd rather have the praise of people whose praise is worth having than twice the money from fools!

MUSIC MASTER. Just so. That's what I think myself. But we can't live on that sort of incense. It takes more than that to give one an easy life. There must be something more solid behind it, and the praise I like best is the jingle of coin in the hand. Of course this man of the new rich hasn't much sense. He gets the wrong end of everything, he always admires the wrong thing. But his money makes up for his want of wit. His purse holds the best sort of intellect, his praises come to us in the shape of gold stamped at the Mint. He is worth more to us than all the wit of that college-bred lord who brought us to his notice.

DANCING MASTER. There's some truth in that. But in my opinion you lean more to the profit side of the business than an artist with self-respect ought to do.

MUSIC MASTER. I don't see that you yourself have any objection to pocketing what he pays.

DANCING MASTER. All the same, I wish he could have been given a little good taste along with his wealth.

MUSIC MASTER. That's what I wish myself, and isn't that what the two of us are trying to put into him? But whether or not, he's giving us the chance of getting our names up in the world.

DANCING MASTER. Here he is coming!

(MR. JORDAIN *comes in centre. He is wearing a dressing-gown and is followed by* TWO FOOTMEN.)

MR. JORDAIN. Well, gentlemen, what have you there? Are you going to show me that funny little performance you were talking of?

DANCING MASTER. What's that? What funny little performance?

MR. JORDAIN. Oh the—what do you call it——? Your prologue, your dialogue of songs and dances.

MUSIC MASTER. We are all quite ready for you.

MR. JORDAIN. I kept you waiting a little, but that is because I was trying on this morning some clothes, such as are worn by people of quality. And the outfitter sent a pair of silk stockings that I give you my word I thought I never could pull on.

MUSIC MASTER. Oh, we are here, sir, to wait for whatever time suits you.

MR. JORDAIN. I will ask you now to wait until my new coat is brought in. I would wish you to see me in it.

MUSIC MASTER. Certainly, sir, whatever you wish.

MR. JORDAIN. You will see me dressed in style from top to toe.

MUSIC MASTER. I am sure of that.

MR. JORDAIN. I've had this Oriental dressing-gown made specially for me.

DANCING MASTER. It's a beauty.

MR. JORDAIN. My tailor tells me people in *real* high society wear this sort of thing of a morning.

MUSIC MASTER. It becomes you greatly.

MR. JORDAIN (*to* FOOTMEN). Hallo, you fellows, come here the two of you!

FOOTMEN (*coming down*). What are you wanting, sir?

MR. JORDAIN. Nothing, only to see if you can hear me calling. (FOOTMEN *retire*.) (*To the* MASTERS) What do you say to my liveries?

DANCING MASTER. They're magnificent.

MR. JORDAIN (*threws open his gown, and displays a pair of red velvet breeches and green velvet jacket*). This is a little lounge suit for my morning exercises.

MUSIC MASTER. It's very tasty.

MR. JORDAIN. Footman!

SERVANT (*coming down*). Sir!

MR. JORDAIN. You other fellow!

OTHER SERVANT (*coming down*). Sir!

MR. JORDAIN. Take my gown. (FOOTMEN *take off his dressing gown, and go back*.) (*To* DANCING MASTER) How do you like me in this suit?

DANCING MASTER. Nothing could be better.

MR. JORDAIN (*taking up* PUPIL'S *music*). Let me have a look at this thing.

MUSIC MASTER. I would wish you first to hear an air he has

composed for the Serenade you ordered. He is one of my pupils. He has a gift for this sort of thing.

MR. JORDAIN. Yes, but you shouldn't have given it to be done by a pupil. Did you think yourself too good to take it in hand yourself?

MUSIC MASTER. You must not think little of him because he is still a scholar, sir. These sort of scholars know as much as the greatest masters, and the air is as good as can be. Just listen to it——

MR. JORDAIN. Give me my dressing-gown. I'll hear better in it—no, stop—I think I'll be as well without it. No, give it here. I think it will be best after all. (*Puts it on.*) A chair.

PUPIL (*sings*)
> O Richard, O my king,
> The world abandons thee!
> On all the earth there is none to bring
> Homage and love but only me!

MR. JORDAIN. That is a dismal sort of a thing—a sort that would send me asleep. I'd be glad now if you could liven it up a bit here and there.

MUSIC MASTER. But, sir, the air should be in accord with the words.

MR. JORDAIN. I learned a *really* pretty song a while ago. Stop a minute—Hum-hum—— How now does it go?——

MUSIC MASTER. That is more than I know.

MR. JORDAIN. There's lamb in it.

MUSIC MASTER. Lamb?

MR. JORDAIN. Yes——ha! (*He sings*)
> Ye friends and ye neighbours, I'm sorry to hear
> There is no money stirring this present new year,
> We thought we'd live well if the markets were down,
> Drink wine and eat lamb like the king with his crown.

Isn't that now very pretty?

MUSIC MASTER. The best I ever heard.

DANCING MASTER. And you sing it so well!

MR. JORDAIN. And without ever learning music!

MUSIC MASTER. You ought to learn it, sir, as you are learning dancing. They are two arts that hold together.

MR. JORDAIN. What! Do people of fashion learn music as well as dancing?

MUSIC MASTER. Yes, sir.

MR. JORDAIN. Then I'll learn it. But I don't know where I'll find the time. For as well as my Fencing Master, I've engaged a Professor of philosophy who should begin with me this morning.

MUSIC MASTER. Well, philosophy is something; but music sir! Music!

DANCING MASTER. Music and dancing. Music and dancing! There you have the whole thing!

MUSIC MASTER. There's nothing so profitable to the State as music.

DANCING MASTER. There's nothing more necessary to any person than dancing!

MUSIC MASTER. A nation cannot exist without music!

DANCING MASTER. A man can do nothing at all without dancing!

MUSIC MASTER. All the disorder—all the wars one sees in the world, come from no other thing than the want of learning music.

DANCING MASTER. All the misfortunes of mankind, all the disasters that fill up the history books—the blunders of politicians, the defeats of great captains all come from the want of knowing how to dance!

MR. JORDAIN. How's that now?

MUSIC MASTER. Doesn't war break out from the want of union among men?

MR. JORDAIN. That's true.

MUSIC MASTER. And if all men learned music wouldn't that be the means of keeping them in tune together, and bringing universal peace into the world?

MR. JORDAIN. That's right.

DANCING MASTER. But when a man has made a slip in his conduct, whether in the affairs of his family, or of the government of his country, or the command of an army, isn't it always said such a one has made a false step?

MR. JORDAIN. So we do say that.

DANCING MASTER. And can making a false step be caused by any other thing than not knowing how to dance?

MR. JORDAIN. That is true, and both of you are right.

DANCING MASTER. We have showed you now the advantage and the use of dancing and of music.

MR. JORDAIN. I understand it now.

MUSIC MASTER. As I was saying, this is a little attempt I made a while ago to show how different passions may be expressed by music.

MR. JORDAIN. Very good.

MUSIC MASTER (*to musicians*). Here—come forward. You must imagine they are dressed like shepherds.

MR. JORDAIN. Why must they always be shepherds? One sees nothing now-a-days but shepherds, shepherds, shepherds.

MUSIC MASTER. When one has to make characters express themselves in music it is necessary to probability that we give a pastoral setting. Singing has at all times been associated with shepherds. It would not be at all natural in a dialogue to hear royal families or shopkeepers singing their passions.

MR. JORDAN. All right, all right. Go ahead.

1ST VOICE. *I am going out a-walking.*

2ND VOICE. *Whither are you walking now?*

1ST VOICE. *Walking out to meet my true love.*

3RD VOICE. *She is not your true love now;*
           She has given me her love.

1ST VOICE. *It will break my heart in twain.*

3RD VOICE. *Find another lover now.*

2ND VOICE. *Go and walk abroad again.*

MR. JORDAIN. It that all?

MUSIC MASTER. That is all.

MR. JORDAIN. I think it is very well put together. There are some very pretty little thoughts in it.

DANCING MASTER. Here now, what I have to show is a little specimen of the most beautiful movements and the loveliest attitudes that can be got into any dance!

MR. JORDAIN. Are they shepherds too?

DANCING MASTER. They are whatever you please, sir. Now begin!

(*Pupils dance to music.*)

MR. JORDAIN. That isn't bad, these do their steps well enough.

MUSIC MASTER. When the dancing is accompanied by its own music it will be better again, and you will see something that will please you.

MR. JORDAIN. That is for bye and bye, mind you, when the lady comes that I am expecting to dine with me. It is in honour of her that I ordered the whole thing.

MUSIC MASTER. But once in a way is not enough, sir. A gentleman like you, and living in the style you do, and having your taste for the fine arts, should give a concert here every Wednesday—or every Thursday.

MR. JORDAIN. Is that what society people do?

MUSIC MASTER. It is, sir.

MR. JORDAIN. So I will give a concert. But it should be a good one.

MUSIC MASTER. You must have three voices—a tenor, a counter-tenor and a bass; and they must be accompanied by a bass viol, a theorbo lute, and a harpsichord for the thorough bass, with two violins for playing the symphonies.

MR. JORDAIN. You must add to those a trumpet marine. That is an instrument that I like, and that is very harmonious.

MUSIC MASTER. We'll manage it all for you.

MR. JORDAIN. And don't forget to send the musicians to sing bye and bye at the dinner.

MUSIC MASTER. Everything will be as you wish.

MR. JORDAN. And mind I want everything of the best.

MUSIC MASTER. You will be well satisfied. Would you wish mariottes?

MR. JORDAN. Ha! Mariottes are my dance. Wait now till you see me dance one—come on, Master.

DANCING MASTER. Now, sir, if you please. La, la, la! La-la-la-la-la-la; la-la-la twice. La-la-la-; la-la. In time, if you please. La-la, the right leg. La-la-la, don't shake your shoulders so much—la-la-la-la-la, la-la-la-la-la: your arms hang as if they were dead— la-la-la-la-la-la: Hold up your head, turn out the toes—la, la, la: Your body straight!

MR. JORDAIN. Hey?

MUSIC MASTER. It couldn't be better than that!

MR. JORDAIN. Look now. Show me what way to make a bow to a Marchioness. I'll have occasion for that bye and bye.

DANCING MASTER. To make a bow to a Marchioness?

MR. JORDAIN. That's it. A Marchioness whose name is Dorimene.

DANCING MASTER. Give me your hand.

MR. JORDAIN. No, you need only show me. I'll remember it all right.

DANCING MASTER. If you want to salute her with great respect you must first make a bow, and fall back a few steps. Then walk towards her, bowing three times, and, as a finish, bow down as low as her knees. (*He does all this.*)

MR. JORDAIN. Show me that again. That's right.

FOOTMAN. Your Fencing Master is here, sir.

MR. JORDAIN. Bid him come in and give me my lesson. You may stop here yourself and see what I can do.

(FENCING MASTER *comes in right centre. Gives* MR. JORDAIN *a foil in his hand.*)

FENCING MASTER. Now, sir, the salute. Body erect. Leaning slightly on the left thigh. The legs not so wide apart. Both feet on the one line. The wrist on the level of the hip. The left hand to the level of the eyes. The point of the sword over against the shoulder. The arm not extended so far. The left shoulder kept square. Hold up your head! Your expression bold. Advance. The body steady! Touch my sword in carte and lunge. One, two! Recover! Now, again, the foot firm—one, two—leap back. When you make a thrust, sir, the sword must quit first, and the body be kept well behind. One, two! Come, thrust tierce and finish tiers. Advance. Spring. Spring from thence. One, two. As you were. Repeat the same. One, two—Leap back! Parry, sir, parry!

(THE FENCING MASTER *gives him two or three thrusts, crying* '*Parry!*')

MR. JORDAIN (*draws a long breath*). Ah-h! (*lays down foil.*)

MUSIC MASTER. You are doing wonders!

FENCING MASTER. I have told you already, sir, the whole secret of arms lies in two things only—to strike and not to be struck. And I showed you the other day by demonstrative reason it is impossible that you should be hit if you know how to turn your adversary's sword from the line of your body. And that depends merely on a slight movement of the wrist, either inward or outward.

MR. JORDAIN. Then that being so, a person without any courage is able to kill his man and not to be killed himself?

FENCING MASTER. Of course. Don't you see that by the demonstration?

MR. JORDAIN. I do.

FENCING MASTER. You may see by this how highly we should be thought of in the State, and how highly the science of arms excels all those useless arts such as music and dancing——

DANCING MASTER. Fair and easy, Mr. Swordsman. I'd thank you not to speak of dancing but with respect.

MUSIC MASTER. And I'll thank you not to disparage music.

FENCING MASTER. Ha, ha! That's a comical idea! Comparing your professions with mine!

MUSIC MASTER. Just listen to that fellow's conceit.

DANCING MASTER. Such a figure of fun with his breastplate!

FENCING MASTER. My little Mr. Skipper, I'll teach you to hop! And you little master Scraper, I'll set you playing a quick march!

DANCING MASTER. With all your clinking and clanking, I'll maybe give you a lesson in your trade!

MR. JORDAIN (*going between them*). Are you out of your senses to go quarrel with a man of his sort that can kill a person by demonstrative reasoning?

DANCING MASTER (*snapping his fingers*). I don't care *that* for his demonstrative reason— or for his tierce or his carte!

MR. JORDAIN. Speak easy now, I tell you!

FENCING MASTER (*to* DANCING MASTER). What's that, Master Impudence!

MR. JORDAIN. Now, now, my dear Fencing Master.

DANCING MASTER (*to* FENCING MASTER). What's that, you big cart horse!

MR. JORDAIN. No, no, my dear good Dancing Master!

FENCING MASTER. If I once lift my hand to you!

MR. JORDAIN. Go easy, now, go easy.

DANCING MASTER. If I get a grip of you!

MR. JORDAIN. Quiet and easy, I say!

FENCING MASTER. I'll curry-comb you!

MR. JORDAIN. For pity's sake!

DANCING MASTER. I'm well inclined myself to thrash you!

MR. JORDAIN. I beg and pray you!

MUSIC MASTER. We'll make him talk with the other side of his mouth!

MR. JORDAIN. Good Lord! Can't you be quiet!

(PROFESSOR OF PHILOSOPHY *comes in left*.)

MR. JORDAIN. Ha! Mr. Philosopher, you've come in the nick of time with your philosophy. Come, see if you can make peace between these fellows.

PHILOSOPHER. What is it all about? What's the matter, gentlemen?

MR. JORDAIN. They have argued themselves into such a passion on the head of their professions that they're calling one another names, and are very near coming to blows.

PHILOSOPHER (*going between* FENCING MASTER *and* DANCING MASTER). Ah, for shame, gentlemen! Where is the use of all this fury? Have you never read the learned *Treatise on Anger*, composed by Seneca? Is there anything lower and more shameful than this wrath and passion that turns a man into a savage brute? Should not reason be the master of all our emotions?

DANCING MASTER. What's that you're saying, sir! He has just been piling abuse on us, running down dancing that is my art, and music that is his! (*Points to* MUSIC MASTER.)

PHILOSOPHER. A wise man is above all the insults that can be put on him. The best answer one can give is patience and moderation.

FENCING MASTER. These two have the impudence to compare their professions with mine!

PHIL. MASTER. Why should that disturb you? It is not about rank or vainglory that men should quarrel with one another. The only qualities that give real distinction are wisdom and virtue.

DANCING MASTER. I stood up to him that dancing is a science it is impossible to think too much of!

MUSIC MASTER. And I say it is music has been held to be highest through all the ages!

FENCING MASTER. And I stick to it, against the two of them, that the science of arms is the best science, and the most necessary of all!

PHIL. MASTER. And what do you say then of Philosophy? In my opinion you are all three very impudent to talk that way in *my* presence! Giving the name of science to things that don't deserve even the name of arts! What do they belong to but the miserable trade of street organ players or dancers?

FENCING MASTER. Get out of that, you fool of a philosopher!

MUSIC MASTER. Get out, you beggar of a bookworm!

DANCING MASTER. Get out, you prating pedant!

PHIL. MASTER. What are you saying? Scum that you are!

(*He falls on them, they all three hit out at him, and at one another.*)

MR. JORDAIN. Mr. Philosopher!

PHIL. MASTER. Scoundrels! Brutes! Insolent dogs!

MR. JORDAIN. Mr. Philosopher!

FENCING MASTER. Plague take the brute!

MR. JORDAIN. Gentlemen!

PHIL. MASTER. Impudent curs!

MR. JORDAIN. Mr. Philosopher!

DANCING MASTER. Devil take the jackass!

MR. JORDAIN. Gentlemen!

PHIL. MASTER. Wretched vermin!

MR. JORDAIN. Mr. Philosopher!

MUSIC MASTER. Let him go to the mischief!

MR. JORDAIN. Gentlemen!

PHIL. MASTER. Rogues! Traitors! Humbugs! Villains!

MR. JORDAIN (*getting up on a chair*). Mr. Philosopher, Gentlemen—Mr. Philosopher! Gentlemen—Mr. Philosopher! Oh, fight one another as much as you like! Fire away! I won't meddle. I'm not going to spoil my new gown for your sakes. What a fool I'd be to go thrust myself between you and maybe get a crack for my pains! (*Gets down.*)

(*All go out, except* PHIL. *and* FOOTMEN.)

PHIL. MASTER. Now, we'll get to our lesson.

MR. JORDAIN. Ah, sir, I'm very sorry for the way they treated you.

PHIL. MASTER. It's nothing at all. A philosopher knows how to put up with all sorts. I'll compose a satire on them that they won't like, in the style of Juvenal——. Let it pass! What have you a mind to learn?

MR. JORDAIN. Everything I can, for I wish beyond everything to be a scholar. Oh! it maddens me that my father and mother didn't make me mind my books when I was a youngster!

PHIL. MASTER. That's right. *Nam sine doctrina vita est quasi mortis inago.* You understand that I suppose? Of course, you know Latin?

MR. JORDAIN. Of course. But you can go on as if I didn't know it. Explain to me now what that means.

PHIL. MASTER. It means that, without learning, life is as it were an image of death.

MR. JORDAIN. That same Latin says the truth.

PHIL. MASTER. Have you not some foundation, some rudiments of learning?

MR. JORDAIN. I can read and write.

PHIL. MASTER. What would you like to begin with. What about Logic?

MR. JORDAIN. What now is Logic?

PHIL. MASTER. It is that which teaches the three operations of the mind.

MR. JORDAIN. What are they, now, those three operations of the mind?

PHIL. MASTER. The first, the second, and the third. The first is the power to understand well by means of Universals. The second to judge well by mean of Categories. And the third is to come to a right conclusion by means of Figures; Barbara, Celarent; Darii, Ferio; Baralipton, etc.

MR. JORDAIN. These now are words that are too crabbed. This logic doesn't suit me at all. Teach me something else; something prettier.

PHIL. MASTER. You would prefer the science of Morality?

MR. JORDAIN. Morals?

PHIL. MASTER. Yes.

MR. JORDAIN. What is it about?

PHIL. MASTER. It treats of happiness; teaches men to moderate their passions and——

MR. JORDAIN. No, leave that alone. I have the devil of a temper, and all your Morals couldn't check it. I'll get into a passion whenever I've a mind to.

PHIL. MASTER. Maybe you would like to learn Physics?

MR. JORDAIN. Physics—What sort is that?

PHIL. MASTER. Physics explain the principles of natural things and the properties of the body. It tells of the nature of the elements, of metals, of minerals, stones, plants and animals, and teaches us the cause of the meteors, the rainbow, falling stars, comets, lightnings, thunder, thunderbolts, rain, snow, hail, winds and whirlwinds.

MR. JORDAIN. There's too much hubble-bubble in that. It would make me giddy.

PHIL. MASTER. What then would you wish me to teach you?

MR. JORDAN. Teach me spelling.

PHIL. MASTER. With pleasure.

MR. JORDAIN. After that you can teach me astronomy, that I'll know when there is or is not a moon.

PHIL. MASTER. As you please. To follow out your thought and treat it philosophically we must begin according to the order of things, with an exact knowledge of the order of letters and the different manner of pronouncing each of them. And in the first place I must tell you that the letters are divided into vowels, called vowels because they express the voice. And into consonants, called consonants because they sound with the vowels, and only mark the different articulations of the voice. There are five vowels or voices —*a, e, i, o, u.*

MR. JORDAIN. I can understand all that.

PHIL. MASTER. The vowel *a* is formed by opening the mouth wide—*a.*

MR. JORDAN. *A—a.* That's it.

PHIL. MASTER. The vowel *e* is formed by drawing the under jaw a little nearer to the upper jaw—*e.*

MR. JORDAIN. *A—e! A—e.* Faith, so it is. Isn't that very nice?

PHIL. MASTER. And the vowel *i* by bringing the jaws nearer to to one another, and stretching the two corners of the mouth towards the ears—*a, e, i.*

MR. JORDAIN. *A, e, i.* So it is! Learning for ever!

PHIL. MASTER. The vowel *o* is formed by opening the jaws again and drawing the lips near together at the two corners, the upper and the under—*o.*

MR. JORDAN. *O—o.* Nothing could be better. *A, e, i, o—i, o.* That's great!

PHIL. MASTER. The opening of the mouth forms a perfect little ring—which resembles an *o.*

MR. JORDAIN. *O—o—o,* you're right. *O.* Ah, what a good thing it is to know something!

PHIL. MASTER. The vowel *u* is formed by bringing the teeth nearly together without joining them altogether, and pouting out both the lips, bringing them near to one another. *U.*

MR. JORDAIN. There's nothing can be truer than that—*u.*

PHIL. MASTER. You pout out the two lips as if you were making a grimace. So that if you should wish to insult anybody by making faces at him you have only to say—*u.*

MR. JORDAIN. *U—u—u.* That's true. Ah, why didn't I take to learning sooner that I might know all this!

PHIL. MASTER. To-morrow we will consider the other letters, the consonants.

MR. JORDAIN. Is there anything so curious in them as in these?

PHIL. MASTER. Certainly. The consonant *d,* for example is formed by striking the tip of your tongue just above the upper teeth—*d.*

MR. JORDAIN. *D—d.* So it is, so it is. O these are lovely things to know!

PHIL. MASTER. The *f* you form by laying the upper teeth upon the lower lip. *F.*

MR. JORDAIN. *F, f, e, f.* Oh my poor father and mother, why did you never teach me that!

PHIL. MASTER. As to the *r,* you must thrust the tip of the tongue up to the roof of the mouth, so that being grazed by the air which bursts out with force it yields to it, and comes back to the same place making a kind of tril—*r—ra*——.

MR. JORDAIN. *R, r, ra. R, r, r, r, r, ra.* So it does. Oh what a clever man you are! And to think of all the time I have lost! *R, r, r, ra.*

PHIL. MASTER. I will explain all those interesting things to you to the very root.

MR. JORDAIN. Very good. But now I am going to tell you a secret.

I have fallen in love with a lady of high quality, and I would wish you to write something for me in a little note that I will drop at her feet.

PHIL. MASTER. Certainly.

MR. JORDAIN. Something in your best style.

PHIL. MASTER. Of course, I will. Is it to be in verse?

MR. JORDAIN. No, no. None of your verse.

PHIL. MASTER. You only want prose?

MR. JORDAIN. No, I will neither have verse nor prose.

PHIL. MASTER. But it must be one or the other.

MR. JORDAIN. Why so?

PHIL. MASTER. Because there is no other way of expressing yourself but by verse or prose.

MR. JORDAIN. Then when you are talking, what is that?

PHIL. MASTER. That is prose.

MR. JORDAIN. What! When I say, "Nicola bring me my slippers, and give my nightcap"—is that prose?

PHIL. MASTER. Yes, sir.

MR. JORDAIN. Faith then these forty years and more I've been speaking prose and never knew it. I am greatly obliged to you for telling me that. Well, I would like to put in the letter, "Beautiful Marchioness, your beautiful eyes are making me die of love." But I want that to be put in a genteel way, and to be well turned.

PHIL. MASTER. Say that the fire of her eyes burns your heart to ashes; that you suffer for her night and day all the torments——

MR. JORDAIN. No, I won't have all that. I'll have nothing but what I tell you—"Beautiful Marchioness your beautiful eyes make me die with love."

PHIL. MASTER. But you must lengthen it out a little.

MR. JORDAIN. No, I tell you I only want those words in the letter, but to give them some sort of a fashionable turn. Tell me now, just to let me know, the different ways they can be set out, so that I can make a choice.

PHIL. MASTER. They can be put just as you say; or, "Of love beautiful Marchioness, your beautiful eyes make me die"; or, "Your beautiful eyes of love make me die"; or, "Make me die your beautiful eyes of love."

MR. JORDAIN. But of all those which would you say is the best?

PHIL. MASTER. What you said yourself. "Beautiful Marchioness your beautiful eyes make me die of love."

MR. JORDAIN. Ha! And I never studied it, and I've made that up myself at the first shot! I'm greatly obliged to you, and I beg you to come early to-morrow.

PHIL. MASTER. I will without fail. (*Goes.*)

MR. JORDAIN (*to* FOOTMAN). Didn't my clothes come yet?

FOOTMAN. No, sir.

MR. JORDAIN. That confounded tailor to keep me waiting on a day when I've so much business to attend to! I'm getting into a passion! That a fever may perish him, and the plague choke him. Let him go to the devil! If I had him here, this ruffian, this hound, this traitor of a tailor, I'd——

(MASTER TAILOR *and* JOURNEYMAN *come in carrying a suit of clothes.*)

MR. JORDAIN. Oh, there you are. I was just near losing my temper with you.

TAILOR. I could come no sooner. I had up to twenty men working on your suit.

MR. JORDAIN. You sent me a pair of stockings so tight that I had the world and all of trouble to get them on. I burst two holes in them.

TAILOR. They will stretch to be only too large.

MR. JORDAIN. They will, if I go on breaking stitches. And along with that you sent me a pair of shoes that pinch me terribly.

TAILOR. Not at all, sir.

MR. JORDAIN. How not at all.

TAILOR. No, they don't pinch you at all, sir.

MR. JORDAIN. I tell you that they do, and hurt me.

TAILOR. That's all imagination.

MR. JORDAIN. I imagine it because I feel it. That's a queer reason to give.

TAILOR. Wait now, here's the handsomest court suit that can be made, and the most artistic. In it I have created a masterpiece. It is no easy thing to invent a suit that is to be serious without being black, and I'll make a bet the six best tailors in the town couldn't equal it.

MR. JORDAIN. What's that I see! You've put the flowers upside down.

TAILOR. You never told me you would prefer them any other way.

MR. JORDAIN. Was there any need to tell you that?

TAILOR. Of course. All fashionable people prefer them this way.

MR. JORDAIN. Do fashionable people like them upside down?

TAILOR. Yes, sir.

MR. JORDAIN. Oh! That will be all right then.

TAILOR. If you wish I will make the alteration.

MR. JORDAIN. No, no.

TAILOR. You only have to say it.

MR. JORDAIN. No, I tell you, you've done quite right. Do you think the coat will fit?

TAILOR. What a question! I defy a painter with his pencil to draw anything that will be a more exact fit. I have a cutter in my place who is the greatest genius in the world at breeches, and another who is the champion of our day in the cut of a waistcoat.

MR. JORDAIN. Is the hat and feather as it should be?

TAILOR. It is quite right, sir.

MR. JORDAIN (*looking closely at the tailor's coat*). Ah ha, Mr. Tailor! I see here some of the stuff of my last suit! I know it's the same!

TAILOR. It is because I admired it so much that I had a mind to have a coat from it myself!

MR. JORDAIN. Yes, but you should not have cribbed it out of mine.

TAILOR. Now, will you try on your coat?

MR. JORDAIN. Yes, give it here to me. (*He begins to put it on.*)

TAILOR. No, that won't do. I have brought this man here to dress you, while others I have brought will play music outside. This is a sort of suit that should be put on with ceremony. Here you——Help the gentleman on with this, the same as you do with the nobility!

MR. JORDAIN (*strutting about, sings to the air of "Malbrough s'en va-t-en guerre"*):

> The hero's going to war,
> Miriton, miriton, mirotaine!
> The hero's going to war,
> Who knows when he'd return?
>
> At Easter he'll be back,
> At Easter he'll be back!
> The hero's going to war,
> A conqueror he'll return!

TAILOR'S MAN. Please good gentleman, give the tailor's men something to drink your health——

MR. JORDAIN. What did you call me?

TAILOR'S MAN. Gentleman!

THE WOULD-BE GENTLEMAN

MR. JORDAIN. Gentleman! See what it is to dress like men of quality. You might go in common clothes all the days of your life, and no one would ever call you gentleman. Here, take this for your civility—Good gentleman!

TAILOR'S MAN. Long life to your lordship!

MR. JORDAIN. Your lordship! Oh, stop a minute—"Your lordship" deserves something. That is a title worth while! Here, this is what his lordship gives you.

TAILOR'S MAN. Your lordship, we'll go drink to the health of your Grace.

MR. JORDAIN. Your Grace! Oh, ho, ho! Stop, don't go away. Calling me your Grace! Faith if he goes as far as your highness he'll empty my purse. Here—that's from his grace!

TAILOR. My lord, we must humbly thank your Grace for your liberality. (*Exit with apprentice.*)

MR. JORDAIN. He behaves well. I was going to give him all I have in my pocket.

(MR. JORDAIN *and two footmen left alone.*)

MR. JORDAIN (*to* FOOTMAN). Follow me now where I'm going to show off my clothes for a while through the town. And mind you walk close behind, the way everyone will know that you belong to me.

FOOTMEN. Yes, sir.

MR. JORDAIN. Stop—call Nicola here, I have some order to give her. No, you needn't go, here she comes.

(*Enter* NICOLA.)

MR. JORDAIN. Nicola!

NICOLA. Yes, sir.

MR. JORDAIN. Listen here——

NICOLA (*giggles*). He, he, he!

MR. JORDAIN. Listen!

NICOLA. He, he, he, he, he!

MR. JORDAIN. What does the fool mean.

NICOLA. He, he, he! The way you are dressed up! Ha, ha, ha!

MR. JORDAIN. What do you mean?

NICOLA. Ah! Ah! Good lord! He, he, he, he!

MR. JORDAIN. Stop that impudence! Is it that you're laughing at me?

NICOLA. No, no, sir! I'd be sorry to do that! Ha, ha, ha, ha, ha!

MR. JORDAIN. If you go on like that I'll give you a slap on the face.

NICOLA. Oh, sir, I can't help it—He, he, he, he, he, he!

MR. JORDAIN. Will you stop!

NICOLA. I beg your pardon, sir—but you are such a comical sight I can't help it! Ha, ha, ha!

MR. JORDAIN. Did anyone ever see such impudence!

NICOLA. You look so funny! he, he!

MR. JORDAIN. I'll——

NICOLA. Oh, please forgive me, sir! Ha, ha, ha, ha!

MR. JORDAIN. Look now. If I hear the least little giggle in the world after this, I give you my word you'll get such a box in the ear as you never had in your life.

NICOLA. Oh, sir, I've done. I'll not laugh any more.

MR. JORDAIN. Mind that you don't. Go now and clean——

NICOLA. Ha, ha!

MR. JORDAIN. Go and clean out properly——

NICOLA. Ha, ha!

MR. JORDAIN. I say go clean out the hall, and——

NICOLA. He, he!

MR. JORDAIN. You're at it again!

NICOLA. Oh, sir, beat me if you like, but let me laugh my fill. That will do me good!

MR. JORDAIN. You will drive me mad!

NICOLA. For mercy's sake let me laugh! He, he, he!

MR. JORDAIN. If I get a hold of you!

NICHOLA. But, sir, if I don't laugh I'll burst! Ha, ha, ha!

MR. JORDAIN. Did ever anyone see such a good for nothing! She laughs in my face in place of taking my orders.

NICOLA. What would you wish me to do, sir?

MR. JORDAIN. To go, girl, and make ready the house for the company that's coming into it bye and bye.

NICOLA. Faith, that'll put an end to laughing. The people you bring in turn everything upside down. The thought of that is enough to put me in bad humour.

MR. JORDAIN. I suppose I should shut the door for your sake, and let nobody in!

NICOLA. It would be as well to shut it against *some* that come here anyway.

MRS. JORDAIN. (*coming in*). Ho, ho! Here's a new story! What in the world is this get up? Have you given up thinking what people say, when you go making yourself such a figure of fun?

MR. JORDAIN. No one will have that opinion, only fools.

MRS. JORDAIN. Let me tell you the town didn't wait until now to make you its laughing-stock. The whole world has done that this good while.

MR. JORDAIN. And who is it, might I ask you, that you're calling the whole world?

MRS. JORDAIN. I call it a world that has sense in it, and is much wiser than yourself. I declare I'm scandalised by the life you lead! I don't know what our house is turned to be. Anyone would think there was a fair going on in it through the year, with this uproar of fiddlers and songsters that disturb the whole district!

NICOLA. The Missis says what's right. I'll never get the place clean again after that gang of people you bring into the house. You'd say they went searching for mud and for dirt in every part of the town, the way they would bring it in upon us. That poor little Fanny has near worn her knees off with scrubbing the floor, after your teachers coming to daub it with their dirty shoes, as regular as the rising of the sun!

MR. JORDAIN. Tut, tut, Miss Nicola, you have a great clatter of words for a servant girl.

MRS. JORDAIN. Nicola is right, and she has better sense than yourself. What are you thinking to do, taking a dancing master at your time of life.

NICOLA. And a big lump of a Fencing Master who goes stamping about, that he shakes the whole house, and knocks to pieces the pavement of the hall.

MRS. JORDAIN. Is it that you are learning to dance against the time you will have no legs?

NICOLA. Is it that you want to learn to kill somebody?

MR. JORDAIN. Hold your tongues. I tell you. You are an ignorant pair, that cannot understand the advantages of all that.

MRS. JORDAIN. You would be better employed looking out for a husband for your daughter that is of an age to be settled!

MR. JORDAIN. I'll think of that when a good match and a suitable match comes forward. But at this time I have my mind made up to get polite learning.

NICOLA. They are telling me he has taken to-day a new teacher to crown all, a philosophy master.

MR. JORDAIN. Very good. I've a mind to polish my wits, and to be able to hold my own with genteel people.

MRS. JORDAIN. Maybe you'll wish to go to school one of these days, and to get a whipping, old as you are!

MR. JORDAIN. Why not? I declare to goodness I'd be glad to be flogged this day before the whole world, if it would give me knowledge of all that is learned at school.

NICOLA. Yes. That would greatly improve the shape of your legs.

MR. JORDAIN. So it might.

MRS. JORDAIN. All this sort of thing is such a great help in the management of your house!

MR. JORDAIN. Of course it is. You are both talking like donkeys, and I'm ashamed of your ignorance. Can you tell me now what it is you are speaking at this minute?

MRS. JORDAIN. I can. I am speaking good sense, and it would be well for you if you would mind me, and live in another fashion.

MR. JORDAIN. I'm not talking of that. I ask you what the words are that you are speaking.

MRS. JORDAIN. They are words with a great deal of sense in them, and that's what your conduct hasn't got.

MR. JORDAIN. I tell you I'm not talking of that. I'm asking you what it is I am speaking to you at this very minute?

MRS. JORDAIN. Stuff and nonsense!

MR. JORDAIN. That's not what I mean. What we are, both of us, saying—the language we are using this very minute?

MRS. JORDAIN. Well?

MR. JORDAIN. What is it called?

MRS. JORDAIN. It is called whatever we like to call it.

MR. JORDAIN. You ignorant woman. It is prose.

MRS. JORDAIN. Prose?

MR. JORDAIN. Yes, prose. Whatever is prose is not verse, and whatever is not verse is prose. Now, see what it is to be a scholar! And you (*to* NICOLA), Do you know what you have to do to say *u*?

NICOLA. What's that?

MR. JORDAIN. Say *u* now to try.

NICOLA. All right, *u*.

MR. JORDAIN. Well, what is it you do?

NICOLA. I do as you bid me.

MR. JORDAIN. A queer thing to have to deal with stupids! You stick out you lips, and bring your under jaw to your upper jaw. Do you see? I make a face—*u*.

NICOLA. Yes. That's great.

MRS. JORDAIN. That is something to admire!

MR. JORDAIN. You would have seen something quite different if you had seen *o* and *dee*—*dee*, and *e-f*—*ef*.

MRS. JORDAIN. What is all this balderdash?

NICOLA. And what good at all is it to us?

MR. JORDAIN. It drives me mad to see such ignorant women!

MRS. JORDAIN. You ought to send all that rubbishy troop to the right about.

NICOLA. And first and foremost that big fencing master that fills the house with dust.

MR. JORDAIN. Oh no. This fencing master seems to stick in your mind. Now, I'll let you see how ignorant you are. (*He takes up the foils and gives one to* NICOLA.) See now. Reason demonstrative, the line of the body. When they thrust in carte, you need only do so. And when they thrust in tierce, one need only do so. That's the way never to be killed. Isn't that now very good, to be on sure ground when you are having a fight with anyone? There—thrust at me a little—just to see——

NICOLA. All right. Is it this way? (*Gives him several thrusts.*)

MR. JORDAIN. Go easy! Oh! Gently! Deuce take the girl!

NICOLA. You bade me to thrust.

MR. JORDAIN (*angrily*). Yes, but you thrust me in tierce before you thrust me in carte—and you hadn't patience to let me parry——

(NICOLA *runs out.*)

MRS. JORDAIN. You are gone off your head with all your fancies. And all this has started since you got the notion of keeping high up company.

MR. JORDAIN. If I keep company with the nobility I show good judgment. It's much better than herding with common towns-people.

MRS. JORDAIN. So it seems. There's a great deal to be gained among your "nobility". You've done something to be proud of, taking up with that Count you are so bewitched with.

MR. JORDAIN. Be quiet. Mind what you're saying. You don't know what you're talking about. He's a more important man than you think. He's made a great deal of at Court—talks to the King just the same as I talk to you. Isn't it something to my credit that such a man can be seen coming so often to my house, calling me his dear friend, treating me as if I was the same as himself. He has a great affection for me. I declare I'm nearly ashamed of the way he makes much of me before the whole world.

MRS. JORDAIN. That's it. He makes much of you and flatters you—but he borrows money from you.

MR. JORDAIN. Even so, isn't it a great honour for me to lend money to a man of his rank. Could I do less for a nobleman who calls me his dear friend?

MRS. JORDAIN. And what has this nobleman done for you?

MR. JORDAIN. Things that would astonish you if you knew them.

MRS. JORDAIN. And what may they be?

MR. JORDAIN. That's enough. There's no need to go into that. It's enough that if I lend him money he'll repay it honestly and before long.

MRS. JORDAIN. All right. Wait till he does.

MR. JORDAIN. He will, of course. Didn't he tell me he would?

MRS. JORDAIN. Ah yes. He won't disappoint you.

MR. JORDAIN. He swore it, on the faith of a gentleman.

MRS. JORDAIN. Stuff and nonsense!

MR. JORDAIN. You're a very obstinate woman. I tell you he'll keep his word.

MRS. JORDAIN. And I tell you he won't, and that he is only humbugging you.

MR. JORDAIN. Hold your tongue! Here he is coming.

MRS. JORDAIN. To borrow more from you! The very sight of him makes me sick.

MR. JORDAIN. Can't you hold your tongue?

COUNT DORANTE (*coming in*). My dear friend, Mr. Jordain, how are you?

MR. JORDAIN. Very well, sir. What can I do for you?

COUNT. And Mrs. Jordain? How is she?

MRS. JORDAIN. Mrs. Jordain keeps as well as she can.

COUNT. Ha, Mr. Jordain, you are dressed in the height of the fashion.

MR. JORDAIN (*to* MRS. J.). Now you see!

COUNT. You look very well in that suit. There's not a young fellow at Court has a better figure than you.

MR. JORDAIN. Aye, aye.

MRS. JORDAIN (*aside*). He touches him in the right place.

COUNT. Turn round. It couldn't be better.

MRS. JORDAIN. He's as great a fool behind as before.

COUNT. I was very impatient to see you, Mr. Jordain. There's no man in the world I think more of. I was talking of you again this morning at the King's levee.

MR. JORDAIN. You do me a great deal of honour, sir. (*To* MRS. JORDAIN). At the King's levee!

COUNT. Now, put on your hat.

MR. JORDAIN. Sir, I am but paying you proper respect.

COUNT. No, no. There must be no ceremony between us.

MR. JORDAIN. Oh, sir!

COUNT. Put it on, Mr. Jordain. We are friends. I won't put mine on if you don't.

MR. JORDAIN (*putting on hat*). Well, it's better to be unmannerly than to be obstinate.

COUNT. I am your debtor as you know.

MRS. JORDAIN (*aside*). Yes, we know that only too well.

COUNT. You have several times very generously lent me money, and in the kindest way in the world.

MR. JORDAIN. You are joking, sir.

COUNT. But I know how to repay a loan.

MR. JORDAIN. I'm certain of that.

COUNT. I want to settle up with you. I've come to make up our accounts together.

MR. JORDAIN (*to* MRS. JORDAIN). Now you see how silly you were.

COUNT. I'm a man who likes to get out of debt as quick as I can.

MR. JORDAIN (*to* MRS. JORDAIN). What did I tell you?

COUNT. Let's see how much I owe you.

MR. JORDAIN (*to* MRS. JORDAIN). You with your nonsensical suspicions!

COUNT. Do you remember how much you have lent me?

MRS. JORDAIN. I think so. I have made a little entry of it. . . . Here it is . . . £300 lent on one occasion.

COUNT. Just so.

MR. JORDAIN. And another time £220.

COUNT. Quite correct.

MR. JORDAIN. And again £140. Altogether £660.

COUNT. That's it.

MR. JORDAIN. Then this little bill to your hatter——

COUNT. Quite true——

MR. JORDAIN. This to your tailor——

COUNT. I remember——

MR. JORDAIN. This to your haberdasher—and your saddler——

COUNT. Very good. What does it all come to?

MR. JORDAIN. Altogether £1,250.

COUNT. Yes, that's the total. Add to that £250 you are going to give me now, that will make exactly £1,500 which I will repay on the very first opportunity!

MRS. JORDAIN (*to* MR. JORDAIN). Didn't I tell you how it would turn out!

MR. JORDAIN. Hush!

COUNT. Will it inconvenience you to let me have it?

MR. JORDAIN. Not at all.

MRS. JORDAIN (*to* MR. JORDAIN). He makes a milch cow of you!

MR. JORDAIN. Hold your tongue!

COUNT. If it is any inconvenience I'll go and get it elsewhere.

MR. JORDAIN. Oh, not at all, sir.

MRS. JORDAIN. He'll never be happy till he ruins you!

MR. JORDAIN. Stop your chat, I tell you.

COUNT. If it would, you have but to say the word——

MR. JORDAIN. Not in the least, sir.

MRS. JORDAIN. He's a born beggar!

MR. JORDAIN. Shut your mouth.

MRS. JORDAIN. He'll squeeze you out of your last farthing!

MR. JORDAIN. Hold your tongue, I say!

COUNT. There are plenty who would be glad to lend it, but as you are my close friend I thought it would hurt you if I went to anyone else.

MR. JORDAIN. That's a great compliment to me, sir. I'll go get what you want.

MRS. JORDAIN. What! Are you going to lend him more again?

MR. JORDAIN. What can I do? Would you have me refuse a man of that rank? Who spoke of me this morning at the King's levee?

MRS. JORDAIN. Go on. Well, you are the fool of the world!

(MR. JORDAIN *goes out*.)

COUNT (*to* MRS. JORDAIN). You seem to be in low spirits. What is the matter, Mrs. Jordain?

(MRS. JORDAIN *goes out*.)

MRS. JORDAIN. If my head is big, it isn't swelled yet.

COUNT. And where is your daughter that I don't see her?

MRS. JORDAIN. My daughter is well enough where she is.

COUNT. How does she get on?

MRS. JORDAIN. She gets about on her two feet.

COUNT. Won't you come with her some day to see the ballet that's being acted at court, and the ball?

MRS. JORDAIN. Yes, indeed, we are much inclined for laughing. Much inclined for it we are.

COUNT. I'm sure Mrs. Jordain you had a great many followers in your early days, so handsome and good-humoured as you were.

MRS. JORDAIN. Early days, indeed! Is it that Mrs. Jordain is crippled with age, and her head shaking with the palsy?

COUNT. Oh, Mrs. Jordain, I beg your pardon. I was forgetting that you are young. I'm often very absentminded. Do please forgive me my mistake!

MR. JORDAIN (*coming back*). Here it is for you. Here's the money.

(MRS. J. *goes out.*)

COUNT. You know I am your devoted friend. I long to do something for you at the court.

MR. JORDAIN. I'm greatly obliged to you.

COUNT (*coming nearer*). As I told you in my note, our lovely Marchioness will be here bye and bye for your little entertainment. I was able to persuade her to come.

MR. JORDAIN. Come a little farther from the door—for a reason I have.

COUNT. I have told you nothing about the diamond ring you sent her a present of. The reason was that I had all the trouble in the world to get her to accept it. It is only to-day she gave in.

MR. JORDAIN. How does she like it?

COUNT. She thinks it beautiful. Beyond everything! I'll be much surprised if it does not bring her to have the same liking for yourself.

MR. JORDAIN. That she may!

COUNT. Of course, I let her know that your admiration for her is no less than the value of the ring.

MR. JORDAIN. What way can I thank you! To think of a man of your rank putting himself out for the sake of a man like me!

COUNT. Oh, you're joking. There should be no thought of such a thing between friends. Wouldn't you do as much for me if you had the chance?

MR. JORDAIN. Indeed I would—and more.

COUNT. I never feel what I do for a friend any burden. The minute you told me you had taken a fancy to the Marchioness and wanted to make her acquaintance didn't I offer to help you?

MR. JORDAIN. You did, you did! I don't know how to thank you.

MRS. JORDAIN (*at the door with* NICOLA). That man will never be gone. I hate the sight of him.

NICOLA. They are very great with one another.

MRS. JORDAIN. What can they be making so much talk about? Go over a little nearer and listen.

(NICOLA *slips in behind the screen,* MRS. JORDAIN *goes.*)

COUNT. You take the right way to her heart. Women like to have money spent on them. All those bouquets you've been sending her —that display of fireworks you arranged for her, the entertainment you are giving her bye and bye. Such things are more likely to win her than all the words you could say.

MR. JORDAIN. There's no expense I wouldn't go to if it would find the way to her heart. A lady of rank! There is nothing I wouldn't do for such an honour.

COUNT. You'll have plenty of time to look at her bye and bye.

MR. JORDAIN. So I will. I've settled that my wife is to go and dine with her sister. She'll be there the whole of the evening.

COUNT. That was a good idea. Your wife might have been rather in the way. I have given the proper orders to your cook, and for everything, music and all. If my ideas are carried out I'm sure it will be a success.

MR. JORDAIN (*catching sight of* NICOLA *behind the screen, gives her a box on the ear*). There Miss Impudence! (*She runs off.*) Come along, Count, it's better for us to go outside. (*They go out as* MRS. J. *comes in, meeting* NICOLA *at the other door.*)

NICOLA. Troth, ma'am, curiosity brought me a box on the ear, but I'm sure there's something queer going on, something underhand, for I heard them saying they didn't want you to see or to know it.

MRS. JORDAIN. Well, now, this is not the first time I've had suspicions of my husband. If he isn't running after some woman, they may call me a fool. But it's my daughter I have on my mind just now, and that young fellow Cleonte who is courting her. I've taking a great liking to him, and I'll help to make the match between him and Lucile, if I can.

NICOLA. Well, now ma'am that just suits myself. For if the master hits your taste, his man Coviel hits mine. And maybe the two weddings might be settled at the one time.

MRS. JORDAIN. There are the very two coming up the street. Go out now and stop them. Give Cleonte a message from me to come in here till we'll ask the father's consent to his marriage with Lucile.

NICOLA. I'll run, ma'am. You couldn't give me a message would please me better. (*Goes to door.*) Stop a minute, Mr. Cleonte! The mistress wants to speak to you! She has something to say——

(MRS. JORDAIN *goes.* CLEONTE *and* COVIEL *come in.*)

NICOLA. Ha! This is a good meeting. I am a lucky messenger. I have good news for you!

CLEONTE. Stop that impudent talk; treachery doesn't amuse me at all.

NICOLA. Is that the way you receive my good message!

CLEONTE. Go back to your deceitful mistress, and tell her that so long as she may live she'll never make a fool of me again!

NICOLA (*to* COVIEL). What on earth has he got in his head? Tell me what all this is about, my dear Coviel?

COVIEL. Your dear Coviel, indeed! Get out of my sight and let me alone.

NICOLA. Are you gone queer, too?

COVIEL. Get away I tell you, and never open your mouth to me as long as you live!

NICOLA (*going*). Well! What fly has stung the two of them? Well, I must go and tell the Missis of this pretty story! (*Goes.*)

COVIEL. A nice way indeed the two of them have treated the two of us!

CLEONTE. I show Lucile all possible devotion! I care for nothing in the world but her! I think of no one but her! All my joys and cares and wishes are on account of her! I talk of nothing, think of nothing, dream of nothing, live for nothing, but her! My heart is entirely hers. And what reward do I get? I am two days without seeing her, days that seem to me as long as centuries! I meet her in the street by chance, my heart starts with joy, my face lights up with it—I hurry to meet her. And what does she do but look the other way and brush past me, as if she had never seen me in her life!

COVIEL. That's the very same way Nicola treated myself.

CLEONTE. Was there ever seen anything to equal Lucile's behaviour!

COVIEL. Or to equal the bad behaviour of Nicola!

CLEONTE. After all the homage I've paid to her beauty!

COVIEL. After all the little jobs I've done in her kitchen!

CLEONTE. All the tears I have shed at her feet!

COVIEL. All the buckets of water I've brought her from the well!

CLEONTE. Such warmth as I've shown, loving her better than myself!

COVIEL. Such scorching as I've put up with, turning the spit for her!

CLEONTE. And now she walks past me with contempt!

COVIEL. She turns her back on me with impudence!

CLEONTE. Such perfidy deserves some great punishment!

COVIEL. Such treachery! She should have her ears boxed!

CLEONTE. Never say a word for her again!

COVIEL. Is it me? Not a fear of it.

CLEONTE. Never try to make excuses for her!

COVIEL. You needn't be uneasy.

CLEONTE. It would be of no use!

COVIEL. Who is thinking to do it?

CLEONTE. I'll write her no more letters!

COVIEL. I give my consent to that.

CLEONTE. It's likely she's dazzled with the good looks and the title of this Count who comes to the house! But I won't give her the chance of throwing me over! I'll not give her the chance to boast. I'll be the first to break away.

COVIEL. Very good. I have that in my own mind too.

CLEONTE. Help me now to keep to that. I want to banish any remnants of my love. Say out anything you can think of against her! Tell me out now all the faults you can find in her.

COVIEL. In her, sir? A mincing piece of affectation, a sort of a dressed up doll. I see nothing much in her more than another. It would be easy to find a hundred better worth looking at. In the first place, she has but small eyes.

CLEONTE. Yes, her eyes are not very large—but then they are full of fire—the brightest, the most loving that were ever seen.

COVIEL. Her mouth is too wide.

CLEONTE. Yes, but it is more attractive than any mouth in the world. It draws me to her! One cannot but long to kiss it!

COVIEL. As to her figure, she's not tall.

CLEONTE. No, but graceful, and beautifully made.

COVIEL. She puts on a sort of careless manner——

CLEONTE. True enough, but she carries it off so well, and her little ways are so taking, she has some charm that winds her into one's heart.

COVIEL. As to her wit——

CLEONTE. Oh, Coviel. She has plenty of that—the most delicate, the most refined!

COVIEL. Her conversation——

CLEONTE. Her conversation is charming.

COVIEL. Too serious she is.

CLEONTE. Would you wish for an endless string of jokes and puns? Is there anything more insufferable than a woman who is always giggling.

COVIEL. Anyway, she's as changeable as anyone can be.

CLEONTE. Yes, she's capricious—but if she is it suits her. Everythings suits a beautiful woman. We put up with anything from beauty.

COVIEL. If that is so, I see you intend to stay in love with her.

170

CLEONTE. I would sooner die. I am going to hate her now as much as I ever loved her!

COVIEL. How will you do that if you think her so perfect?

CLEONTE. My revenge will show out all the better. I will show my strength of mind in leaving her, hating her—lovely and lovable as she may be. Here she is coming—I won't speak to her——

COVIEL. I'll treat Nicola the same way.

(LUCILE *and* NICOLA *come in.*)

LUCILE. What's the matter, Cleonte? What has happened you?

NICOLA. What ails you, Coviel?

LUCILE. Are you in any trouble?

NICOLA. What makes you so cross?

LUCILE. Are you dumb, Cleonte?

NICOLA. Have you lost your tongue, Coviel?

CLEONTE. Oh, the wretch!

COVIEL. Oh, the traitor!

LUCILE. I am sure what happened when we met this morning has put you out.

CLEONTE (*to* COVIEL). Ah, ha, she knows what she has done.

NICOLA (*to* COVIEL). Our not stopping to talk with you has made you touchy.

COVIEL (*to* CLEONTE). She has guessed our grievance.

LUCILE. Is not that what has vexed you, Cleonte?

CLEONTE. Yes, you deceitful girl, that is it. And I can tell you you'll gain nothing by your behaviour. I am the first to break with you, and you won't be able to boast of having thrown me over. I daresay I'll suffer for a while, I can't get over my love in a day. But I'll carry the thing through! I would sooner kill myself than give in to the weakness of coming back to you.

COVIEL. I say the same. Like master like man.

LUCILE. What a fuss about nothing! I'll give you, Cleonte, the reason we wouldn't speak to you this morning.

CLEONTE (*turning as if to go*). No, I won't listen to you.

LUCILE. I tell you, this morning——

CLEONTE. No, you needn't——

NICOLA (*to* COVIEL). Let me tell you——

COVIEL. No, you traitor!

LUCILE. Listen!

CLEONTE. Not a bit of it! (*He walks away.*)

NICOLA. Let me speak. (*Follows him.*)

COVIEL. I am deaf! (*He follows* CLEONTE.)

LUCILE. Cleonte!

CLEONTE. No!

NICOLA. Coviel!

(ALL *follow each other round and round the room.*)

COVIEL. I won't!

LUCILE. Stop——

CLEONTE. Rubbish!

NICOLA. Listen now——

COVIEL. Stuff and nonsense!

LUCILE. A moment!

CLEONTE. Not one!

NICOLA. Have patience!

COVIEL. Fiddlesticks!

LUCILE. Two words——

CLEONTE. No, it's over——

NICOLA. One word——

COVIEL. No more dealings——

LUCILE (*stopping*). Very well. If you won't hear me keep your own opinion, and do as you please.

NICOLA (*stopping*). If that's the way with you, do as you like.

CLEONTE. Let us hear the reason of your behaviour.

LUCILE. I don't want to give it now. (LUCILE *walks away, going round as* CLEONTE *had done, he following her.*)

CLEONTE. Tell me——

LUCILE. No, I'll tell you nothing.

COVIEL. Say, now——

NICOLA. No, I'll say nothing. (*She walks away—he following her.*)

CLEONTE. For goodness sake——

LUCILE. No, I say.

COVIEL. For charity's sake.

NICOLA. Not a word.

CLEONTE. I beg and pray——

LUCILE. Let me alone——

COVIEL. For all the sakes!

NICOLA. Get out of that!

CLEONTE. Lucile!

LUCILE. No!

COVIEL. Nicola!

NICOLA. Not at all!

CLEONTE. In heaven's name!

LUCILE. I will not!

COVIEL. Speak to me!

172

NICOLA. No, I won't!

CLEONTE. Clear up my doubts!

COVIEL. Pacify my mind!

NICOLA. It doesn't suit me!

CLEONTE (*stopping*). Very well. You care so little to ease my pain and to justify yourself as to the unworthy way you have treated me, it is the last sight you will have of me, you ungrateful girl! I am going far away, to die of grief and love!

COVIEL (*stopping*). And I'll do the same thing!

LUCILE. Cleonte!

NICOLA. Coviel!

CLEONTE. Aye?

COVIEL. What is it?

LUCILE. Where are you going?

CLEONTE. Where I said.

COVIEL. We are going to die!

LUCILE. Are you going to die, Cleonte?

CLEONTE. Yes, you cruel girl, since you wish it.

LUCILE. *I* wish you to die?

CLEONTE. Yes, you wish it.

LUCILE. Who said that?

CLEONTE. Didn't you wish it when you wouldn't explain to me——

LUCILE. Is that my fault? If you would have listened to me I would have told you that the matter you make such a fuss about was not my fault—I could not stop to speak to you because my old aunt was with us. She will have it, right or wrong, that even to look at a man or to talk with him is a disgrace to a girl. She is always preaching sermons to us on that head, she tells us that all men are demons that we must fly from.

NICOLA. That is the whole secret of the matter.

CLEONTE. Are you deceiving me, Lucile?

COVIEL. Are you playing me a trick, Nicola?

LUCILE. That is the whole truth.

NICOLA. It is just as she says.

COVIEL. Are we to give in to that?

CLEONTE. Ah, Lucile, how you can banish my anger with one little word! How easily we can be persuaded by the one we love!

COVIEL. How easily we can be coaxed by these cunning humbugs!

MRS. JORDAIN (*coming in*). I'm delighted to see you, Cleonte.

You are come in the nick of time. My husband is just coming in. Take the opportunity, and ask for his consent to your marriage.

CLEONTE. Oh, ma'am, that is a good thought. That is just what I would wish. Nothing could be more welcome than leave to do this.

(MR. JORDAIN *comes in.*)

CLEONTE. Sir, I did not wish anyone to say for me something I have had in mind for a long time. I have come to make a request of you. And without beating about the bush I'll tell you at once that the great favour I beg you to grant me is, that I may have the honour of becoming your son-in-law.

MR. JORDAIN. Before I give you my answer I would wish you to tell me if you are a gentleman.

CLEONTE. Well, sir, most people would answer that question without much hesitation. It is an easy word to say. People don't scruple to take the name, and the custom of to-day seems to authorize the theft. But as to myself I confess I feel differently. I think that any imposture is unworthy of an honest man. It is cowardly to deny the station to which one is born; to claim to be something one is not. I come of men who have filled honourable employments. I had the honour of serving for six weeks in the army. I keep, I may say, good company. But for all that I won't give myself a name that others in my place would probably take, and I'll tell you straight out that I am not a gentleman.

MR. JORDAIN. Stop now, sir. My daughter is not for you.

CLEONTE. How so?

MR. JORDAIN. You are not a gentleman, and you'll not get my daughter.

MRS. JORDAIN. What are you at now, with your *gentleman*? Do you think we ourselves are descended from St. Louis?

MR. JORDAIN. Hold your tongue, now. I see what you're at.

MRS. JORDAIN. Aren't the two of us descended from plain towns-people?

MR. JORDAIN. That's no way to be talking.

MRS. JORDAIN. Wasn't your father a tradesman the same as my own?

MR. JORDAIN. Bad luck to the woman! She's always going on at this! If your father was a shopkeeper so much the worse for him. But as for mine, no one would say that of him but a fool. All I have to say to you is, that for my son-in-law I'll have a gentleman.

MRS. JORDAIN. Your daughter should have a husband that's fitting for her. She would be better off with an honest man that's well made and well to do, than with a gentleman who was badly made and a beggar.

NICOLA. That is so. The son of the big gentleman in our parish is the most awkward lout, the biggest ninny I ever laid an eye on.

MR. JORDAIN. Hold your tongue, Miss Insolence! You are always pushing yourself into the conversation. I have money enough for my daughter! All I want for her is rank, and I'll make her a Marchioness.

NICOLA. A Marchioness!

MRS. JORDAIN. Did I ever! The Lord be between us and harm!

MR. JORDAIN. It is a thing I've determined on.

MRS. JORDAIN. It's a thing I myself will never consent to. Marriage with people above your station always brings down every sort of annoyance. It's not my wish that my son-in-law should run down his wife's relations, and his children be ashamed to call me grandmama. If she'd come visiting me in her carriage as a great lady, and didn't take proper notice of the neighbours, they would be sure to say this and that. "Look," they'd say, "what airs she gives herself! And she Mr. Jordain's daughter, and was happy enough, when she was little, to play children's play with us. She was not always so lofty as we see her now, and her two grandfathers drapers near St. Innocent's Gate! They heaped no great riches for their children, that they're maybe paying dear enough for now, in the other world. For it isn't often by being honest that people grow so rich as that!" I don't want to have all that tittle tattle! What I want is a man that will be thankful to me for my daughter, and that I can say: "Sit down there, son-in-law, and eat your dinner with us!"

MR. JORDAIN. Those are the thoughts of a poor mean little mind, that never wishes to raise itself. Let me have no back answers! My daughter is to be a Marchioness in spite of everyone. And if you put me in a passion I'll make her a Duchess! (*He goes off.*)

MRS. JORDAIN. Now, Cleonte, don't lose courage. Come along with me my girl, and tell your father straight and fair, that if you can't have him you won't marry anyone at all.

(ALL *go out but* CLEONTE *and* COVIEL.)

COVIEL. You made a pretty piece of work, sir, with your fine ideas.

CLEONTE. What could I do? I feel very strongly about this matter.

COVIEL. You are wrong to be serious with such a man as that.

Don't you see he's a cracked fool. Would it cost you anything to give in to his follies?

CLEONTE. You're right enough. But I never thought it would be necessary to bring proofs of nobility, before one could be son-in-law to Mr. Jordain.

COVIEL. Ha, ha, ha!

CLEONTE. What are you laughing at?

COVIEL. At a thought that's come into my head, to play a trick on him, and get what you want.

CLEONTE. In what way?

COVIEL. It's a very comical idea. But I think it will do the trick.

CLEONTE. What trick do you mean?

COVIEL. You must be a Turk——

CLEONTE. I don't know what you're talking about.

COVIEL. If he won't give his daughter to you, and wants a big title, let him give her to the son of a Grand Turk.

CLEONTE. You're talking nonsense.

COVIEL. Wait a minute. Those playactors he has engaged to amuse his lofty friends have sent in a lot of their costumes—costumes of Turks some of them are. We'll put you into one of them. I myself will be a rich merchant coming to introduce you, and he will be taken in.

CLEONTE. I don't think so. He will recognise me.

COVIEL. Another man might, but his head is so full of folly we may risk anything, he'll swallow any nonsense we put before him. The dresses are here quite handy. Come along with me. (*They go out.*)

(MR. JORDAIN *and a* FOOTMAN *come in.*)

MR. JORDAIN (*sitting down at the table*). What are they all making such a fuss about! What have they against me unless keeping high company? I think nothing can be better than keeping company with the nobility. There's nothing among *them* but honour and civility. I declare I would give two fingers off my hand to have been born a Count or a Marquis!

FOOTMAN. Here, sir, is the Count and a lady he is bringing in.

MR. JORDAIN (*rising*). Good Lord! I've some orders to give yet! Tell them I'll be back in a minute. (*Goes.*)

(*The* COUNT *and* DORIMENE *come in.*)

FOOTMAN. The master told me to tell you, sir, he'll be back in a minute. (*Goes.*)

COUNT. That's all right.

DORIMENE. I am afraid, Dorante, I have done something very

unusual in letting you bring me to a strange house where I don't know anyone.

COUNT. Where then, Marchioness, would you let your admirer entertain you? You forbid both your own house and mine for fear of gossip.

DORIMENE. But what can I do when you never cease running after me? I refuse this and that, you weary me until I give in, you have a pleasing kind of obstinacy that gets you your way in spite of me. First your visits, then serenades and entertainments, and presents—I forbade all these things, but you would not take no for an answer. You get your way step by step. I do believe you will bring me at last to accept you, little as I was thinking of a second marriage.

COUNT. Upon my word, ma'am, you ought to have made up your mind to it before this. You have no one to interfere with you, being a widow, I am my own master, and I love you better than life. Why shouldn't you say yes to me this very day?

DORIMENE. Ah, Dorante, there must be a great many good qualities on each side to make two people live happily together. It has often failed the wisest people in the world to do that.

COUNT. Ah, ma'am, you're making too much of it all. If your first marriage wasn't happy that doesn't mean that another won't be so.

DORIMENE. Another thing. The expense you are putting yourself to disturbs me for two reasons. One is, it seems to bind me to accepting you. Don't be offended if I say I'm sure you can't afford to go to all this expense, and I don't like to see you do it.

COUNT. Ah, ma'am, that's nothing at all.

DORIMENE. I know what I'm talking about. This diamond ring you have forced me to take is of great value.

COUNT. Oh don't talk to me about that! It is not worthy of you. Ah—here is the master of the house.

(MR. JORDAIN *comes in.*)

MR. JORDAIN (*having made two low bows finds himself close to* DORIMENE). A little farther back, ma'am——

DORIMENE. What?

MR. JORDAIN. One step back, if you please.

DORIMENE. What then?

MR. JORDAIN. Fall back a little for the third——

COUNT. Mr. Jordain is a Society man.

MR. JORDAIN. Madam, it is a very great glory to see myself so fortunate—to have the felicity—you should have the goodness, to grant me the favour, to do me the honour, to honour me with the favour of your presence; and if I had but the merit to merit a favour like yours—and that Heaven, envious of my happiness had granted me the advantage—of seeing myself worthy——

COUNT. Mr. Jordain, that's enough. This lady doesn't care for too many compliments, and she knows already you are a man of fine wit. (*To* DORIMENE, *aside*) He's not a bad sort of fellow, though ridiculous, as you see, in his ways and manners.

DORIMENE (*aside*). One can easily see that.

COUNT. Madam, this is my best friend.

MR. JORDAIN. You are showing me too much honour.

COUNT. A very well-bred man——

DORIMENE. I can see he is that, every inch of him.

MR. JORDAIN. Oh I've done nothing yet, ma'am, to deserve your good opinion.

COUNT (*in a whisper to* JORDAIN). Take care not to say anything about that diamond you sent her.

MR. JORDAIN. Mightn't I just ask her how she likes it?

COUNT. No, no! Take care you don't do that! It would be a very mean thing to do. As a gentleman in society you should act as if it was not you who sent it to her at all. (*To* DORIMENE) Mr Jordain is saying, Marchioness, how delighted he is to see you in his house.

DORIMENE. It is very kind of him. (*Moves away to a mirror.*)

MR. JORDAIN (*to* COUNT). What way can I thank you for saying that so nicely for me!

COUNT. I had all the trouble in the world to get her to come.

MR. JORDAIN. Indeed I don't know how to thank you enough.

COUNT (*to* DORIMENE). He is saying, ma'am, that he thinks you the most beautiful person in the whole world.

DORIMENE. That is too kind of him.

MR. JORDAIN. Oh, ma'am, it is you who are kind—and——

COUNT. It is time to think of eating something. (*Goes to the table.*)

MR. JORDAIN. The dinner will be set out in the next room. These are just some little nick-nacks to begin on till it is ready.

COUNT. I can tell you it will be a good dinner, as it was I who ordered it.

DORIMENE. Those things look very tempting. (*Sits down.*)

MR. JORDAIN. Ah, ma'am, I wish they were more worthy of you.

COUNT. I feel like Mr. Jordain, I wish all this were more worthy of your acceptance.

DORIMENE. I will make no answer to your compliments, but by enjoying what is here. (*Takes a morsel in her fingers.*)

MR. JORDAIN. Ah, what a beautiful hand!

DORIMENE. The hands are just so-so. You are thinking of the diamond, it is very beautiful——

MR. JORDAIN. Is it, ma'am! Do you think I would mention that! It would not be acting like a gentleman, and the diamond is no great thing.

DORIMENE. You are very hard to please——

MR. JORDAIN. You are too kind.

COUNT (*making signs to* MR. JORDAIN, *hurriedly calls to* SERVANTS). Here, give some wine to Mr. Jordain, and to this lady. (*To* MUSICIANS) Will these gentlemen favour us with a song?

The MUSICIANS *sing:*

> Rascal Time is deceitfully flying,
> Rascal Time is deceitfully flying,
> For lost Youth soon our hearts will be sighing,
> For lost Youth soon our hearts will be sighing,
> Time, let me catch you and bind you and keep you,
> The years of my youth, the days of my love.
> So to love and delight, to love and delight,
> While Youth and Time delay.

DORIMENE (*as they finish, to* MR. JORDAIN). Music adds a wonderful relish to all this. I am enjoying myself immensely.

MR. JORDAIN. Ah, my lady, it is not worthy of you.

COUNT (*to* SERVANTS). Here, give some wine to the musicians. They'll give us another song.

MR. JORDAIN. Madam, it is not——

COUNT. Mr. Jordain, let us listen to these singers. They will entertain us with something better than anything we can possibly say.

> (MUSICIANS *take the glasses filled for them, and sing, walking round the room as they sing*)
>
> > To Burgundy I give my voice,
> > And Champagne has my equal choice,
> > Pommard, Veuve Cliquot, in their kind
> > To each I bring an equal mind.

Heidsieck, Musigny,
Violet, amber, as may be,
All are welcome unto me,
If I see them flowing free.
But of all are sold,
The greatest I uphold
Is this that I enfold.
If to Champagne I give my voice,
Dark Pommard holds an equal choice,
To Chambertin, to Veuve Cliquot,
I doff my hat before I go!

(*As they finish they empty their glasses with a shout.* COUNT
and MR. JORDAIN *applaud.*)

DORIMENE (*clapping her hands*). I don't think anything could be
better sung. It is quite charming.

MR. JORDAIN. But I see something still more charming.

DORIMENE. Well, well! Mr. Jordain is more of a lady's man than
I expected.

COUNT. Why, what did you take him for?

MR. JORDAIN. I wish indeed she would take me.

DORIMENE. There he is again!

COUNT. You don't know him.

MR. JORDAIN. She can know more of me if she likes.

DORIMENE. Oh! He beats me in repartee!

COUNT. He is quick with his give and take.

DORIMENE. I am very much taken with Mr. Jordain.

MR. JORDAIN. If I could but take your heart, I'll be——
(MRS. JORDAIN *comes in.* MUSICIANS *run away.*)

MRS. JORDAIN. Ha, ha, I find good company here! It's easily
seen I wasn't expected. It was for this pretty business you were in
such a hurry to send me off to dine with my sister! In one room
I find no less than a stage full of actors, and in the next (*points to
door*) a feast set out that's fit for a wedding breakfast! That's the
way you spend your money! Entertaining fine ladies in my
absence! Giving them plays and music while you send me abroad
in the street!

COUNT. What are you talking about, Mrs. Jordain! What fancies
have you got into your head that your husband is spending his
money, and that it's he who is giving this little treat to this lady?
Get it into your mind now that it is I who am doing it, it is *my*

party, that he only lends me his house, and that you ought to take better care what you say!

MR. JORDAIN. Yes, you impudent woman, it is the Count who does all this for that lady, who is a titled lady. He pays me the compliment of using my house and of inviting me to join their company.

MRS. JORDAIN. Stuff and nonsense! I know what I know.

COUNT. You must put on better spectacles, Mrs. Jordain.

MRS. JORDAIN. I don't want spectacles. I can see clear enough. I guessed this long time there was something going on. I'm no fool! It's a very ugly thing for you, a titled man, to lend a hand as you do to my husband's follies. And as to you, ma'am, a lady of quality, it is neither right nor honourable to bring trouble into a household, and to allow my husband to make love to you!

DORIMENE. What is the meaning of all this? It is wrong of you, Dorante, to expose me to the imaginations of this raving woman. (*She goes out of the room.*)

COUNT. Oh, Dorimene, where are you going?

MR. JORDAIN. Oh, ma'am; O Count, make my excuses to her and try to bring her back. (COUNT *goes after her.*) Ah, you impertinent woman, look at your fine doings! Coming to put insults on me before the whole world, and drive away people of quality!

MRS. JORDAIN. Little I care for their quality!

MR. JORDAIN. I don't know what hinders me from splitting your head with a plate of the little meal you came disturbing! (*Takes one up.*)

(SERVANTS *take away the table hurriedly.*)

MRS. JORDAIN (*going*). It's my rights I'm defending! And there's not a wife in the country but will be on my side.

MR. JORDAIN. You do well to get out of my way! (*She goes.*) Well, she chose a very unlucky time to come in. I was in the humour for saying pretty things. I never felt myself so witty— who now is this?

COVIEL (*comes is as a traveller, with cloak and hat. He wears a mask which he raises at the door, to let audience see who he is*). I don't know, sir, if I have the honour of being recognised by you?

MR. JORDAIN. No, sir.

COVIEL. I saw you when you were no bigger than *that*! (*Holds out his hand.*)

MR. JORDAIN. Me?

COVIEL. Yes. I was a great friend of that gentleman, your late father.

MR. JORDAIN. Of that *gentleman*, my father?

COVIEL. Yes. He was a very polished gentleman.

MR. JORDAIN. My father?

COVIEL. Yes.

MR. JORDAIN. You knew him well?

COVIEL. Certainly.

MR. JORDAIN. And you knew him to be a gentleman?

COVIEL. Of course.

MR. JORDAIN. Then I don't know what sort the world is!

COVIEL. Why so?

MR. JORDAIN. There is a class of stupid people going, who will face me down that he was but a tradesman.

COVIEL. A tradesman? That's sheer scandal. He never was any such thing. It was all that he did, he was very obliging, very civil and kind, and as he was a great judge of stuffs, he used to go here and there, and have them brought to his house, and gave them to his friends for money.

MR. JORDAIN. Well now, I'm delighted to have made your acquaintance, for now you can bear witness that my father was a gentleman.

COVIEL. I will stand to that before the world.

MR. JORDAIN. I'm greatly obliged to you. What business has brought you here?

COVIEL. Since the time I knew that gentleman your father—a very civil gentleman he was, as I have said—I have travelled through the whole world.

MR. JORDAIN. Through the whole world?

COVIEL. Yes.

MR. JORDAIN. That must be a long way off.

COVIEL. It is surely. I only came back from my long journey four days ago, and on account of the interest I take in everything that concerns you, I have come to tell you the best news that can be told.

MR. JORDAIN. What now is that?

COVIEL. You know the son of the Grank Turk is here.

MR. JORDAIN. Is that so? I didn't know it.

COVIEL. How is that? He has a magnificent train of servants. Everyone is calling on him. He has been received here as a great personage.

MR. JORDAIN. Faith I knew nothing of that.

COVIEL. And what concerns you, and is to your advantage, is that he has fallen in love with your daughter.

MR. JORDAIN. The son of the Grand Turk!

COVIEL. Yes. And he wants to be your son-in-law.

MR. JORDAIN. My son-in-law! The son of the Grand Turk!

COVIEL. The son of the Grand Turk your son-in-law. As I went to see him, and as I understand his language perfectly, he had a talk with me, and after some other conversation he says to me *Accian croc soler onch alla moustaph gidelum amanabem verahini cussere carbulath.* That is to say, "Have you not seen a young handsome person who is the daughter of Mr. Jordain, a gentleman?"

MR. JORDAIN. The son of the Grand Turk said that of me?

COVIEL. Yes. When I answered that I knew you extremely well, and that I had seen your daughter, "Ah," says he, "*Marababa sahem.*" That is to say, "Ah, I have fallen head over ears in love with her!"

MR. JORDAIN. *Marababa sahem* means, "I have fallen head over ears in love with her"?

COVIEL. Yes.

MR. JORDAIN. Faith you do well telling me that, for I never have believed that *Marababa sahem* meant "I have fallen head over ears in love with her." That is a wonderful language, that same Turkish.

COVIEL. No one could believe how wonderful! Do you know what this means: *Cacaramouchem?*

MR. JORDAIN. *Cacaramouchem?* No.

COVIEL. It is as you would say, "My dear soul."

MR. JORDAIN. *Cacaramouchem* means, "My dear soul?"

COVIEL. Yes.

MR. JORDAIN. That now is wonderful—*Cacaramouchem*, "my dear soul." Would anyone ever think it? That beats all.

COVIEL. Well, to finish what I was sent for, he is anxious to ask for your daughter in marriage. And that he may have a suitable father-in-law he intends to make you a Mamamouchi, that is a great dignitary of his country.

MR. JORDAIN. Mamamouchi?

COVIEL. Yes. Mamamouchi. That is what we in this country would call Paladin. Paladins are those ancient—Paladins, in short. There is no higher rank in the world, and you will be all one with a royal duke.

MR. JORDAIN. The son of the Grand Turk is doing me a great honour. I would wish you to bring me where he is, that I may thank him.

COVIEL. Not at all. He is just on his way here.

MR. JORDAIN. He is coming here?

COVIEL. Yes. And he is bringing everything needful for the ceremony of your installation.

MR. JORDAIN. Well, he is in a great hurry.

COVIEL. His love will not put up with any delay.

MR. JORDAIN. All that bothers me is, that daughter of mine has a will of her own, and she has taken a fancy to a young fellow called Cleonte. She takes her oath she will marry no other one.

COVIEL. She'll change her mind when she sees the Grand Turk's son. And then it's a very curious thing that he has a sort of look of Cleonte, he was pointed out to me a while ago. It's likely the fancy she has for the one may turn around to the other. Stop! He is coming to the door. Here he is!

(*Enter* CLEONTE *as a Turk. The* TWO FOOTMEN *follow him, their livery in part disguised.*)

CLEONTE. *Ambousahim oqui boraf, Jordina, salamalequi.*

COVIEL. He is saying, "Mr. Jordain, may your heart be all the year like a rose tree in flower." This is their pleasing way of speaking in those countries.

MR. JORDAIN. I am his Turkish Highness's most humble servant.

COVIEL. *Carigar camboto oustin moraf.*

CLEONTE. *Oustin yoc catamalequi basum base alla moran.*

COVIEL. He says that Heaven has given you the strength of lions, and the prudence of serpents.

MR. JORDAIN. His Turkish Highness does me too much honour, and I wish him every sort of prosperity.

COVIEL. *Ossa binamen sadoc babally oracaf ouram.*

CLEONTE. *Bal-men.*

COVIEL. He says you must go at once with him to make ready for the ceremony of ennobling you, that you may then see your daughter and arrange the wedding.

MR. JORDAIN. So many things in two words?

COVIEL. Yes. That's the way with the Turkish language. It says a great deal in a few words. Go with him now.

(CLEONTE *and* MR. JORDAIN *go out. The* COUNT *comes in.*)

COVIEL. Ha, ha, ha! Faith, that's a good joke! What a fool he is! If he had learned the part by heart he couldn't have played it better! I hope, sir, you will give us your help in this affair.

COUNT. Ah ha, Coviel! Who could have known you, dressed up as you are.

COVIEL. There you see! Ha, ha!

COUNT. What are you laughing at?

MR. JORDAIN. Listen to her impudence! To be talking that way to a Mamamouchi!

MRS. JORDAIN. A what?

MR. JORDAIN. Yes. You will have to treat me with respect now I have just been made a Mamamouchi.

MRS. JORDAIN. And what sort of an animal is that?

MR. JORDAIN. Mamamouchi—that is to say in our language a Paladin.

MRS. JORDAIN. A Balladin—what ballet? Are you of an age to go be a ballet dancer?

MR. JORDAIN. You ignorant woman! I said Paladin. It is a dignity. I went through a ceremony.

MRS. JORDAIN. What sort of a ceremony?

MR. JORDAIN. Volgar far un Palandina Giordina.

MRS. JORDAIN. What?

MR. JORDAIN. Dar turbanta con galera.

MRS. JORDAIN. What meaning has that gibberish?

MR. JORDAIN. Per difender Palestina——

MRS. JORDAIN. What at all are you trying to say?

MR. JORDAIN (*struts and sings*):

> The Hero's going to war,
> Miroton, Mirotan, Mirotaine!

MRS. JORDAIN. My bitter grief! My husband has gone mad!

MR. JORDAIN (*walking off angrily*). Hold your tongue you piece of insolence! Show respect to the Paladin—Mamamouchi!

MRS. JORDAIN. What made him lose his senses? I must run and stop him from going out. I see nothing but worry all around—and here now come the rest of the gang. (*She goes.*)

(*The* COUNT *and* DORIMENE *come in.*)

COUNT. Now, you'll see something that will amuse you greatly. We must try and help Cleonte in his masquerade. And besides, there is that little entertainment I planned for you.

DORIMENE. I really can't permit this any longer. I must put a stop to your extravagance. Yes, I have made up my mind to do that at once, and to put an end to all you are spending on my account. And to do this I will marry you. All these things come to an end, as you know, with marriage.

COUNT. Oh, is it possible you have come to such a sweet decision!

DORIMENE. I am only doing it to save you from going bankrupt. If you go on as you are doing you won't have a farthing left.

COUNT. How can I thank you enough for the interest you are taking in preserving my estate! I lay it at your feet with my heart. You may make what use you like of the one and the other!

DORIMENE. I will do that. But here comes your friend. What a wonderful figure!

(MR. JORDAIN *comes in.*)

COUNT. We have come, the Marchioness and I, to pay homage to your new dignity, and to rejoice with you at the marriage you have arranged between your daughter and the son of the Grand Turk.

MR. JORDAIN (*making his bow in the Turkish manner*). Sir, I wish you the strength of serpents and the wisdom of lions!

DORIMENE. I am so glad to be one of the first to congratulate you on the high degree of glory to which you have attained.

MR. JORDAIN. Madam, may your rose-tree flower all the year round! I am greatly obliged to you for taking notice of the honours that have come to me. And I am very glad to see you are come back, ma'am, that I may make excuses for the foolishness of my wife.

DORIMENE. Oh, that doesn't matter. I can forgive her little jealous outbreak. Your affection must be precious to her. And it is no wonder that the possession of such a husband as *you* must keep her in a perpetual fright!

COUNT. But where is his Turkish Highness? We should like, as your friends, to pay him our respects.

MR. JORDAIN. Here he is coming. And I've sent for my daughter that I may give her to him as his bride.

(CLEONTE *comes on in his Turkish dress.*)

COUNT. Sir, we are come to pay our very humble respects to your Highness as friends of this gentleman, your father-in-law.

MR. JORDAIN. Where is that traveller, the interpreter, to tell him who you are, and to make him understand what you say? He is a wonder at speaking Turkish. Hallo there! Where at all is he gone? (*To* CLEONTE.) Stref, strif, strof, straf. The gentleman is a grand Signor—grand signore. And Madame is a granda Dama, granda dama. Oh dear—Sir, he is a French Mamamouchi, and Madame is a French Mamamouchess. I can't speak any plainer.

(COVIEL *comes in.*)

Good, here's the Traveller. Where were you going? We can't say anything without you. Just tell him this lady and gentleman are people of great quality who are come as my friends to show

188

respect to him, and to offer him their services. Now you're going to see how he will answer.

COVIEL. *Alabala crociam, acci boram alabamen.*

CLEOTE. *Catalequi tubal ourin sotor Amalouchan.*

MR. JORDAIN. Do you see?

COVIEL. He says that the rain of prosperity waters at all times the garden of your family.

MR. JORDAIN. Didn't I tell you that he speaks Turkish?

COUNT. This is splendid! (LUCILE *comes in.*)

MR. JORDAIN. Come on, daughter, come here and give your hand to this gentleman, who does you the honour of asking to marry you.

LUCILE. What, father? Why are you dressed up like that? Are you playacting in a comedy?

MR. JORDAIN. No, no, it's not a comedy, it's a very serious matter, and the greatest honour for you that anyone could wish. This is the husband I bestow upon you!

LUCILE. Oh no, father!

MR. JORDAIN. Yes, on you. Come here, now, take him by the hand, and thank Heaven for your good luck.

LUCILE. But I don't want to marry.

MR. JORDAIN. But I that am your father want it.

LUCILE. I'll have nothing to do with it!

MR. JORDAIN. Oh, what a fuss. Come along I tell you. Give out your hand.

LUCILE. No, father. I've told you already no power can force me to take any husband but Cleonte, I would go to any length—— (CLEONTE *raises his mask for a moment. She recognises him.*) It is true, you are my father, I owe you entire obedience. It is for you to dispose of me according to your own wish.

MR. JORDAIN. Ah, I'm well pleased to see you come back so quick to your duty. That now delights me, to have such an obedient daughter.

MRS. JORDAIN (*bursting in*). What's this now? What is going on here? They are saying you want to give your daughter to some sort of a dressed-up buffoon.

MR. JORDAIN. Will you hold your tongue, Impudence! You always come poking your folly into everything, and there's no way of teaching you to have sense.

MRS. JORDAIN. It is yourself will never learn sense! You go on from folly to folly. What now is your plan? And what do you want with all this gathering of people?

MR. JORDAIN. It is my intention to marry our daughter to the son of the Grand Turk.

MRS. JORDAIN. To the son of the Grand Turk!

MR. JORDAIN. Yes. Give him your compliments through this interpreter.

MRS. JORDAIN. I'll have nothing to do with interpreters! And I'll tell him myself to his face, that he will never get my daughter.

MR. JORDAIN. Will you hold your tongue for one minute!

COUNT. What, Mrs. Jordain? You are opposing such a piece of good luck! You refuse his Turkish Highness for a son-in-law!

MRS. JORDAIN. I'll thank you, sir, not to trouble yourself about what doesn't concern you!

COUNT. It is our friendly feeling for you that makes us anxious for what is for your good.

MRS. JORDAIN. I can get on very well without your friendliness!

COUNT. See how your daughter has given in to her father's wish.

MRS. JORDAIN. My daughter has consented to marry a Turk!

COUNT. Certainly.

MRS. JORDAIN. Does she forget Cleonte?

COUNT. What wouldn't one forget to become a great lady?

MRS. JORDAIN. I would choke her with my own hands if she had done such a thing as that!

MR. JORDAIN. That's enough of prattling and chattering! I tell you this marriage is to be brought off.

MRS. JORDAIN. And I tell you it shall not come off!

MR. JORDAIN (*stopping ears*). Was there ever heard such a noise!

LUCILE. Mother!

MRS. JORDAIN. Get away you good for nothing girl.

MR. JORDAIN. What! You are attacking her for obeying me!

MRS. JORDAIN. If I am, she belongs to me as much as to you.

COVIEL. Madam.

MRS. JORDAIN. What have you to say to me, you.

COVIEL. Only one word——

MRS. JORDAIN. I'll have nothing to do with your one word!

COVIEL (*to* MR. J.). Look sir, if she'd only consent to let me say one word to her I'd engage to get her consent.

MRS. JORDAIN. I will not consent.

COVIEL. Only listen to me——

MRS. JORDAIN. No!

MR. JORDAIN Can't you give him a hearing.

MRS. JORDAIN I will not hear him!

MR. JORDAIN. He'll tell you——

MRS. JORDAIN. I won't let him tell me anything.

MR. JORDAIN. Did ever anyone see such an obstinate woman! What harm can it do you to listen to him!

COVIEL. Only listen and then you can take your own way——

MRS. JORDAIN. Well—what?

COVIEL (*drawing her aside*). I've been making signs to you ma'am this half hour. Can't you see that all this is a trick to fit in with your husband's great visions? We are taking him in with our disguise. It is Cleonte himself is the son of the Grand Turk!

MRS. JORDAIN. Oh, ho!

COVIEL. And I, Coviel, am the Interpreter!

MRS. JORDAIN. Well, if that is so, I give in.

COVIEL. But don't seem to know anything.

MRS. JORDAIN (*to* MR. JORDAIN). Yes, that is settled. I give my conset to the marriage.

MR. JORDAIN. Ah, now, everybody has seen reason, and has learned sense. I knew he would explain to you what is the son of the Grand Turk.

MRS. JORDAIN. He has explained it clear enough, and I'm satisfied. Let us go now and get them married.

COUNT. Very good. And Mrs. Jordain, to make your mind quite easy, and that you may give up any jealous thoughts or suspicions of your husband let me tell you that this lady and myself will be joined in marriage at the same time.

MRS. JORDAIN. I consent to that too!

MR. JORDAIN. Come on, now. Let the music strike up!

(*They march round the room before going out, to the air of Malbrook se'n va-t-en guerre!*)

Curtain.

MIRANDOLINA
BY
CARLO GOLDONI

MIRANDOLINA

PERSONS
  MARQUIS OF FORLIPOPOLI
  COUNT OF ALBAFIORITA
  CAPTAIN RIPAFRATTA
  MIRANDOLINA. *An Innkeeper*
  FABRIZIO. *Servant at the Inn*
  CAPTAIN'S SERVANT

ACT I

SCENE: *Large room at an Inn, with rough furniture and three doors.* COUNT *and* MARQUIS.

MARQUIS. There is some difference, Count, between you and myself!

COUNT. How do you make that out?

MARQUIS. Are you setting yourself up to be my equal?

COUNT. My money is worth as much as yours . . . at an Inn.

MARQUIS. I am the Marquis of Forlipopoli!

COUNT. And I am the Count of Albafiorita!

MARQUIS. You only got your title through buying an estate.

COUNT. If I bought my estate you sold yours.

MARQUIS. I should be treated with respect.

COUNT. Who is showing you disrespect?

MARQUIS. What is keeping you at this Inn?

COUNT. The same thing that keeps yourself.

MARQUIS. I don't know what you're talking about.

COUNT. I am talking of Mirandolina.

MARQUIS. Mirandolina! The Innkeeper! What have you to do with her?

COUNT. That's a good joke! You think no one but yourself may look at Mirandolina!

MARQUIS. She will never look at you while she has a chance of a Marquis.

COUNT. What is a Marquis against money? In these times a handle to the name counts less than pence in the pocket.

MARQUIS. I'll back my rank against your riches.

COUNT. It isn't riches I think of, but what they will buy.

MARQUIS. Go on buying till you break your neck! You won't be able to do anything with her. She doesn't care *that* for you. (*Snaps his fingers.*)

COUNT (*sarcastically*). I won't, and you will!

MARQUIS. I am what I am!

COUNT. I have what I have! She sees more of my money than of yours.

MARQUIS. I don't go about talking of what I do.

COUNT. Everybody knows what you *don't* do. Even the servants are talking about it.

MARQUIS. Servants! I suppose you mean that low fellow Fabrizio . . . I have my suspicions of him.

COUNT. I think I hear him outside. (*Opens the door and calls*): Fabrizio!

FABRIZIO (*coming in.*) What is it you are wanting, Sir?

COUNT. What way is the little Missis to-day?

FABRIZIO. She is well, Sir.

MARQUIS. Is she in the house?

FABRIZIO. She is, Sir.

COUNT. Ask her to come here, I want to speak to her.

FABRIZIO. I will, Sir. (*Goes.*)

MARQUIS. What do you want with her?

COUNT. Don't you know it's her birthday? Mirandolina comes of age to-day.

MARQUIS. What's that to you?

COUNT. I'm going to give her a birthday present . . . aren't you?

MARQUIS. It's worth more to her than presents that I patronize her Inn: I bring it into fashion.

COUNT (*tossing a handful of money*). I bring it what is better!

MARQUIS. You don't understand what you're talking about.

COUNT. You are talking nonsense.

MARQUIS. Hold your tongue, Sir.

COUNT. Hold your own!

CAPTAIN (*coming in*). What's all this noise about? Are you quarrelling?

COUNT. Only arguing.

CAPTAIN. What on earth about?

COUNT. Something you would laugh at.

MARQUIS. It's no laughing matter!

COUNT. The Marquis has taken a fancy to our landlady.

MARQUIS. I am only thinking of her interests.

COUNT. He thinks of them . . . I spend for them.

CAPTAIN. I never heard of anything so little worth a quarrel. To grow angry about a woman! To lose one's temper about a woman! Whoever heard of such a thing? I will never have words with any-one about a woman. I have never looked at one, and never thought much of any one of them. A weakness for women is a ridiculous thing.

MARQUIS. For all that, there is something very taking about Mirandolina.

COUNT. The Marquis is right. Our landlady is a very charming little thing.

MARQUIS. You may be sure any woman *I* lose my heart to must be something out of the common.

CAPTAIN. Stuff and nonsense! What could there be out of the common in a woman of that sort?

MARQUIS. She has a very taking manner.

COUNT. She is pretty and very conversable, she dresses with very good taste.

CAPTAIN. All things that are not worth twopence. I have been three days in this Inn and I give you my word I wouldn't know her if I met her in the street.

COUNT. Take a look at her, and she may make an impression on you yet.

CAPTAIN. Rubbish: I've seen her well enough; she's like any other woman.

MARQUIS. She is not like any other woman. She is something more than others. I have known ladies in the best society, and I give you my word I've never met her equal.

COUNT. I know women well enough. I know them and their fol-lies. But I tell you in spite of the length of time I have been run-ning after Mirandolina and all the money I have spent, I haven't so much as touched her little finger.

CAPTAIN. Tricks, all tricks. You are fools to be taken in by her. She would never try her tricks on me! Believe me, all women are the same in the long run. They don't know anything. They are no use; and I don't like them.

COUNT. You have never been in love.

CAPTAIN. Never, and never will be. My people have worked heaven and earth to make me marry, but I never would give in to it.

MARQUIS. But you are the only one of your family. Don't you think it a pity your property should go to strangers?

CAPTAIN. I do think it. But whenever I remember that to have an heir I must put up with a wife, I banish the thought quick enough.

COUNT. And what will you do with all your money?

CAPTAIN. I'll enjoy spending it in my own way.

COUNT. And you will spend nothing at all on women?

CAPTAIN. Not a penny. I will never give a woman the chance to come nibbling at it.

COUNT (*looking from door*). Here she is coming. Here is Mirandolina. Look at her! Isn't she adorable?

CAPTAIN. Oh, a great beauty! I would think a great deal more of a good greyhound.

MARQUIS. If you don't think much of her, I do.

CAPTAIN. I would leave her there if she was handsomer than Venus.

(MIRANDOLINA *comes in.*)

MIRANDOLINA (*curtseys*). Good morning to you, gentlemen. Do you want anything of me?

MARQUIS. I have something to ask of you but not now . . . bye-and-bye . . . but not here.

MIRANDOLINA. If you want anything from me, I will send a servant with it.

MARQUIS (*aside to* CAPTAIN). What do you think of that now?

CAPTAIN. What you call behaviour I call impudence.

(*The* MARQUIS *takes a silk handkerchief from his pocket, opens it and shows it to her.*)

MIRANDOLINA. That's a pretty handkerchief, Sir.

MARQUIS (*to* MIRANDOLINA). Ah! it's a fine one! I have good taste—aye?

MIRANDOLINA. It is certainly very tasty.

MARQUIS. It is from London.

MIRANDOLINA. Is it indeed?

MARQUIS (*folding up his handkerchief carefully*). It must be properly folded, that it may not be creased, a thing of this sort should be taken great care of. (*Gives it to* MIRANDOLINA.) Take it.

MIRANDOLINA. Do you want it sent to your room?

MARQUIS. No, to yours.

MIRANDOLINA. Why to mine?

MARQUIS. Because I am making you a present of it. A birthday present.

MIRANDOLINA. But I won't take it.

MARQUIS. Don't make me angry.

MIRANDOLINA. Oh! if it comes to that, you know, Sir, I don't wish to disoblige anyone. So, just to keep you from losing your temper, I will take it.

COUNT. Dear Mirandolina, look at these earrings. Do you like them?

MIRANDOLINA. They are beautiful.

COUNT. Those are diamonds, do you know?

MIRANDOLINA. Oh, I know that. I know what diamonds are.

COUNT. And they are for you.

CAPTAIN (*aside to* COUNT). A fool and his money are soon parted!

MIRANDOLINA. Why are you giving them to me?

MARQUIS. A great present, indeed! In its own way the handkerchief is in better taste.

COUNT. Maybe so, but from way to way there is a good distance. These are set in the fashion. I want you to take them for my sake.

CAPTAIN. He has lost his wits!

MIRANDOLINA. No, indeed, Sir.

COUNT. It is for your birthday. If you refuse you will vex me.

MIRANDOLINA. I don't know what to say. I would wish to be friendly with my guests. Not to vex the Count, I *will* take them.

CAPTAIN. What a schemer!

COUNT (*to* CAPTAIN). Hasn't she a ready wit?

CAPTAIN. Very ready indeed. She will eat you up and never say thank you.

MARQUIS. Now, Mirandolina, *I* have a word to say to you. I am a nobleman.

MIRANDOLINA (*aside to* COUNT). What a fiery declaration! It won't burn him up altogether. If there is nothing else wanted, I will go.

CAPTAIN. Here, ma'am I don't think much of the table linen you have given me. (*Angrily.*) If you have none better I will send out for some.

MIRANDOLINA. I will give you better, Sir; it shall be sent up to you, but I think you might have asked it with a little more politeness.

CAPTAIN. Where I am spending my own money, there is no need of paying compliments.

COUNT (*to* MIRANDOLINA). You should pity him. He is a great enemy of all women.

CAPTAIN. What's that? I don't want to be pitied by her.

MIRANDOLINA. Poor women! What way have they treated him? Why are you so hard on us, Sir?

CAPTAIN. That will do. There is no more to be said about it. Change the cloth for me, I will send my servant to fetch it. (*Goes.*)

MIRANDOLINA. That man is no better than a bear.

COUNT. Dear Mirandolina, if he knew you he would be at your feet.

MIRANDOLINA. I don't want him at my feet, but I don't like to be made little of.

COUNT. He is a woman hater. He can't bear the sight of them.

MIRANDOLINA. The poor foolish creature! He hasn't met yet with the woman who knows how to manage him—but he'll find her—he'll find her or maybe . . . maybe . . . he *has* found her! I hope she will punish him and put him down . . . and conquer him and get the better of him and teach him not to run down the best thing Mother Nature ever put a hand to!

COUNT. Don't waste another thought on him.

MIRANDOLINA. Indeed, I am so put out by his bad manners I will give him notice to leave the Inn.

MARQUIS. Do so, and if he refuses to go, tell me and I will send him about his business. Make what use you will of my protection.

COUNT. And as to any money you may lose by it, you must allow me to make it up to you. (*Aside.*) Listen, send away the Marquis along with him, and I promise I will make up for his loss.

MIRANDOLINA. Thank you, gentlemen, many thanks; but I am well able to tell a guest when I don't want him. And as to business, there is never an empty room in the house.

FABRIZIO (*coming in, to* COUNT). There is someone wanting you, Sir.

COUNT. Do you know who it is?

FABRIZIO. I think he is a jeweller. (*Aside to* MIRANDOLINA) Have sense, Mirandolina; this is no company for you. (*Goes.*)

COUNT. Oh, yes, he has an ornament to show me. I want it to go with these ear-rings, Mirandolina.

MIRANDOLINA. Oh, no, Sir.

COUNT. You deserve the best of everything, and I don't care a straw what it costs. I am going to take a look at it. (*Goes out.*)

MARQUIS. That Count is a nuisance with all his money!

MIRANDOLINA. Indeed the Count is giving himself too much trouble.

MARQUIS. There are some people who have no more than twopence and will spend it for a show off! I know them; I know the ways of the world.

MIRANDOLINA. I know the ways of the world myself.

MIRQUIS. They think a woman like you can be come round with presents!

MIRANDOLINA. Presents don't disagree with me at all.

MARQUIS. I would be afraid of offending you if I pressed things on you.

MIRANDOLINA. Indeed, Sir, you have never offended me in that way.

MARQUIS. And I never will.

MIRANDOLINA. I believe that indeed.

MARQUIS. But if there is anything I can do for you, tell me of it.

MIRANDOLINA. But I should have to know first in what way you could help me.

MARQUIS. In every way.

MIRANDOLINA. But, tell me, for instance . . .

MARQUIS. By Jove, you are a wonder of a woman.

MIRANDOLINA. You are too kind, your Excellency.

MARQUIS. Ah, I could almost commit a folly; I could almost curse my nobility.

MIRANDOLINA. Why is that, Sir?

MARQUIS. There are times when I wish I could change places with the Count.

MIRANDOLINA. I suppose because he is so rich?

MARQUIS. Rich! I don't care a pin for that! . . . but if I were like him . . . a mere Count . . .

MIRANDOLINA. What would you do then, Sir?

MARQUIS. By all that's damnable . . . I would marry you! (*Goes out.*)

MIRANDOLINA (*looking out of door after him*). Oh! What is it he said? Your High Excellency the Marquis Misery would think of marrying me! But if you should wish to marry me, there is one little bar in the way . . . I myself would not wish it.

FABRIZIO (*enters*). Are you there, ma'am?

MIRANDOLINA. What is it?

FABRIZIO. That Captain Ripafratta in the middle room is crying out against the table cloths; he says they are common, and that he won't use them.

MIRANDOLINA. I know, I know; he told me about it and I'll change them.

FABRIZIO. All right. Come and put out whatever you have for him, and I'll carry them up.

MIRANDOLINA. Never mind . . . that will do . . . I will give them to him myself.

FABRIZIO. You will bring them to him yourself!

MIRANDOLINA. Just so, myself.

FABRIZIO. That is showing him great attention.

MIRANDOLINA. I pay attention to everything. Mind your own business.

FABRIZIO. It is quite plain to me, you will do nothing for me . . . you lead me on just to make a fool of me.

MIRANDOLINA. You are a goose, but you are a very honest servant.

FABRIZIO. It is always the custom that I should attend the lodgers.

MIRANDOLINA. You are a little too rough for them.

FABRIZIO. And you are maybe a little too smooth.

MIRANDOLINA. I know very well what I am doing. I want no advice.

FABRIZIO. All right. You may look for another serving man.

MIRANDOLINA. Why so, Mr. Fabrizio? Are you out with me? (*Takes his hands.*)

FABRIZIO. Do you remember what your father said to the two of us at the time of his death?

MIRANDOLINA. I do . . . and whenever I think of marrying I will bring it to mind.

FABRIZIO. But I am someway thin-skinned. There are some things I cannot put up with. Sometimes it seems as if you will have me, and other times that you will not have me. You say you are not giddy but you always take your own way.

MIRANDOLINA. But what sort of an owl do you take me for? A bit of vanity? A fool? I'm astonished at you . . . What are strangers to me, that are here to-day and gone to-morrow? If I treat them well it is for my own interest and the credit of the house. I live honestly and I like my freedom; I amuse myself with everybody but I fall in love with nobody. But I know who suits me and who is worth while. And when my time comes for marriage I will not forget my father. And whoever has served me well won't have to complain of me. I am not ungrateful. I know him, but he doesn't know me. That is enough, Fabrizio. You may understand me, if you can. (*Goes.*)

FABRIZIO. Whoever can understand her is a very clever man.

But, after all, if lodgers come, they go away again, and I am here always. The best chance will always be with me. (*Goes.*)

SCENE II. *Captain's Parlour.* (CAPTAIN *sitting. His* SERVANT *comes in with a letter.*)

SERVANT. If you please, Sir, this letter has come for you.

CAPTAIN (*opening letter*). Who is writing to me? "The sincere friendship I have for you." It's another of these meddling friends of mine wants me to marry an heiress . . . £10,000 . . . I can do without that while I am a bachelor . . . if I were married, that and as much again wouldn't be enough . . . *I* take a wife . . . I'd sooner take an ague. Bring in the chocolate.

(SERVANT *goes out.*)

MARQUIS (*coming in*). May I come in for a minute?

CAPTAIN. Certainly.

MARQUIS. You and I can have a sensible talk. That donkey of a Count is not fit to join in with us at all. You know my way, I try to get on with everyone, but as to that man, I cannot stand him.

CAPTAIN. You can't stand him because he is your rival . . . For shame! A man of your rank in love with an Innkeeper! A sensible man like you.

MARQUIS. My dear Sir, she has bewitched me!

CAPTAIN. All folly! Weakness! What bewitchments? How is it that women don't bewitch me? Their bewitchings are in their humbug and flatteries. Anyone keeping out of their way as I do is in no danger of finding himself bewitched.

MARQUIS. I agree with you, and I don't agree . . . but what is worrying me more than that just now, is that agent of mine in the country.

CAPTAIN. Has he robbed you?

MARQUIS. He has broken his word to me.

(SERVANT *enters with chocolate.*)

MARQUIS. Ha! what's this? Chocolate?

CAPTAIN (*to* MARQUIS). Perhaps you will take it?

MARQUIS (*takes and sips chocolate without ceremony, talking and drinking*). This agent of mine, as I was saying . . . (*Drinks.*) He promised to send me my money as usual . . . (*Sipping*) but he has not sent it.

CAPTAIN. He'll send it another time.

MARQUIS. The fact is . . . the fact is (*finishes chocolate*) that I am in a great difficulty, and I don't know what to do.

CAPTAIN. Oh, a week more or less . . .

MARQUIS. But you who are a man of position and breeding, know what a trying thing it is to have to break one's word . . . I am in a difficulty. Good God! What am I to do?

CAPTAIN. I am sorry to see you so much put out. (*Aside.*) If I could but escape with decency!

MARQUIS. You would not be able to oblige me? . . . for a week . . . ?

CAPTAIN. My dear Marquis, if I could, you should make use of me with the greatest pleasure. I would have offered it to you at once if I had it. I am looking out for my own supplies, but they have not come in yet.

MARQUIS. Surely *you* are not short of money?

CAPTAIN. See here; this is all I have . . . it doesn't amount to much. (*Shows him a gold piece and some change.*) Yes, it is the last I have left.

MARQUIS. Lend it to me . . .

CAPTAIN. But what am I to do?

MARQUIS. I will pay you back.

CAPTAIN. I don't know what to say . . . well . . . take it. (*Gives coin.*)

MARQUIS. I have to keep an appointment . . . I must be off . . . We shall meet again at dinner. (*Goes.*)

CAPTAIN (*to* SERVANT). Bravo! He was in hopes of borrowing ten guineas and contented himself with one in the end . . . Well, if he doesn't pay, it will keep him from bothering me. I think worse of his having drunk my chocolate!

(MIRANDOLINA *comes to door with linen.*)

MIRANDOLINA. May I come in, Sir?

CAPTAIN (*harshly*). What do you want?

MIRANDOLINA (*coming a little further*). Here is some finer linen.

CAPTAIN (*pointing to table*). All right, leave it there.

MIRANDOLINA. Will you see, if you please, Sir, if it is what you like?

CAPTAIN. What sort is it?

MIRANDOLINA. There are cambric sheets.

CAPTAIN. Sheets?

MIRANDOLINA. Yes, Sir, the very finest; look at them.

CAPTAIN. I did not ask that . . . I only asked for some better cloths than what you gave me.

MIRANDOLINA. I got this linen for those I should think worthy of it, who would know the difference. I give it to you because you are yourself . . . but I would give it to no other one.

CAPTAIN. "Because you are yourself." I don't know what you mean——

MIRANDOLINA. Look at this tablecloth . . . it is from Flanders.

CAPTAIN. It's a pity to use it at all.

MIRANDOLINA. I would not grudge so small a thing to a gentleman of your quality. I have napkins of the same; they are here for you.

CAPTAIN (*turns his back*). Give the things to my servant, or leave them there. You need not put yourself to so much trouble.

MIRANDOLINA (*making a grimace behind him mimicking his manner*). Oh, it is no trouble at all, when it is for someone like you.

CAPTAIN. Well, well, that will do; I don't want anything more.

MIRANDOLINA. I will put it in the cupboard.

CAPTAIN. Wherever you like.

MIRANDOLINA (*having arranged linen*). What would you like, Sir, for your dinner?

CAPTAIN. Whatever there is will do.

MIRANDOLINA. I would wish to know your tastes, Sir. If there is any dish you have a liking for more than another tell me of it.

CAPTAIN. If I want anything I will tell the waiter.

MIRANDOLINA. Men don't give the same attention to these things as we do. If there is any dish you have a fancy for, or any dressing, tell me what it is, if you please.

CAPTAIN. I am obliged to you. But even this civility will not help you to do with me what you have done with the Marquis and the Count.

MIRANDOLINA. Oh, why should you talk of that folly? If people who come to an Inn pretend to have fallen in love with the landlady . . . we have something else to think of than to give heed to their nonsense. We try to serve our own interest. If they give us soft words we turn it to the good of the business. As for myself, when I hear them beginning their flatteries I laugh myself tired.

CAPTAIN. Well done! I like to hear you speak the truth.

MIRANDOLINA. I always do. That is the only good thing about me.

CAPTAIN. For all that you are ready enough to make believe with your admirers.

MIRANDOLINA. I, to make believe! Heaven preserve me from any such thing! Go and ask those two gentlemen who are making love to me if I have ever given them any sign of liking at all, or if I have amused myself with them in any way that could deceive them . . . I don't drive them away, because it would not be to my interest to do that, but I sometimes come very near it. I hate the sight of men of that sort. Look here, I am not a young girl, I have left some years behind me; I'm no great beauty, but I have had good chances, but I never had a mind to marry, because I think it a fine thing to be free.

CAPTAIN. Yes, indeed; freedom is a treasure well worth having.

MIRANDOLINA. And there are many who are foolish enough to part with it.

CAPTAIN. I know what suits me best; liberty suits me.

MIRANDOLINA. Has your Excellency a wife?

CAPTAIN. God forbid! I don't want one.

MIRANDOLINA. That's right, keep to that always; as to women . . . No, that's enough . . . I have no mind to speak ill of them.

CAPTAIN. You are the first woman I ever heard say that.

MIRANDOLINA. I tell you, we Inn-keepers see plenty and hear plenty, and I pity those men that are taken in by any woman at all.

CAPTAIN. That is an odd thing for you to say.

MIRANDOLINA. With your leave, Sir. (*Is going.*)

CAPTAIN. You are in a hurry.

MIRANDOLINA. I don't want to be troublesome.

CAPTAIN. Not at all; you amuse me.

MIRANDOLINA. You see now for yourself, Sir, that is the way I go on with others . . . I keep them in chat for a few minutes . . . I joke a little to entertain them . . . and then all of a minute . . . you understand me, Sir? they begin to make love to me.

CAPTAIN. That happens because you have a taking manner.

MIRANDOLINA (*with a curtsey*). You are too kind, Sir.

CAPTAIN. And then they lose their hearts.

MIRANDOLINA. What folly to be in such a hurry to lose their hearts!

CAPTAIN. It is a thing I never could understand.

MIRANDOLINA. Talk of strength, indeed! Fine strong men they are.

CAPTAIN. Their weakness is a disgrace to humanity——

MIRANDOLINA. That is right talk for a man . . . I would like, Sir, to shake you by the hand.

CAPTAIN. Why do you want to shake hands with me?

MIRANDOLINA. If you would condescend, Sir . . . see . . . mine is clean.

CAPTAIN. Here is my hand.

MIRANDOLINA. This is the first time I ever had the honour to touch the hand of a man who had the real mind of a man . . .

CAPTAIN. That will do.

MIRANDOLINA. Look now, if I had held out my hand to either one of that feather-brained pair downstairs, he would have been full sure I was dying for him. He would have lost his heart then and there! I would not have taken any such liberty with them for all the gold of the world. They have no understanding; oh, it's a blessing to be able to say things out without raising suspicion or doing mischief. I beg your pardon, Sir, for my forwardness. Whenever I can serve you, just give the order, and I will pay more attention to it than I have ever done for anyone in the whole world.

CAPTAIN. Why should you think so well of me?

MIRANDOLINA. Because you being a well-reared gentleman, I know I can say out my mind to you and have no fear you will think I have an object, or that you will torment me with follies and absurdities.

CAPTAIN. Now, if you want to attend to your business, don't let me keep you here.

MIRANDOLINA. Yes, Sir, I will go and look after the housework. That is my delight and my joy. In case you should want anything I will send the serving-man.

CAPTAIN. All right. But you might look in at some other time.

MIRANDOLINA. I am not in the habit of attending on my guests ... but it will be different with you.

CAPTAIN. Why so?

MIRANDOLINA. Because, Sir, I like you.

CAPTAIN. You like me!

MIRANDOLINA. I like you because you are not weak, you are not a fool, you are a strong man, you will never give in to love. (*Goes.*)

Curtain.

ACT II

SCENE. *The Captain's room, with a table laid for dinner.* CAPTAIN *is walking with a book.* SERVANT *standing near door.* FABRIZIO *brings in soup.*

FABRIZIO (*to* SERVANT). Tell your master the soup is on the table.

SERVANT. You can tell him as easy as myself.

FABRIZIO. He is so queer, I don't like to be speaking to him.

SERVANT. He is not altogether bad for all that . . . he can't bear the sight of a woman, but he is civil enough with men.

FABRIZIO. Your dinner is on the table, Sir. (*Goes.*)

> (CAPTAIN *puts down book and comes to sit at table. The* SERVANT *stands behind his chair with a plate under his arm.*)

CAPTAIN (*eating, to* SERVANT). It seems to me dinner is earlier than usual to-day.

SERVANT. This room was served before the others, Sir; the Count of Albafiorita made a great noise when he was not served the first, but the mistress would not give in to putting you after him.

CAPTAIN. I am obliged to her for that.

SERVANT. She is a very perfect woman, Sir. I never saw so civil a one in any part of the world I travelled.

CAPTAIN. You admire her then? (*Turning a little.*)

SERVANT. If it was not for disobliging my master I would come and take service with Mirandolina.

CAPTAIN. You are a fool. What am I to do with you? (*Gives him plate and he changes it.*)

SERVANT. Such a woman! I would obey her just the same as a little lapdog she would have. (*Goes for a dish.*)

CAPTAIN. By Jove! She puts her enchantment on you all. It would be a very laughable thing if she should put it on me! I think to-morrow I'll go on to Livorno.

SERVANT (*bringing boiled fowl and another dish*). The mistress says if you do not like the pullet she will send you a pigeon.

CAPTAIN. I like everything so far . . . What is this?

SERVANT. The mistress says I am to say to your Excellency she hopes you will like this sauce she has made with her own hands.

CAPTAIN. She is doing a great deal for me. (*Takes it.*) It is excellent. It is a capital sauce . . . I have never tasted a better. If Mirandolina goes on like this she will never be in want of guests. A good table, a good laundry . . . and there's no denying she is pleasing . . . but what I think most of is her truthfulness; that is the great thing.

SERVANT. It is, Sir.

CAPTAIN (*taking more sauce*). Tell her I am enjoying this sauce and much obliged to her.

SERVANT. I will, Sir.

CAPTAIN. Go and tell her at once.

SERVANT. At once, Sir. (*Goes.*)

(CAPTAIN *goes on eating.*)

SERVANT (*coming back*). She thanks you Excellency for receiving her poor attempt so kindly. She is at this moment making ready another dish with her own hands, but I don't know what it is.

CAPTAIN. She is making it herself?

SERVANT. Yes, Sir.

CAPTAIN. Give me something to drink.

SERVANT (*goes to sideboard, brings bottle*). Here it is, Sir. (*Brings it to table.*)

CAPTAIN. I must make a return for all this . . . it is too much. I must pay double . . . I will treat her well; but I'll go to Livorno. (SERVANT *gives him wine.*) The Count has gone to dinner? (*Drinks.*)

SERVANT. He went out, Sir; he is not back yet.

(MIRANDOLINA *comes to the door with a plate in her hand.*)

MIRANDOLINA. May I come in?

CAPTAIN. Who is there?

SERVANT. Come in, Ma'am; let me have it.

CAPTAIN. Take the dish from her.

MIRANDOLINA. No . . let me have the pleasure of putting it on the table myself. (*Does so.*)

CAPTAIN. You ought not to do that.

MIRANDOLINA. Ah, Sir, who am I? Am I a lady? I am the servant of whoever comes into my Inn.

CAPTAIN. What humility!

MIRANDOLINA. To tell the truth, it would be no trouble to me to attend all my guests at table, but I don't do it for certain reasons. I don't know if you understand me? But I have no scruple in coming to you, quite simply.

CAPTAIN. I am obliged to you. What dish is this?

MIRANDOLINA. It is a haricot made with my own hands.

CAPTAIN. Very good. If it is made by you it is sure to be good.

MIRANDOLINA. Oh, you are too kind, Sir; I don't know how to do anything right. But I would wish to give so good a gentleman something to his liking.

CAPTAIN (*aside to* SERVANT). To Livorno to-morrow. . . . If you have anything to do now don't waste your time on me.

MIRANDOLINA. It doesn't matter, Sir, the house is well provided with servants. I would be glad to know if this dish is to your taste.

CAPTAIN. Certainly. . . . I will try it. . . . (*Tastes.*) Good! It couldn't be better. What a flavour, what is it?

MIRANDOLINA. I have secrets of my own, Sir. This hand knows how to make good things.

CAPTAIN (*to* SERVANT *with some passion*). Give me some wine.

MIRANDOLINA. After this dish, Sir, you ought to drink something good.

CAPTAIN (*to* SERVANT). Give me some Burgundy.

MIRANDOLINA. Bravissimo! Burgundy is a splendid wine. In my opinion it is the best of all at dinner. (SERVANT *puts down bottle and glass.*)

CAPTAIN. You are a good judge of everything.

MIRANDOLINA. Sure enough, I don't often make a mistake.

CAPTAIN. But this time you are making a mistake.

MIRANDOLINA. In what way, Sir?

CAPTAIN. In thinking I deserve to be made much of by you.

MIRANDOLINA (*sighing*). Ah! Sir.

CAPTAIN (*altered*). What is it? What do these sighs mean?

MIRANDOLINA. I will tell you. I show these little attentions to everybody, and I am sorry to think they displease you.

CAPTAIN (*quietly*). I will not be ungrateful to you.

MIRANDOLINA. I do not want to win gratitude from you . . . I am doing no more than my duty.

CAPTAIN. No, no, I know that very well. I am not so bad as you think. You will not have to complain of me. (*Pours wine in his glass.*)

MIRANDOLINA. But . . . Sir . . . I don't understand.

CAPTAIN. Your good health! (*Drinks.*)

MIRANDOLINA. I am greatly obliged . . . it is too much honour.

CAPTAIN. The wine is beyond praise.

MIRANDOLINA. Burgundy is my favourite.

CAPTAIN. Take some and welcome.

MIRANDOLINA. Oh! No, thank you, Sir.

CAPTAIN. Have you had your dinner?

MIRANDOLINA. Yes, Sir.

CAPTAIN. Won't you try a little glass?

MIRANDOLINA. I don't deserve such a favour.

CAPTAIN. You are very welcome.

MIRANDOLINA. I don't know what to say . . . I am not worthy of your kindness.

CAPTAIN (*to* SERVANT). Bring a glass.

MIRANDOLINA. No, no; if you will allow me I will take this. (*Takes the* CAPTAIN'S *glass.*)

CAPTAIN. Oh, but I have used that one.

MIRANDOLINA (*smiling*). I drink to your good looks, Sir. (*The* SERVANT *puts another glass on the tray.*)

CAPTAIN. Eh! By Jove! (*Pours out wine.*)

MIRANDOLINA. But it is some time since I have eaten anything. I'm afraid it might go to my head.

CAPTAIN. There's no danger.

MIRANDOLINA. If you would favour me with a mouthful of bread.

CAPTAIN. Certainly. (*Gives her a piece.*) Take it.

(MIRANDOLINA *with the glass in one hand and a piece of bread in the other, stands awkwardly as if not able to drink.*)

CAPTAIN. You will be more comfortable if you sit down.

MIRANDOLINA. Oh! That is too much, Sir.

CAPTAIN. Come, come; there is no one here. (*To* SERVANT) Put a chair.

SERVANT (*aside*). The master must be near his death. I never saw him this way before. (*Goes for a chair.*)

MIRANDOLINA. If the Count should hear this . . . or the Marquis . . . woe betide me.

CAPTAIN. Why so?

MIRANDOLINA. A hundred times they have pressed me to eat or drink something with them and I would not.

CAPTAIN. Come, sit down. (*She sits down and sips the wine.*) (*To* SERVANT) Listen. . . . (*Speaking low*) Don't mention to anyone that our landlady has been sitting at my table.

SERVANT. Never fear, Sir.

MIRANDOLINA. May the Captain have his heart's desire!

CAPTAIN. Thank you, my polite little landlady.

MIRANDOLINA. This toast has nothing to do with women.

CAPTAIN. No, and why?

MIRANDOLINA. Because I know you hate the sight of women.

CAPTAIN. That is true. I never wish to see one.

MIRANDOLINA. Is it so with you still?

CAPTAIN. I don't want . . . (*Looks at* SERVANT.)

MIRANDOLINA. What don't you want?

CAPTAIN. Listen. (*Leans across table.*) I don't want you to make me change my nature.

MIRANDOLINA. I Sir? How could I do that?

CAPTAIN (*to* SERVANT). You may go and have a couple of eggs cooked for me, and bring them up when they are ready.

SERVANT. What way should the eggs be done?

CAPTAIN. Whatever way you like, you fool!

SERVANT (*aside*). I understand, Sir. (*Goes.*)

CAPTAIN. Mirandolina, you are a very pretty young person.

MIRANDOLINA. Oh, Sir! You are making fun of me.

CAPTAIN. Listen . . . I am going to say a true word . . . a very true word that will be to your honour.

MIRANDOLINA. I shall be well pleased hearing it.

CAPTAIN. You are the first woman I have ever enjoyed talking to in this world.

MIRANDOLINA. I will tell you why, Sir; not that I would make too much of myself, but people that have something akin know one another when they meet; this sympathy, this feeling for one another is sometimes to be found even between people who have never met. I myself feel for you what I have felt for no other.

CAPTAIN. I am afraid you want to take away my peace of mind.

MIRANDOLINA. Oh, Sir, you are a sensible man; you would never give in to the weaknesses others fall into. Indeed if I saw any sign of it I would never come in here again. I myself feel . . . as well as you . . . I don't know what . . . inside me . . . something I never felt before . . . but I will not give in to being foolish about a man . . . much less for one who is against us all . . . and he maybe . . . maybe, to try me, and then to laugh at me, has been talking in a way to lead me on . . . if you please, Sir, give me another drop of Burgundy.

CAPTAIN. Eh? I know, I know . . . (*Pours out wine.*) (*Giving her the glass of wine*) Take it.

MIRANDOLINA. Thank you, Sir, but you yourself are not taking any.

CAPTAIN. Yes. I will take some. (*Aside*) The one devil may drive out the other! (*Pours wine into his glass.*) And tell me, do you dislike men?

MIRANDOLINA. As you detest women.

CAPTAIN. My enemies are getting their revenge.

MIRANDOLINA. How is that, Sir?

CAPTAIN. Ah, you little humbug, you know very well. (MARQUIS *heard calling "Captain".*) (*Drinks.*)

MIRANDOLINA (*caressingly*). Captain!

CAPTAIN. What is it?

MIRANDOLINA. Touch it . . . (*Makes her glass touch his.*) To those who live in good fellowship!

CAPTAIN (*languidly*). In good fellowship. (MARQUIS *calls nearer "Captain."*)

MIRANDOLINA. With no ill thought!

CAPTAIN. I drink to that.

(MARQUIS *comes in.*)

MARQUIS. Here I am. Whose health are you drinking?

CAPTAIN (*changing manner*). What do you want to know?

MARQUIS. Excuse me, my dear Sir. I had been calling out, and no one answered.

MIRANDOLINA. With your leave. (*Is going.*)

CAPTAIN (*to* MIRANDOLINA). Don't go. (*To* MARQUIS) I don't take such liberties with you.

MARQUIS. I beg pardon. I thought you were alone. I am delighted to see our admirable hostess here . . . ah! What do you say? Isn't she perfection?

MIRANDOLINA. I had brought up some things for the Captain . . . a little faintness came over me and he came to my help with a glass of Burgundy.

MARQUIS (*to* CAPTAIN). Is that Burgundy?

CAPTAIN. Yes, it is Burgundy.

MARQUIS. Is it really?

CAPTAIN. At least I paid for it as such.

MARQUIS. I am a judge. Let me try it and I'll tell you if it is or not.

CAPTAIN (*calls at door*). Here! (SERVANT *enters.*) A glass for the Marquis. (SERVANT *gives it and goes.*)

MARQUIS. That glass is too small; Burgundy is not a liqueur; one can't judge without getting enough to judge by. (*Takes a larger glass.*)

SERVANT (*comes in with plate*). Here are the eggs, Sir. (*Puts them on the table.*)

CAPTAIN. I don't want anything more.

MARQUIS. What have you there?

CAPTAIN. Eggs.

MARQUIS. I don't care about eggs. (SERVANT *takes them away to sideboard.*)

MIRANDOLINA. Marquis, if the Captain will allow me . . . will you taste this haricot . . . made with my own hands.

MARQUIS. Oh, very well, here . . . a chair . . . (SERVANT *hands him a chair and puts glass on tray.*) A fork . . .

CAPTAIN. Lay a place there. (SERVANT *does so.*)

MIRANDOLINA. I am feeling better now, Sir . . . I will go. (*Gets up.*)

MARQUIS. Do me the pleasure of stopping a little longer.

MIRANDOLINA. But I have my own business to attend to; and then, the Captain . . .

MARQUIS (*to* CAPTAIN). You will allow her to stay a little longer.

CAPTAIN. Why do you want her to stay?

MARQUIS. I will ask you to taste a glass of Cyprus wine, the equal of which you have never tasted in this world, and I would wish Mirandolina to try it also and to give her opinion.

CAPTAIN (*to* MIRANDOLINA). You must stay to oblige the Marquis.

MIRANDOLINA. The Marquis will excuse me.

MARQUIS. Won't you just taste it?

MIRANDOLINA. Another time, your Excellency.

CAPTAIN. Oh, you had better stay.

MIRANDOLINA (*to* CAPTAIN). Is that a command?

CAPTAIN. I say you are to stay here.

MIRANDOLINA (*sitting down*). I obey.

MARQUIS (*eating*). Oh, what a good dish! What a savoury smell! What a flavour! Your health, Captain. (*Drinks Burgundy.*)

CAPTAIN. Well, what do you think of it?

MARQUIS. With all due respect, it is very poor . . . Try my Cyprus wine . . .

CAPTAIN. But where is this Cyprus wine?

MARQUIS. I have it here . . . I brought it with me . . . we must enjoy it together; there's no mistake about it. (*Takes from pocket a very small bottle.*)

MIRANDOLINA. By what I see, Sir, you don't want your wine to go to our heads.

MARQUIS. This! It should be tasted drop by drop like Tokay. Where are the glasses? (*Opens bottle;* SERVANT *brings glasses.*) Eh! Those are too big . . . have you no smaller?

(*He covers the bottle with his hand.*)

CAPTAIN (*to* SERVANT). Bring the liqueur glasses.

MIRANDOLINA. I think smelling it will be enough.

MARQUIS (*smelling it*). Oh, dear! It has a very comforting smell. (SERVANT *brings three glasses on the tray, the* MARQUIS *very slowly fills the glasses, giving one to the* CAPTAIN, *one to* MIRANDO-LINA *and keeping one, carefully re-corking the bottle.*) What Nectar! (*Takes a sip.*) What Ambrosia! What distilled manna !

CAPTAIN (*aside to* MIRANDOLINA). What do you think of this filth?

MIRANDOLINA (*aside to* CAPTAIN). Bottle rinsings.

MARQUIS (*to* CAPTAIN). Eh! What do you think?

CAPTAIN. Very good! Delicious!

MARQUIS. Do you like it, Mirandolina?

MIRANDOLINA. Well, Sir, as you ask me, I can't make a pretence. I think it nasty and I won't say it's nice. Let whoever pleases pretend to like it, but I won't. To deceive in one thing, is to be ready to deceive in other things.

CAPTAIN. You say that as a reproach to me and I don't know why.

MARQUIS. Mirandolina, you are no judge at all of wine of this sort; I am sorry for you. You were able to understand the handkerchief I gave you, and to admire it—(*rises*)—but you know nothing at all about Cyprus wine. (*Finishes his glass.*) May I call your servant? (*Goes to door and talks to* SERVANT.)

MIRANDOLINA (*moves nearer to* CAPTAIN). It is amusing to hear him praise his own goods.

CAPTAIN (*aside to* MIRANDOLINA). That is not my habit.

MIRANDOLINA (*aside to* CAPTAIN). Your boasting is of your contempt for us poor women.

CAPTAIN (*aside to* MIRANDOLINA). And yours is bringing to your feet every man.

MIRANDOLINA (*carelessly*). Not all men.

CAPTAIN (*with some passion*). Yes all.

MARQUIS (*returning from door*). Here is a clean glass. (SERVANT *brings them on a tray.*)

MIRANDOLINA. I don't want any more.

MARQUIS. No, never fear, it's not for you . . . Here, my man, with your Master's leave, go to the Count of Albafiorita and tell him out *loud*, so that anyone may hear, that I beg him to try a little of this.

SERVANT. I will, Sir.

CAPTAIN. Marquis, you are very generous.

MIRANDOLINA. Take care it doesn't upset him, Sir.

MARQUIS (*to* MIRANDOLINA). Do you know what it is upsets me?

MIRANDOLINA. What is it?

MARQUIS. Your beautiful eyes.

MIRANDOLINA. Is that so, indeed?

MARQUIS. Captain, I have entirely lost my heart to her. And I am as jealous as a bear. I don't mind her being here, because I know what you are, but otherwise I wouldn't let her near you for a hundred thousand pounds. (*Exit.*)

CAPTAIN. The poor Marquis is going crazy.

MIRANDOLINA. He has taken away his little bottle to comfort him.

CAPTAIN. He is mad, I tell you, and it is you who have driven him mad.

MIRANDOLINA. Am I one of those who make men mad?

CAPTAIN (*troubled*). Yes, you are.

MIRANDOLINA (*getting up*). Sir . . . with your leave . . .

CAPTAIN. Stay here.

MIRANDOLINA (*going*). I beg pardon, I don't trouble the wits of any one. (*Goes towards door.*)

CAPTAIN. Listen to me . . . (*He gets up but stands before her.*)

MIRANDOLINA (*tries to brush past him*). Excuse me.

CAPTAIN (*imperiously*). Stay here I tell you.

MIRANDOLINA (*turning, with pride*). What do you want with me?

CAPTAIN. Nothing . . . (*Is confused.*) Take another glass of Burgundy . . .

MIRANDOLINA. Well, be quick, for I am going.

CAPTAIN. Sit down.

MIRANDOLINA. Standing, standing!

CAPTAIN (*giving her the glass gently*). Take it.

MIRANDOLINA. I will give a toast, and then I will be off . . . a toast my nurse taught me . . .

> "Wine comes in at the mouth,
> And Love comes in at the eye,
> That's all we shall know for truth,
> Before we grow old and die;
> I lift the glass to my mouth
> I look at you and I sigh."

(*Goes.*)

CAPTAIN. Well done . . . Come back! Ah, the wretch, she has made off . . . and she has left a hundred devils to torment me! "I lift the glass to my mouth, I look at you and I sigh." What does that mean? Ah! you little villain. I know what you are at! You want to put me down, to get the better of me. But you do it so charmingly; you know so well how to wind yourself in. The devil, the devil, you can do as you like with me. No, I will go away. I will never see her again. Let her not come in my way again; my curse upon women! I never will set foot again in any place where there is one to be found.

SERVANT (*coming in*). Shall I put the fruit on the table, Sir?

CAPTAIN. Go to the devil!

SERVANT. Are you speaking to me, Sir?

CAPTAIN. I'll leave this to-morrow.

SERVANT. Very well, Sir.

CAPTAIN. Yes, or to-night.

SERVANT. It will be hard to be ready, Sir.

CAPTAIN. I will not stay here another night. I am determined. I have made up my mind like a man. Go to Fabrizio and tell him to bring my bill.

SERVANT. I will do that, Sir.

CAPTAIN. Listen—have the luggage ready within two hours. What's the matter? Do you hear me . . . ?

SERVANT. Oh, Sir, my heart is broken going away, on account of Mirandolina! (*Goes.*)

CAPTAIN (*walking to door and returning as if undecided*). For all that I feel a sort of unwillingness to leave, that is quite new to me. So much the worse for me if I should stay; Mirandolina might get hold of me. I ought to set out. I am determined to get away this very minute.

(FABRIZIO *coming in, meets him at door.*)

FABRIZIO. Is it true, Sir, that you are wanting your bill?

CAPTAIN. Yes, have you brought it?

FABRIZIO. The mistress is just making it out.

CAPTAIN. She makes up the accounts?

FABRIZIO. She does always. She did it living with her father. She can write and can make up figures better than any young fellow in business.

CAPTAIN. She is a wonderful woman.

FABRIZIO. And will you be going so soon from us?

CAPTAIN. Yes, I've business to attend to.

FABRIZIO. I hope you will remember the waiter.

CAPTAIN. Bring the bill and I'll know what I should do.

FABRIZIO. Is it here you want the bill brought? I'll bring it without any delay. (*Goes.*)

CAPTAIN. You are all bewitched by Mirandolina! It is no wonder if even I myself catch fire . . . but I'll make my escape! I will go away. Who do I see? Mirandolina? What does she want with me? She has a sheet of paper in her hand. She is bringing the bill. What can I do! I must put up with this last attack. In two hours from this I set out.

MIRANDOLINA (*coming in with bill*). . . . (*Sadly.*) Sir . . .

CAPTAIN. What is it, Mirandolina?

MIRANDOLINA (*standing in background*). I beg your pardon.

CAPTAIN. Come over here.

MIRANDOLINA (*sadly*). You asked for your bill. I have brought it.

CAPTAIN. Give it here.

MIRANDOLINA. Here it is. (*Wipes her eyes with her apron as she is giving it.*)

CAPTAIN. What is the matter? You are crying.

MIRANDOLINA. Nothing, Sir. The smoke has got into my eyes.

CAPTAIN. The smoke got into your eyes? Ah, that will do. What does the bill matter. (*Reads it.*) Two guineas in four days! Such a liberal table . . . only two guineas!

MIRANDOLINA. That is your account, Sir.

CAPTAIN. And those two special dishes you gave me this morning? They are not put down.

MIRANDOLINA. I beg your pardon, Sir. What I give I do not charge for.

CAPTAIN. You've been feasting me for nothing.

MIRANDOLINA. Forgive the liberty. I thank you for an act of kindness. (*Covers her face appearing to cry.*)

CAPTAIN. But what is the matter?

MIRANDOLINA. I don't know if it's the smoke or if it's some weakness of the eyes.

CAPTAIN. I would not like you to suffer through cooking those two priceless dishes for me.

MIRANDOLINA. If it was for that, I would suffer very willingly.

(*She falls as if unconscious into a chair.*)

CAPTAIN. . . . Mirandolina! Oh, my dear Mirandolina! She has fainted. Have you fallen in love with me? But so quickly . . . And why not? Am I not in love with you? Dear Mirandolina! I saying "dear" to a woman! But it is for my sake you have fainted. Oh! how beautiful you are. If I had but something to bring you round . . . ! I, not being used to weak women, have no salts or scent-bottles. Who is there? Nobody. Quick, I will go. Bless you, my poor little thing. (*He goes.*)

MIRANDOLINA (*sitting up*). I've got him this time! I thought a faint would do it. Back to it now. (*Falls as before.*)

CAPTAIN (*coming back with a glass of water*). Here I am! Here I am. She has not come to herself yet. Ah! there can be no doubt she likes me. I will sprinkle the water on her face. She ought to

awake. (*He sprinkles and she moves.*) Courage, courage . . . I am
here, my dear. I will not go away now or ever.

SERVANT (*with sword and belt*). Here are the sword and the
belt.

CAPTAIN (*to* SERVANT). Go away.

SERVANT. The portmanteaus.

CAPTAIN. Get away; confound you!

SERVANT. Mirandolina! (*Comes towards her.*)

CAPTAIN (*seizing sword*). Go or I'll split your head! (SERVANT
goes.) Not come round yet? Her forehead is moist. Come, dear
Mirandolina, take courage. Open your eyes. . . . Tell me everything.

(MARQUIS *and* COUNT *come in.*)

MARQUIS. Captain!

COUNT. What on earth!

CAPTAIN. Oh, confound it.

MARQUIS (*excitedly*). Mirandolina!

MIRANDOLINA (*getting up*). Ah, dear me.

MARQUIS. It was my voice that brought her round.

COUNT. I am glad, Captain . . .

MARQUIS. Well done. Sir . . . after all your talk!

CAPTAIN. That's impertinence.

COUNT. Have you given in at last?

CAPTAIN. Go to the devil, the two of you! (*He throws jug at
them and goes towards them in a fury.*)

COUNT. He has gone mad! (*They rush out, followed by*
CAPTAIN.)

MIRANDOLINA (*getting up*). I've done it! His heart is on fire, in
flames, in cinders. I have but to carry through my victory to teach
a lesson to all unmannerly men!

Curtain.

ACT III

SCENE. *Room with three doors, as in Act I, with a table, and
linen to be ironed.* MIRANDOLINA *alone.*

MIRANDOLINA. Eh, Fabrizio!

FABRIZIO (*coming in*). Ma'am?

MIRANDOLINA. Do something for me; bring me the hot iron.

FABRIZIO (*gravely, as he is going*). Yes, Ma'am.

MIRANDOLINA. You must excuse me for giving you this trouble.

FABRIZIO. Not at all, Ma'am. So long as I am eating your bread it is my duty to obey you. (*Is going.*)

MIRANDOLINA. Stop, listen; you are not bound to obey me in these things . . . but I know you do it willingly for me, and I . . . that's enough, I'll say no more.

FABRIZIO. As for me, I would do the world and all for you . . . but I see all I can do is but thrown away.

MIRANDOLINA. How is it thrown away? Am I so ungrateful?

FABRIZIO. You have no respect for poor men . . . you are too much taken up with the quality.

MIRANDOLINA. Ah, you poor goose! If I could but tell you all . . . ! Come, come . . . go and get me the iron.

FABRIZIO. But what I have seen with my own eyes . . .

MIRANDOLINA. Come along . . . not so much chattering; get the iron.

FABRIZIO (*going*). All right, all right. I will do your bidding but not for long.

MIRANDOLINA (*pretending to speak to herself, but meaning to be heard*). With these men the more one wants to please them, the less one succeeds.

FABRIZIO (*with tenderness, turning round*). What did you say?

MIRANDOLINA. Go away; bring me that smoothing iron.

FABRIZIO. I'll bring it. I don't understand you at all; one time you are for putting me up; another time for knocking me down. I don't understand it at all. (*Goes.*)

MIRANDOLINA. You poor silly! You have to obey me in spite of yourself.

SERVANT (*coming in*). Mistress Mirandolina . . .

MIRANDOLINA. What is it, friend?

SERVANT. My master sends his compliments . . . and to know how you are.

MIRANDOLINA. Tell him I am very well.

SERVANT (*giving her a smelling bottle*). He says that if you will smell these salts, they will be very serviceable to you.

MIRANDOLINA. This bottle seems to be made of gold.

SERVANT. It is, Ma'am, of gold; I can answer for that.

MIRANDOLINA. Why didn't he give me his smelling salts when I was in that terrible faint?

SERVANT. He had not the little bottle at that time.

MIRANDOLINA. And where did he get it now?

SERVANT. Listen, and I will tell you a secret: he sent me just now to bring a goldsmith and he bought it, and he paid seven guineas for it . . . and after that he sent me to an apothecary for the salts.

MIRANDOLINA. Ah! Ah! Ah!

SERVANT. Are you laughing?

MIRANDOLINA. I am laughing because he is so ready to cure me now the faint is over.

SERVANT. It will be good for another time.

MIRANDOLINA. Well, I'll smell it as a safeguard. (*She smells it and gives him back the bottle.*) Take it and say I am obliged to him.

SERVANT. Oh, the bottle is your own.

MIRANDOLINA. How is it mine?

SERVANT. The master bought it on purpose.

MIRANDOLINA. On purpose for me?

SERVANT. For you; but hush, be quiet.

MIRANDOLINA. Take him back his bottle and say I am obliged to him.

SERVANT. Ah, that won't do.

MIRANDOLINA. Give it to him, I tell you . . . I don't want it.

SERVANT. Would you wish to offend him?

MIRANDOLINA. Not so much talk. Do as I bid you; take it.

SERVANT. I suppose I must. I will bring it to him. Oh! what a woman! To refuse pure gold! I never met your equal, Ma'am. And I should travel far to find it! (*Goes.*)

MIRANDOLINA. He is boiled, baked, and roasted!

FABRIZIO (*comes in stiffly, with an iron in his hand*). Here is the smoothing iron.

MIRANDOLINA. Is it very hot?

FABRIZIO. It is, Ma'am. It is so hot it might have scorched me.

MIRANDOLINA. Is there any new grievance?

FABRIZIO. This gentleman of a Captain has sent you messages and has sent you presents by his servant.

MIRANDOLINA. Yes, Mr. High-and-Mighty . . . he sent me a little smelling bottle and I sent it back to him.

FABRIZIO. You sent it back to him?

MIRANDOLINA. I did . . . you can ask the same servant.

FABRIZIO. Why now did you do that?

MIRANDOLINA. Because Fabrizio . . . I can't tell you . . . Let us talk of some other thing.

FABRIZIO. My dear Mirandolina, you should have pity on me.

MIRANDOLINA. Go away . . . Have done. . . . Let me do my ironing.

FABRIZIO. I'm not stopping you from doing it.

MIRANDOLINA. Go and heat another iron, and, when it's hot, bring it to me.

FABRIZIO. I will. Believe now what I am saying . . .

MIRANDOLINA. Don't say another word; I am getting vexed.

FABRIZIO. I'll say nothing. You have a flighty little head, but I like you all the same. (*Goes.*)

MIRANDOLINA. That is all right. I'm getting credit with Fabrizio for having refused the Captain's gift. That shows I know how to live and what to do.

CAPTAIN (*coming in at back*). There she is. I didn't want to come . . . it's the devil that has dragged me.

MIRANDOLINA (*seeing him with the corner of her eye and ironing*). There he is, there he is.

CAPTAIN. Mirandolina?

MIRANDOLINA (*ironing*). Oh, Sir! I beg your pardon.

CAPTAIN. How are you?

MIRANDOLINA (*stepping back without looking at him*). Very well, thank you, Sir.

CAPTAIN. I have reason to complain of you.

MIRANDOLINA (*looking at him a moment*). Why so, Sir?

CAPTAIN. Because you have refused the smelling bottle I sent you.

MIRANDOLINA (*ironing*). What would you have me do?

CAPTAIN. I would have you accept what was offered to you.

MIRANDOLINA. Thank Heaven I am not subject to fainting fits. (*Ironing.*) What happened to me to-day is a thing that will never happen to me again.

CAPTAIN. Dear Mirandolina, I hope I was not the cause of it.

MIRANDOLINA (*ironing*). But I am afraid it is you yourself who were the cause of it.

CAPTAIN (*with passion*). I? Is that so?

MIRANDOLINA (*ironing with fury*). You made me drink that unlucky wine and it upset me.

CAPTAIN (*mortified*). What! Is it possible?

MIRANDOLINA. It was that and no other thing. I will never go near your parlour again.

CAPTAIN (*tenderly*). I understand; you will not come near me; I understand the mystery. Yes, I understand it. But come, my dear, and you will not regret it.

MIRANDOLINA. This iron is getting cold. Here, Fabrizio! (*Calls very loud from the door*) If the other iron is heated, bring it in.

CAPTAIN. Do me this kindness now. Take this bottle. (*Holds it out.*)

MIRANDOLINA (*with displeasure . . . ironing*). Indeed, Sir, I don't accept presents.

CAPTAIN. But you took one from the Count.

MIRANDOLINA (*ironing*). I was forced to take it, not to offend him.

CAPTAIN. And you would offend and disoblige me?

MIRANDOLINA. What does it matter to you if a woman offends you? You can't dislike them more than you do.

CAPTAIN. Ah! Mirandolina, I cannot say that now.

MIRANDOLINA. Tell me, Sir, when will there be a new moon?

CAPTAIN. It is not the moon that has worked the change; it is your own beauty and your own charm.

MIRANDOLINA (*laughing and ironing*). Ha! Ha! Ha!

CAPTAIN. You are laughing?

MIRANDOLINA. You don't want me to laugh? You make fun of me and then you don't want me to laugh!

CAPTAIN. That's all nonsense; here, take it.

MIRANDOLINA (*ironing*). No, thank you; no, thank you.

CAPTAIN. Take it . . . or you'll make me angry.

MIRANDOLINA (*ironing with exaggeration*). Fabrizio! The iron!

CAPTAIN (*angrily*). Will you take it, or will you not take it?

MIRANDOLINA. Oh! fie! Temper, temper! (*Takes bottle and throws it contemptuously into linen basket.*) (*Loud as before*) Fabrizio!

FABRIZIO (*comes in with the iron*). Here I am. (*Seeing the* CAPTAIN, *he grows jealous.*)

MIRANDOLINA (*taking the iron*). Is it very hot?

FABRIZIO (*dignified*). It is, Ma'am.

MIRANDOLINA (*tenderly to* FABRIZIO). What is the matter with you? You seem to be put out?

FABRIZIO. Nothing, Ma'am; nothing at all.

MIRANDOLINA (*as before*). Are you not well?

FABRIZIO. Give me the other iron if you want it brought to the fire.

MIRANDOLINA (*as before*). Indeed I am afraid there is something wrong with you.

CAPTAIN. Give him the iron and let him go.

MIRANDOLINA (*to* CAPTAIN). I think a great deal of him, as you know. He is my good helper.

CAPTAIN (*aside, furious*). I can stand no more of this.

MIRANDOLINA (*giving the iron to* FABRIZIO). Take it, my dear, and heat it.

FABRIZIO (*tenderly*). Ah, Ma'am.

MIRANDOLINA (*driving him away*). Get along, hurry.

FABRIZIO. What a life this is; I can stand no more of it. (*Goes.*)

CAPTAIN. Great civility to your own servant.

MIRANDOLINA. Well, what have you to say about it?

CAPTAIN. I say you are in love with him.

MIRANDOLINA. In love with a serving man! You are paying me a fine compliment, Sir. . . . I have not such bad taste as you think. . . . When I want to fall in love I won't throw myself away foolishly.

CAPTAIN. You are worthy of a King's love.

MIRANDOLINA. The King of Spades or the King of Hearts?

CAPTAIN. Let us leave joking, Mirandolina, and talk sense.

MIRANDOLINA (*ironing*). Talk on them and I'll listen.

CAPTAIN. Can't you leave off your ironing for a few minutes?

MIRANDOLINA. Oh, no, I must get ready this linen for to-morrow.

CAPTAIN. You think more of it than of me?

MIRANDOLINA. To be sure I do.

CAPTAIN. Can you say that?

MIRANDOLINA. Certainly. This linen is useful to me, and I see no use at all I can put you to.

CAPTAIN. On the contrary, you can do what you like with me.

MIRANDOLINA. Eh? You woman-hater?

CAPTAIN. Don't torment me any more . . . you have had your full revenge. . . . I think well of you; I would think well of any woman like you if she were to be found . . . I admire you, I love you, and I ask your pity.

MIRANDOLINA. Oh, yes Sir, I understand. (*She lets a sleeve drop.*)

CAPTAIN. You may believe me. (*Picks up sleeve and gives it to her*).

MIRANDOLINA. Don't take that trouble.

CAPTAIN. You are well worth waiting on.

MIRANDOLINA. Ha! Ha! Ha!

CAPTAIN. Why are you laughing?

MIRANDOLINA. Because you are talking nonsense.

CAPTAIN. Mirandolina, I can bear no more.

MIRANDOLINA. Are you feeling ill?

CAPTAIN. Yes, I can't stand it.

MIRANDOLINA (*throwing him the bottle with contempt*). Take a sniff of your own salts!

CAPTAIN. Don't treat me so harshly. (*Tries to take her hand but she touches him with the iron*). Damn!

MIRANDOLINA. I beg your pardon. I didn't do it on purpose.

CAPTAIN. Never mind . . . this is nothing. . . . You have given me a worse wound than that.

MIRANDOLINA. Where, Sir?

CAPTAIN. In the heart.

MIRANDOLINA (*calls laughingly*). Fabrizio!

CAPTAIN. For pity sake, don't call that man.

MIRANDOLINA. But I want the other iron.

CAPTAIN. Wait and I will call my servant.

MIRANDOLINA. Eh! Fabrizio!

CAPTAIN. I swear to Heaven if that man comes in I will break his head.

MIRANDOLINA. Oh, that's a good joke! I am not to be attended by my own servant!

CAPTAIN. Call someone else. . . . I won't have that fellow come here.

MIRANDOLINA. It seems to me, Sir, you are going a little too far. (*She draws back from table with the iron in her hand.*)

CAPTAIN. Oh, forgive me! I am outside myself.

MIRANDOLINA. I had better go into the kitchen.

CAPTAIN. No, my dear, stay here.

MIRANDOLINA (*moving on round table*). This is a strange thing to happen.

CAPTAIN (*following her*). Take pity on me.

MIRANDOLINA (*passing back*). I am not to call who I like?

CAPTAIN. I tell you I am jealous of that man. This is the first time I have known what love is.

MIRANDOLINA (*still walking*). No one has ever given me orders.

CAPTAIN (*following her*). I don't want to give you orders.

MIRANDOLINA (*turning, with a change of manner*). What do you want of me?

CAPTAIN. Love, compassion, pity.

MIRANDOLINA. A man that could not put up with me this very morning to be calling out for love and pity! It is all nonsense. I am not giving heed to you. I don't believe a word of it. (*Goes.*)

CAPTAIN (*alone*). My curse upon the hour I first looked at her! There is no help for me now, I have tumbled into the net! (*Goes.*)

COUNT (*coming in*). What do you say, Marquis, to the great news?

MARQUIS. To what news?

COUNT (*to* MARQUIS). That unmannerly Captain, that woman hater, has fallen in love with Mirandolina!

MARQUIS. Likely enough. He saw that anyone I cast my eye upon must be worth admiring. But he will be well punished for his impudence.

COUNT. But if Mirandolina encourages him?

MARQUIS. That cannot happen. She would not think it right towards me. She knows who I am. She knows all I have done for her.

COUNT. I have done a great deal more for her. But it is all thrown away. Mirandolina is making up to Captain Ripafratta. She has shown him attention she has never shown to either of us. That's the way with women, the more you do for them the less thanks you get, and they run off after somebody who has never thrown them a civil word.

MARQUIS. If it were true . . . but it cannot be.

COUNT. Why can it not be true?

MARQUIS. Would she put that man on a level with me?

COUNT. Didn't you see her yourself sitting at his table? Did she ever do as much as that for us? The best linen for him, his table served the first. Dishes made for him with her own hands; the servants all notice it and talk about it. Fabrizio is raging with jealousy. And that fainting fit, whether it was real or a pretence, what was that but a declaration of love?

MARQUIS. What! She herself made that delicious ragout for him and gave me a dish of leathery beef and potatoes? This is a great insult, indeed.

COUNT. I, who spent so much on her?

MARQUIS. And I who was always giving her presents! Why I gave her a glass of my Cyprus wine!

COUNT. I see she is a thankless creature. I have made up my mind to give her up. I will leave this wretched Inn this very day.

MARQUIS. Yes, you will do well to go away.

COUNT. And you had better do the same.

MARQUIS. But . . . where can we go?

COUNT. Leave that to me.

MARQUIS. All right. I'll punish this fool of a woman. I will give up her Inn!

(*Both go out.*)

226

SCENE II. *The same room.* MIRANDOLINA *rushes in by centre door—bangs and locks it.*

MIRANDOLINA (*panting*). What an escape!
(CAPTAIN *heard rushing to door and knocking at it.*)
CAPTAIN. Mirandolina! Let me in, Mirandolina.
MIRANDOLINA. What do you want, Sir?
CAPTAIN. Open the door!
MIRANDOLINA. Wait a while. . . . I will be with you directly.
CAPTAIN. Why can't you let me in?
MIRANDOLINA. There are people coming. Go if you please. I am coming at once.
CAPTAIN. I am going. If you don't come, it will be the worse for you. (*Goes.*)
MIRANDOLINA (*looking through keyhole*). Yes, yes, he is gone. (*Goes to another door.*) Here, Fabrizio!
FABRIZIO (*coming in*). Did you call?
MIRANDOLINA. Come here; I want to tell you something.
FABRIZIO. I'm here.
MIRANDOLINA. Do you know that the Captain has fallen in love with me?
FABRIZIO. Oh, I know that.
MIRANDOLINA. What! You know it? But I myself didn't know it.
FABRIZIO. You poor innocent! You never knew it. You did not take notice, the time you were handling your smoothing irons, of the eyes he was throwing on you and the jealousy he was showing towards myself.
MIRANDOLINA. I was thinking of my work. I didn't think much of what he was doing. (*Goes to door and listens.*) But since then, Fabrizio, he has said things to me that make me blush.
FABRIZIO. Look here, now. That is because you are young, and you are alone without father or mother or anybody at all. If you had a husband things would not turn out that way.
MIRANDOLINA. Well, it may be you are saying what is true. I have been thinking of marrying.
FABRIZIO. Remember what your father said to you.
MIRANDOLINA. Yes, I remember.
(CAPTAIN *heard again beating at door.*)
MIRANDOLINA (*to* FABRIZIO). Listen . . . Listen!
FABRIZIO (*loud, towards door*). Who is that knocking?
CAPTAIN. Open the door!

MIRANDOLINA (*to* FABRIZIO). Don't let him in!

FABRIZIO (*goes nearer to door*). What do you want?

MIRANDOLINA. Wait till I go away.

FABRIZIO. What are you afraid of?

MIRANDOLINA. Dear Fabrizio, I don't know . . . I am afraid. . . .

FABRIZIO. Don't be uneasy. . . I'll take care of you.

CAPTAIN. Let me in, I say!

(MIRANDOLINA *goes*.)

FABRIZIO. What do you want, Sir? What is this noise? That is no behaviour for a respectable Inn.

CAPTAIN. Open the door. (*He is heard trying to force it.*)

FABRIZIO. The devil! I am in no hurry to open it. Are any of the men about? There's nobody!

(MARQUIS *and* COUNT *come in at third door.*)

COUNT. What is it?

MARQUIS. What is this noise?

FABRIZIO (*low that the* CAPTAIN *may not hear*). I beg your pardon, gentlemen. This Captain that wants to get in.

CAPTAIN. Open the door, or I'll break it open!

MARQUIS (*to* COUNT). Is he mad? Let us go away.

COUNT (*to* FABRIZIO). Open it; I have something to say to him.

FABRIZIO. I will open it, but I ask of you——

COUNT. Don't be afraid. You have us here.

(FABRIZIO *opens door and the* CAPTAIN *comes in.*)

CAPTAIN. The devil! Where is she?

FABRIZIO. Who are you looking for, Sir?

CAPTAIN. Mirandolina. Where is she?

FABRIZIO. I don't know.

CAPTAIN. The good-for-nothing baggage! I'll find her! (*Comes further into the room and sees* COUNT *and* MARQUIS.)

COUNT (*to* CAPTAIN). What has gone wrong with you?

FABRIZIO. What do you want with the Mistress, Sir?

CAPTAIN. That is no business of yours. When I give orders I expect to be obeyed. That is what I pay for.

FABRIZIO. You pay your money to be served in straight things and honest things.

CAPTAIN. What are you saying? What do you know about it? Get out of that you rascal or I'll knock you down.

FABRIZIO. I wonder at you.

MARQUIS (*to* FABRIZIO). Be quiet.

COUNT (*to* FABRIZIO). Leave the room.

CAPTAIN (*to* FABRIZIO). Get away out of this.

FABRIZIO (*getting warm*). I tell you, gentlemen . . .

MARQUIS. Be off!

CAPTAIN. Making me wait in my room! (*They all push him away—he goes.*)

MARQUIS. What the deuce ails you?

CAPTAIN. She has been talking with Fabrizio. Was she talking of marrying him?

COUNT. Well, your heart is very easy to touch, after all.

CAPTAIN. What do you mean by saying that?

COUNT. I know why you're angry.

CAPTAIN (*to* MARQUIS). Do you know what he is talking about?

MARQUIS. I don't know anything.

COUNT. I am talking about you. Under pretence of despising women you tried to come between me and Mirandolina.

CAPTAIN (*confused, to* MARQUIS). I?

COUNT. Look at me and answer me. Perhaps you are ashamed of your behaviour.

CAPTAIN. I should be ashamed to listen to you any longer without saying that you are telling a lie.

COUNT. I, telling a lie?

MARQUIS. Things are getting worse.

CAPTAIN (*to* MARQUIS, *angrily*). The Count doesn't know what he is talking about.

MARQUIS. I don't want to mix myself with it at all.

COUNT (*to* CAPTAIN). You yourself are a liar.

MARQUIS. I'm going away. (*Tries to go.*)

CAPTAIN (*holding him by force*). Stop here.

COUNT. And you will account to me.

CAPTAIN. Yes, I will account to you. . . . (*To* MARQUIS) Lend me your sword.

MARQUIS. Come now, quiet yourselves, both of you. My dear Count, what does it matter to you if the Captain is in love with Mirandolina.

CAPTAIN. I, in love? That's not true . . . whoever says that is a liar.

MARQUIS. I, a liar? That does not refer to me . . . it was not I who said it.

CAPTAIN. Who says it, then?

COUNT. I say it, and hold to it, and I will not be put down by you.

CAPTAIN (*to* MARQUIS). Give me your sword.

MARQUIS. I will not, I say.

CAPTAIN. Are you another enemy?

MARQUIS. I am everybody's friend.

CAPTAIN. Damn! (*Takes sword from* MARQUIS, *who gives it with scabbard.*) (*To* MARQUIS) If you take offence I will settle with you as well.

MARQUIS. Go away! You are too hot tempered and (*grumbles to himself*) I don't like it.

COUNT. I want satisfaction. (*Puts himself on guard.*)

CAPTAIN. I will let you have it! (*Tries to take sword out of scabbard but can't.*)

MARQUIS. That sword does not know you!

CAPTAIN (*trying to force it out*). Confound it!

MARQUIS. Captain, you will never do it.

COUNT. I am out of patience.

CAPTAIN. Here it is! (*Draws sword, but sees it has no blade.*) What is this?

MARQUIS. You have broken my sword.

CAPTAIN. Where is the rest of it? There is nothing in the scabbard.

MARQUIS. Yes, that is true. . . . I broke it in my last duel. . . . I had forgotten.

COUNT. I swear to Heaven you shall not escape me.

CAPTAIN. Who wants to escape? I am not afraid to stand up to you with nothing but this inch of blade.

MARQUIS. It is a Spanish blade. . . . It does not know fear.

CAPTAIN. Yes, with this blade. (*Goes towards* COUNT.)

COUNT (*putting himself at defence*). Back!

(MIRANDOLINA *and* FABRIZIO *come in.*)

FABRIZIO. Stop, stop, gentlemen!

MIRANDOLINA. Stop, stop, Sir!

COUNT. It is all your fault!

MIRANDOLINA. Oh, poor me!

MARQUIS. It is on your account.

COUNT (*pointing at the* CAPTAIN). He has fallen in love with you.

CAPTAIN. That's a lie.

MIRANDOLINA. The Captain in love with me! He denies it, and his denying it mortifies me and makes little of me and makes me understand his politeness and my own weakness . . . To tell the truth, if I had made him care for me I should have taken credit for the greatest victory in the world; a man who can't bear the sight of a woman, who despises them, and makes nothing of them, how could we ever expect to see such a one fall in love. Gentlemen, I am very straight and truthful; when I ought to speak I speak out, and I cannot hide the truth. I wanted to punish the Captain for his scorn of us all. I tried to touch his heart, but I failed to do it. (*To* CAPTAIN) Is not this true, Sir? I tried and tried and didn't succeed after all.

CAPTAIN. What can I say? . . . I can't say anything.

COUNT (*to* MIRANDOLINA). What do you think of him now?

MARQUIS (*to* MIRANDOLINA). He has not courage to say no.

CAPTAIN (*angrily to* MARQUIS). You don't know what you are talking about.

MIRANDOLINA. Oh, the Captain didn't give way! He sees through all arts, he knows the roguery of women, he doesn't give heed to what they say, he is not taken in by their tears; if they faint, he only makes fun of it.

CAPTAIN. Are all women's tears a lie, then, and their faintings a cheat?

MIRANDOLINA. What! Don't you know, or are you making pretence not to know?

CAPTAIN. Good heavens! Such deceit deserves a knife across the throat!

MIRANDOLINA. Oh, Sir, don't be angry because these gentlemen think you were really in love!

COUNT. You are still, you can't deny it.

MARQUIS. One can see it in your eyes.

CAPTAIN (*angrily to* MARQUIS). No, you can't!

MIRANDOLINA. No, gentlemen, I say he is not. I say it. I stick to it, and I am ready to prove it.

CAPTAIN. I can stand this no longer! Count, at some other time you will find me with a proper sword. (*Throwing away* MARQUIS'S *half sword.*)

MARQUIS (*picking it up*). Eh, the hilt is worth money.

MIRANDOLINA. Stay here, Captain, for your own sake. These gentlemen believe you are in love with me. You must undeceive them.

CAPTAIN. There is no need for that.

MIRANDOLINA. Oh, yes Sir, there is. . . . Wait a minute.

CAPTAIN. What is she going to do?

MIRANDOLINA. The surest sign of love is jealousy; no one who does not know jealousy can have any knowledge of love. If this gentleman cared for me, he could not bear the thought that I was going to another . . . but, as you shall see, he will bear it.

CAPTAIN. Who are you going to marry?

MIRANDOLINA. The husband chosen for me by my father.

FABRIZIO. You are maybe speaking of me?

MIRANDOLINA. Yes, my dear Fabrizio, in the presence of all these gentlemen I give you my hand as a token.

CAPTAIN (*angrily to himself*). Marry *him*! I won't bear it.

COUNT. If she is marrying Fabrizio she has no fancy for the Captain. . . Yes, marry him, and I will give you what will pay for the wedding.

MARQUIS. Mirandolina, an egg to-day is worth more than a chicken to-morrow; marry him and I will give you—this very minute—my blessing.

MIRANDOLINA. Thank you, gentlemen, but I have no need of anything. I am but a poor woman, without graces, without liveliness, not able to kindle any love or any passion at all. But Fabrizio wants me and I will take him.

CAPTAIN. Yes, you wretched woman, marry whoever you will, I know that you deceived me. I know you are triumphing in yourself at having dragged me down. . . . . But I will go away out of your sight. . . I leave my curse upon your cajoleries and your tears and your pretences. You have made me know what an unlucky power you have over us, you have made me learn at my own expense that to get the better of you it is not enough to despise you, but to run away. (*Goes.*)

COUNT. And you said just now that he was not in love!

MIRANDOLINA. Hush, hush. He is gone and he will not return, and if the matter is over now, I call myself very lucky. Poor man, I succeeded only too well in making him care for me, and I ran an ugly risk. I don't want to do it again. Fabrizio, come here, dear, and give me your hand.

FABRIZIO. Go gently, Ma'am. You take delight in drawing men on in this way, and then you think that I am ready to take you all the same!

MIRANDOLINA. Ah, get along, you goose; it was a joke, a fancy, a play-game. I was like a child having no one to keep me in order. When I am married I know what I will do.

FABRIZIO. What will you do?

(CAPTAIN'S SERVANT *comes in.*)

SERVANT. Mistress Mirandolina, I am come to pay my respects before I go. They are putting the horses to the carriage.

MIRANDOLINA (*gives him the gold bottle*). Good-bye, take this little bottle as a remembrance, and forgive me for anything I may have done.

SERVANT. Good luck to you, Ma'am. . . . Good-bye. (*Goes weeping.*)

MIRANDOLINA. Thank God, the Captain is gone! I do feel sorry. I won't try any more of those tricks to the end of my life.

COUNT. Mirandolina, child, married or single, I will always be the same to you.

MARQUIS. You may always make use of my protection.

MIRANDOLINA. Dear gentlemen, now that I am marrying, I don't want patrons. I don't want amusement. I have been amusing myself up to this, and I was foolish and I ran into danger. I won't do so any more! This is my husband.

FABRIZIO. But go easy now.

MIRANDOLINA. Go easy! What are you talking about? What difficulties are there? What is to hinder us? Give me your hand.

FABRIZIO. We had best make out our contract first.

MIRANDOLINA. What contract? This is our contract. . . . Give me your hand or get away with you to your own district.

FABRIZIO. I will give you my hand . . . but after . . .

MIRANDOLINA. But after . . . yes, my dear, I will belong to you altogether. Don't be doubting me. I will always love you; you will be my very life.

FABRIZIO (*giving her his hand*). Take it, my dear. I cannot but give in.

MIRANDOLINA. That is another thing settled.

COUNT. Mirandolina, you are a great woman; you are able to bring men to whatever you will.

MIRANDOLINA. If that is so, I may make one request of you, there is just one last favour I will ask.

COUNT. You have but to tell it.

MARQUIS. Speak out.

FABRIZIO. What is she going to ask for this time?

MIRANDOLINA. I ask you as a favour to find for yourselves rooms at another inn.

FABRIZIO. Bravo! I see you are in earnest.

MIRANDOLINA. I thank you very much for all your kind words. In changing my state I mean to change my manners, and you yourselves may also learn a lesson. If you are ever in danger of losing your hearts, think of the humbug you have seen practised and the trickeries, and remember Mirandolina!

Curtain.

233

SANCHO'S MASTER
AFTER
MIGUEL DE CERVANTÈS

To
F. J. McCormick

SANCHO'S MASTER

PERSONS
  THE HOUSEKEEPER.
  SAMPSON CARASCO. *A Notary.*
  SANCHO PANZA.
  DON QUIXOTE.
  MULETEERS (4).
  PRISON GUARD.
  PRISONERS (3).
  THE DUCHESS.
  HER DUENNA.
  THE DUKE.
  A BOY.
  A BARBER.
  A TRUMPETER.
  A VEILED LADY.
  TWO GIRLS.
  SERVANTS.
  ATTENDANT.
  TWO PAGES.

ACT I

SCENE. *An old-fashioned sitting-room belonging to a gentleman in easy circumstances; the wall covered with canvas; a gun and sword hanging on a rack on the wall and an empty birdcage; a cupboard in the wall. Window at back. Two doors. That on right leading to a passage at end of which is* QUIXOTE'S *room; that on left to garden path. The* HOUSEKEEPER *is unfolding a frilled shirt.*

HOUSEKEEPER (*having looked from window goes to inner door, opens it and calls out*). Are you nearly ready, sir? I see Sampson Carasco the Notary coming up the road. He only came back to the village yesterday. He will be happy seeing you so much improved. Put on now, sir, your frilled shirt I have aired for you.

(*She goes through door.* CARASCO *comes in. She comes back.*)
CARASCO. Fine morning. How is the Master?

HOUSEKEEPER. You are welcome, Mr. Carasco. He will be able to welcome you himself to-day. It is the first time he has been fit to move from his room these six weeks.

CARASCO. So I heard from the Priest and from the Doctor. I was sorry to be so long away, and not able to look in and give him advice. This new regulation about the boundaries is calling me here and there.

HOUSEKEEPER. So they were telling me.

CARASCO. I am to go and see the Duke one of these days at his new hunting lodge about some business of the sort. Now that is good news that Mr. Quesada is better. (*Goes towards door right.*)

HOUSEKEEPER (*stopping him*). He will be coming in here within a few minutes. He is putting on the frilled shirt I had aired for him. But his strength is greatly reduced. Though as to all the eggs I spent getting it up a little, God and the world is my witness, and my hens that will not let me lie!

CARASCO. That fever should have left him very weak in the limbs.

HOUSEKEEPER. It did so. (*Nods mysteriously.*)

CARASCO. More than that maybe?

HOUSEKEEPER. Ah, he'll be all right now he is leaving the bed.

CARASCO. You can speak out to me, I being his close friend and his adviser. You did not take notice of there being any queer way in his mind?

HOUSEKEEPER. Ah, what would ail his mind, and he so full of learning?

CARASCO. Tush—with all his learning a child might nearly persuade him it was night at noonday. It is well for him to have *me* at hand.

HOUSEKEEPER. Was the Priest saying anything?

CARASCO. He was. And the Doctor was saying that he got to be very cloudy and changeable. They thought it right to warn me he might be neglecting his little property, I having the management of his niece's estate who is his next heir.

HOUSEKEEPER. If there is anything wrong with him it is books that did it. Reading and reading he is this good while back. No one could have good sense keeping his eyes from dawn to dark upon a printed page.

CARASCO. Oh, he is a very educated man. But I wish I could give him more of *my* company. He is too much alone.

HOUSEKEEPER. That is what they were saying, that it was time

238

for him to take a wife and to rear up a family. But maybe books make less trouble in the house, little profit as they are to anyone.

CARASCO. Tut tut. There are books and books.

HOUSEKEEPER. Whatever may be within the cover I have no liking for the dust that had gathered on those he brought down from the loft overhead, and that he kept in piles on the floor till I turned out all my linen I had in the cupboard. (*Opens it.*) Will you look at them?

CARASCO (*taking out one or two books*). These are just the very sort that have filled his head with tales of follies and knight errantry.

HOUSEKEEPER. That's it. He has strange giddy talk of the champions he lays down went out in search of adventures in the early days of the world.

CARASCO. The priest was talking of that. He is of opinion it is these queer tales he is stuffing himself with, that have gone near to turning his brain.

HOUSEKEEPER. That might be so. Blows and slashes, and complaints the knights make when they are absent from their lady. That is what I hear him giving out. Indeed you would nearly feel pity for them—king's daughters so hard-hearted that sooner than bestow a kind look on an honest gentleman, would let him die or run mad.

CARASCO. I've heard of those sort of foolish romances. Stuffed with stories of an unprofitable race of people. Dreams told by men half asleep.

HOUSEKEEPER. Wizards and enchanters, he reads out stories of, doing every folly and every bad thing. I thought they were gone out of the world this good while, or only in the old people's folktales. I'd nearly wish one of them to come here now, and carry away the whole of these books that are filled with stories of their cunningness and their deeds and my joy go with them——

CARASCO. There is more sense in what you are saying than you know.

HOUSEKEEPER. I didn't wait till now to get a name for good sense!

CARASCO. It is not far from what I myself, and the priest, and the doctor, were saying this morning.

HOUSEKEEPER. About the good sense I have?

CARASCO (*going to door, opening it and looking out, shuts it and comes back*). About doing away with the whole bulk of them, that whole rabble of knights and enchanters, the contrivance and invention of idle wits.

239

HOUSEKEEPER. And did his Reverence say that?

CARASCO. He did. "Can't he be content," he said, "to read in the Holy Scriptures the exploits in the Book of Judges? And the devil take all such books," he said, "that have spoiled the finest understanding in the whole province of La Mancha."

HOUSEKEEPER. That was very nice talk.

CARASCO. "Throw out," he said, "those accursed romances that are all falsehoods and folly, before they have altogether driven away his wits."

HOUSEKEEPER. Talking's easy. The Master wouldn't let us do away with one of them.

CARASCO. Would you wish to see him altogether lose his mind?

HOUSEKEEPER. Wait till he'll do something out of the way.

CARASCO. That might be too late. Listen now. It is the opinion of the Doctor and the Priest, and of myself, that if this folly goes on, it will be right to put him for a while in the charge of a Holy Brotherhood.

HOUSEKEEPER. To give him to be locked up! There is no loyalty in whoever made that thought. That is not in the nature of friendship!

CARASCO. It would be to save himself and his estate.

HOUSEKEEPER. To put him within walls! I would never give in to see him wronged! There is no one can say any mad drop is attached to him through his father or his mother——

CARASCO. It would only be, maybe, for a short time.

HOUSEKEEPER. I'd sooner God to have taken him than to see him brought out from his own house and his home! He that never was for drinking or cards or nothing, but was a noble gentleman through his whole lifetime!

CARASCO. Be quiet for one moment!

HOUSEKEEPER. Let him come out now before you—and God grant he may have put on his frilled shirt—and you'll see has he any of the signs of a half-wit!

CARASCO (jumping up and stamping his foot). Do you think I am against him? I tell you all I want is to separate him clear and clean from what has played the mischief with him—those books!

HOUSEKEEPER. Ah, my curse upon them! If I knew they'd bring him under such a danger they'd be at the bottom of the well before this!

CARASCO. They might come up again in the bucket. Water is no safe element for getting quit of such things.

HOUSEKEEPER. And to bury them, they would be maybe scrabbled up by rabbits, or by boys who would be ferreting for rats.

CARASCO. There is only one way to make an end of them—that is by fire. And it has to be done on the minute, before he comes in here from his sick bed. Stop! I took notice as I came in of a bonfire by the roadside.

HOUSEKEEPER. So there is—where Sancho Panza is burning the old withered stalks from the field.

CARASCO. Sancho Panza from the village? A simple fellow without brains or wit. (*Shouts from window.*) Hi! Sancho Panza. Come in here—be quick! Hurry! That's right. (*Turns back.*) The priest laid down they should be burned by fire the same as if they were written by heretics——

HOUSEKEEPER. I'd like well to see them in the heart of it, and the lies in them going harmlesss on the breeze. But what at all will the master say, missing them!

CARASCO. He might not remember to ask for them.

HOUSEKEEPER. Not remember! He'd easier forget the nature of the four elements. (CARASCO *is piling the books near the window.*) It's easy talking for you, that will not be in reach of his passion. To see the shelves empty he will maybe take my life!

CARASCO. Here, hurry, Sancho! (*Calls and beckons from window.*) We might think of a plan.

HOUSEKEEPER. There is no plan possible unless you think to put a plaster over his eyes——

CARASCO. That's it! Over his eyes. No, but to shut the cupboard and to pin a bit of that stuff over it. (*Points to a piece of canvas on a chair, same as that on the walls.*) If he goes looking for it, I'll engage I'll make him believe some magical enchanter has carried it away to the Eastern world.

SANCHO (*at window*). What is wanting, Mr. Carasco?

CARASCO. Take hold of these books (*holds out a bundle*), they are dangerous.

SANCHO. I wouldn't wish to meddle with them if that is so——

CARASCO. Hurry, hurry, there is nothing will be a danger to yourself. Put them now with no delay on that bonfire outside on the road—come back quick for more.

SANCHO. So long as the danger won't catch on to myself——?

CARASCO. It's only a danger that catches to people who give more attention to romances than to their food.

SANCHO. I'm safe so. Give them here to me. (*Takes an armful and trots off.*)

CARASCO (*to* HOUSEKEEPER). Hand me here those other mischief-makers. (*Takes one and reads title.*) *Amadis of Gaul*—he was the father of an innumerable rabble of descendants. (*Throws it out of window.*) Let that author of mischief go into the heart of the bonfire!

HOUSEKEEPER. This is one with a nice cover I often saw in his hand.

CARASCO (*taking it*). *Amadis of Greece*. In the fire with it! These two books are great liars. I declare I would burn my own father in the flames if I met him in the dress of a knight errant!

HOUSEKEEPER. So you would do well, sir. (*Gives him other.*)

CARASCO. *Morte d'Arthur*. If he had a strange death let him have a strange burial. (*Throws.*) *Roncesval*. In the fire with him without any remission. *Tirant*—That's not so bad, for I heard that in it the knights eat and sleep and die in their beds, and make their wills before they die. Take care of it, and I'll bring it away. Let it have the benefit of transportation.

HOUSEKEEPER. Hurry on now or he'll be coming.

CARASCO (*putting out an armful*). Throw all the big ones out, this whole generation of knights and enchantments. (*She throws.*) As to this little book of pastorals, it seems to have in it poems about pipes and shepherds, pleasing enough, it won't do any harm.

HOUSEKEEPER. Oh, sir, it's best make a clean sweep of them, or he may take a fancy to turn shepherd and go wandering and playing on a flute—or worse again, he'll turn to be a poet, and that's a disease there's no cure for!

CARASCO. True enough. Throw this stumbling-block out for the fire!

SANCHO (*at window*). The flame is catching on them, but it will be choked if I put more on for a while.

CARASCO. Well, we have done enough to satisfy the Priest. Put the rest of this savoury reading out of sight, to be dealt with later by the secular arm of the housekeeper.

(*Flings the last lot out while* HOUSEKEEPER *finishes plastering the piece of stuff over the cupboard door.*)

HOUSEKEEPER. I hear him coming! (*Hides paste-pot.*) I declare I'm shaking!

CARASCO. Put up that map over the place. I'll go out that he may suspect nothing. (*She hangs up map, then as he goes out, opens inner door.*)

(QUIXOTE *comes in, very weak and stooping.*)

HOUSEKEEPER (*setting out a chair for him*). Ah, sir, you never put on your aired shirt after all. Sit down now for a while. You must mind your health and build it up with good heartening things. I'll bring in a fat pigeon I have roasted for you. A mouthful of meat and a drop of wine will help to make blood in your veins, and to bring back your strength.

QUIXOTE. Be easy, woman. I do not need food.

HOUSEKEEPER. Ah, Sir, your stomach will close up if you give it no nourishment at all!

QUIXOTE. One of the best knights of Arthur's Round Table went fasting through twenty-five days.

HOUSEKEEPER. Believe me he ate a good meal at the end of his fast. But as to yourself, you don't use what would go in the eye of a midge!

QUIXOTE. Cuchulain of Ireland went for a twelve-month without any bit at all, his soul being away through enchantment, with a Queen.

HOUSEKEEPER. Ah, that was in the long ago. Maybe men were made with bodies different from what they are to-day.

QUIXOTE. I could tell you of Perseus of the Greeks if you had an intellect to understand—or of Arthur who broke open prison doors with the might of his flaming sword; or the valiant Lauricalce, Lord of the Silver Bridge.

HOUSEKEEPER. So I could tell you plenty myself of a champion that with one stroke cut asunder five giants as if they had been so many bean pods. And of witches and wizards, and a hero that went riding over mountains of ice, and through a lake of fire. Wasn't my grandfather giving out stories of them in the half-dark when I was but a child?

QUIXOTE (*interested*). Yes, tyrants and enchanters. If they are not among us yet, where does all the oppression come from and all the misery? Mountains of ice and lakes of fire—they are surely around us still.

CARASCO (*knocking at the door, and coming in*). Well, Alonso Quesada, I am glad, sir, to see you are yourself again. It is company you want now, and to be moving about and taking the air.

QUIXOTE (*giving him his hand*). Indeed I am nearly strong enough now to go out, and find how I can help to do away with some of the troubles of the world.

CARASCO. Oh, yes. It is fresh air you are in need of—going out of a morning as you used, with your brace of greyhounds or your angle-rod.

QUIXOTE. No, I have wasted enough of my days in that way, while so many who are doing unkindnesses are left walking the world at their ease.

CARASCO. Tut tut. It would not look well for a man in your position, a gentleman of good standing, to go meddling with custom, going maybe against your own class. It would be more likely to do harm than good. (*Sits down.*)

QUIXOTE. Yet those old knights went out against anyone, high or low, who was doing wrong.

CARASCO. There may have been great tyrants at that time, but it has gone by. There is no need now for meddlers to go settling troubles. There are courts of law and judges, and justice to be had for all. It is best to trust to the law.

QUIXOTE. I don't know. I think Amadis would have found some work to his hand—or Lancelot who went near to death, putting down the slanderers of a queen. They did not wait for courts and judges.

CARASCO. Those were things suitable to be done at that time. Our old fathers fought their battles that the generations after them might live at ease.

QUIXOTE. I would never wish to live at ease, so long as there is any injustice left unchecked.

CARASCO (*impatiently*). Can't you be content to give what you wish in charity, and say a few prayers for the poor?

QUIXOTE. The religious, with all peace and quietness implore Heaven for the good of the world. But soldiers and knights, of whom I would be one, defend it with the strength of arms, the edge of the sword. And so are God's ministers on earth, and the arm by which He executes justice.

CURASCO (*impatiently*). I that have travelled and been in college have better knowledge of the world than you. Listen to reason!

QUIXOTE (*getting up*). That is enough now. I will read my books for a while. I will be so happy to have them in my hand again, to turn the pages, every one of them giving the story of some great deed enrolled in the temple of immortality. No one would bring them to me when I was in my bed, but now they cannot be kept from me.

CARASCO. Well, if you won't listen I'll be going. I have the Duke's business to attend to.

HOUSEKEEPER (*holding him at door*). Oh, wait a while, sir! Do not leave us till we see what happens.

QUIXOTE (*goes where cupboard was, looks around, then looks back at the wall*). This is where they were—on the shelves of the press. Where is it? (*Passes hands over his eyes.*) It was at this side of the room——

HOUSEKEEPER (*low to* CARASCO). I am getting uneasy. I'm in dread he will find out.

QUIXOTE. I must be weaker than I knew—my memory is failing me. I was sure it was just here—it is not here. (*Goes feeling the wall around.*) It is nowhere—— Has madness come upon me?

CARASCO. It is not in the room. You may likely have had some dream about it as you lay in the bed.

QUIXOTE. It was no dream. I am certain it was here, and the shelves in it, and the books. Where is it? What has happened? (*Seizes* HOUSEKEEPER *by the shoulder.*) Tell me where it is gone! (*Shakes her roughly.*)

HOUSEKEEPER (*whimpering*). How would I know? Maybe it never was there at all.

QUIXOTE. You are lying! I am in my senses. I see the room, and the table, and the sword upon the wall. Where is the press with my books?

HOUSEKEEPER. Leave go of me, and I'll tell all I know.—They were maybe carried off by the Old Boy himself as they were likely written at his bidding! (*Looks at* CARASCO *for help.*)

QUIXOTE (*still holding her*): Tell me the truth!

(*She whimpers.*)

CARASCO (*releasing her*). I will tell you that. It's no use looking for them, cupboards, or shelves, or books. It was not a devil carried them away. It was an enchanter that came upon a cloud. (*To* HOUSEKEEPER): Wasn't that so?

HOUSEKEEPER. It was so—the very day you took to your bed! He called out that he was your secret enemy, and away with him, shelves and books and all. All he left after him was a cloud of smoke——

CARASCO. There is some smell of it in the room yet. (*Sniffs.*)

QUIXOTE (*leaning on chair*). A secret enemy. Merlin the French enchanter it might be—or some other. He must have been watching me—he put that sickness on me. He knows I will some day surely vanquish him or some champion he has under his protection, or release some lady he has in his power. That is the reason he has done me this unkindness! Oh I will pay him what I owe! I will surely get my revenge! (*He totters and sits down with head in hands.*)

SANCHO (*coming in*). The bonfire made a great blaze up to the skies!

HOUSEKEEPER. Go out now! (*Pushes him.*) And mind your own business.

SANCHO. I thought you might have some more fuel to put on it —of the same sort——

HOUSEKEEPER. That's enough now. (*Tries to push him out.*)

SANCHO (*to* CARASCO). There is no person passing the road but stopped to take a look at it—even to a chain of prisoners that were on their way to the galleys.

QUIXOTE. What did you say?

HOUSEKEEPER (*pushing* SANCHO *again*). Go back to your work!

QUIXOTE. What was that about *prisoners*?

SANCHO. They are after passing the road, about a dozen of them, strung like beads in a row, on a great iron chain.

QUIXOTE. Ha! Chained! Where were they going?

SANCHO. Where they are forced by the King. That is to row in the galleys.

QUIXOTE. Forced?

SANCHO. Condemned for their crimes to serve the King as galley slaves.

QUIXOTE. Brought there against their will?

SANCHO. Anyway, it is not with their own liking.

QUIXOTE. It seems this is some of my business. To defeat violence —to succour and help the miserable——(*starts up.*)

CARASCO (*putting hand on his arm*). Have sense, sir.

QUIXOTE. That is no sense, to sit idle, while all the oppressors of the world make slaves of their fellow men at their ease! There is no one of those old knights but would have gone out hearing that!

CARASCO. If they did they were used to fighting, and they had good armour to protect them.

QUIXOTE. Armour! Yes, so they had.

CARASCO. And where do *you* think to go looking for armour? (*laughs.*)

QUIXOTE. Stop, stop! I have it in my mind I saw armour somewhere—somewhere in this house.

HOUSEKEEPER. And where would it be?

QUIXOTE. It is long ago I handled it—it was heavy.

SANCHO. So it was heavy. (*To* HOUSEKEEPER.) Didn't I bring it in at your bidding ma'am, not long ago, from the corner of the old forge where it had been through the years, for to make a place there for your wheel?

QUIXOTE. Go get it. Bring it to me! Make no delay. It is Heaven sent the thought of it! Hurry, hurry—no I will go myself. (*Goes towards inner door.*)

HOUSEKEEPER (*holding him back*). For pity's sake! (*He breaks away, she follows him.*)

(SANCHO *is going after them, but* CARASCO *holds him back.*)

CARASCO. This is a bad business.

SANCHO. Him getting the armour? What harm could there be in that?

CARASCO. Can't you see the poor gentleman is losing his wits, or has lost them.

SANCHO. Is it to go mad you think he did?

CARASCO. He is on the road to be shut up in a Brotherhood.

SANCHO. To lock him up! Why now would they do that? He's as harmless as a piece of bread.

CARASCO. I am going out to bring the Priest and Doctor to judge of him, whether he can be left at large. Now mind this. You must not let him leave the house until we come. I am acting for his own good. Just keep him quiet and humour him.

SANCHO. To be sure I will; and keep him in chat.

(*A clatter outside.*)

HOUSEKEEPER (*outside door*). They're very weighty; they're slipping from me!

(SANCHO *goes out to help.* QUIXOTE *comes in, greaves in hand.* CARASCO *turns back from door.*)

QUIXOTE. Bring in the rest.

(SANCHO *and* HOUSEKEEPER *come in carrying armour which they pile on the floor.*)

HOUSEKEEPER (*taking a brush*). I'll sweep the cobwebs from it. But it will be hard to banish the rust.

SANCHO. If I had a fistful of sand I could scour it where it is thick.

QUIXOTE (*handling it*). The buckler—that is good. The gauntlets —the corselet, the gorge too—that wants a lace. Where is the helmet?

SANCHO. It is not in it. It was maybe used to make a nest for the hens.

HOUSEKEEPER. It was not. They have plenty of nests without that! Here is some sort of a little cap.

QUIXOTE. That is the leather morion. But I would wish it to have more the appearance of a helmet. It should have a visor.

SANCHO. Give me here that old birdcage and I'll put a face on it. (*Turns his back and works at it.*)

QUIXOTE (*taking sword from wall*). Now I can go out like Arthur's knights, or Orlando and the twelve peers of France. (HOUSEKEEPER *goes, gloomily.*)

CARASCO (*with an impatient gesture and sneer*). You are expecting, I suppose, to have your own name, Alonso Quesada, added to that catalogue.

QUIXOTE. You are right—Quesada—that is not a fitting name—Quixote would have a sharper sound—Don Quixote de la Mancha—that would not be out of tune with Lancelot du Lake.

CARASCO. Of all the folly! This must be stopped! (*Goes quickly out.*)

QUIXOTE. Lancelot went out fighting for a queen's sake——

SANCHO. Faith, I'd sooner go fighting for myself.

QUIXOTE. A knight without a lady to fight for is like a tree without leaves or fruit, a sky without moon or stars. If I chance to meet some tyrant, and force him to yield, will it not be proper to have some lady to send him to that she may dispose of him as she thinks best? (*Walks up and down.*) I will make her famous, as Tristram did Iseult of the White Hand.

SANCHO. Faith sir, you would look long enough in this place, before you would find a queen's daughter, or anyone at all having a white hand.

QUIXOTE. Whoever I, a knight errant, choose for my lady will have a hand no man in the world dare see a spot on without my leave!

SANCHO. Well, I don't know where your worship will go look, unless among the girls reaping and binding in the field outside.

QUIXOTE. Look you yourself from the window and give me the name of whatever fitting maiden you may see!

SANCHO (*hurrying to window*). There's a neighbour's daughter from the parish of Toboso—a strong mettlesome girl with a good blush in her cheeks. Will I call her in till your honour will take a look at her?

QUIXOTE. No, I will take no look at her, nor so much as kneel to kiss her hand, until I bring her the arms and the sword of some one of the tyrants I am going out to destroy.

SANCHO. Dulcie her name is.

QUIXOTE. That is not a name for a poet to put in his rhymes, or a knight to bind upon his arm. She must take another—Dulcinea

248

—Dulcinea del Toboso. That is a more fitting name. Here, give me my armour—I will make that name known through all the provinces of Spain!

SANCHO (*helping him to put on gorget*). And what way will your Honour travel the road?

QUIXOTE. As every knight errant has done—on horseback.

SANCHO. Faith, if it's old Rosinante outside in the meadow you are thinking to go ride, it's likely he won't carry you far. So lean and feeble as he is—so sharp in the backbone.

QUIXOTE. He will do as well as another, while there is no other to be found. Give me that helmet.

SANCHO (*holding it up*). Look at it now how strong it is. Try it now with a stroke till we see what way it will bear a blow.

QUIXOTE (*putting it on*). No, it is not likely the enemy will ever come near enough to strike it— hurry now and help me on with this bodycoat.

SANCHO (*helping him*). Faith, it's all for luck your worship is so much reduced with the fever. They must not have been very bulky in the olden times.

QUIXOTE. Go on with the fastenings.

SANCHO. Aren't you the great warrior now, sir, to go out with nothing but your sword and your armour, against gunpowder that might blow you up into the elements! (*Kneels to fasten greaves.*)

QUIXOTE. Ah, gunpowder! My curse on this age where we live! But the will of Heaven be done.

SANCHO. Are you in earnest, sir, thinking to go out fighting alone, and no one to care you through hardships and the howling of the wolves?

QUIXOTE. That is so. Yet the knights had squires to attend them. Every knight had a squire. Sancho, will you be mine?

SANCHO. I don't know. I have a wife at home and a daughter. I must make provision for them, and not go rambling. How much now did the squire of a knight errant get in those times? Did they agree by the month, or by the day the same as labourers?

QUIXOTE. I never read that any knight errant allowed his squire set wages, and to think I will force the ancient usage off its hinges is a very great mistake.

SANCHO. Your worship is always right, and I am but an ass. But I want no more than to pass this life in credit and in comfort. I wouldn't wish to go wandering away in a wilderness till we'd be turned into mummy. And another thing, if I did go, it would be on condition your worship would battle it out yourself, and I would have but to look to your clothes and your diet. I am as good to fetch and carry as any house-dog. But to think I will lay a hand on the sword, is a very great mistake.

QUIXOTE. As to that I forbid you to raise a hand to defend me whatever peril I may be in, unless it may be against any rascally rabble or low common mob. If they should be knights like myself it is not allowed by the laws of chivalry that you should meddle at all.

SANCHO. I will give you my oath, sir, I'll obey you in that. I am a quiet peaceable man and an enemy to thrusting myself into quarrels and brangles. I'll keep that law as religiously as to stop work on Sunday. (*Stands up.*) And from this time forward in the presence of God I forgive all injuries anyone has done or shall do me hereafter, rich or poor, gentle or simple. For it is in my mind that whatever may happen for the knight in a battle, for the poor squire he must sing sorrow.

QUIXOTE. But at some time or other such an adventure may befall, that an island may be won in the turn of a hand, and my squire be made its governor.

SANCHO. Ha! An island! I'd like well to taste what it is to be a governor. Let me alone to lick my own fingers! I'll live on my rents like any duke and let the world rub!

QUIXOTE. It may even be that I may win such a territory as will fit my squire to be crowned a king.

SANCHO (*speaking low*). A king! Tell me sir, if by some of those miracles I should be made a king, would Teresa my crooked rib be made a queen, and my children princes?

QUIXOTE. Who can doubt it?

SANCHO (*turning his back and muttering as he puts away tools*). For I'm certain that if golden crowns were to rain down from the skies not one of them would fit well on the head of my wife Teresa. For good as she is as a woman I am certain she would not be worth two farthings as a queen!

HOUSEKEEPER (*bursting in*). Oh! Sir, you would put terror on the world in those battle clothes! I declare you put my heart across, seeing you. But it's best for your honour to put on your boots that are well cleaned for you, before Mr. Carasco will come back, and the Priest.

QUIXOTE. Ha! They are coming? I must make haste. (*Goes back to his room.*)

HOUSEKEEPER (*closing door after him, stands with her back against it*). You look to be in good spirits, *Mr.* Sancho Panza!

SANCHO. Is it me? Why wouldn't I?

HOUSEKEEPER. It is likely you won't eat your bread for nothing! I heard your talk, and you giving in to blind vagaries. Yourself and your islands!

SANCHO. Well, if I covet islands there are some that covet worse things!

HOUSEKEEPER. And you so cock sure! Making much of yourself, thinking to govern it! Let it come and let us see, as one blind man said to another.

SANCHO. I wish I may get it as quick as I'll know how to govern it!

HOUSEKEEPER. A governor! Good luck to you! Without a government you came into the world, and without one you'll be laid in your grave. Thinking yourself fit for such an office. What a hurry you're in!

SANCHO. Why wouldn't I hurry when fortune is knocking at my door! If I am not able to govern now I won't be at the age of Methuselah. If I fail it won't be for the want of a head to govern it!

HOUSEKEEPER. And what will they say to the governor's wife, that went to Mass yesterday with the tail of her petticoat over her head?

SANCHO. Honours change manners. Wait till you'll see her sitting on a sofa with velvet cushions and tapestries, in under a canopy of state!

HOUSEKEEPER. And the little girl you have? Will she be Frenchified too?

SANCHO. My little daughter is fit to be presented to the Pope himself in person!

HOUSEKEEPER. You'll be looking for a great match for her?

SANCHO. Well, why would you hinder me from marrying her to one that'll maybe bring me grandchildren that will be called your lordships!

HOUSEKEEPER (*advances into room.* QUIXOTE *appears at door listening*). God grant I may see you dumb before I die! (*Looks from window.*) Look out now and you'll see Mr. Carasco and the Doctor and the Priest coming! They will be here within five minutes to put a stop to your grand notions and to banish all your great hopes and plans! They have *their* plan made to put the master in safe keeping, that he will stop quiet under locks within a Brotherhood from this out, and quit his notion of rambling over hills and valleys, till he'll learn that this whole business of knights errant is all invention and lies!

QUIXOTE (*bursting in*). If you were not a woman I would make such an example of you for that blasphemy that the whole world would ring with it!

(HOUSEKEEPER *falls back whimpering*.)

SANCHO. Now maybe, my lady, you'll hold your peace!

HOUSEKEEPER (*turning back*). If your honour would but bring with you your good shirt!

QUIXOTE. I will burden myself with nothing! I am going out for the doing away with tyranny; to face danger whenever it may come! And along with that I will send the name of Dulcinea del Toboso sounding through the ages of the world!

(*He rushes out.* SANCHO *slowly follows.* HOUSEKEEPER *gives a wail of lamentation.*)

Curtain.

ACT II

SCENE: *A wooded background; a well near centre: Armour piled beside it.*

SANCHO (*coming in on right with a large sack, and one or two smaller bags*). Are you here your worship? (*Calls out.*) I followed the track of the horse as far as the brink of the wood. I saw him grazing below in the meadow. I left my poor ass, Dapple, along with him. (*Listens.*) He cannot be far off—here is his armour on the brink of the well. (*Raises his voice.*) It is me, Sancho Panza is calling your honour! You need not go fasting, I have a good share of provisions I brought away from the inn!

(*He lays his bags down, throws the sack behind the well. Walks to left of stage.*)

A VOICE (*shouting from right*). Here is the thief! Come on, lads!

(*More shouts, and three men, muleteers, rush in.*)

SANCHO (*turning*). It's those mule drivers I saw in the stable yard of the inn.

IST MAN. Here's the fat fellow, sure enough!

2ND MAN (*seizing him*). No wonder he's fat, if he has eaten all he brought away!

3RD MAN (*seizing him*). Here we have him safe enough. Tickle him with a touch of the whip!

1ST MAN. No, but get a rope and hang him from a tree!

SANCHO. What at all are you doing?

1ST MAN. If you have any prayer to say, say it before the rope will choke you!

SANCHO. Have a care what you do! My master is at hand—Don Quixote de la Mancha!

2ND MAN. Don Robber you should say! Don thief!

3RD MAN. He that would not pay his night's lodgings at the inn!

1ST MAN. Threatened the landlord with a sword when he asked for honest dealing!

2ND MAN. Said he would make no payment, he being a knight errant!

SANCHO. So he is that! And when he wouldn't pay why would I pay? That goes by rule and reason. Like master like man! Do you think I would let so good a custom be lost through me?

1ST MAN. Hay and barley for your two beasts, and your own supper and your bed!

2ND MAN. Besides what you brought away with you in the bags! (*Seizes and opens one.*) Look here, lads, the plunder he brought away with him! Beef and cheese—and a wine bottle—that beats all!

3RD MAN. Put a rope around his neck, and he'll swallow no more stolen goods!

1ST MAN. Turn him upside down and shake him till we see what he has in his pocket!

SANCHO. Shake away! For I swear on my oath I have no penny at all, or no halfpenny, if you were to strip the skin off me in your search!

1ST MAN. Here, we'll toss him in the horse-blanket till we'll see is he empty! (*Unfolds it.*)

2ND MAN. Bring it out from the trees, here to where there is no boundary but the sky!

SANCHO (*shouting*). Master! Master! Come, come and save me!

MEN. Do you think we care two farthings for your master? Up with him! (*They put him in the blanket.*)

SANCHO. Stop! Stop! You'll have me killed.

ALL THE MEN. One—two—three—away! (*They toss him.*)

1ST MAN. Up with him again till he'll hit the stars!

QUIXOTE (*coming from the right, brandishing sword*). What is this outrage?

SANCHO. Help, help! Master! I have no bone but is broken!

QUIXOTE. Impudent scoundrels! How dare you lay a hand upon my squire!

3RD MAN. We were but canting him nearer to heaven. One, two, three——

QUIXOTE (*rushing at him*). Out of my presence! (*They all run off laughing.*) Ignorant monsters. I would flay you alive were you worthy of my sword!

1ST MAN (*calling back*). Never fear, Sancho, but the next time we get a hold of you we'll hoist you to the clouds!

QUIXOTE. I will follow the scoundrels and teach them what it is to meddle with anyone under my protection!

SANCHO (*holding him*). Do not, sir, or it might be worse for us. They spoke very bad of your worship as well as myself, for not paying the reckoning at the inn.

QUIXOTE. The low-born crew! What knight errant ever paid customs, porterage, or ferry-boat? These are their due in recompense of all the hardships they endure, by night and by day, in heat and in cold, subject to all the inclemencies of heaven and all the inconveniences of earth.

SANCHO. I said the same thing myself, though I am not so well read as your worship in scriptures errant. (*Rubs himself ruefully.*) And I'd lay my curse upon all knights of the sort, if it wasn't that your worship is one.

QUIXOTE. Talk on, my son, and you won't feel the pain; and if you wish to go back from this high aim to your wife and children, I will not hinder you. Honey is not for an ass's mouth.

SANCHO. Dear sir of my soul, I confess that to be a complete ass, I want nothing but a tail.

QUIXOTE. It is time to go on. I will not rest until I have a story to tell of great deeds done.

SANCHO. Your worship will make no hand of doing deeds if you go on fasting. For by your appearance I'd say you have hardly strength to feed a cat. I brought away a bit in my wallet those robbers near had me robbed of. (*Takes up bag, and pulls food out.*) Such misusage and such mishaps! But bread is relief for all sorts of grief. And let us get to our meal, for all besides is idle talk of which we must give an account in the next world. Eat a bit, sir, it will keep the life in you.

QUIXOTE. No, no. I, Sancho, was born to live dying; but you to die eating.

SANCHO (*with mouth full*). Well, I will stretch my life by using food till it reaches the end Heaven has allotted to it. For the greatest madness a man can commit in this life, is to suffer himself to die.

QUIXOTE. Stop that foolish chatter. There is one thing only I want to hear from you. Before you touch another morsel give me the news I crave of my lady Dulcinea. Did you see her before you set out?

SANCHO. I did. For she is a good girl to work, and early and all as it was, she was out beside her father's barn.

QUIXOTE. Did she send me any letter?

SANCHO. It would be hard for her to do that, unless she had tossed it over the palings of the haggard.

QUIXOTE. Palings of a haggard! Did you fancy those to be palings that surrounded her? You mean galleries or arcades of some rich palace?

SANCHO. As your worship pleases. But to me they seemed palings, unless I have a very shallow memory.

QUIXOTE. I will go back there now, for however I may see her, through crannies or through lattice windows, one ray of her beauty, should it reach me, will enlighten my understanding and fortify my heart.

SANCHO. Faith, when I had a sight of that sun it was not so bright as to send out many rays. For her ladyship was winnowing a sack of wheat, and the dust that flew out of it overcast her face like a cloud.

QUIXOTE. Can you believe what you say, that my lady Dulcinea was winnowing wheat? That was not wheat but grains of oriental pearls!

SANCHO. That is what I saw her doing. A good hardworking girl.

QUIXOTE (*threatening him*). I tell you Sancho, you are the greatest little liar and rascal in all Spain! I declare to heaven I have a mind to castigate you in a way that will teach honesty to all the lying squires of times to come! You forget the record of all the poets and chroniclers of romance. If the lady worshipped by a knight has to do any labour, it is but to sit in a green meadow embroidering rich stuffs with silk and precious stones. There is not a doubt my lady Dulcinea was so employed, and whoever says otherwise lies like a very great rascal! (*Moves a step towards him with sword.*)

SANCHO (*jumping up and backing*). All right so. Maybe when I saw her at any time making a leap up on an ass, or salting a barrel of pork, it was an enchanter that changed all that picture in my eyes.

QUIXOTE. Yes, yes. Why did I not think of that. It is that wizard, my secret enemy.

SANCHO. Very well. But if enchanters are going to put lies and deceptions on me, my character and my good name will be knocked about the same as a tennis ball. What way did your worship see her yourself?

QUIXOTE. You will put me out of all patience. Don't you know I never saw the beautiful Dulcinea, and never stepped across her threshold in all the days of my life!

SANCHO. If that is so maybe I never saw her myself. Anyway it seems I'm as well able to give an account that pleases you, as to box the moon.

(*Shouts heard and rattling of chains.*)

QUIXOTE. What is the noise? An enemy coming near?

SANCHO (*looking out*). It is not, but a chain of galley slaves. The very same troop that passed the road ere yesterday beside your honour's own house.

QUIXOTE. The very men I came out to save!

SANCHO. It's best leave them alone.

QUIXOTE. To loose the chains of captives—to raise the fallen and cast down. This is my business.

SANCHO. Believe me they are a bad class or they wouldn't be sent to the galleys.

(*A GUARD and three PRISONERS come on chained to one another. The chain extends and the rattling as of other prisoners is heard.*)

QUIXOTE (*gently to guard*). Stop a minute, friend. I would ask why it is you have put chains on these men—where are you leading them?

GUARD. They are slaves going to the galleys by order of the king.

QUIXOTE. And for what reason?

GUARD. For their crimes. That should be reason enough. Hurry on! (*Pokes* 1ST PRISONER.)

QUIXOTE. (*holding up hand to stop him*). I would ask you, sir, to tell me the cause of this misfortune that has come upon them?

GUARD. I have no time to lose telling out crimes and causes.

QUIXOTE (*putting hand on sword*). If you knew who I am, and what is my purpose, you would not refuse me.

GUARD. I'll stop here for no one. I am fasting since the break of day—delayed on the road, and not bringing meat or drink with me as you yourself would seem to have done! (*Points to* SANCHO'S *provision.*)

SANCHO (*hurriedly*). If the Captain would take a share of the provisions my master would be well pleased. He never begrudged food or drink to anyone, rich or poor. (*Holds out bottle and food.*)

GUARD. Give a drink so, and he can put his questions while I eat a mouthful of meat. Come ask themselves, sir, and it's likely they'll answer you, for they are a class that take as great a pleasure boasting of their rogueries as they do in committing them. (*Puts down his gun, and eats and drinks.*)

QUIXOTE (*to first galley slave*). Tell me my friend what crime it was that brought you into these chains?

1ST PRISONER. Well your worship—it was through falling in love.

QUIXOTE. For being in love! If that is a crime I myself, like all knights errant, might be sent to the galleys.

PRISONER. It was not just the same sort your worship has in mind. My crime was falling head over ears in love with a roll of fine linen, and holding it so close in my arms that if it had not been taken from me by force I would not have parted with it to this day.

QUIXOTE (*to* 2ND PRISONER). And what was the cause of your misfortune?

(PRISONER *shakes his head, but says nothing.*)

1ST PRISONER. He is ashamed to answer, sir. He was a cattle stealer.

QUIXOTE. Is that the most shameful of crimes?

1ST PRISONER. It is not, sir. But when he was threatened with the torture he confessed to it. And for that reason the rest of the gang abuse him, and will have nothing to do with him, for confessing, and not having the courage to say no.

QUIXOTE (*going to the third, who is more heavily chained than the others, and whose hands are fastened with a padlock*). Why is this man fettered and shackled so much more heavily than the rest?

GUARD (*with his mouth full*). He has committed more villainies than all the rest put together. He is that desperate criminal Parapatta.

3RD PRISONER. Fair and softly now. Let you not be lengthening my name. Passanante is my name, and not Parapatta. Let everyone turn himself round and look at home, and he'll find enough to do.

GUARD. Keep a civil tongue in your head, thief that you are, or I'll make you keep silence to your sorrow!

PASSANANTE. Some people will learn some day what is or is not my name! (*To* QUIXOTE.) As to you, Mister, if you have anything to give us, give it out, and God be with you, for we've had enough of your questions—and I've had enough of being called out of my name by that policeman. But misfortunes always fall upon the best!

GUARD (*threatening him*). Upon the worst! And that is what you are.

PASSANANTE. I told you to go fair and easy. For it wasn't to ill-use us poor prisoners your masters gave you this authority, but to lead and bring us to wherever the king commands. So let everyone hold his tongue, and live well, and speak better; and let us march on, for we have been kept here long enough.

GUARD (*striking at him with knife he has been cutting meat with*). Hold that glib tongue of yours!

QUIXOTE (*seizing the knife*). No, do not strike him. It is only fair that he who has his hands chained up should have his tongue a little at liberty. (*Turns to* PRISONERS.) I see my dear brothers that you are going to your punishment against your liking, and against your will. But it may be that the judge, by some twisting or wresting of the law has led to your condemnation; or the want of money or of friends.

PRISONERS. That's it! That is so.

QUIXOTE (*to* GUARD, *taking his arm*). And so I beg you, sir, to loose these prisoners, and let them go in peace. For it seems to be a hard case to make slaves of those whom God and nature made free.

GUARD (*trying to free his arm*). Have done with meddling, whoever you are!

QUIXOTE. These poor men have done nothing against you. Let them answer for their sins in another world. I ask this of you gently, but if you do not grant it, this sword in my hand will compel you.

GUARD. To let the king's prisoners go! That's a good joke. Go out of this, sir, and mend your wits, and do not go looking for five legs on a cat!

QUIXOTE (*furious*). You are a cat and a rat and a rascal along with it! (*He attacks him so suddenly that he falls wounded and crawls away.*)

PASSANANTE. Catch hold of the gun, boys, it's the only one they have! Here's our chance! Take from him the key of our chains. (*They snatch the key from* GUARD *as he crawls, one of them opens* PASSANANTE'S *chains, he seizes gun.*) Now come on ye guards at the back! I'm ready for you! (*Fires it.*) There they run!

(*The* PRISONERS, *having thrown off their chains, cheer, and also those off stage.*)

A PRISONER. They are running like hares! They'll never stop till they get to the holy Brotherhood!

PASSANANTE. Give a cheer now for our deliverer!

(*All shout and cheer clustering round* QUIXOTE.)

ANOTHER. PRISONER. Anything we ever can do for you, we'll do it.

QUIXOTE. That is well. To be thankful for benefits received is the property of persons well born. (*They are snatching up and eating remains of* SANCHO'S *food.*) And what I ask of you as my reward is, that loaded with the chains I have taken off your heels you go now at once to the City of Toboso to present yourselves before the lady Dulcinea, and tell her the story of your deliverance, and that her knight sends you to present his service to her. Having done this you may go in God's name wherever you will.

PASSANANTE. What! Go show ourselves on the road! And all in a string! Not at all. What we have to do is to go alone, every man by himself, and hide ourselves in the very holes of the earth from the hue and cry that will be made after us. What we will do for your worship in place of that, is to say a few prayers for you on our beads as we find time, running or resting, by day or by night. But to expect us to go travelling the open road to Toboso by broad daylight is what we will not do!

QUIXOTE (*threatening*). On my oath then, you, you ill-born ruffian, or whatever you may call yourself, will go alone on my message with your tail between your legs, and the whole chain upon your back.

PASSANANTE (*giving a sign to the others*). Give him something to remember us by boys! And away with us!

(*They attack him. He stumbles and falls. All the* PRISONERS *shout and run off.* SANCHO, *who had gone to end of stage and shrunk almost out of sight, comes back.*)

SANCHO. Oh my dear master, are you dead or living, after the way they have treated you!

(QUIXOTE *tries to rise but cannot. Groans.*)

259

SANCHO. Do not stir at all now—all blood and bruises as you are —and your cheek looking very pale and wan. (*Wipes his face.*)

QUIXOTE. Help me to stand up.

SANCHO. How can you rise up, and so battered as you are?

QUIXOTE. Get a little water from the well.

(SANCHO *goes to it, comes back and helps him to sit up. He moans.*)

SANCHO. It is no thanks to those villains if the whole of your bones are not broken. (*Goes on bathing his wounds.*)

QUIXOTE. If I do not complain of pain, it is because it is not the custom of knight errants to cry out, when they are wounded and bruised.

SANCHO. God knows I'd be glad to hear your worship complain. As to myself, I must complain of the least pain I feel—unless this business of not complaining of bangs or encounters is a part of the duty of squires.

QUIXOTE. The wounds would be little to bear had they been given me by the gaoler from whom I set the prisoners free. But those slaves to have turned on me! Oh, there is nothing so bitter to bear as ingratitude.

SANCHO. Ah, to expect thankfulness from that class, is to go looking for mushrooms at the bottom of the sea.

QUIXOTE (*sitting up*). And yet, toil, disquietude, and arms were designed for what the world calls knights errant, of whom I, though unworthy, am the last. And so I count myself a happy man.

SANCHO. In my opinion your worship is better fitted for plaster than discourses. And it's what I'm thinking, it would be best return to our village now while it is reaping time, and not go running into disadventures till we won't know which is our right foot. To retire is not to run away.

QUIXOTE. Adventures Sancho! And you having nothing to complain of, being sound and sane.

SANCHO. Nothing to complain of? Maybe he that was tossed in a blanket a while ago, was not my father's son!

QUIXOTE (*rising with difficulty*). I know the reason of my misfortune. I should not lawfully have taken up this business until I have received the order of knighthood.

SANCHO. And what way will your honour receive that?

QUIXOTE. I should spend the night watching by my armour in a chapel——

SANCHO (*looks around*). Faith I see no chapel here around.

QUIXOTE. In place of that I watched beside the well. But the other virtue of knighthood lies in the stroke of the sword.

SANCHO. If that is so, couldn't I give your honour a stroke myself?

QUIXOTE. That is folly. It must be given by some one who already belongs to the order. I will await a rightful hand.

SANCHO (*getting up*). Let us get out of this now sir, knighthood or no knighthood. For with these ruffians you let loose, and the soldiers and gaolers that will be coming looking for them, we have more use for heels than hands. But to say that to your worship, I might as well be hammering on cold iron.

QUIXOTE. Silence, Sancho. You have no authority to meddle or to question what I do.

(*Horn heard from the wood.*)

QUIXOTE. What is that? A trumpet?

SANCHO (*listening*). It would sound like a party of hunters following after their prey.

QUIXOTE. It may be rather some champions setting out to fight against the Moors. Go, Sancho! See if there is any knight among them who will admit me to his order. I will stay and watch over my armour, as is fitting, as I did through the night time beside the well.

SANCHO. Faith, it would be best for your worship to go and put it on you beyond, under the shade of the trees. For indeed you are no way dressed for company.

QUIXOTE. I will do that. (SANCHO *goes off left.*)

QUIXOTE (*takes up armour and stands leaning on the sword*). I am about to join that great company of Saints and Christian adventurers; Diego who went against the Moors, one of the most valiant knights the world ever had, or heaven has now; St. George, one of the best errants in the divine warfare; St. Martin who divided his cloak with the beggar. These professed what I profess, that is the exercise of arms. The only difference is, that they were saints, and fought after a heavenly manner; and I am a sinner and must fight after an earthly manner. They conquered heaven by force of arms, and I cannot tell what I may conquer by force of suffering. (*Goes off left.*)

(*Voices heard right.* DUCHESS *and* LADIES *come on right, as* SANCHO *comes back left.*)

DUCHESS. I think you must be Sancho Panza?

SANCHO. That is so, ma'am.

DUCHESS. But where is your master?

SANCHO. He is within among the trees, your honour, my ladyship, putting on his armour. Readying himself to be made a knight errant.

DUCHESS. It is a pity I am no queen to make knights. I must call to the duke, my husband, to do that.

SANCHO. My master, Don Quixote de la Mancha, is well worthy to have that honour, or any honour, given to him by the king himself.

DUCHESS. Then he is really that Don Quixote whose story I have been hearing from the Notary who has come to our lodge. And we have just got word that he has set free a whole string of galley slaves?

SANCHO. If he did, they had a queer way of showing their thanks. Eaten bread is soon forgotten. And at his first start he has got more kicks than ha'pence. It's likely he is another sort of knight from those now in fashion.

DUCHESS. Tell me now, as we are alone, and he cannot hear, is this wonderful master of yours altogether in his right mind, or a little touched in the head?

SANCHO (goes, finger on lips, towards left, listens, comes back). Now, ma'am that I'm sure no one hears us, I'll give you a straight answer. At some times he has so much sense that Aristotle himself could not speak better. There's not a history in the world he has not at his fingers' ends, and pasted down in his memory.

DUCHESS. But this story about Dulcinea; I hear he claims she is the most beautiful lady in the world.

SANCHO. That's it. When he begins his raving about her you would nearly say him to be stark, staring, mad. He nearly knocked the head off me a while ago when I said I left her winnowing in the barnyard. Never fear the next time he'll ask me, I'll say I saw her covered with diamonds riding on a white palfrey, and her dress one blaze of flaming gold.

DUCHESS (laughing). You have a good imagination to make such a picture as that.

SANCHO. I often heard him raving out of his books about people of the sort, when I was bringing in sticks for the fire, or a thing of the kind. It is no sin to lie to him when he is out of his mind. It's a lot better do that than to let him drive me away for truth-telling, and be left with no one to tie up his wounds or put the saddle on his horse. I did well a while ago, putting in his head that she was changed by enchantment—and she as much enchanted as my father!

DUCHESS. But something whispers in my ear, if Don Quixote

de la Mancha is a fool or out of his mind, and Sancho Panza knowing this, follows him, he must be yet more foolish than his master.

SANCHO. It's hard to tell. There are but two families in the world,
my grandmother used to say, the Haves and the Have Nots; and
she stuck to the Haves. It's early days yet. If he is cudgelled to-day
he might be an emperor to-morrow. To-day without a crust to
nourish him, and to-morrow with two or three kingdoms in his
hand, and the government of an island to give to his squire. Hammer on stoutly, and pray to God devoutly. And it's what I'll pray,
that heaven will direct him to whatever is best for him, and will
enable him to bestow most favours on myself.

DUCHESS. You are a brave man, Sancho.

SANCHO. I am not. It was allotted to me to follow him. We are
of the same townland. I have eaten his bread, I love him, he returns
my kindness. He has promised me an island. And so it is impossible
anything would part us, but the sexton's spade and shovel.

(*The* DUKE *comes in left in hunting dress and gun with*
CARASCO, *who, seeing* SANCHO, *falls back.*)

DUCHESS. Here is the duke.

(SANCHO *goes aside.*)

DUKE. Our men have gone home carrying the boar I killed. I
thought you might have found some game in this thicket?

DUCHESS. So I have. Something you will never guess. This very
Don Quixote we have been hearing of is close at hand waiting for
you to knight him.

DUKE. Ha, ha, ha! How could I do that?

DUCHESS. Just give him his own way, and strike him on the
shoulder as if in earnest, and we'll have all the fun in the world.
And this is Sancho Panza, his squire. Quixote has promised to
make him governor of an island.

DUKE. Ha, ha, ha! That's very good. Does he think he really
will get it?

SANCHO (*offended*). If I do not, I am not one to fret. It might be
all for luck. It might be easier for Sancho the servant to get into
heaven than Sancho the governor. And I love the little black nail
of my soul better than my whole body! (*Goes off with dignity, left.*)

DUKE. Here's the Toboso Notary, he came after us when his
work was done, hearing there was news of this poor cracked
Quixote.

CARASCO (*bowing to* DUCHESS). Your grace, I am determined
to bring home my poor friend Alonso Quesada, who is transformed
from a sober gentleman to a knight errant run mad.

263

DUCHESS. He will never go with you till he has had some more adventures. What a pity he can't have a real encounter, with another knight errant!

CARASCO. Yes, one who would conquer him, and would make him wish for his bed, and command him to go home and put an end to his wandering folly!

DUKE. Ha, ha, ha! That would be very good. But I don't suppose there's another madman of his kind to be found in the kingdom.

DUCHESS. And perhaps Quixote would not be beaten after all.

CARASCO. Of course he'd be beaten. It would be strange if a man in his full sense could not put down one who is out of his mind. I would engage to do it myself if I could but meet him in disguise, though I never handled a gun!

DUCHESS. That would be easy. We brought some dresses for our stage players to the lodge. Go quickly with my Duenna—she'll show you what you want. Quick, quick—he is coming! (*Pushes him and* DUENNA *off.*)

(QUIXOTE *comes on with* SANCHO.)

DUKE. He looks a queer doleful figure.

DUCHESS. Now for a real play-game! The knighthood! Don Quixote de la Mancha, the duke and I myself bid you welcome to our forest. (*Holds out her hand.*)

QUIXOTE (*holding out his*). Take, madam, this hand, this chastiser of the evil-doers of the world, that no woman's hand has touched until now, even hers who has the right to my whole body.

DUCHESS. I am told you had rough treatment from those you freed from their chains.

QUIXOTE. I am well pleased to have been delayed in my journey, since I may now obtain knighthood from such noble hands.

DUKE. There is no hurry. It would be better if you would wait till I am at my castle.

QUIXOTE (*kneeling*). I will never rise from my knees until your courtesy has admitted me to that high order, that I may be qualified to travel through the four quarters of the world, to use my whole strength in aid of the persecuted and the weak!

DUCHESS (*taking his sword, gives it to the* DUKE *coaxingly*). Here, it is all for fun.

DUKE (*striking him*). Arise Don Quixote de la Mancha, Knight of the Sorrowful Countenance.

SANCHO. Rise up now, sir, as the gentleman bids you. I'll give you a hand. (*He rises.*)

DUCHESS. Heaven make you a fortunate knight!

QUIXOTE (*standing up*). I will fight for the weak against the strong; for the poor against the rich, for the oppressed against the oppressor. I will make the surpassing beauty of the lady I love to be acknowledged through the whole of the living world!

DUCHESS. She must surely be happy to know she is loved and served by the light and mirror of Manchean chivalry.

QUIXOTE (*with a sigh*). I cannot say for certain if she, my sweet enemy, is pleased or not that the world should know I am her servant. I can but say her name is Dulcinea; her country Toboso; her quality is at least equal to that of a princess, since she is my queen and sovereign lady. All the beauty the poets have imagined is realised in her. If her lineage is not that of the Roman Curii or the later Colonna, it may yet give a noble beginning to the most illustrious families of the ages to come.

(A BOY *bareheaded runs on, his clothes torn.*)

BOY. Save me! Save me!

(DUCHESS *goes aside avoiding him.*)

QUIXOTE. I will do that. What tyrant is ill-using you?

(BARBER, *basin in hand, runs in after him, with a stick.*)

BARBER. Come on, now! I didn't give you enough of the stick yet!

BOY. Oh, I won't ask it again—I promise! (*He goes behind* QUIXOTE.)

BARBER. Let me at him! I owe him more strokes than he got! I'll flay him like any St. Bartholomew!

QUIXOTE. Unmannerly knight, it is not fitting you should meddle with this lad who cannot defend himself! Come, take your lance, and I will make you know it is a shameful thing you are doing, and that you are no better than a coward!

BARBER (*falling back*). Oh, sir, this lad I am chastising is my servant boy—I employ him to wait on my customers, and he is so heedless I am losing money and customers every day. And when I correct him, he says I do it out of roguery and for an excuse to keep back his wages.

BOY. So it is an excuse!

BARBER. I declare to heaven he is telling lies!

QUIXOTE. Lies in my presence! Pitiful rascal! I have a mind to run this sword through your body! Pay him directly with no more delay, or by the heaven above us I will make an end of you in this very minute! (*Flourishes sword.*)

BARBER (*shrinking back*). There is no justice in this! I am an honest barber.

QUIXOTE. A treacherous knight of Barbary! (*To* BOY.) How much does he owe you?

BOY. Sixty pence.

BARBER. By the oath of a man in danger of his life, it is not. For I must deduct from it the price of two blood-lettings when he was sick.

QUIXOTE. Very good. But put the blood-lettings against the undeserved blows you have given him. For if some surgeon drew blood from him when he was sick, you have drawn it when he is well. So upon that account he owes you nothing. I command you to pay him this very minute!

BARBER. How can I pay him having no money about me? Let him come back with me, and I'll pay him to the last penny.

BOY. Go with him! The devil a bit! No, sir, I will not, for when he gets me alone he'll skin me!

QUIXOTE. No fear of that. I have laid my commands on him. Let him swear by his order of knighthood, and I will let him go free, and will go bail for the payment.

BOY. A queer sort of a knight, refusing me the wages of my work and my sweat!

BARBER. I am not refusing you! Come along now, and I'll swear by all the orders in the universe to pay you every penny down, and a luckpenny into the bargain.

QUIXOTE. I am satisfied with that. But see that you perform what you promise, or I swear to you by the same oath to come back and chastise you. And, believe me, I will find you out if you hide yourself closer than a lizard! For I am Don Quixote de la Mancha, the redresser of abuses and wrongs!

BARBER (*to* BOY). Come along now till I pay you.

(BARBER *and* BOY *go off, leaving basin on the ground.*)

DUCHESS (*taking* DUKE'S *arm*). Come and meet Carasco. (DUCAL *party go off laughing.*)

QUIXOTE (*holding up his sword*). Well mayest thou think thyself happy, O Dulcinea del Toboso, beauty above all beauties, since it has been thy lot to have subject and obedient to thy will and pleasure so valiant and renowned a knight, who has wrested the scourge out of the hand of the pitiless enemy who so undeservedly lashed the tender stripling!

SANCHO (*taking basin*). That chap will be in no good humour when he misses his brass basin that he has left after him.

266

QUIXOTE. Sancho! Your wits are wandering! That is no brass basin! It is a golden helmet. Give it here to me.

SANCHO (*giving it*). Gold or brass, it is but a barber's basin. Look at the bit out of it.

QUIXOTE. You think it to be a basin? It is some enchantment that has been put upon your eyes. But I know it to be a helmet. Being so large it is likely it was made for the gigantic head of Malbrino the Saracen. I will wear it as I can, for something is better than nothing, and it will serve to protect me against stones. (*Puts it on.*)

SANCHO (*examining his empty bags*). I would be better pleased if we had something to protect us against hunger. Those galley slaves have us robbed.

QUIXOTE. Put the saddle on Rosinate. Now we may thrust our hands up to the elbows in adventures! (*Goes off, right.*)

SANCHO. I wish I could thrust my hand into a good pot of bacon —with beans and onions.

(*The* BOY *rushes back sobbing and stops.*)

SANCHO. What ails you, now?

BOY. Where is that master of yours?

SANCHO. What do you want of him? To save you another beating?

BOY. No, no! Let him quit saving me! I had enough of saving! (*Turns to go.*)

SANCHO (*holding him*). What happened you?

BOY. We had hardly got around the corner of the wood, and my master was speaking very kind and very nice, saying he would pay me all he owed. And I said I was thankful to that good gentleman that helped me, and that I wished he might live a thousand years (*sobs*), and that if I was not paid he would come back and do all he had promised. (*Sobs again.*)

SANCHO. Go on, go on.

BOY. All of a sudden, and when we were well out of sight, he made a step and took a hold of me by the arm, and tied me to a tree——

SANCHO. Ah, the low villain, I wouldn't doubt him!

BOY. "I owe you more than you asked," says he, "and this is how I'll pay you!" And whatever thrashing he gave me before, he gave me twice as much this time. And he said I might call now to that redresser of wrongs, and welcome, and that he had not done with me yet, and he would skin me alive. And when he was tired beating me he went away laughing. And I am left worse off than

I was before. If he ever meets with me again let him not save me, though he is beating me to bits! (*Sobs again.*)

SANCHO. That now is a queer way of doing good to the world.

(*Sounds of trumpet. A* TRUMPETER *appears.*)

BOY. Oh! Is that him coming! Let me run! (*Runs off.*)

TRUMPETER. Where is your master? Go tell him there is a knight errant coming to challenge him!

SANCHO. Oh! That is no good news!

TRUMPETER. Go, call him to come here, and face him.

SANCHO. I will not. I will not. Is it to call him to be killed?

QUIXOTE (*coming on*). What is that sound of trumpets?

(DUKE, DUCHESS, *and* LADIES *come in, and stand at back, left.*)

TRUMPETER. A knight errant come to challenge the Knight of La Mancha!

(CARASCO, *dressed in armour and masked comes on.*)

SANCHO. The Lord be between us and harm!

CARASCO (*clasping hands, and looking up in the air*). Oh, Casildea de Vandalia, most ungrateful lady! How can you suffer me to pine in hard toils!

SANCHO (*to* QUIXOTE). He would seem to be in love with some lady.

QUIXOTE. It is as natural for a knight to be in love as for the night to be full of stars!

DUCHESS (*clapping hands*). Oh, that is splendid!

(ATTENDANT *spreads cloak on tree-trunk for her and* DUKE.)

DUKE. This is likely to be as good sport as a bullfight.

CARASCO. It is not enough that I have caused you to be acknowledged as the surpassing beauty of the world by the knights of Navarre and of Leon and of Andalusia!

QUIXOTE (*advancing*). I deny it. Nor would I ever confess that any beauty is beyond that of the lady I myself serve!

CARASCO. I have done great labours for my lady's sake and to win her love. And now she has commanded me to travel through all the provinces of Spain to force every knight I meet to confess that I am the most valiant of men, and she the most beautiful of all women, in the living world!

QUIXOTE. I say again, I deny it!

CARASCO. I can boast that having conquered in single combat that famous knight Don Quixote de la Mancha I have made him confess that my Casildea is more beautiful than his Dulcinea! And

I claim that in this conquest alone, I have overcome all the knights of the world!

QUIXOTE (*restraining himself*). Whatever may be the number of the knights you have overcome, Don Quixote de la Marcha was not one of them.

CARASCO. I swear by the canopy of heaven I overcame him and made him submit. By the same token he is tall, thin faced, grizzle-haired, hawk-nosed, going by the name of the Knight of the Sorrowful Figure. If that is not enough to convince you here is my sword! (*Flourishes it.*)

QUIXOTE. This Don Quixote is the dearest friend I have, and I deny what you say. Now listen. Here is Don Quixote himself and he says: Let the whole world stand if the world does not confess that there is not in the whole world a maiden more beautiful than the peerless Dulcinea del Toboso!

CARASCO. If she is so great a beauty as you say let me see her and I will confess it!

QUIXOTE. If I should show her to you where would be the merit of confessing so notorious a truth? The business is that without seeing, you believe and confess, affirm and maintain it!

CARASCO. I am ready for the fight. I make but one condition, that whoever is conquered shall be entirely at the command of the conqueror, to do whatever he may please, provided it is nothing against honour.

QUIXOTE. I am satisfied. Put up your bevoir now that I may see your face.

CARASCO. You will have time enough to look at my face when you are my prisoner and my captive, and forced to obey my commands!

SANCHO. Let me go climb into a corktree till I'll be out of the way of the fight. (*Runs to side and calls from there*) Sir, hold up the basin before your face.

(*They rush at each other.* CARASCO *falls.*)

QUIXOTE (*putting sword to his throat*). You are a dead man, Sir Knight, if you do not confess that the beauty of my lady is far beyond the pretensions of yours!

CARASCO (*pushing back sword*). I confess, and declare, that the lady Dulcinea's torn and dirty shoe is worth more than my Casildea's whole head of hair!

(QUIXOTE *puts up his sword, satisfied.*)

SANCHO. Ha, ha, sir! You have put this champion in pickle anyway!

(*As* QUIXOTE *turns away,* CARASCO *pushes back his bevoir and gasps.*)

SANCHO (*looking at him cautiously*). That is the very spit and image of Sampson Carasco—more enchantments!

Curtain.

ACT III

SCENE. *A terrrace at the* DUKE'S *Castle. Door at the back into the house. Steps to the garden at the left.*

(DUKE *and* DUCHESS *sitting idle.*)

DUKE (*yawning*). What a curse it is having to stay in the country once the hunting is over.

DUCHESS. That boundary business can't last much longer; the Notary has brought the last plans—and then we'll be off to the city!

DUKE. If we don't die of dullness before then.

DUCHESS. You are forgetting our new guests. It was a lucky season for them to come!

DUKE. Ha! Ha! I don't know which to laugh at most, the madness of the master or the foolishness of the man.

DUCHESS. The girls have been planning such a comical trick to play upon the Don——

DUKE. Take care—that may be him coming——

DUCHESS (*jumps up and looks out of door*). No, it is only Carasco.

CARASCO (*coming in, bowing*). I have brought these papers for your Grace to look at.

(DUKE *takes and looks at them.*)

DUCHESS. Have you seen our friend the Knight Errant?

CARASCO. Your Grace, I don't want to hear his name mentioned. I am at my wits' end. Idlers coming to Toboso through these months past, wanting news of "Don Quixote"; thinking we ought to be pleased at possessing a fellow townsman who is rambling up and down the provinces, shattered in body and in brains.

DUCHESS. I hope they have not heard of that unlucky fight in the wood?

CARASCO (*with impatient gesture*). They have heard how he attacked a windmill, taking it to be a giant waving his arms. No one could make that mistake unless he had the like in his head!

DUKE. Ha, ha! Very good.

CARASCO. If I had but got him into my care I would have brought him to his senses by this time.

DUCHESS. Oh! Heaven forgive you the injury you would do to the whole world, trying to restore to his senses the most diverting madman in it!

CARASCO. Sancho, too, that eternal babbler, encouraging his delusion for his own profit!

DUCHESS. Oh, you must have patience. We can't spare our jesters yet. Perhaps the tricks our girls are making up will show them the folly of knight errantry.

DUENNA (*coming in*). Sancho Panza is saking to come in. He says by your Grace's orders.

DUKE. Let him come in.

(DUENNA *goes*.)

CARASCO. I won't stay and lose my temper listening to him throwing his pert sayings into the world like fritters. Your Grace, there is someone come with me who is anxious to see poor Quixote —his housekeeper. She thinks he must be tired of roaming, and that she may carry him home.

DUCHESS. Oh, poor woman, send her in here. Sancho will be so pleased to see an old neighbour.

(CARASCO *bows and goes*.)

DUKE. Ha! Ha! He doesn't like to think of Sancho having seen him beaten in the fight. (*Sits down on couch*.)

SANCHO (*coming in*). My respects to your Grace, my ladyship.

DUCHESS. Welcome, Sancho. You have not told us yet half the deeds of your wonderful master.

SANCHO (*scratching his head and thinking*). Going through hardships—in the hunger of forests and wildernesses—sleeping out on thyme and rushes—his companions solitude and the night dew——

DUCHESS. But his adventures?

SANCHO. As to them, some turned out well and some cross and unlucky.

DUCHESS. Did he ever have a lucky one?

SANCHO. He had, ma'am. Didn't he rescue a lady of a princess that was being brought away to the sea by enchanters——

DUCHESS. Oh, Sancho—enchanters——

SANCHO. Anyway by five men on horseback, and an armed bully from Biscay, talking gibberish. Making no more of the Biscayner that fell on him like a mountain than a cat does of a mouse. A great victory! It was in that fight he lost a part of his ear, and all but lost his life.

DUCHESS. Yes, we had news of it here, and that he did not get any more gratitude from the lady than from the Biscayan.

(HOUSEKEEPER *comes in at back*.)

SANCHO. Another time he faced a raging ravenous lion——

DUKE. Ha! Ha! A lion. Did he make *it* confess Dulcinea's beauty?

SANCHO. So he would make it confess, if it could say anything beyond a roar. He forced the keeper to set open the cage——

HOUSEKEEPER (*coming forward*). And where were you at that time, Sancho Panza? Up in a tree, I'll engage, or down in a furrow of the field, the time the lion made its spring!

SANCHO. Not a spring in the world, but turned its back to the company, and laid itself down again behind the bars!

HOUSEKEEPER. Is it belittling your master's courage you are now, to show yourself out as the braver man of the two?

SANCHO. If courage could bring him to his death he would have met with it there and then, for he bade the keeper give it some blows that would provoke it to come out. But he refused, and shut the door, saying no one could do more than to challenge his foe, and if the lion would not come out in the field, let the disgrace be left on its own head.

DUCHESS (*clapping hands*). Oh, that is very good!

HOUSEKEEPER (*seeing* DUCHESS). I beg your pardon, your honour, my ladyship, for coming into your grandeur, and your palace of mahoganies and jewelleries, where everything is better than another, in search of my master that got demented in the head and in the mind, and was led away by that vagabond before you!

DUCHESS. Oh, we must not meddle in your little quiet talk with Sancho. Come away, duke. (*They go*.)

SANCHO (*calls out*). Don't mind her, ma'am. That one has a tongue that would hang the Pope!

HOUSEKEEPER. My respect to their honours, but it's little I care for any of them, beside my poor master's four bones, that is my only best friend next to God!

SANCHO. Isn't he well off to be here where there is everything better than another? This kind of a life squares and corners with *me* very well. I tell you, you'd hear more crackling in the pan in this house than you'd hear in our whole parish within the year! As much of leavings as I couldn't eat in five days!

HOUSEKEEPER. Long you took coming to it! It is you led him astray; bringing him this dance up and down the province, rambling through highways and byways, through deserts without a road! I'll engage it's seldom he ate bread on a table-cloth—he that is noble and high-blooded—or laid himself down on a bed!

SANCHO. Be easy, can't you. Wasn't I there to care him?

HOUSEKEEPER. You! that haven't a hand to take up a stitch in his stocking, or so much as put a patch upon his shoe!

SANCHO. Get home you sack of mischief! My master is no whimperer to make complaints!

HOUSEKEEPER. Get home yourself, you bag of rogueries! Go mind your cart and your plough! You with your islands and your highlands! That you may be choked with that same island! Is it something you can eat that you are such a glutton after it?

SANCHO. Take care how you speak to me that am used to face armies!

HOUSEKEEPER. You and your armies! Great armies! It is said on the road they were but a flock of sheep!

SANCHO. To say nothing of enchanters and goblins!

HOUSEKEEPER. Let him who says that eat the lie and swallow it with his bread. I'd never believe you saw anything worse than yourself!

SANCHO. Don't you cock up your nose at me, or I'll give you such a gag as will shut your mouth for a year!

HOUSEKEEPER. Oh, I'm such a barbarian that will never do anything right while I live! But if I get no grandeurs or govern-ments, I'm not set cutting capers in a blanket like some I know, for all the world to see!

SANCHO. Hold your noise! What matters? He that falls to-day may rise to-morrow! We must all have our ups and downs. But there's sunshine on the walls yet!

HOUSEKEEPER. You that went hiding your body behind a tree the time he had the great fight in the wood.

SANCHO. Who the mischief can start fighting without anger or provocation? Don't be so pettish now. Let our masters fight and hear of it in another world, but let us drink and live!

HOUSEKEEPER. You look good yourself indeed, and no sign on

you of having a broken head or the loss of an ear. It's likely he was often faint with hunger, while you are grown fat with pure cramming!

SANCHO. Ah, you treasure of mischief, you have the sting in you yet. Mind yourself; though I am a poor man I am an old Christian!

HOUSEKEEPER. Letting on to have such love and such nature for him, and your heart as hard as a stone of ice!

SANCHO. If it is, everyone is as God made him.

HOUSEKEEPER. He is, and often a great deal worse!

SANCHO. You have too much to say. Big voice and little head!

HOUSEKEEPER. If this is the civility you learned on the road you had best have stopped with the brute beasts in the cowshed where you were reared.

SANCHO (*huriedly*). Have done with your quirks and quillets and go hide yourself out of sight, for I hear our master coming and the company—go back now and I'll bring you to him in the bye and bye. (*They go as* QUIXOTE, DUKE *and* DUCHESS *come in.*)

DUCHESS (*sitting down and giving him a chair near her*). I was longing to ask what news you have of the lady Dulcinea.

QUIXOTE. My misfortunes, madam, though they have had a beginning will never have an end. If I conquer enemies and send them to her, by whom I am taken in the inextricable net of love, how can they find her, if she has by enchantment turned from comely to rustic, from light to darkness, from the north star of my travels to a clumsy jumping Joan?

DUCHESS. But there are some who say that you, sir, never saw the lady Dulcinea, that there is no such lady, she having been the creation of your own brain, dressed up with all the perfections you could imagine.

QUIXOTE. There is something to be said for that. God knows whether there is or is not a Dulcinea in the world, and whether she is or is not imaginary. But whether or no, I contemplate her as a lady endowed with all those qualities which may make her famous over the whole world. And I give her the praise of high birth, because beauty shines and displays itself with greater degrees of perfection when matched with noble blood, than in subjects that are of mean extraction.

DUCHESS (*clapping her hands*). Well done, Don Quixote! I will from this time believe, and make all my people believe, and even my lord Duke if need be, that there is a Dulcinea, living and beautiful, well born and well deserving such a knight as you should be her servant. I can say nothing more than that!

(*A doleful noise heard outside, rattle of wheels, and melancholy music.*)

DUKE. What is happening——?

DUCHESS (*putting finger on her lips, and making signs to him*). Someone in trouble! (*To* DUENNA) Go and see—there must be someone in great hurry or distress coming to the door!

DUENNA (*coming*). It is a lady of rank, your grace—a Countess, a person of quality. She seems to be in great affliction.

DUCHESS. Oh, poor thing—what can we do for her?

DUENNA. She would not tell me—but only that she was in sore trouble, and that it is only here there is help for her to be found.

(QUIXOTE *puts hand on sword.*)

DUKE. Bring her in here till we have a look at her.

DUENNA. She is here on my heels, your Grace. She followed me. She must be in very urgent need of help.

QUIXOTE. This now is likely to be some of my business! (*Stands up.*)

(*A* VEILED LADY *is led in. She stands and sobs.*)

DUCHESS (*going to her*). You seem to be very troubled——

LADY. Oh, indeed I am! Such trouble has never come upon anyone in the whole world!

DUCHESS. Will you not lift up this heavy veil? Here is a handkerchief to wipe away your tears.

LADY. I dare not uncover my face—I dare not let anyone see it!

DUCHESS. We will do our utmost to help you if you will but tell us your grief.

LADY (*more composed*). I am a Countess of the Province of Catalonia. I was guardian to a young girl, the niece of the Queen of Candya, who, dying, left her in my charge. (*Sobs.*)

DUKE. We could hear your story better, madam, if we could see you——

LADY. No, No! (*Holds veil very slightly asunder that they may hear better*). It is hard for me to explain. An unheard of trouble has set my mind astray.

DUKE. Go on, madam. Go on.

LADY. This beautiful young girl fell in love with a young gentleman of the court—one Don Clavigo. And there is excuse for her, for though he was not rich he was young and handsome and witty —could touch a guitar so as to make it speak (*sobs*). Besides that he was a poet—and a fine dancer—and could make birdcages so well that he could get his living by it in case of need.

DUCHESS. No wonder she took a fancy to him; all this sounds very charming.

LADY. Oh, the bitter is to come! No sooner had the marriage taken place when there appeared—riding on a wooden horse—a cruel enchanter as tall as a giant, called Malambrino, who was cousin to her. He broke into a great fury hearing that the young princess was already wed, and by his enchantments he turned her into a monkey made of brass! (*Sobs.*) And the bridegroom into a fearful crocodile of some unknown metal. He called out then: "These two presumptuous lovers shall never come back to their own shape until I have fought in single combat with the valiant Knight of La Mancha. For this adventure has been kept by destiny for his great valour alone!"

QUIXOTE (*coming forward*). I am here, ready. Did he send any sign or token?

LADY. Alas, he put on me a punishment he said would be a sign —and indeed it is one that is worse than death.

QUIXOTE. He shall be made to repent that!

LADY. On the instant I felt a pricking pain cover my face—like the pricking of needles. Oh, that he had rather struck off my head! (*She lifts her veil and shows a thick beard.*)

DUKE. A beard! Ha, ha! This is something new in the way of enchantments.

LADY. Where can I hide myself! Where can I go! Was there ever such a punishment put on any woman! My father and mother would disown me! My curse on the wretched hour in which I was born. Am I to be carried bearded to the grave?

(*She faints: all surround her.* DUCHESS *covers her face.*)

SANCHO. This is the queerest enchantment ever I saw! Would it not have been enough for him to cut off the half of her nose, even if it made her snuffle all through her lifetime?

QUIXOTE. Madam, let every hair of my own head be plucked from me by my enemies if I fail to free you from this curse!

LADY (*sitting up, but keeping beard covered*). Oh! that word has brought me back to life!

QUIXOTE. Tell me where I am to find this outrageous Malambrino?

LADY. That is easy. For he has sent his own magical wooden horse, that was made by the enchanter Merlin in the time gone by. The same horse can be here to-day, to-morrow in Potosi, the third day in France. And although he ambles at such a pace through the air, he is so smooth and easy that his rider may carry a cup of water in his hand without spilling a drop.

(*Exit* QUIXOTE, *right*.)

SANCHO. For smooth and easy going I'd back against him my own ass Dapple—so long as he may go by earth and not in the skies. And where now, ma'am, is this magic charger to be found?

LADY (*rising*). He is here, outside on the grass plot ready to make his start with the knight in the saddle, and the squire on the crupper behind—and a covering over their eyes——

SANCHO. I would like well to see him. But to think I will go ride on him, with or without a saddle, is to go look for pears on an elm-tree!

LADY. Indeed you must go, or we are likely to do nothing at all.

SANCHO. Soft and easy, ma'am. What have squires to do with their master's adventures? Did you ever hear the name of the squire put with the name of his master in any of the romances of the world?

(QUIXOTE *comes back from right, with armour on*.)

LADY. Oh, that you would set out, sir! For if this beard is still on me when the heat of summer comes, what will happen to my poor face!

QUIXOTE. I will set out on the moment, I am all impatience to put an end to your great trouble. Come, Sancho.

SANCHO. I will not come, with a bad or a good will, or anyway at all. Let this lady find some other way to smooth her face. For I am no witch to take delight in travelling through the air. And if the horse would get tired, or the enchanter be out of humour, it might take us half a dozen years to come back again. And where will my island be by that time? Melted away, maybe, like salt in a shower.

DUKE. Go with your master, Sancho, and I give you my word your island shall not be lost by it.

SANCHO. All right, sir, I am thankful; but I am a poor squire, and have no fine words. Let my master get up in the saddle. Let my eyes be hoodwinked, as the saying is, and commend me to the protection of heaven.

DUCHESS. Here is a handkerchief to bind over your eyes, Sancho. (*Ties it on him.*)

SANCHO. I'm obliged to you, ma'am. And that there may be someone to do the same for you if ever you would come to the same end of needing it!

QUIXOTE. Follow me. Win or lose, no one can take from us the glory of having made the attempt!

(*He and* SANCHO *and* LADY *go off down steps.*)

A SHOUT FROM BELOW. Now they are up! Bravo Sancho!

DUKE (*looking down*). What on earth is that they are riding?

DUCHESS (*laughing*). Some stuffed horse's head from the saddle room, put on to a barrel filled full of fireworks, crackers and squibs.

A GIRL (*running on with a bellows*). This is to blow the north wind on them! (*Blows it from steps.*)

(*Cries of "Up they go! Sit tight, sir! Up with you! Good man, Sancho!"*)

DUCHESS. Play now a good galloping tune! (*Music strikes up.*)

VOICE OF QUIXOTE (*as the music has grown fainter*). We must have left the earth. I never was on the back of an easier steed. We have the wind behind us.

VOICE OF SANCHO. So we have, indeed. I feel it as strong as the blast of a blacksmith's bellows.

DUCHESS AND OTHERS. Up they go! (*Growing fainter.*) Farewell! (*Very faint.*) They're out of sight among the clouds!

DUKE. Isn't it time to put an end to this adventure? They will find out——

CARASCO (*at top of steps blowing through a megaphone*). I, Malambrino, am satisfied! I only wanted a proof. Don Quixote's bravery has won the day. Clavigo and his bride have regained their human forms!

DUKE. The adventure is at a glorious end.

DUCHESS. Now blow up the wonder horse!

(*A loud explosion. Shouts and cries.* QUIXOTE *and* SANCHO *come up the steps.*)

DUCHESS. Oh, what has happened. We thought the sky had fallen!

QUIXOTE. My Lord Duke, the adventure is over. I have passed through the region of air and of fire. The lady's beauty is restored. Where is she? She vanished as we fell to the ground.

SANCHO. Calling out that her face was as smooth as a melon.

QUIXOTE. I will go and put away my sword. (*Goes off.*)

DUCHESS. Now, tell me, Sancho, how did *you* get on in that journey to the skies?

SANCHO. Very well, ma'am. When the noises of earth grew to be silent, and we felt the cold air blowing on us, I had a great wish to peep out and see where we were.

DUCHESS. Oh, but that was foolish.

278

SANCHO. Well, ma'am, whatever way it is, I have some little spice of curiosity, and a desire to know what is hidden from me. So I just pushed up, being behind my master and no one to see me, a little corner of the handkerchief and looked down towards the earth.

DUCHESS. Oh, naughty Sancho! What did you see?

SANCHO. I give you my oath it looked no bigger than a grain of mustard seed, and the people walking on it but a little bigger than hazel nuts.

DUCHESS. Take care, Sancho. If that was so one man must have covered the whole face of the earth.

SANCHO. Maybe so, ma'am. But for all that, I had a side view of it, and saw it all. And if we flew by enchantment why couldn't I see the whole earth by enchantment, whichever way I looked?

DUKE. Ha, ha! Right, Sancho. What did you do after that?

SANCHO. Well, your grace, we were getting very close to heaven, and we passed near the stars where the seven little goats live. And I, that was a goat herd in my own district, had such a longing and such a desire to go play for a while with those little kids that were for all the world like violets, and every one a different colour— blue—and speckled—and carnation—that if I had not, I think I would have died. So I gambolled with them three-quarters of an hour, and I give you my word the horse stopped in the air without moving the entire time.

DUKE. You are romancing, Sancho. *I* have never heard of goats with such colours.

SANCHO. No, your grace. But must there not be a difference between the goats of earth and the goats of heaven?

(QUIXOTE *returns and sits down.*)

(*Notes of bugle heard from within the house.*)

DUCHESS. That is the call to dinner. Let us make ready.

(TWO GIRLS *come in with basin and ewer and a towel.*)

LADY. I am come to make his Excellency Don Quixote ready.

(*She empties the basin over his head, a lather of soap falling over his face. He starts up.*)

DUCHESS (*to* DUKE, *smothering her laughing*). This is not of my ordering, it is those giddy girls.

DUKE. This is too unmannerly a jest. Come here, girl. Wash me as you have washed Don Quixote.

(*She splashes a little water over him.* SANCHO *leads* QUIXOTE *from the room.*)

DUKE (*to* DUCHESS). If I had not turned it off, calling for the

same treatment, they should have been punished for their impertinence.

(*A commotion outside, and* SANCHO *runs in followed by the*
GIRLS *with water and a dirty towel.*)

DUKE. What is going on now?

GIRL. Your Grace, this gentleman will not suffer himself to be
washed as his master has been.

SANCHO. I will not until I have cleaner towels, and cleaner suds,
and not those filthy rags. There is no such difference between me
and my master that he should be washed with clean water and I
get the rinsings of the sink. I have no need of such refreshing, and
whoever will offer to scour me, I will smash in their skulls with my
fists! For such ceremonies and scrapings look more like jibes than
good manners.

DUCHESS (*smothering laughter*). Sancho is in the right, and as
he says needs no washing. Get away you ministers of cleanliness,
you have been presumptuous in bringing your jug and dish-cloths
instead of fine linen and gold.

(*Exit* GIRLS.)

SANCHO (*falling on his knees before* DUCHESS). For great folk
great favours are fitting. A peasant I am; married I am; children
I have, and I serve my master. But if in any way at all I can be
serviceable to your grandeur I will not be slower in obeying, than
your ladyship in giving the command.

DUCHESS. Why it seems you have learned to be courteous in the
very school of courtesy. Rise, friend Sancho, for I will reward your
civility by prevailing with my Lord Duke to carry out at once the
promise he has made.

DUKE. I will do that. This very moment you may set out to
become governor of the island. The inhabitants are longing for you
as for rain in springtime.

SANCHO. Long live the givers!

DUCHESS. The Island of Barataria. It will fit you like a ring.
The boat is waiting.

SANCHO. When they give you a heifer make haste with the
halter! Believe me I'll make no delay.

DUCHESS. That's right. There are edicts waiting for you to sign.

SANCHO. To sign! Sure I don't know the first letter of the
A, B, C. Well, at the worst, I can pretend my right hand is lame,
and make another sign for me. For there is a remedy for everything
but death.

DUCHESS. I am sure you will govern it well.

SANCHO. I will feel its pulse. My subjects may come for wool and go back shorn. Aye, aye. Let them put their finger in my mouth, and they'll see if I can bite. And if they should be blacks, I can ship them off to sell!

DUKE (*calls over balustrade*). Is the ship ready? (*Shouts of—Aye, aye, your Grace.*) Then conduct His Excellency to the cabin and set sail at once.

(SANCHO *trots off down steps pompously.*)

DUCHESS. Come, let us eat our meal very quickly—we have to turn this room into the Island of Barataria!

(*Curtain drops, music is heard. Curtain rises after some minutes. As it goes up* ALL *are seen changing the position of furniture, putting a table across, laying it as a dinner table, putting a large armchair at back. They draw a curtain across back. One of the* DUENNAS *has brought in a basket of costumes and masks and they are putting them on.*)

DUCHESS. I can only stand in the background. Sancho would know my voice.

DUKE. Don't you think he will recognise the place?

DUCHESS. No, he will be too bewildered—and then the change of furniture. Duke, you must be the Chamberlain to receive him. He has never heard you say much. You are not a chatterbox like me.

CARASCO. What I would ask is to be the doctor in charge of his excellency's health.

DUCHESS. That will do very well. The footmen can read their cases of law, and the hall porters will be the mob outside.

CARASCO. I'll pay him off, giving him a diet that won't please him.

DUKE. But will he ever think this is really an island?

DUCHESS. Of course he will. He is at this moment going shut up in the cabin of the little pleasure boat on the river. They will put a hood over his head when he lands, telling him it is the custom with new governors on arrival, that all may see they will not judge by the sight of the eye, but by wisdom of the mind.

DUKE (*to* CARASCO). Those are good law cases you have made up to puzzle him. It will be a comical sight, the giving out of justice by Sancho Panza! Ha, ha, ha!

(*A trumpet is heard outside.*)

DUCHESSS. Here he is coming! Take your places.

(*They arrange themselves.* SANCHO *is led in, his hood is removed, he rubs his eyes.*)

SANCHO. That was a troublesome journey if it was not a long one. I am well pleased to be on dry land. I got a great tossing on the waves.

DUKE (*reads*). Your excellency is welcome to the State and Government of Barataria. We, the inhabitants, hope you will find happiness in this great office.

SANCHO. It is likely I will. It is not covetousness brought me to it, but a thought I have that it is good to command, if it be but a flock of sheep.

DUENNA. We feel assured that your excellency will be a wise and good ruler.

SANCHO. Well, it will go hard with me, but I will be such a governor that in spite of rogues I shall get to heaven. All bribes refuse, but insist on your dues. That will be my motto.

DUENNA. Here is your excellency's professor of medicine, who will attend to your excellency's health, and here is your excellency's chamberlain who will put on your excellency's robes! (CHAMBER-LAIN *does so*.)

SANCHO. You may dress me as you will and welcome. But whatever coat I wear, I will still be Sancho Panza.

DUENNA. I understand your excellency has been fully instructed as to justice and behaviour by the famous Knight Don Quixote.

SANCHO. I was that, and all the advice he gave me was good, as you would expect from one who was reared a gentleman, and is now made much of in a duke's palace. He wrote it out, too, but I chanced to lose it, likely in that tossing I got in the boat. Anyway, it has gone from me, and I remember no more of it than of last year's clouds, only that I was not to let my nails grow, and if I should have occasion to marry again not to choose a covetous wife, for whatever the judge's wife receives, the husband must account for at the day of judgment—and not to chew with both sides of my mouth. And that reminds me it is my dinner time, and I have a mind to eat something warm, for cold-treat has been my fare long enough in field and in forest.

CARASCO (*in foreign accent*). Certainly, your excellency. All is ready here.

(*Table with dishes is pushed before him.* CARASCO *ties a napkin under his chin. A dish is handed to him.*)

SANCHO. That looks good. (*Is about to help himself when it is snapped away from him.*)

CARASCO. Here is another dish, and a better one.

SANCHO. It has a savoury smell. (*As he puts fork in the dish it is snatched away.*)

SANCHO. Is this a conjuring show?

CARASCO. My lord governor, there must be no eating here but what is customary in other islands where there are governors.

SANCHO. A man can't live on air! Governors are made of flesh and blood.

CARASCO. I am responsible for your excellency's health as court physician. I ordered the first dish to be taken away because it was too moist—and that stewed beef as being too much spiced, thereby causing thirst. For he who drinks much destroys and consumes the radical moisture of which life consists. The health of the whole body is tempered in the forge of the stomach.

SANCHO. Then say out which of all the dishes on the table will do me most good, and will not throw my stomach off the hinges, for I am starving with hunger; and whatever you, Mr. Physician, may say, this starvation is more likely to shorten my life than to lengthen it.

CARASCO. Your worship is right. But I must forbid you that breast of veal because its dressing is too rich; we don't know what may have gone into it. But there can be no mistake in simple things, and what I would advise is a wafer biscuit or two thinly spread with marmalade. That is food that will help digestion, and sit light on the stomach. There are cases coming to trial, and to eat but little quickens the judgment.

(*Puts a small plate before him. All the rest is cleared away.*)

SANCHO (*throwing himself back in the chair, and looking at* CARASCO). What now is your name?

CARASCO. I am Don Pedro Rezio D'Agnero. I took my doctor's degree at the University of Ossuna.

SANCHO. Then, doctor, whatever you call yourself, get out of my sight this very minute or by my oath I'll take a cudgel and so use it that there will not be one of your profession left in the island! (*Gets up.*) Quit this or I will take this chair I am sitting on and fling it at your head! (CARASCO *goes back hurriedly. To* SERVANTS) Give me food, I say! Are you expecting to see me nourish myself taking up grapestones on the point of a fork? Do you want me to leave my bones here in this island? Give me food, or I'll give back the government. For an office that will not find a man in victuals is not worth two beans!

(*A loaf of bread is put before him and he seizes and devours it.*)

283

CHANCELLOR. There are cases waiting to be heard, your excellency—a tailor to lay his case before you.

SANCHO. A strange thing a man of business would not know such things should not have jurisdiction over the time that is spent in eating and drinking! What does the tailor want?

CHANCELLOR. He says, your excellency, a stingy man came to him with a piece of cloth, and asked if there was enough in it for the makings of a cap. He said there was, and the man thought to get more than the one out of him, and went on asking could he make two or three till he came to five, and the tailor let him have his way. And when they were made, there were five sure enough, but they would but go on his four fingers and his thumb. (*Holds up his hand with the five caps*). And now he refuses to pay for the making, seeing they are of no use to him.

SANCHO. I can give you that judgment while you'd snuff a candle. Let the miser lose the caps, and the tailor his work, and let the caps be confiscated and given to whoever they will fit.

CHANCELLOR. There is another case waiting.

SANCHO. Tell it out then.

CHANCELLOR. It is a very hard one. There is a certain river, and over the river there is a bridge, and at the head of the bridge a gallows. Now the law of that place is that whoever passes over the bridge must first take an oath where and on what business he is going. If he swears true they will let him pass, but if he tells a lie he must be hanged without any remission. It has happened that a certain man having taken the oath, swore by the oath he had taken, he was going to die on the gallows. But the judge says: "If we let this man pass through, he will have sworn a lie, and by the law he ought to die. But if we hang him he ought to go free, as he swore the truth that he was going to die on that way, and so by the same law he ought to go free." And so having heard of your excellency's high understanding, they have sent me to beseech your lordship to give your opinion on so intricate and doubtful a case.

SANCHO. That is plain enough. Let them let pass that part of the man that told the truth, and hang that part that told the lie.

CHANCELLOR. But then they would cut the man in two parts and he would die.

SANCHO. Then tell these gentlemen who sent you that since the reasons for condemning him and acquitting him are equal, they should let him pass free. For it is a precept given me by my master, Don Quixote, before I set out for this island, that when justice happens to be in the least doubt, I should incline and lean to the side of mercy. And God has brought it to my mind at this very moment where it comes in so pat.

CHANCELLOR. It does so. Lycurgus himself, who gave laws to the Macedonians, could not have given a better judgment. And let us have no more business to-day. And I will give orders that his Excellency the Governor shall dine now to his satisfaction.

SANCHO. That is good news. Let us have fair play. Let me eat my fill, and you may bring me cases and questions as thick as you please, and I'll despatch them while you'd snuff a candle.

(*A dish is being put before him when a horn blows.*)

1ST PAGE (*rushing in*). The enemy is coming! The enemies of the Governor of the Island! (*Goes off.*)

(*Noise and shouts outside.*)

2ND PAGE (*rushing in*). Arm, arm, your excellency! Take arms! A whole host of your enemies have landed. We are destroyed, unless you put them down and save us! (*Runs off.*)

(*Noise increases.*)

1ST PAGE (*returning*). Arm, arm yourself, or you will be killed, and the whole of us with you!

SANCHO. What have I to do with arming? I am not used to those hurly burlies!

2ND PAGE (*returning with arms, bag, etc.*). Come out, sir! Be our captain, and our leader!

CARASCO. It is your place to lead us as our governor!

1ST PAGE. Lead us on! Encourage us!

(*They tie a clumsy buckler on him; he cannot walk.*)

SANCHO. I cannot stir! I am hindered by these ropes!

1ST PAGE. Fie, sir! It is fear more than the ropes that hinders you. For shame, sir! Bestir yourself! It is late.

2ND PAGE. The enemy increases! The danger presses! Here is a helmet.

(*They put the bag over his head and tie it. They ill-use him, making game of him, and then drag him out. The DUCAL party take off their disguises.*)

DUKE. Ha, ha! It seems to me Sancho is the wisest judge since Solomon.

DUCHESS. Poor Sancho. It went to my heart not letting him enjoy his food. But we'll make up for it bye and bye! He shall have such a supper as never was seen.

DUKE. You had better do away with these things. The Don will be coming in.

(SERVANTS *move table, gather up costumes, dishes, etc., and go.*)

DUCHESS. Oh, you haven't heard yet of all the fun the girls had with him while we were settling out this island for Sancho. They had left a little lute in his room, and he found it by the window, and began to sing in his poor hoarse voice a love song to his Dulcinea.

DUKE. Ha, ha! I should have liked to hear that.

DUCHESS. It was just the usual thing. (*Sings*)

"Whether fortune smile or frown:
"Constancy's the lover's crown."

DUKE. I think indeed he never looked at any other woman.

DUCHESS. Perhaps that is why they played the trick on him. They let down a rope to the open window, and pushed in a sack full of cats——

DUKE. Why cats?

DUCHESS. Oh, just for fun—they had bells tied to their tails. I wish I had not missed it—the girls nearly died with laughter.

DUKE. I am afraid that was going rather too far.

DUCHESS. Oh, he will never bear malice. He will think it was all an enchantment. Hush! I see his housekeeper coming back——

HOUSEKEEPER (*coming in*). I ask pardon my noble lord and lady for pushing in on you. I have no one to draw to but yourselves.

DUCHESS. Oh, tell me what is the matter. Have you any complaint to make?

HOUSEKEEPER. It is not for myself I have any complaint to make, but for my master.

DUCHESS. I hope he has not sent you to complain?

HOUSEKEEPER. He has not. He spoke no word. He did but lay himself down on the bed with a deep sigh. You couldn't knock a smile out of him. There has gone from him his liveliness and his strength.

DUKE. What! Is he ill? He was quite well an hour ago.

HOUSEKEEPER. It is no illness, sir, sent upon him by God. But he was greatly tossed. There are some in this house that have done a great wrong to him. To treat him in the way they did is a disgrace to the world.

DUKE. I am sorry to hear that.

DUCHESS. I suppose it was that jest with the cats.

HOUSEKEEPER. A cat pent up in a room and frightened will turn to a tiger. And Sancho that should be there to guard him being gone as governor—God save the mark! Well, there's One above that rubs the thunder, if here they give him no fair play.

DUKE. Who are you speaking of?

HOUSEKEEPER. Some bold girls in your lordship's house.

DUCHESS. Oh, I am sorry if they went too far.

HOUSEKEEPER. I will tell you, ma'am, for you are not haughty like town ladies, but treat people more upon the level. I would say nothing if he met with cruelty upon the road in some of his en- counters and bangs. But in a big gentleman's house, that was no fitting thing to do.

DUKE (to DUCHESS). I am vexed about this. You should not have encouraged that trick.

DUCHESS (taking HOUSEKEEPER's hand). Say no more about it. I will see that these girls are punished and made repent.

HOUSEKEEPER. I am thankful to you, ma'am. You are a good plain humble lady. Let me be buried with such ladies as these!

(HOUSEKEEPER goes.)

DUENNA (coming in). Here is his excellency coming, Sancho Panza. He lost his senses for a while through a fall he got when they pushed him down the steps.

DUCHESS (clapping hands). He will think he got through the journey here during a trance! I long to hear his account of the mock attack on the island.

(SANCHO coming in bows to them gravely.)

DUCHESS. Welcome, welcome Governor Sancho! I am afraid you were given a rough end to your government by these rebels. We must manage things better for your next time. What can we do for you now?

SANCHO. All I ask of your grace is to be allowed to go back to my old way of life.

DUCHESS. Oh, no, we will make all pleasant for you here.

DUKE. You must try your hand at another government.

SANCHO. I was not born to be a governor, or to defend cities. I better understand how to plough and to dress vines than to give laws and judgments. I have had enough of mounting upon the towers of pride and ambition. Naked I came into the world, and naked I am. Without a penny I went into that government and without a penny I come out. I return to walk upon plain ground with a plain foot and to take the spade, take the scythe, and go into the field like a gentleman.

DUKE. I am afraid you have not been well treated, Sancho, but this will not happen again.

SANCHO. My respects to you my Lord Duke, but jests that hurt are no jests. These are not tricks to be played twice. I say no more though I could. All I will ask is a little barley for Dapple my ass, and a handful of bread and cheese for the road. (*Turns away.*)

DUCHESS. Oh, what will Don Quixote say to this!

CARASCO (*coming in gravely*). Your Grace, he asks leave to come in.

DUCHESS. Why, bring him in at once. (CARASCO *and* SANCHO *go out together.*)

DUKE. I am sorry about Sancho. That adventure turned out too heavy and too hard.

QUIXOTE (*coming in leaning on* CARASCO *and* SANCHO). I am come to ask on my own behalf to go on my way.

DUKE. I hope, sir, nothing has happened to offend you.

QUIXOTE. I was not born for this idle life, I would go out on the road again.

DUCHESS. Oh, you are not fit for it. You look weary. Your cheeks are pale.

QUIXOTE. I thank your grace, but I have committed a great fault, spending idle days for which I must give my account to God.

DUCHESS (*taking his hand*). We will do all we can to please you. There will be no more romping and teasing. It was never meant to annoy. I promise you comfort and ease.

QUIXOTE. Freedom is best. It is one of the best gifts heaven has bestowed upon men. The treasures that the earth encloses or the sea covers are not to be compared with it. Life may and ought to be risked for liberty as well as for honour. I have had a fine lodging; I have had banquets here. But the obligation of returning favours received are ties that obstruct the free agency of the mind. I will go back to my own poor place. (*He reels and catches at back of a chair.*)

DUCHESS. Oh, do not leave us in this way! I will do all that is possible for your healing and ease.

QUIXOTE (*to* SANCHO *faintly*). Lead me home—to my house—for I think I am not very well.

DUCHESS. Oh, stay! Forgive us all and forgive me! I never meant to hurt you. Stay and I will care you myself better than any other one could do! (*She takes hold of his hand.*)

QUIXOTE. I hear someone speaking as through a dream—Lead me home.

SANCHO. That's right, sir. You got your own scourge. Come leave this rambling among strange places and strangers.

DUCHESS. Oh, say some word of kindness—say that you forgive me! I was thoughtless—that was all—I will not be so foolish any more. Tell me you will not think harshly of me. Keep some kind thought of me—say some kind word!

QUIXOTE (*to* SANCHO). My strength is failing. I think I will not fight again.

DUCHESS. Just say one comfortable word!

QUIXOTE (*standing straight up and speaking with difficulty*). It is not fitting that my weakness should discredit the truth (*calls out*) —Dulcinea del Toboso is the most beautiful woman in the world!

Curtain.

Collaborations

THE POORHOUSE
BY
DOUGLAS HYDE AND LADY GREGORY

THE POORHOUSE

PERSONS
  COLUM.
  PAUDEEN.
  THE MATRON.
  THE DOORKEEPER.
  A COUNTRY WOMAN.

SCENE. *A Poorhouse Ward. Two beds with a little space between them. An old man in each bed of them. There are other beds at the side; they are not seen, but one hears now and again voices of the men that are in them.*

MATRON (*comes in and stoops over one of the beds*). Are you better to-day, Paudeen? Would you like anything?

PAUDEEN. I am better than I was yesterday, may good be with you.

MATRON. Is there anything you are wanting?

PAUDEEN. Not a ha'porth, I am thankful to you.

(*The MATRON goes to the other bed.*)

MATRON. And are you better, Colum?

COLUM. No loss at all on me, ma'am, thank you, but the cough that is sticking to me always, and the sort of itching on my heart. It seems to me that if it could be pulled out and scoured, and put back again, I would have some ease.

MATRON. Ah, Colum, I am afraid there is no doctor in Dublin itself could do that feat for you. Is there anything you are wanting?

COLUM. There is not, but a vessel of water or of milk to be beside me; the thirst is attacking me always. I cannot satisfy it.

MATRON. Did the doctor give you leave to have milk?

COLUM. He did not say against it.

DOORKEEPER (*coming in, to* MATRON). There is a woman below asking to say a couple of words to you. She came to take some old man with her out of this house, if she got leave from you.

MATRON. That'll do. I will come down with you. And, Colum,

I will be back at the end of a half hour, and I will put a vessel of milk at the head of your bed.

PAUDEEN. Don't give the whole of the milk to that man; give a share of it to me.

MATRON. I will, when I come back.

(*She and the* DOORKEEPER *go out.*)

COLUM. Aurah, aren't you the devil to be asking milk of the mistress and you not wanting it?

PAUDEEN. And why would I not be wanting it the same as yourself?

COLUM. There is no thirst on you no more than on the post of my bed, but envying me and jealous of me you are, the way you always were for threescore years, and as you will be for ever.

PAUDEEN (*raising his voice*). Envying you and jealous of you. Ha! ha! ha! Aurah, isn't it a pretty old schemer I'd be jealous of! An old corpse of speckled shins that is in you.

A VOICE (*on* PAUDEEN'S *side of the ward*). Oh murder! There is the pair of them beginning again.

ANOTHER VOICE. Shut your mouth, and we'll have the sport.

COLUM. Old corpse of speckled shins does he say? Aurah! O Lord, if I could rise out of this bed, it is short till he would know what sort of a corpse I am.

A VOICE. Stick to him, Colum.

ANOTHER VOICE. Don't leave it with Colum, Paudeen.

PAUDEEN (*rising on his elbow*). I will not leave it, and it is not right to leave it, when he knows, in the middle of his heart, there is no old *sprealaire* in Ireland could be put beside him for lying, for knavery, for softheadedness, and for brutishness.

COLUM (*rising on his elbow*). *Maiseadh,* it's I who knows who is quarrelsome and lying from nature, that had not but knavery in his heart and lies in his mouth since he was put out of the cradle. The poor widow that had nothing of the store and cost of the world but the three ducks only, who stole them from her? Answer me that! I saw him doing it. Now!

PAUDEEN. If I did that trick itself and I a boy, it wasn't to the Souper school I used to be going to get my share of learning like yourself. Now!

COLUM. To the Souper school! O, listen to that! The most respectable man in Ireland it was that taught me my share of learning. He did not teach me to go backbiting other people and telling lies about them, to get the place for myself, the way you did about Seumas O'Connor.

PAUDEEN. And who burned Seaghan Ban's barn? Answer me that.

A VOICE. That's it, Paudeen.

ANOTHER VOICE. Now, Colum, give it to him.

COLUM. And if I set fire to Seaghan's barn, it wasn't by myself I was, but I was along with the honestest and the most respectable people in the parish, that would do nothing but the thing would be honest and right. A company that you were never in the like of, for you would not be let into it!

A VOICE. Long life to you, Colum.

ANOTHER VOICE. Now, Paudeen, give him a prick.

PAUDEEN. It's true for you. I never practised to be among the thieves and the destroyers and the rapparees of the world like yourself. I had no acquaintance with them. It's not burning barns or robbing people I used to be, but giving heed to my own work.

COLUM. I know well what your own work was. Who was it put a good appearance on the two bullocks that had the disease on them, and sold them, and they died on the morrow? You went bail for them that they were sound, and you denied it after.

PAUDEEN. Who drove Seumas Ruadh's ass before him when he found it on the road, and said that it was his own?

COLUM. And who hung his old shirt out of the window the time the King came? Seeking to be made a magistrate he was! (*Great laughter from the beds on each side.*) And you without the use of your feet.

PAUDEEN. I had once the use of my feet and it's a thing you never had. Didn't Nora O'Brien say of your dancing long ago it was a better dance you'd make to leave your legs at home, and to be dancing on your head?

COLUM. But what did Nora say when she saw you scratching and scrapin' yourself at the Mass? She said there wasn't a girl in the seven parishes that you wouldn't scare.

PAUDEE. How well I didn't scare Red Sarah when you thought you had her yourself.

COLUM. And the creature! It's little of the pleasure of the world she had after that.

PAUDEEN (*sitting up*). I never lay for three hours of the clock in the middle of the street a fair day, and I red drunk, till the peelers brought me with them to the barracks.

COLUM (*sitting up*). That's true for you. It was never drunkenness or anything half as respectable brought you to the barracks, but betraying and spying and telling lies on the neighbours.

PAUDEEN (*gnashing his teeth at him*). It's finely I'd leather your bones now if I could rise up, but remember, you vagabone, the fine welting I gave you thirty years ago at the fair of Dunmore, that left your stump of a nose crushed and broken from that out.

COLUM. Isn't it fine memory entirely you have! but don't forget the day I threw you down from the top of the bridge in the big river. You were drowned that time surely, but that it was your hanging you were born for.

PAUDEEN. You be choked! (*Takes up his pillow and throws it at the other man.*)

COLUM. The binding of death on you, you old *sprealaire.* (*He throws his own pillow.*)

A VOICE. That's it now! Hit him, Paudeen!

ANOTHER VOICE. Give it to him, Colum.

ANOTHER VOICE. That pair are fighting one another since the day they were born, like two whelps, and they're going at one another's throats yet, and they two lame old dogs.

PAUDEEN (*throwing his pipe at the other man that it breaks*). Och, if I had but the use of my two feet, you'd catch it from me!

COLUM (*throwing his prayerbook at* PAUDEEN). O Lord! I not to be able to rise.

PAUDEEN (*throwing his tin mug*). If I was able to knock that crooked eye out of you altogether, it would be better to me than a sight of heaven.

COLUM (*throwing his own can*). It failed you as it always failed you. Here's at you with the can.

A VOICE. The Pooka'll take you.

ANOTHER VOICE. Quiet, quiet!

ANOTHER VOICE. Quit your noise! The Mistress is coming.

MANY VOICES. Whist, she's coming.

PAUDEEN (*settling* COLUM'S *pillow hastily under his own head and lying down*). My grief, the ridge of the whole world not to be between myself and yourself, you rogue of ill luck!

COLUM (*doing the same thing*). It is a hard case you to be beside me here through the length of two months now; it would be better to me the Old Boy himself to be in your bed than you.

(*The* MATRON *comes in again and a woman from the country with her, comely and comfortably dressed.*)

THE MATRON. Colum, here is your sister.

WOMAN (*stooping down and kissing* COLUM). Aurah, Colum, achree! Isn't it a poor place that I see you? Aurah, what way are you, or are you living at all?

COLUM. Well, Kate, you never asked after me this five years, and what is on you now to be coming to me?

WOMAN. Didn't you hear, Colum? My poor man died, and I am alone with myself now, with none but me in it. I was that lonely I could not stand it. I said to myself that I would come seeking you, and that I would bring you out of this place.

COLUM. Oh! the blessing of God on you, Kate!

WOMAN. You will be better with me than you are here.

COLUM. And what way of living have you now, Kate? are you middling well off?

WOMAN. I have a good house, and I have three lambs to send to the fair of Dunmore after to-morrow.

COLUM. And you will bring me with you to-day?

WOMAN. It is what I was saying to myself, it would take a share of the loneliness from me you to be with me. You could be sitting in the corner, and minding the pot, and the fire; and throwing a little grain of meal to the chickens while I would be out in the fields.

COLUM. Oh! the blessing of God on you, Kate.

WOMAN. There is a neighbour of my own without, and a cart with him, and he promised me to bring you home with him as far as my house, if you come now. I got leave from the Mistress to bring you with me.

COLUM. It's I that will come. May God reward you, Kate, astore!

PAUDEEN (*sits up and begins to sigh and to groan*). Ochone! ochone! Is it going away from me you are now, Colum, and leaving me here after you! I that was near you ever since you were born. You are leaving me among strangers now. Ochone! ochone!

(*He begins to cry.*)

COLUM. Kate avourneen——

WOMAN. You will not.

COLUM. I won't anger you if I ask a little thing of you?

WOMAN. You will not.

COLUM. *Maiseadh*, God bless you, and bring the two of us with you.

WOMAN. Is it out of your senses you are, Colum? Why would I bring that man with me?

COLUM. Because it's I am asking you.

WOMAN. Indeed, I will not, sorra foot. Let him stop in the place where he is, and it's good enough for him.

COLUM. Kate.

WOMAN. What is it now?

COLUM. It is what I am considering, this place is not too bad entirely, not as bad you know as they say.

WOMAN. Maybe you'd sooner be in it than in my house.

COLUM. That's not so, that's not so; but it is what I was thinking to myself, I am not certain, certain as you might say, how . . .

(*He begins stammering.*)

WOMAN. Speak out.

COLUM. I wasn't certain you know, what way I would be with you. . . .

WOMAN. O, if you would sooner be here. . . .

COLUM. That's not it, that's not it; but, Kate, will you bring this man along with me?

WOMAN. I see now that you are out of your senses altogether.

COLUM. That's not so, Kate, but . . .

WOMAN. Oh! if you would sooner be here, it's the same to me. If it's lonesome I am, I won't be long by myself. If I wanted a husband, I wouldn't have far to go to get him, and the comfortable way of living I have, and my three lambs going to the fair after to-morrow.

COLUM. O Kate, astore, bring the both of us with you.

WOMAN. No fear of me. You have your choice now. Come with me, or stop where you are.

COLUM. Kate, I am thinking I will stop.

WOMAN (*angrily turning her back to him*). That will do, I gave you your own choice. I am going.

A THIN, WEAK, BROKEN LITTLE VOICE (*from an old man in another bed*). Oh, ma'am, look ma'am. . . .

WOMAN (*half turning*). What is that?

THE VOICE. If you are lonesome, it is I myself would make the kind, fitting husband to you.

WOMAN. P'suit.

THE VOICE. I am ready to go with you; take me, and I will make the kind husband, day and night to you. (*Laughter from the other beds.*)

WOMAN (*turning to* COLUM). You will not come with me, so?

COLUM. I will stop, Kate; I will stop, unless you will bring this other man with you.

WOMAN. *Maiseadh*, that there may be no luck to you. Good-bye to you. (*She goes away.*)

THE SAME VOICE. It is I that would have made the good, kind husband to her. (*Laughter.*)

COLUM. She is gone.

A VOICE. Why didn't you go with her?

COLUM. That old vagabone would be lonesome without some person to be fighting him.

PAUDEEN. You lie.

COLUM. He must always be quarrelling with some person. He would be lonesome without me to go against him.

PAUDEEN. You are beginning on your share of lies again.

COLUM. That is no lie, you old glugger, you.

PAUDEEN. Old glugger! O, wait a while!

(*He takes his pillow and threatens the other man.*)

COLUM. You ugly *Rogaire!*

(*He takes up his own pillow.*)

VOICES. Oh, God save us! Look at them at the old work again!

(*They threaten one another with their pillows.*)

Curtain.

THE UNICORN FROM THE STARS
BY
W. B. YEATS AND LADY GREGORY

THE UNICORN FROM THE STARS

PERSONS
FATHER JOHN
THOMAS HEARNE. *A coachbuilder*
ANDREW HEARNE. *His brother*
MARTIN HEARNE. *His nephew*
JOHNNY BOCACH ⎫
PAUDEEN   ⎪
BIDDY LALLY   ⎬ *Beggars*
NANNY   ⎭

Period: early nineteenth century

ACT I

SCENE: *Interior of a coachbuilder's workshop. Parts of a gilded coach, among them an ornament representing a lion and unicorn. THOMAS working at a wheel. FATHER JOHN coming from door of inner room.*

FATHER JOHN. I have prayed over Martin. I have prayed a long time, but there is no move in him yet.

THOMAS. You are giving yourself too much trouble, Father. It's as good for you to leave him alone till the doctor's bottle will come. If there is any cure at all for what is on him, it is likely the doctor will have it.

FATHER JOHN. I think it is not doctor's medicine will help him in this case.

THOMAS. It will, it will. The doctor has his business learned well. If Andrew had gone to him the time I bade him and had not turned again to bring yourself to the house, it is likely Martin would be walking at this time. I am loth to trouble you, Father, when the business is not of your own sort. Any doctor at all should be able and well able to cure the falling sickness.

FATHER JOHN. It is not any common sickness that is on him now.

THOMAS. I thought at the first it was gone to sleep he was. But when shaking him and roaring at him failed to rouse him, I knew

305

well it was the falling sickness. Believe me, the doctor will reach it with his drugs.

FATHER JOHN. Nothing but prayer can reach a soul that is so far beyond the world as his soul is at this moment.

THOMAS. You are not saying that the life is gone out of him!

FATHER JOHN. No, no, his life is in no danger. But where he himself, the spirit, the soul, is gone, I cannot say. It has gone beyond our imaginings. He is fallen into a trance.

THOMAS. He used to be queer as a child, going asleep in the fields, and coming back with talk of white horses he saw, and bright people like angels or whatever they were. But I mended that. I taught him to recognise stones beyond angels with a few strokes of a rod. I would never give in to visions or to trances.

FATHER JOHN. We who hold the Faith have no right to speak against trance or vision. Saint Elizabeth had them, Saint Benedict, Saint Anthony, Saint Columcille. Saint Catherine of Siena often lay a long time as if dead.

THOMAS. That might be so in the olden time, but those things are gone out of the world now. Those that do their work fair and honest have no occasion to let the mind go rambling. What would send my nephew, Martin Hearne, into a trance, supposing trances to be in it, and he rubbing the gold on the lion and unicorn that he had taken in hand to make a good job of for the top of the coach?

FATHER JOHN (*taking up ornament*). It is likely it was that sent him off. The flashing of light upon it would be enough to throw one that had a disposition to it into a trance. There was a very saintly man, though he was not of our Church, he wrote a great book called *Mysterium Magnum*, was seven days in a trance. Truth, or whatever truth he found, fell upon him like a bursting shower, and he a poor tradesman at his work. It was a ray of sunlight on a pewter vessel that was the beginning of all. (*Goes to the door and looks in.*) There is no stir in him yet. It is either the best thing or the worst thing can happen to any one, that is happening to him now.

THOMAS. And what in the living world can happen to a man that is asleep on his bed?

FATHER JOHN. There are some would answer you that it is to those who are awake that nothing happens, and it is they that know nothing. He is gone where all have gone for supreme truth.

THOMAS (*sitting down again and taking up tools*). Well, maybe so. But work must go on and coachbuilding must go on, and they

306

will not go on the time there is too much attention given to dreams. A dream is a sort of a shadow, no profit in it to any one at all. A coach, now, is a real thing and a thing that will last for generations and be made use of to the last, and maybe turn to be a hen-roost at its latter end.

FATHER JOHN. I think Andrew told me it was a dream of Martin's that led to the making of that coach.

THOMAS. Well, I believe he saw gold in some dream, and it led him to want to make some golden thing, and coaches being the handiest, nothing would do him till he put the most of his fortune into the making of this golden coach. It turned out better than I thought, for some of the lawyers came looking at it at Assize time, and through them it was heard of at Dublin Castle . . . and who now has it ordered but the Lord Lieutenant! (FATHER JOHN *nods*.) Ready it must be and sent off it must be by the end of the month. It is likely King George will be visiting Dublin, and it is he himself will be sitting in it yet.

FATHER JOHN. Martin has been working hard at it, I know.

THOMAS. You never saw a man work the way he did, day and night, near ever since the time six months ago he first came home from France.

FATHER JOHN. I never thought he would be so good at a trade. I thought his mind was only set on books.

THOMAS. He should be thankful to myself for that. Any person I will take in hand, I make a clean job of them the same as I would make of any other thing in my yard—coach, half-coach, hackney-coach, ass-car, common-car, post-chaise, calash, chariot on two wheels, on four wheels. Each one has the shape Thomas Hearne put on it, and it in his hands; and what I can do with wood and iron, why would I not be able to do it with flesh and blood, and it in a way my own?

FATHER JOHN. Indeed, I know you did your best for Martin.

THOMAS. Every best. Checked him, taught him the trade, sent him to the monastery in France for to learn the language and to see the wide world; but who should know that if you did not know it, Father John, and I doing it according to your own advice?

FATHER JOHN. I thought his nature needed spiritual guidance and teaching, the best that could be found.

THOMAS. I thought myself it was best for him to be away for a while. There are too many wild lads about this place. He to have stopped here, he might have taken some fancies, and got into some trouble, going against the Government maybe the same as Johnny

Gibbons that is at this time an outlaw, having a price upon his head.

FATHER JOHN. That is so. That imagination of his might have taken fire here at home. It was better putting him with the Brothers, to turn it to imaginings of Heaven.

THOMAS. Well, I will soon have a good hardy tradesman made of him now that will live quiet and rear a family, and be maybe appointed coachbuilder to the Royal Family at the last.

FATHER JOHN (*at window*). I see your brother Andrew coming back, from the doctor; he is stopping to talk with a troop of beggars that are sitting by the side of the road.

THOMAS. There, now, is another that I have shaped. Andrew used to be a bit wild in his talk and in his ways, wanting to go rambling, not content to settle in the place where he was reared. But I kept a guard over him; I watched the time poverty gave him a nip, and then I settled him into the business. He never was so good a worker as Martin, he is too fond of wasting his time talking vanities. But he is middling handy, and he is always steady and civil to customers. I have no complaint worth while to be making this last twenty years against Andrew.

(ANDREW *comes in.*)

ANDREW. Beggars there outside going the road to the Kinvara Fair. They were saying there is news that Johnny Gibbons is coming back from France on the quiet; the King's soldiers are watching the ports for him.

THOMAS. Let you keep now, Andrew, to the business you have in hand. Will the doctor be coming himself or did he send a bottle that will cure Martin?

ANDREW. The doctor can't come, for he's down with the lumbago in the back. He questioned me as to what ailed Martin, and he got a book to go looking for a cure, and he began telling me things out of it, but I said I could not be carrying things of that sort in my head. He gave me the book then, and he has marks put in it for the places where the cures are. . . . Wait now. . . . (*Reads.*) "Compound medicines are usually taken inwardly, or outwardly applied; inwardly taken, they should be either liquid or solid; outwardly, they should be fomentations or sponges wet in some decoctions."

THOMAS. He had a right to have written it out himself upon a paper. Where is the use of all that?

ANDREW. I think I moved the mark maybe. . . . Here, now, is the part he was reading to me himself. . . . "The remedies for diseases belonging to the skins next the brain, headache, vertigo, cramp, convulsions, palsy, incubus, apoplexy, falling sickness."

THOMAS. It is what I bid you to tell him, that it was the falling sickness.

ANDREW (*dropping book*). O, my dear, look at all the marks gone out of it! Wait, now, I partly remember what he said . . . a blister he spoke of . . . or to be smelling hartshorn . . . or the sneezing powder . . . or if all fails, to try letting the blood.

FATHER JOHN. All this has nothing to do with the real case. It is all waste of time.

ANDREW. That is what I was thinking myself, Father. Sure it was I was the first to call out to you when I saw you coming down from the hillside, and to bring you in to see what could you do. I would have more trust in your means than in any doctor's learning. And in case you might fail to cure him, I have a cure myself I heard from my grandmother—God rest her soul! —and she told me she never knew it to fail. A person to have the falling sickness, to cut the top of his nails and a small share of the hair of his head, and to put it down on the floor, and to take a harrypin and drive it down with that into the floor and to leave it there. "That is the cure will never fail", she said, "to rise up any person at all having the falling sickness."

FATHER JOHN (*hand on ear*). I will go back to the hillside, I will go back to the hillside; but no, no, I must do what I can. I will go again, I will wrestle, I will strive my best to call him back with prayer. (*Goes in and shuts door.*)

ANDREW. It is queer Father John is sometimes, and very queer. There are times when you would say that he believes in nothing at all.

THOMAS. If you wanted a priest, why did you not get our own parish priest that is a sensible man, and a man that you would know what his thoughts are? You know well the Bishop should have something against Father John to have left him through the years in that poor mountainy place, minding the few unfortunate people that were left out of the last famine. A man of his learning to be going in rags the way he is, there must be some good cause for that.

ANDREW. I had all that in mind and I bringing him. But I thought he would have done more for Martin than what he is doing. To read a Mass over him I thought he would, and to be convulsed in the reading it, and some strange thing to have gone out with a great noise through the doorway.

THOMAS. It would give no good name to the place such a thing

309

to be happening in it. It is well enough for labouring-men and for half-acre men. It would be no credit at all such a thing to be heard of in this house, that is for coachbuilding the capital of the county.

ANDREW. If it is from the Devil this sickness comes, it would be best to put it out whatever way it would be put out. But there might no bad thing be on the lad at all. It is likely he was with wild companions abroad, and that knocking about might have shaken his health. I was that way myself one time.

THOMAS. Father John said that it was some sort of a vision or a trance, but I would give no heed to what he would say. It is his trade to see more than other people would see, the same as I myself might be seeing a split in a leather car-hood that no other person would find out at all.

ANDREW. If it is the falling sickness is on him, I have no objection to that—a plain straight sickness that was cast as a punishment on the unbelieving Jews. It is a thing that might attack one of a family, and one of another family, and not to come upon their kindred at all. A person to have it, all you have to do is not to go between him and the wind, or fire, or water. But I am in dread trance is a thing might run through the house the same as the cholera morbus.

THOMAS. In my belief there is no such thing as a trance. Letting on people do be to make the world wonder the time they think well to rise up. To keep them to their work is best, and not to pay much attention to them at all.

ANDREW. I would not like trances to be coming on myself. I leave it in my will if I die without cause, a holly-stake to be run through my heart the way I will lie easy after burial, and not turn my face downwards in my coffin. I tell you I leave it on you in my will.

THOMAS. Leave thinking of your own comforts, Andrew, and give your mind to the business. Did the smith put the irons yet on to the shafts of this coach?

ANDREW. I will go see did he.

THOMAS. Do so, and see did he make a good job of it. Let the shafts be sound and solid if they are to be studded with gold.

ANDREW. They are, and the steps along with them—glass sides for the people to be looking in at the grandeur of the satin within— the lion and the unicorn crowning all. It was a great thought Martin had the time he thought of making this coach!

THOMAS. It is best for me to go see the smith myself and leave it to no other one. You can be attending to that ass-car out in the yard wants a new tyre on the wheel—out in the rear of the yard it is. (*They go to door.*) To pay attention to every small thing, and to fill up every minute of time shaping whatever you have to do, that is the way to build up a business. (*They go out.*)

FATHER JOHN (*bringing in* MARTIN). They are gone out now—the air is fresher here in the workshop—you can sit here for a while. You are now fully awake, you have been in some sort of a trance or a sleep.

MARTIN. Who was it that pulled at me? Who brought me back?

FATHER JOHN. It is I, Father John, did it. I prayed a long time over you and brought you back.

MARTIN. You, Father John, to be so unkind! O leave me, leave me alone!

FATHER JOHN. You are in your dream still.

MARTIN. It was no dream, it was real. Do you not smell the broken fruit—the grapes? The room is full of the smell.

FATHER JOHN. Tell me what you have seen, where you have been.

MARTIN. There were horses—white horses rushing by, with white shining riders—there was a horse without a rider, and some one caught me up and put me upon him and we rode away, with the wind, like the wind—

FATHER JOHN. That is a common imagining. I know many poor persons have seen that.

MARTIN. We went on, on, on. We came to a sweet-smelling garden with a gate to it, and there were wheatfields in full ear around, and there were vineyards like I saw in France, and the grapes in bunches. I thought it to be one of the townlands of Heaven. Then I saw the horses we were on had changed to unicorns, and they began trampling the grapes and breaking them. I tried to stop them, but I could not.

FATHER JOHN. That is strange, that is strange. What is it that brings to mind? I heard it in some place, *monoceros de astris*, the unicorn from the stars.

MARTIN. They tore down the wheat and trampled it on stones, and then they tore down what were left of the grapes and crushed and bruised and trampled them. I smelt the wine, it was flowing on every side—then everything grew vague. I cannot remember clearly, everything was silent; the trampling now stopped, we were all waiting for some command. O! was it given? I was trying to hear it; there was some one dragging, dragging me away from that. I am sure there was a command given, and there was a great burst of laughter. What was it? What was the command? Everything seemed to tremble round me.

FATHER JOHN. Did you awake then?

MARTIN. I do not think I did, it all changed—it was terrible, wonderful! I saw the unicorns trampling, trampling, but not in the wine-troughs. O, I forget! Why did you waken me?

FATHER JOHN. I did not touch you. Who knows what hands pulled you away? I prayed, that was all I did. I prayed very hard that you might awake. If I had not, you might have died. I wonder what it all meant? The unicorns—what did the French monk tell me?—strength they meant, virginal strength, a rushing, lasting, tireless strength.

MARTIN. They were strong. O, they made a great noise with their trampling.

FATHER JOHN. And the grapes, what did they means? It puts me in mind of the psalm, *Et calix meus inebrians quam praeclarus est.* It was a strange vision, a very strange vision, a very strange vision.

MARTIN. How can I get back to that place?

FATHER JOHN. You must not go back, you must not think of doing that. That life of vision, of contemplation, is a terrible life, for it has far more temptation in it than the common life. Perhaps it would have been best for you to stay under rules in the monastery.

MARTIN. I could not see anything so clearly there. It is back here in my own place the visions come, in the place where shining people used to laugh around me, and I a little lad in a bib.

FATHER JOHN. You cannot know but it was from the Prince of this world the vision came. How can one ever know unless one follows the discipline of the Church? Some spiritual director, some wise learned man, that is what you want. I do not know enough. What am I but a poor banished priest, with my learning forgotten, my books never handled and spotted with the damp!

MARTIN. I will go out into the fields where you cannot come to me to awake me. I will see that townland again; I will hear that command. I cannot wait, I must know what happened, I must bring that command to mind again.

FATHER JOHN. (*putting himself between* MARTIN *and the door*). You must have patience as the Saints had it. You are taking your own way. If there is a command from God for you, you must wait His good time to receive it.

MARTIN. Must I live here forty years, fifty years . . . to grow as old as my uncles, seeing nothing but common things, doing work . . . some foolish work?

FATHER JOHN. Here they are coming; it is time for me to go. I must think and I must pray. My mind is troubled about you (*To* THOMAS *as he and* ANDREW *come in.*) Here he is; be very kind to him for he has still the weakness of a little child. (*Goes out.*)

THOMAS. Are you well of the fit, lad?

MARTIN. It was no fit. I was away—for a while—no, you will not believe me if I tell you.

ANDREW. I would believe it, Martin. I used to have very long sleeps myself and very queer dreams.

THOMAS. You had, till I cured you, taking you in hand and binding you to the hours of the clock. The cure that will cure yourself, Martin, and will waken you, is to put the whole of your mind on to your golden coach; to take it in hand and to finish it out of face.

MARTIN. Not just now. I want to think—to try and remember what I saw, something that I heard, that I was told to do.

THOMAS. No, but put it out of your mind. There is no man doing business that can keep two things in his head. A Sunday or a holy-day, now, you might go see a good hurling or a thing of the kind, but to be spreading out your mind on anything outside of the workship on common days, all coachbuilding would come to an end.

MARTIN. I don't think it is building I want to do. I don't think that is what was in the command.

THOMAS. It is too late to be saying that, the time you have put the most of your fortune in the business. Set yourself now to finish your job, and when it is ended maybe I won't begrudge you going with the coach as far as Dublin.

ANDREW. That is it, that will satisfy him. I had a great desire myself, and I young, to go travelling the roads as far as Dublin. The roads are the great things, they never come to an end. They are the same as the serpent having his tail swallowed in his own mouth.

MARTIN. It was not wandering I was called to. What was it? What was it?

THOMAS. What you are called to, and what every one having no great estate is called to, is to work. Sure the world itself could not go on without work.

MARTIN. I wonder if that is the great thing, to make the world go on? No, I don't think that is the great thing—what does the Munster poet call it?—"this crowded slippery coach-loving world". I don't think I was told to work for that.

ANDREW. I often thought that myself. It is a pity the stock of the Hearnes to be asked to do any work at all.

THOMAS. Rouse yourself, Martin, and don't be talking the way a fool talks. You started making that golden coach, and you were set upon it, and you had me tormented about it. You have yourself wore out working at it, and planning it, and thinking of it, and at the end of the race, when you have the winning-post in sight, and the horses hired for to bring it to Dublin Castle, you go falling into sleeps and blathering about dreams, and we run to a great danger of letting the profit and the sale go by. Sit down on the bench now, and lay your hands to the work.

MARTIN (*sitting down*). I will try. I wonder why I ever wanted to make it; it was no good dream set me doing that. (*He takes up wheel.*) What is there in a wooden wheel to take pleasure in it? Gilding it outside makes it no different.

THOMAS. That is right, now. You had some good plan for making the axle run smooth.

MARTIN (*letting wheel fall and putting his hands to his head*). It is no use. (*Angrily.*) Why did you send the priest to awake me? My soul is my own and my mind is my own. I will send them to where I like. You have no authority over my thoughts.

THOMAS. That is no way to be speaking to me. I am head of this business. Nephew or no nephew, I will have no one come cold or unwilling to the work.

MARTIN. I had better go; I am of no use to you. I am going—I must be alone—I will forget if I am not alone. Give me what is left of my money and I will go out of this.

THOMAS (*opening a press and taking out a bag and throwing it to him*). There is what is left of your money! The rest of it you have spent on the coach. If you want to go, go, and I will not have to be annoyed with you from this out.

ANDREW. Come now with me, Thomas. The boy is foolish, but it will soon pass over. He has not my sense to be giving attention to what you will say. Come along now, leave him for a while; leave him to me, I say, it is I will get inside his mind.

(*He leads* THOMAS *out.* MARTIN *bangs door angrily after them and sits down, taking up lion and unicorn.*)

MARTIN. I think it was some shining thing I saw. What was it?

ANDREW (*opening door and putting in his head*). Listen to me, Martin.

MARTIN. Go away, no more talking; leave me alone.

ANDREW. O, but wait. I understand you. Thomas doesn't understand your thoughts, but I understand them. Wasn't I telling you I was just like you once?

MARTIN. Like me? Did you ever see the other things, the things beyond?

ANDREW. I did. It is not the four walls of the house keep me content. Thomas doesn't know. O no, he doesn't know.

MARTIN. No, he has no vision.

ANDREW. He has not, nor any sort of a heart for a frolic.

MARTIN. He has never heard the laughter and the music beyond.

ANDREW. He has not, nor the music of my own little flute. I have it hidden in the thatch outside.

MARTIN. Does the body slip from you as it does from me? They have not shut your window into eternity?

ANDREW. Thomas never shut a window I could not get through. I knew you were one of my own sort. When I am sluggish in the morning. Thomas says, "Poor Andrew is getting old". That is all he knows. The way to keep young is to do the things youngsters do. Twenty years I have been slipping away, and he never found me out yet!

MARTIN. That is what they call ecstasy, but there is no word that can tell out very plain what it means. That freeing of the mind from its thoughts; when we put those wonders into words, those words seem as little like them as blackberries are like the moon and sun.

ANDREW. I found that myself the time they knew me to be wild, and used to be asking me to say what pleasure did I find in cards, and women, and drink.

MARTIN. You might help me to remember that vision I had this morning, to understand it. The memory of it has slipped from me. Wait, it is coming back, little by little. I know that I saw the unicorns trampling, and then a figure, a many-changing figure, holding some bright thing. I knew something was going to happen or to be said, something that would make my whole life strong and beautiful like the rushing of the unicorns, and then, and then—

JOHNNY BOCACH'S VOICE (*at window*). A poor person I am, without food, without a way, without portion, without costs, without a person or a stranger, without means, without hope, without health, without warmth—

ANDREW (*looking towards window*). It is that troop of beggars. Bringing their tricks and their thieveries they are to the Kinvara Fair.

315

MARTIN (*impatiently*). There is no quiet—come to the other room. I am trying to remember.

(*They go to door of inner room, but* ANDREW *stops him.*)

ANDREW. They are a bad-looking fleet. I have a mind to drive them away, giving them a charity.

MARTIN. Drive them away or come away from their voices.

ANOTHER VOICE. I put under the power of my prayer
　　　　　　All that will give me help.
　　　　　　Rafael keep him Wednesday,
　　　　　　Sachiel feed him Thursday,
　　　　　　Hamiel provide him Friday,
　　　　　　Cassiel increase him Saturday.

Sure giving to us is giving to the Lord and laying up a store in the treasury of Heaven.

ANDREW. Whisht! He is entering by the window! (JOHNNY *climbs up.*)

JOHNNY. That I may never sin, but the place is empty.

PAUDEEN (*outside*). Go in and see what can you make a grab at.

JOHNNY (*getting in*). That every blessing I gave may be turned to a curse on them that left the place so bare! (*He turns things over.*) I might chance something in this chest if it was open.

(ANDREW *begins creeping towards him.*)

NANNY (*outside*). Hurry on, now, you limping crabfish, you! We can't be stopping here while you'll boil stirabout!

JOHNNY (*seizing bag of money and holding it up high in both hands*). Look at this, now, look!

(ANDREW *comes behind, seizes his arm.*)

JOHNNY (*letting bag fall with a crash*). Destruction on us all!

MARTIN (*running forward seizes him. Heads at the window disappear*). That is it! O, I remember. That is what happened. That is the command. Who was it sent you here with that command?

JOHNNY. It was misery sent me in, and starvation and the hard ways of the world.

NANNY (*outside*). It was that, my poor child, and my one son only. Show mercy to him now and he after leaving gaol this morning.

MARTIN (*to* ANDREW). I was trying to remember it—when he spoke that word it all came back to me. I saw a bright many-changing figure; it was holding up a shining vessel (*holds up arms*); then the vessel fell and was broken with a great crash; then I saw the unicorns trampling it. They were breaking the world to pieces—

when I saw the cracks coming I shouted for joy! And I heard the command, 'Destroy, destroy, destruction is the life-giver! destroy!'

ANDREW. What will we do with him? He was thinking to rob you of your gold.

MARTIN. How could I forget it or mistake it? It has all come upon me now; the reasons of it all, like a flood, like a flooded river.

JOHNNY (*weeping*). It was the hunger brought me in and the drouth.

MARTIN. Were you given any other message? Did you see the unicorns?

JOHNNY. I saw nothing and heard nothing; near dead I am with the fright I got and with the hardship of the gaol.

MARTIN. To destroy, to overthrow all that comes between us and God, between us and that shining country. To break the wall, Andrew, to break the thing—whatever it is that comes between; but where to begin—?

ANDREW. What is it you are talking about?

MARTIN. It may be that this man is the beginning. He has been sent—the poor, they have nothing, and so they can see Heaven as we cannot. He and his comrades will understand me. But how tc give all men high hearts that they may all understand?

JOHNNY. It's the juice of the grey barley will do that.

ANDREW. To rise everybody's heart, is it? Is it that was your meaning all the time? If you will take the blame of it all, I'll do what you want. Give me the bag of money then. (*He takes it up.*) O, I've a heart like your own. I'll lift the world, too. The people will be running from all parts. O, it will be a great day in this district.

JOHNNY. Will I go with you?

MARTIN. No, you must stay here; we have things to do and to plan.

JOHNNY. Destroyed we all are with the hunger and the drouth.

MARTIN. Go, then, get food and drink, whatever is wanted to give you strength and courage. Gather your people together here, bring them all in. We have a great thing to do, I have to begin—I want to tell it to the whole world. Bring them in, bring them in, I will make the house ready.

(*He stands looking up as if in ecstasy;* ANDREW *and* JOHNNY BOCACH *go out.*)

ACT II

SCENE: *The same workshop.* MARTIN *seen arranging mugs and bread, etc., on a table.* FATHER JOHN *comes in, knocking at open door as he comes; his mind intensely absorbed.*

MARTIN. Come in, come in, I have got the house ready. Here is bread and meat—everybody is welcome.

(*Hearing no answer, turns round.*)

FATHER JOHN. Martin, I have come back. There is something I want to say to you.

MARTIN. You are welcome, there are others coming. They are not of your sort, but all are welcome.

FATHER JOHN. I have remembered suddenly something that I read when I was in the seminary.

MARTIN. You seem very tired.

FATHER JOHN (*sitting down*). I had almost got back to my own place when I thought of it. I have run part of the way. It is very important; it is about the trance that you have been in. When one is inspired from above, either in trance or in contemplation, one remembers afterwards all that one has seen and read. I think there must be something about it in Saint Thomas. I know that I have read a long passage about it years ago. But, Martin, there is another kind of inspiration, or rather an obsession or possession. A diabolical power comes into one's body, or overshadows it. Those whose bodies are taken hold of in this way, jugglers, and witches, and the like, can often tell what is happening in distant places, or what is going to happen, but when they come out of that state they remember nothing. I think you said—

MARTIN. That I could not remember.

FATHER JOHN. You remembered something, but not all. Nature is a great sleep; there are dangerous and evil spirits in her dreams, but God is above Nature. She is a darkness, but He makes everything clear; He is light.

MARTIN. All is clear now. I remember all, or all that matters to me. A poor man brought me a word, and I know what I have to do.

FATHER JOHN. Ah, I understand, words were put into his mouth. I have read of such things. God sometimes uses some common man as His messenger.

MARTIN. You may have passed the man who brought it on the road. He left me but now.

318

FATHER JOHN. Very likely, very likely, that is the way it happened. Some plain, unnoticed man has sometimes been sent with a command.

MARTIN. I saw the unicorns trampling in my dream. They were breaking the world. I am to destroy; destruction was the word the messenger spoke.

FATHER JOHN. To destroy?

MARTIN. To bring again the old disturbed exalted life, the old splendour.

FATHER JOHN. You are not the first that dream has come to. (*Gets up, and walks up and down.*) It has been wandering here and there, calling now to this man, now to that other. It is a terrible dream.

MARTIN. Father John, you have had the same thought.

FATHER JOHN. Men were holy then, there were saints everywhere. There was reverence; but now it is all work, business, how to live a long time. Ah, if one could change it all in a minute, even by war and violence! There is a cell where Saint Ciaran used to pray; if one could bring that time again!

MARTIN. Do not deceive me. You have had the command.

FATHER JOHN. Why are you questioning me? You are asking me things that I have told to no one but my confessor.

MARTIN. We must gather the crowds together, you and I.

FATHER JOHN. I have dreamed your dream, it was long ago. I had your vision.

MARTIN. And what happened?

FATHER JOHN (*harshly*). It was stopped; that was an end. I was sent to the lonely parish where I am, where there was no one I could lead astray. They have left me there. We must have patience; the world was destroyed by water, it has yet to be consumed by fire.

MARTIN. Why should we be patient? To live seventy years, and others to come after us and live seventy years, it may be; and so from age to age, and all the while the old splendour dying more and more.

(*A noise of shouting.* ANDREW, *who has been standing at the door, comes in.*)

ANDREW. Martin says truth, and he says it well. Planing the side of a cart or a shaft, is that life? It is not. Sitting at a desk writing letters to the man that wants a coach, or to the man that won't pay for the one he has got, is that life, I ask you? Thomas arguing at you and putting you down—"Andrew, dear Andrew, did you put the tyre on that wheel yet?' Is that life? No, it is not. I ask you all, what do you remember when you are dead? It's the sweet cup in the corner of the widow's drinking-house that you remember. Ha, ha, listen to that shouting! That is what the lads in the village will remember to the last day they live.

MARTIN. Why are they shouting? What have you told them?

ANDREW. Never you mind; you left that to me. You bade me to lift their hearts and I did lift them. There is not one among them but will have his head like a blazing tar-barrel before morning. What did your friend the beggar say? The juice of the grey barley, he said.

FATHER JOHN. You accursed villain! You have made them drunk!

ANDREW. Not at all, but lifting them to the stars. That is what Martin bade me to do, and there is no one can say I did not do it.

(*A shout at door, and* BEGGARS *push in a barrel. They cry,* 'Hi! for the noble master!' *and point at* ANDREW.)

JOHNNY. It's not him, it's that one! (*Points at* MARTIN.)

FATHER JOHN. Are you bringing this devil's work in at the very door? Go out of this, I say! get out! Take these others with you!

MARTIN. No, no; I asked them in, they must not be turned out. They are my guests.

FATHER JOHN. Drive them out of your uncle's house!

MARTIN. Come, Father, it is better for you to go. Go back to your own place. I have taken the command. It is better perhaps for you that you did not take it. (FATHER JOHN *and* MARTIN *go out.*)

BIDDY. It is well for that old lad he didn't come between ourselves and our luck. Himself to be after his meal, and ourselves staggering with the hunger! It would be right to have flayed him and to have made bags of his skin.

NANNY. What a hurry you are in to get your enough! Look at the grease on your frock yet, with the dint of the dabs you put in in your pocket! Doing cures and foretellings, is it? You starved pot-picker, you!

BIDDY. That you may be put up to-morrow to take the place of that decent son of yours that had the yard of the gaol wore with walking it till this morning!

NANNY. If he had, he had a mother to come to, and he would know her when he did see her; and that is what no son of your own could do and he to meet you at the foot of the gallows.

JOHNNY. If I did know you, I knew too much of you since the first beginning of my life! What reward did I ever get travelling with you? What store did you give me of cattle or of goods? What provision did I get from you by day or by night but your own bad character to be joined on to my own, and I following at your heels, and your bags tied round about me!

NANNY. Disgrace and torment on you! Whatever you got from me, it was more than any reward or any bit I ever got from the father you had, or any honourable thing at all, but only the hurt and the harm of the world and its shame!

JOHNNY. What would he give you, and you going with him without leave! Crooked and foolish you were always, and you begging by the side of the ditch.

NANNY. Begging or sharing, the curse of my heart upon you! It's better off I was before ever I met with you to my cost! What was on me at all that I did not cut a scourge in the wood to put manners and decency on you the time you were not hardened as you are!

JOHNNY. Leave talking to me of your rods and your scourges! All you taught me was robbery, and it is on yourself and not on myself the scourges will be laid at the day of the recognition of tricks.

PAUDEEN. 'Faith, the pair of you together is better than Hector fighting before Troy!

NANNY. Ah, let you be quiet. It is not fighting we are craving, but the easing of the hunger that is on us and of the passion of sleep. Lend me a graineen of tobacco now till I'll kindle my pipe— a blast of it will take the weight of the road off my heart.

(ANDREW *gives her some.* NANNY *grabs at it.*)

BIDDY. No, but it's to myself you should give it. I that never smoked a pipe this forty year without saying the tobacco prayer. Let that one say did ever she do that much.

NANNY. That the pain of your front tooth may be in your back tooth, you to be grabbing my share!

(*They snap at tobacco.*)

ANDREW. Pup, pup, pup! Don't be snapping and quarrelling now, and you so well treated in this house. It is strollers like yourselves should be for frolic and for fun. Have you ne'er a good song to sing, a song that will rise all our hearts?

PAUDEEN. Johnny Bocach is a good singer, it is what he used to be doing in the fairs, if the oakum of the gaol did not give him a hoarseness within the throat.

ANDREW. Give it out so, a good song, a song will put courage and spirit into any man at all.

JOHNNY (*singing*).

'O come all ye airy bachelors,
    A warning take by me,
A sergeant caught me fowling,
    And he fired his gun so free.

His comrades came to his relief,
    And I was soon trepanned,
And bound up like a woodcock
    That had fallen into their hands.

The judge said transportation,
    The ship was on the strand;
They have yoked me to the traces
    For to plough Van Diemen's Land!"

ANDREW. That's no good of a song but a melancholy sort of a song. I'd as lief be listening to a saw going through timber. Wait, now, till you will hear myself giving out a tune on the flute.

(*Goes out for it.*)

JOHNNY. It is what I am thinking, there must be a great dearth and a great scarcity of good comrades in this place, a man like that youngster, having means in his hand, to be bringing ourselves and our rags into the house.

PAUDEEN. You think yourself very wise, Johnny Bocach. Can you tell me, now, who that man is?

JOHNNY. Some decent lad, I suppose, with a good way of living and a mind to send up his name upon the roads.

PAUDEEN. You that have been gaoled this eight months know little of this countryside. It isn't a limping stroller like yourself the Boys would let come among them. But I know. I went to the drill a few nights and I skinning kids for the mountainy men. In a quarry beyond the drill is—they have their plans made—it's the Square House of the Brownes is to be made an attack on and plundered. Do you know, now, who is the leader they are waiting for?

JOHNNY. How would I know that?

PAUDEEN (*singing*)

'O, Johnny Gibbons, my five hundred healths to you!
    It's long you are away from us over the sea!'

JOHNNY (*standing up excitedly*). Sure, that man could not be Johnny Gibbons that is outlawed!

PAUDEEN. I asked news of him from the old lad, and I bringing in the drink along with him. 'Don't be asking questions,' says he;

'take the treat he gives you,' says he. 'If a lad that has a high heart has a mind to rouse the neighbours', says he, 'and to stretch out his hand to all that pass the road, it is in France he learned it', says he, 'the place he is but lately come from, and where the wine does be standing open in tubs. Take your treat when you get it', says he, 'and make no delay or all might be discovered and put an end to.'

JOHNNY. He came over the sea from France! It is Johnny Gibbons, surely, but it seems to me they were calling him by some other name.

PAUDEEN. A man on his keeping might go by a hundred names. Would he be telling it out to us that he never saw before, and we with that clutch of chattering women along with us? Here he is coming now. Wait till you see is he the lad I think him to be.

MARTIN (*coming in*). I will make my banner, I will paint the unicorn on it. Give me that bit of canvas, there is paint over here. We will get no help from the settled men—we will call to the law-breakers, the tinkers, the sievemakers, the sheepstealers.

(*He begins to make banner.*)

BIDDY. That sounds to be a queer name of an army. Ribbons I can understand, Whiteboys, Rightboys, Threshers, and Peep o' Days, but Unicorns I never heard of before.

JOHNNY. It is not a queer name but a very good name. (*Takes up lion and unicorn.*) It is often you saw that before you in the dock. There is the unicorn with the one horn, and what is it he is going against? The lion of course. When he has the lion destroyed, the crown must fall and be shivered. Can't you see it is the League of the Unicorns is the league that will fight and destroy the power of England and King George?

PAUDEEN. It is with that banner we will march and the lads in the quarry with us, it is they will have the welcome before him! It won't be long till we'll be attacking the Square House! Arms there are in it, riches that would smother the world, rooms full of guineas, we will put wax on our shoes walking them; the horses themselves shod with no less than silver!

MARTIN (*holding up banner*). There it is ready! We are very few now, but the army of the Unicorns will be a great army! (*To* JOHNNY.) Why have you brought me the message? Can you remember any more? Has anything more come to you? You have been drinking, the clouds upon your mind have been destroyed. . . . Can you see anything or hear anything that is beyond the world?

JOHNNY. I can not. I don't know what do you want me to tell you at all.

MARTIN. I want to begin the destruction, but I don't know where to begin. . . . You do not hear any other voice?

JOHNNY. I do not. I have nothing at all to do with Freemasons or witchcraft.

PAUDEEN. It is Biddy Lally has to do with witchcraft. It is often she threw the cups and gave out prophecies the same as Columcille.

MARTIN. You are one of the knowledgeable women. You can tell where it is best to begin, and what will happen in the end.

BIDDY. I will foretell nothing at all. I rose out of it this good while, with the stiffness and the swelling it brought upon my joints.

MARTIN. If you have foreknowledge you have no right to keep silent. If you do not help me I may go to work in the wrong way. I know I have to destroy, but when I ask myself what I am to begin with, I am full of uncertainty.

PAUDEEN. Here now are the cups handy and the leavings in them.

BIDDY (taking cups and pouring one from another). Throw a bit of white money into the four corners of the house.

MARTIN. There! (Throwing it.)

BIDDY. There can be nothing told without silver. It is not myself will have the profit of it. Along with that I will be forced to throw out gold.

MARTIN. There is a guinea for you. Tell me what comes before your eyes.

BIDDY. What is it you are wanting to have news of?

MARTIN. Of what I have to go out against at the beginning . . . There is so much . . . the whole world, it may be.

BIDDY (throwing from one cup to another and looking). You have no care for yourself. You have been across the sea, you are not long back. You are coming within the best day of your life.

MARTIN. What is it? What is it I have to do?

BIDDY. I see a great smoke, I see burning . . . There is a great smoke overhead.

MARTIN. That means we have to burn away a great deal that men have piled up upon the earth. We must bring men once more to the wildness of the clean green earth.

BIDDY. Herbs for my healing, the big herb and the little herb, it is true enough they get their strength out of the earth.

JOHNNY. Who was it the green sod of Ireland belonged to in the olden times? Wasn't it to the ancient race it belonged? And who has possession of it now but the race that came robbing over the

324

sea? The meaning of that is to destroy the big houses and the towns, and the fields to be given back to the ancient race.

MARTIN. That is it. You don't put it as I do, but what matter? Battle is all.

PAUDEEN. Columcille said, the four corners to be burned, and then the middle of the field to be burned. I tell you it was Columcille's prophecy said that.

BIDDY. Iron handcuffs I see and a rope and a gallows, and it maybe is not for yourself I see it, but for some I have acquaintance with a good way back.

MARTIN. That means the Law. We must destroy the Law. That was the first sin, the first mouthful of the apple.

JOHNNY. So it was, so it was. The Law is the worst loss. The ancient Law was for the benefit of all. It is the Law of the English is the only sin.

MARTIN. When there were no laws men warred on one another and man to man, not with machines made in towns as they do now, and they grew hard and strong in body. They were altogether alive like Him that made them in His image, like people in that unfallen country. But presently they thought it better to be safe, as if safety mattered or anything but the exaltation of the heart, and to have eyes that danger had made grave and piercing. We must overthrow the laws and banish them.

JOHNNY. It is what I say, to put out the laws is to put out the whole nation of the English. Laws for themselves they made for their own profit, and left us nothing at all, no more than a dog or a sow.

BIDDY. An old priest I see, and I would not say is he the one was here or another. Vexed and troubled he is, kneeling fretting and ever-fretting in some lonesome ruined place.

MARTIN. I thought it would come to that. Yes, the Church too— that is to be destroyed. Once men fought with their desires and their fears, with all that they call their sins, unhelped, and their souls became hard and strong. When we have brought back the clean earth and destroyed the Law and the Church, all life will become like a flame of fire, like a burning eye . . . O, how to find words for it all . . . all that is not life will pass away.

JOHNNY. It is Luther's Church he means, and the hump-backed discourse of Seaghan Calvin's Bible. So we will break it, and make an end of it.

MARTIN. We will go out against the world and break it and unmake it. (*Rising.*) We are the army of the Unicorn from the

325

Stars! We will trample it to pieces.—We will consume the world, we will burn it away—Father John said the world has yet to be consumed by fire. Bring me fire.

ANDREW (*to* BEGGARS). Here is Thomas. Hide—let you hide.

(*All except* MARTIN *hurry into next room.* THOMAS *comes in*).

THOMAS. Come with me, Martin. There is terrible work going on in the town! There is mischief gone abroad. Very strange things are happening!

MARTIN. What are you talking of? What has happened?

THOMAS. Come along, I say, it must be put a stop to. We must call to every decent man. It is as if the Devil himself had gone through the town on a blast and set every drinking-house open!

MARTIN. I wonder how that has happened. Can it have anything to do with Andrew's plan?

THOMAS. Are you giving no heed to what I'm saying? There is not a man, I tell you, in the parish and beyond the parish but has left the work he was doing whether in the field or in the mill.

MARTIN. Then all work has come to an end? Perhaps that was a good thought of Andrew's.

THOMAS. There is not a man has come to sensible years that is not drunk or drinking! My own labourers and my own serving-men are sitting on counters and on barrels! I give you my word, the smell of the spirits and the porter, and the shouting and the cheering within, made the hair to rise up on my scalp.

MARTIN. And yet there is not one of them that does not feel that he could bridle the four winds.

THOMAS (*sitting down in despair*). You are drunk too. I never thought you had a fancy for it.

MARTIN. It is hard for you to understand. You have worked all your life. You have said to yourself every morning, 'What is to be done to-day?' and when you were tired out you have thought of the next day's work. If you gave yourself an hour's idleness, it was but that you might work the better. Yet it is only when one has put work away that one begins to live.

THOMAS. It is those French wines that did it.

MARTIN. I have been beyond the earth. In Paradise, in that happy townland, I have seen the shining people. They were all doing one thing or another, but not one of them was at work. All that they did was but the overflowing of their idleness, and their days were a dance bred of the secret frenzy of their hearts, or a battle where the sword made a sound that was like laughter.

THOMAS. You went away sober from out of my hands; they had a right to have minded you better.

MARTIN. No man can be alive, and what is Paradise but fulness of life, if whatever he sets his hand to in the daylight cannot carry him from exaltation to exaltation, and if he does not rise into the frenzy of contemplation in the night silence. Events that are not begotten in joy are misbegotten and darken the world, and nothing is begotten in joy if the joy of a thousand years has not been crushed into a moment.

THOMAS. And I offered to let you go to Dublin in the coach!

MARTIN (*giving banner to* PAUDEEN). Give me the lamp. The lamp has not been lighted, and the world is to be consumed! (*Goes into inner room.*)

THOMAS (*seeing* ANDREW). Is it here you are, Andrew? What are these beggars doing? Was this door thrown open too? Why did you not keep order? I will go for the constables to help us!

ANDREW. You will not find them to help you. They were scattering themselves through the drinking-houses of the town, and why wouldn't they?

THOMAS. Are you drunk too? You are worse than Martin. You are a disgrace!

ANDREW. Disgrace yourself! Coming here to be making an attack on me and badgering me and disparaging me! And what about yourself that turned me to be a hypocrite?

THOMAS. What are you saying?

ANDREW. You did, I tell you! Weren't you always at me to be regular and to be working and to be going through the day and the night without company and to be thinking of nothing but the trade? What did I want with a trade? I got a sight of the faery gold one time in the mountains. I would have found it again and brought riches for it but for you keping me so close to the work.

THOMAS. O, of all the ungrateful creatures! You know well that I cherished you, leading you to live a decent, respectable life.

ANDREW. You never had respect for the ancient ways. It is after the mother you take it, that was too soft and too lumpish, having too much of the English in her blood. Martin is a Hearne like myself. It is he has the generous heart! It is not Martin would make a hypocrite of me and force me to do night-walking secretly, watching to be back by the setting of the seven stars! (*He begins to play his flute.*)

THOMAS. I will turn you out of this, yourself and this filthy troop! I will have them lodged in gaol.

JOHNNY. Filthy troop, is it? Mind yourself! The change is coming. The pikes will be up and the traders will go down.

(ALL *seize* THOMAS *and sing*)
'O the lion shall lose his strength,
And the bracket-thistle pine,
And the harp shall sound sweet, sweet at length,
Between the eight and nine!'

THOMAS. Let me out of this, you villains!

NANNY. We'll make a sieve of holes of you, you old bag of treachery!

BIDDY. How well you threatened us with gaol, you skim of a weasel's milk!

JOHNNY. You heap of sicknesses! You blinking hangman! That you may never die till you'll get a blue hag for a wife!

(MARTIN *comes back with lighted lamp.*)

MARTIN. Let him go. (*They let* THOMAS *go, and fall back.*) Spread out the banner. The moment has come to begin the war.

JOHNNY. Up with the Unicorn and destroy the Lion! Success to Johnny Gibbons and all good men!

MARTIN. Heap all those things together there. Heap those pieces of the coach one upon another. Put that straw under them. It is with this flame I will begin the work of destruction. All nature destroys and laughs.

THOMAS. Destroy your own golden coach!

MARTIN (*kneeling before* THOMAS). I am sorry to go a way that you do not like and to do a thing that will vex you. I have been a great trouble to you since I was a child in the house, and I am a great trouble to you yet. It is not my fault. I have been chosen for what I have to do. (*Stands up.*) I have to free myself first and those that are near me. The love of God is a very terrible thing! (THOMAS *tries to stop him, but is prevented by* BEGGARS. MARTIN *takes a wisp of straw and lights it.*) We will destroy all that can perish! It is only the soul that can suffer no injury. The soul of man is of the imperishable substance of the stars!

(*He throws wisp into heap—it blazes up.*)

Curtain.

ACT III

Before dawn. A wild rocky place. NANNY *and* BIDDY LALLY *squatting by a fire. Rich stuffs, etc., thrown about.* PAUDEEN *watching by* MARTIN, *who is lying as if dead, a sack over him.*

NANNY (*to* PAUDEEN). Well, you are great heroes and great warriors and great lads altogether, to have put down the Brownes the way you did, yourselves and the Whiteboys of the quarry. To have ransacked the house and have plundered it! Look at the silks and the satins and the grandeurs I brought away! Look at that now! (*Holds up a velvet cloak.*) It's a good little jacket for myself will come out of it. It's the singers will be stopping their songs and the jobbers turning from their cattle in the fairs to be taking a view of the laces of it and the buttons! It's my far-off cousins will be drawing from far and near!

BIDDY. There was not so much gold in it all as what they were saying there was. Or maybe that fleet of Whiteboys had the place ransacked before we ourselves came in. Bad cess to them that put it in my mind to go gather up the full of my bag of horseshoes out of the forge. Silver they were saying they were, pure white silver; and what are they in the end but only hardened iron! A bad end to them! (*Flings away horseshoes.*) The time I will go robbing big houses again it will not be in the light of the full moon I will go doing it, that does be causing every common thing to shine out as it for a deceit and a mockery. It's not shining at all they are at this time, but duck-yellow and dark.

NANNY. To leave the big house blazing after us, it was that crowned all! Two houses to be burned to ashes in the one night. It is likely the servant-girls were rising from the feathers and the cocks crowing from the rafters for seven miles around, taking the flames to be the whitening of the dawn.

BIDDY. It is the lad is stretched beyond you have to be thankful to for that. There was never seen a leader was his equal for spirit and for daring. Making a great scatter of the guards the way he did. Running up roofs and ladders, the fire in his hand, till you'd think he would be apt to strike his head against the stars.

NANNY. I partly guessed death was near him, and the queer shining look he had in his two eyes, and he throwing sparks east and west through the beams. I wonder now was it some inward wound he got, or did some hardy lad of the Brownes give him a tip on the skull unknownst in the fight? It was I myself found him, and the troop of the Whiteboys gone, and he lying by the side of a wall as weak as if he had knocked a mountain. I failed to waken him trying him with the sharpness of my nails, and his head fell back when I moved it, and I knew him to be spent and gone.

BIDDY. It's a pity you not to have left him where he was lying and said no word at all to Paudeen or to that son you have, that kept us back from following on, bringing him here to this shelter on sacks and upon poles.

NANNY. What way could I help letting a screech out of myself, and the life but just gone out of him in the darkness, and not a living Christian by his side but myself and the great God?

BIDDY. It's on ourselves the vengeance of the red soldiers will fall, they to find us sitting here the same as hares in a tuft. It would be best for us follow after the rest of the army of the Whiteboys.

NANNY. Whisht! I tell you. The lads are cracked about him. To get but the wind of the word of leaving him, it's little but they'd knock the head off the two of us. Whisht!

(*Enter* JOHNNY BOCACH *with candles.*)

JOHNNY (*standing over* MARTIN). Wouldn't you say now there was some malice or some venom in the air, that is striking down one after another the whole of the heroes of the Gael?

PAUDEEN. It makes a person be thinking of the four last ends, death and judgment, Heaven and Hell. Indeed and indeed my heart lies with him. It is well I knew what man he was under his byname and his disguise.

(*Sings*)

'O, Johnny Gibbons, it's you were the prop to us.
You to have left us, we are foals astray!'

JOHNNY. It is lost we are now and broken to the end of our days. There is no satisfaction at all but to be destroying the English, and where now will we get so good a leader again? Lay him out fair and straight upon a stone, till I will let loose the secret of my heart keening him!

(*Sets out candles on a rock, propping them up with stones.*)

NANNY. Is it mould candles you have brought to set around him, Johnny Bocach? It is great riches you should have in your pocket to be going to those lengths and not to be content with dips.

JOHNNY. It is lengths I will not be going to the time the life will

330

be gone out of your own body. It is not your corpse I will be wishful to hold in honour the way I hold this corpse in honour.

NANNY. That's the way always, there will be grief and quietness in the house if it is a young person has died, but funning and springing and tricking one another if it is an old person's corpse is in it. There is no compassion at all for the old.

PAUDEEN. It is he would have got leave for the Gael to be as high as the Gall. Believe me, he was in the prophecies. Let you not be comparing yourself with the like of him.

NANNY. Why wouldn't I be comparing myself? Look at all that was against me in the world. Would you be matching me against a man of his sort, that had the people shouting him and that had nothing to do but to die and to go to Heaven?

JOHNNY. The day you go to Heaven that you may never come back alive out of it! But it is not yourself will ever hear the saints hammering at their musics! It is you will be moving through the ages, chains upon you, and you in the form of a dog or a monster. I tell you that one will go through Purgatory as quick as lightning through a thorn-bush.

NANNY. That's the way, that's the way.

(*Croons*)

> Three that are watching my time to run,
> The worm, the Devil, and my son,
> To see a loop around their neck,
> It's that would make my heart to lep!

JOHNNY. Five white candles. I wouldn't begrudge them to him indeed. If he had held out and held up, it is my belief he would have freed Ireland!

PAUDEEN. Wait till the full light of the day and you'll see the burying he'll have. It is not in this place we will be waking him. I'll make a call to the two hundred Ribbons he was to lead on to the attack on the barracks at Aughanish. They will bring him marching to his grave upon the hill. He had surely some gift from the other world, I wouldn't say but he had power from the other side.

ANDREW (*coming in very shaky*). Well, it was a great night he gave to the village, and it is long till it will be forgotten. I tell you the whole of the neighbours are up against him. There is no one at all this morning to set the mills going. There was no bread baked in the night-time, the horses are not fed in the stalls, the cows are not milked in the sheds. I met no man able to make a curse this night but he put it on my head and on the head of the boy that is lying there before us. . . . Is there no sign of life in him at all?

JOHNNY. What way would there be a sign of life and the life gone out of him this three hours or more?

ANDREW. He was lying in his sleep for a while yesterday, and he wakened again after another while.

NANNY. He will not waken, I tell you. I held his hand in my own and it getting cold as if you were pouring on it the coldest cold water, and no running in his blood. He is gone, sure enough, and the life is gone out of him.

ANDREW. Maybe so, maybe so. It seems to me yesterday his cheeks were bloomy all the while, and now he is as pale as wood ashes. Sure, we all must come to it at the last. Well, my white-headed darling, it is you were the bush among us all, and you to be cut down in your prime. Gentle and simple, every one liked you. It is no narrow heart you had, it is you were for spending and not for getting. It is you made a good wake for yourself, scattering your estate in one night only in beer and in wine for the whole province; and that you may be sitting in the middle of Paradise and in the chair of the Graces!

JOHNNY. Amen to that. It's a pity I didn't think the time I sent for yourself to send the little lad of a messenger looking for a priest to overtake him. It might be in the end the Almighty is the best man for us all!

ANDREW. Sure, I sent him on myself to bid the priest to come. Living or dead I would wish to do all that is rightful for the last and the best of my own race and generation.

BIDDY (*jumping up*). Is it the priest you are bringing in among us? Where is the sense in that? Aren't we robbed enough up to this with the expense of the candles and the like?

JOHNNY. If it is that poor starved priest he called to that came talking in secret signs to the man that is gone, it is likely he will ask nothing for what he has to do. There is many a priest is a Whiteboy in his heart.

NANNY. I tell you, if you brought him tied in a bag he would not say an Our Father for you, without you having a half-crown at the top of your fingers.

BIDDY. There is no priest is any good at all but a spoiled priest. A one that would take a drop of drink, it is he would have courage to face the hosts of trouble. Rout them out he would, the same as a shoal of fish from out the weeds. It's best not to vex a priest, or to run against them at all.

NANNY. It's yourself humbled yourself well to one the time you were sick in the gaol and had like to die, and he bade you to give over the throwing of the cups.

BIDDY. Ah, plaster of Paris I gave him. I took to it again and I free upon the roads.

NANNY. Much good you are doing with it to yourself or any other one. Aren't you after telling that corpse no later than yesterday that he was coming within the best day of his life?

JOHNNY. Whisht, let ye. Here is the priest coming.

(FATHER JOHN *comes in.*)

FATHER JOHN. It is surely not true that he is dead?

JOHNNY. The spirit went from him about the middle hour of the night. We brought him here to this sheltered place. We were loth to leave him without friends.

FATHER JOHN. Where is he?

JOHNNY (*taking up sacks*). Lying there stiff and stark. He has a very quiet look as if there was no sin at all or no great trouble upon his mind.

FATHER JOHN (*kneels and touches him*). He is not dead.

BIDDY (*pointing to* NANNY). He is dead. If it was letting on he was, he would not have let that one rob him and search him the way she did.

FATHER JOHN. It has the appearance of death, but it is not death. He is in a trance.

PAUDEEN. Is it Heaven and Hell he is walking at this time to be bringing back newses of the sinners in pain?

BIDDY. I was thinking myself it might be away he was, riding on white horses with the riders of the forths.

JOHNNY. He will have great wonders to tell out, the time he will rise up from the ground. It is a pity he not to waken at this time and to lead us on to overcome the troop of the English. Sure, those that are in a trance get strength that they can walk on water.

ANDREW. It was Father John wakened him yesterday the time he was lying in the same way. Wasn't I telling you it was for that I called to him?

BIDDY. Waken him now till they'll see did I tell any lie in my foretelling. I knew well by the signs, he was coming within the best day of his life.

PAUDEEN. And not dead at all! We'll be marching to attack Dublin itself within a week. The horn will blow for him, and all good men will gather to him. Hurry on, Father, and waken him.

FATHER JOHN. I will not waken him. I will not bring him back from where he is.

JOHNNY. And how long will it be before he will waken of himself?

FATHER JOHN. Maybe to-day, maybe to-morrow, it is hard to be certain.

BIDDY. If it is *away* he is, he might be away seven years. To be lying like a stump of a tree and using no food and the world not able to knock a word out of him, I know the signs of it well.

JOHNNY. We cannot be waiting and watching through seven years. If the business he has started is to be done we have to go on here and now. The time there is any delay, that is the time the Government will get information. Waken him now, Father, and you'll get the blessing of the generations.

FATHER JOHN. I will not bring him back. God will bring him back in His own good time. For all I know he may be seeing the hidden things of God.

JOHNNY. He might slip away in his dream. It is best to raise him up now.

ANDREW. Waken him, Father John, I thought he was surely dead this time, and what way could I go face Thomas through all that is left of my lifetime, after me standing up to face him the way I did? And if I do take a little drop of an odd night, sure, I'd be very lonesome if I did not take it. All the world knows it's not for love of what I drink, but for love of the people that do be with me! Waken him, Father, or maybe I would waken him myself.

(Shakes him.)

FATHER JOHN. Lift your hand from touching him. Leave him to himself and to the power of God.

JOHNNY. If you will not bring him back why wouldn't we our-selves do it? Go on now, it is best for you to do it yourself.

FATHER JOHN. I woke him yesterday. He was angry with me, he could not get to the heart of the command.

JOHNNY. If he did not, he got a command from myself that satis-fied him, and a message.

FATHER JOHN. He did—he took it from you—and how do I know what devil's message it may have been that brought him into that devil's work, destruction and drunkenness and burnings? That was not a message from Heaven! It was I awoke him, it was I kept him from hearing what was maybe a divine message, a voice of truth, and he heard you speak and he believed the message was brought by you. You have made use of your deceit and his mistak-ing—you have left him without house or means to support him, you are striving to destroy and to drag him to entire ruin. I will not help you, I would rather see him die in his trance and go into God's hands than awake him and see him go into Hell's mouth with vagabonds and outcasts like you!

JOHNNY (*turning to* BIDDY). You should have knowledge, Biddy Lally, of the means to bring back a man that is away.

BIDDY. The power of the earth will do it through its herbs, and the power of the air will do it kindling fire into flame.

JOHNNY. Rise up and make no delay. Stretch out and gather a handful of an herb that will bring him back from whatever place he is in.

BIDDY. Where is the use of herbs, and his teeth clenched the way he could not use them?

JOHNNY. Take fire so, in the Devil's name, and put it to the soles of his feet. (*Takes a lighted sod from fire.*)

FATHER JOHN. Let him alone, I say! (*Dashes away the sod.*)

JOHNNY. I will not leave him alone! I will not give in to leave him swooning there and the country waiting for him to awake!

FATHER JOHN. I tell you I awoke him! I sent him into thieves' company! I will not have him wakened again and evil things, it may be, waiting to take hold of him! Back from him, back, I say! Will you dare to lay a hand on me? You cannot do it! You cannot touch him against my will!

BIDDY. Mind yourself, do not be bringing us under the curse of the Church.

(JOHNNY *steps back.* MARTIN *moves.*)

FATHER JOHN. It is God has him in His care. It is He is awaking him. (MARTIN *has risen to his elbow.*) Do not touch him, do not speak to him, he may be hearing great secrets.

MARTIN. That music, I must go nearer—sweet marvellous music—louder than the trampling of the unicorns; far louder, though the mountain is shaking with their feet—high joyous music.

FATHER JOHN. Hush, he is listening to the music of Heaven!

MARTIN. Take me to you, musicians, wherever you are; I will go nearer to you; I hear you better now, more and more joyful; that is strange, it is strange.

FATHER JOHN. He is getting some secret.

MARTIN. It is the music of Paradise, that is certain, somebody said that. It is certainly the music of Paradise. Ah, now I hear, now I understand. It is made of the continual clashing of swords!

JOHNNY. That is the best music. We will clash them sure enough. We will clash our swords and our pikes on the bayonets of the red soldiers. It is well you rose up from the dead to lead us! Come on, now, come on!

MARTIN. Who are you? Ah, I remember—where are you asking me to come to ?

PAUDEEN. To come on, to be sure, to the attack on the barracks at Aughanish. To carry on the work you took in hand last night.

MARTIN. What did I take in hand last night? O yes, I remember —some big house—we burned it down—but I had not understood the vision when I did that. I had not heard the command right. That was not the work I was sent to do.

PAUDEEN. Rise up now and bid us what to do. Your great name itself will clear the road before you. It is you yourself will have freed all Ireland before the stooks will be in stacks!

MARTIN. Listen, I will explain—I have misled you. It is only now I have the whole vision plain. As I lay there I saw through everything, I know all. It was but a frenzy, that going out to burn and to destroy. What have I to do with the foreign army? What I have to pierce is the wild heart of time. My business is not reformation but revelation.

JOHNNY. If you are going to turn back now from leading us, you are no better than any other traitor that ever gave up the work he took in hand. Let you come and face now the two hundred men you brought out daring the power of the Law last night, and give them your reason for failing them.

MARTIN. I was mistaken when I set out to destroy Church and Law. The battle we have to fight is fought out in our own mind. There is a fiery moment, perhaps once in a lifetime, and in that moment we see the only thing that matters. It is in that moment the great battles are lost and won, for in that moment we are a part of the host of Heaven.

PAUDEEN. Have you betrayed us to the naked hangman with your promises and with your drink? If you brought us out here to fail us and to ridicule us, it is the last day you will live!

JOHNNY. The curse of my heart on you! It would be right to send you to your own place on the flagstone of the traitors in Hell. When once I have made an end of you I will be as well satisfied to be going to my death for it as if I was going home!

MARTIN. Father John, Father John, can you not hear? Can you not see? Are you blind? Are you deaf?

FATHER JOHN. What is it? What is it?

MARTIN. There on the mountain, a thousand white unicorns trampling; a thousand riders with their swords drawn—the swords

336

clashing! O, the sound of the swords, the sound of the clashing of the swords!

(*He goes slowly off stage.* JOHNNY *takes up a stone to throw at him.*)

FATHER JOHN (*seizing his arm*). Stop—do you not see he is beyond the world?

BIDDY. Keep your hand off him, Johnny Bocach. If he is gone wild and cracked, that's natural. Those that have been wakened from a trance on a sudden are apt to go bad and light in the head.

PAUDEEN. If it is madness is on him, it is not he himself should pay the penalty.

BIDDY. To prey on the mind it does, and rises into the head. There are some would go over any height and would have great power in their madness. It is maybe to some secret cleft he is going, to get knowledge of the great cure for all things, or of the Plough that was hidden in the old times, the Golden Plough.

PAUDEEN. It seemed as if he was talking through honey. He had the look of one that had seen great wonders. It is maybe among the old heroes of Ireland he went, raising armies for our help.

FATHER JOHN. God take him in His care and keep him from lying spirits and from all delusions!

JOHNNY. We have got candles here, Father. We had them to put around his body. Maybe they would keep away the evil things of the air.

PAUDEEN. Light them so, and he will say out a Mass for him the same as in a lime-washed church.

(*They light the candles.*)

(THOMAS *comes in.*)

THOMAS. Where is he? I am come to warn him. The destruction he did in the night-time has been heard of. The soldiers are out after him, and the constables—there are two of the constables not far off—there are others on every side—they heard he was here in the mountain—where is he?

FATHER JOHN. He has gone up the path.

THOMAS. Hurry after him! Tell him to hide himself—this attack he had a hand in is a hanging crime. Tell him to hide himself, to come to me when all is quiet—bad as his doings are, he is my own brother's son; I will get him on to a ship that will be going to France.

FATHER JOHN. That will be best; send him back to the Brothers and to the wise Bishops. They can unravel this tangle, I cannot. I cannot be sure of the truth.

337

THOMAS. Here are the constables; he will see them and get away. Say no word. The Lord be praised that he is out of sight.

(CONSTABLES *come in.*)

CONSTABLE. The man we are looking for, where is he? He was seen coming here along with you. You have to give him up into the power of the Law.

JOHNNY. We will not give him up. Go back out of this or you will be sorry.

PAUDEEN. We are not in dread of you or the like of you.

BIDDY. Throw them down over the rocks!

NANNY. Give them to the picking of the crows!

ALL. Down with the Law!

FATHER JOHN. Hush! He is coming back. (*To* CONSTABLES) Stop, stop—leave him to himself. He is not trying to escape, he is coming towards you.

PAUDEEN. There is a sort of a brightness about him. I misjudged him calling him a traitor. It is not to this world he belongs at all. He is over on the other side.

MARTIN (*standing beside the rock where the lighted candles are*). *Et calix meus inebrians quam praeclarus est!*

FATHER JOHN. I must know what he has to say. It is not from himself he is speaking.

MARTIN. Father John, Heaven is not what we have believed it to be. It is not quiet, it is not singing and making music, and all strife at an end. I have seen it, I have been there. The lover still loves, but with a greater passion, and the rider still rides, but the horse goes like the wind and leaps the ridges, and the battle goes on always, always. That is the joy of Heaven, continual battle. I thought the battle was here, and that the joy was to be found here on earth, that all one had to do was to bring again the old wild earth of the stories—but no, it is not here; we shall not come to that joy, that battle, till we have put out the senses, everything that can be seen and handled, as I put out this candle. (*He puts out candle.*) We must put out the whole world as I put out this candle (*puts out another candle*). We must put out the light of the stars and the light of the sun and the light of the moon (*puts out the rest of the candles*), till we have brought everything to nothing once again. I saw in a broken vision, but now all is clear to me. Where there is nothing, where there is nothing—there is God!

CONSTABLE. Now we will take him!

JOHNNY. We will never give him up to the Law!

PAUDEEN. Make your escape! We will not let you be followed.

338

(*They struggle with* CONSTABLES; *the* WOMEN *help them; all disappear struggling. There is a shot.* MARTIN *stumbles and falls.* BEGGARS *come back with a shout.*)

JOHNNY. We have done for them; they will not meddle with you again.

PAUDEEN. O, he is down!

FATHER JOHN. He is shot through the breast. O, who has dared meddle with a soul that was in the tumults on the threshold of sanctity?

JOHNNY. It was that gun went off and I striking it from the constable's hand.

MARTIN (*looking at his hand, on which there is blood*). Ah, that is blood! I fell among the rocks. It is a hard climb. It is a long climb to the vineyards of Eden. Help me up. I must go on. The Mountain of Abiegnos is very high—but the vineyards—the vineyards!

(*He falls back dead. The* MEN *uncover their heads.*)

PAUDEEN (*to* BIDDY). It was you misled him with your fore-telling that he was coming within the best day of his life.

JOHNNY. Madness on him or no madness, I will not leave that body to the Law to be buried with a dog's burial or brought away and maybe hanged upon a tree. Lift him on the sacks, bring him away to the quarry; it is there on the hillside the boys will give him a great burying, coming on horses and bearing white rods in their hands.

(NANNY *lays the velvet cloak over him. They lift him and carry the body away singing*)

'Our hope and our darling, our heart dies with you,
    You to have failed us, we are foals astray!'

FATHER JOHN. He is gone and we can never know where that vision came from. I cannot know—the wise Bishops would have known.

THOMAS (*taking up banner*). To be shaping a lad through his lifetime, and he to go his own way at the last, and a queer way. It is very queer the world itself is, whatever shape was put upon it at the first.

ANDREW. To be too headstrong and too open, that is the beginning of trouble. To keep to yourself the thing that you know, and to do in quiet the thing you want to do. There would be no disturbance at all in the world, all people to bear that in mind!

Curtain.

HEADS OR HARPS
BY
W. B. YEATS AND LADY GREGORY

HEADS OR HARPS

A COMEDY

PERSONS
  MR. HOWARD PATTERSON. *A barrister.*
  MRS. HOWARD PATTERSON.
  MATTHEW PATTERSON. *Their nephew.*
  DR. MEADOWS. *Professor of Moral Philosophy in Trinity College.*

SCENE. *A study in Merrion Square. A writing table. A small table with tray with cold meat, decanter of sherry, etc.*

MR. PATTERSON (*who has just come in*). Well, Louisa, I think everything is going well. How will you like appearing at the next Drawing Room as the Solicitor General's wife?

MRS. PATTERSON. I hope the good luck is really coming, and that there is no mistake about it.

MR. PATTERSON. O yes, I mustn't tell you the particulars of all the Chancellor said, but I know it's all right. (*He takes her hand.*) I am more glad for your sake and the children's than my own. If we have worked hard they will have the best of everything, and be able to take life easy. (*Takes out his watch.*) By the way, that nephew of mine should be here by this. I am glad to be able to give him a helping hand.

MRS. PATTERSON. You are always very kind, Howard. It is good of you to think of your brother's children as well as your own.

MR. PATTERSON. I hope to be able to do a good deal for them now I am getting on so well. But I wish he had come by the early train. This unpunctuality is a bad beginning. I want to set at work with him at once.

MRS. PATTERSON. He should be here in a few minutes, I hope he will be able to help you. It will be a great help to himself if he does so, for he seems to be only idling where he is, and living on his father. . . . I hear the hall door opened, he must have come . . . I'll bring him in here. (*She rises and opens door.*) Yes, it's Matthew. Come in here, Matthew, and see your uncle.

343

(MATTHEW PATTERSON *comes in, a young man unfashion-ably dressed, carrying a small bag.*)

MR. PATTERSON. How are you, Matthew. I hope you left all well at home. It's a long time since I've seen any of you.

MRS. PATTERSON. But I hope we shall see a good deal of you for the future, and that you will become one of ourselves. Won't you have some lunch? (*Points at tray.*) You have had a long journey from the west.

MATTHEW. I'm not hungry, I can wait awhile. (*To his* UNCLE) You said you had something for me to do. I can begin now if you like.

MR. PATTERSON. That's just as well, for we have no time to waste. How was it you did not come by the early train?

MATTHEW Oh, I missed it; it was an early start, there's no one gets up very early in our house.

MR. PATTERSON. You must get into punctual habits here or you won't do much good.

MATTHEW. It was just as well. The guard of the next train was a friend of my own, and he let me pass without a ticket as far as the junction.

MR. PATTERSON. That was not honest. That was cheating the company.

MATTHEW. We don't think much of that in my place. They can afford it.

MRS. PATTERSON. When you know your uncle better Matthew you will find he is very particular about little things of that sort.

MR. PATTERSON. And no wonder. This slipperiness in little things is one of the worst faults of this country. It sometimes makes me despair of its future. Better education is the only hope I see.

MRS. PATTERSON. Matthew is young, he has plenty of time to learn.

MATTHEW (*who has been looking embarrassed, taking up a paper*). The Mayo Champion! I thought you would not have taken that in this house. (*Turns it over.*) Did you know it was I wrote that article on the Government prosecutions? (*Puts his finger on one.*)

MR. PATTERSON. I knew you had been writing for those papers lately, but your father tells me you don't make much by it.

MATTHEW. No indeed, I don't make anything out of it. They gave me a little at first, but I thought they couldn't afford it, and I wouldn't take it of late. They are doing a great deal for the people.

344

MR. PATTERSON. Ah, for the people. That is just what I wanted to hear about. You will be surprised to hear I have been reading these papers very carefully the last few days. In fact, that has led to my sending for you to come to town. Louisa, as Matthew won't have lunch we may as well begin work at once. Tell the servants not to let me be disturbed.

MRS. PATTERSON. Yes, I'm going to the drawingroom, you'll have the room to yourselves. (*She goes out.*)

MR. PATTERSON. (*to* MATTHEW). Sit down . . . now, you must understand that what I am telling you is in strict confidence. I have heard on the best authority that the Government are going to accede to the demands of the National leaders . . .

MATTHEW (*clapping his hands together*). To give Home Rule?

MR. PATTERSON. I won't say so much as that, but they will go as far as they safely can in that direction. Now, they want a lawyer of high reputation, who will take the Nationalist side, to help them in framing their measure, and a hint has been conveyed to me from a very high quarter that the Solicitor Generalship will be given to me if I can change my politics, that is if I can take the same view as the Government, and without losing the confidence of the public.

MATTHEW. You are coming over to the National side? That's grand, it will have an immense effect.

MR. PATTERSON. I have to make a speech tomorrow to my constituents, and it is most important I should lose no time in beginning to explain my change.

MATTHEW. There will be great rejoicing in Essronan when this is heard. You are remembered there yet. I wish I was there when the news comes in. If you will come down and speak there we'll give you a great reception. I often thought so great a man as you would see the right side if only you set your mind to think about it.

MR. PATTERSON. Never mind that now. Take that piece of paper, I am going to dictate my speech to you, that will be the beginning of your work as secretary. You are used to writing and reporting for the papers, and you have been at so many political demonstrations you will know what I want. I thought of you at once when I made up my mind to change. You will be able to keep me from making any slips, and you will be able to help me presently with a few telling facts. (*Gets up to pace up and down the room.*) Are you ready?

MATTHEW. Am I ready? I am indeed. There is no earthly thing I wouldn't be ready to do for you from this day out.

MR. PATTERSON. I am going to begin rather quietly. Mr. Chairman and gentlemen. . . no, fellow countrymen. Hadn't I better say fellow countrymen? (MATTHEW *nods*.) I feel that what I am about to say may be misconstrued by some of you, but I assure you that I have not made up my mind upon the subject without deep consideration, without I may say much anxiety and searching of heart. (*He takes another pace or two*.) That will do for a first sentence; I can put in something when the time comes, the usual compliments, etc. Perhaps I should have spoken sooner upon this matter, but it is a serious thing to break with old associations, to separate oneself from old traditions, and it may even be from old friends.

There is no one here who can say that I have not loyally supported the Government, the division lists are there to be my witness . . . That will do for the moment, we will go on to the more important part, to the reasons for my change. Now, here is where you might help me. I have always recognised from my first entrance into public life that the country must be governed either by English or by Irish ideals. There is no one who can say I have ever faltered between these two courses. I still hold that it was right that the one policy should be tried—tried to the utmost, before the other was attempted, but that the change if ever attempted should be complete and unhesitating . . . I will here make a pause,—quite a long pause. English policy in Ireland has broken down, the policy of Ireland for the Irish remains, and I am ready from this moment to support that policy with all the strength of my convictions. Could you give me an idea now, you have heard so many attacks on English policy and its results?

MATTHEW. There's emigration, and there's coercion, and then the thorny path of Kathleen ni Houlihan.

MR. PATTERSON. Perhaps that is a little coloured . . .

MATTHEW. Put in something about the British policy of extermination. Say they have taken as many lives as Cromwell, and that they are more underhand.

MR. PATTERSON. No, no, these exaggerated phrases are a part of the untruthfulness which is so deplorable in Irish character, that want of exactness has always harmed your cause.

MATTHEW. Well, I don't see why we should be too particular, after the way they have treated us.

MR. PATTERSON. Is there not something about Government by sympathy we could put in? . . . Can you give me an idea? Who is this coming? I said we were not to be disturbed.

(*Enter* MRS. PATTERSON *and* PROFESSOR MEADOWS.)

346

MRS. PATTERSON. I have brought the professor, he has something to tell you at once.

PROFESSOR. My dear Howard, you were very nearly in a hole. It's all up with the new policy. The Manchester election has been lost, and has scared the Government.

MR. PATTERSON. All up with the new policy! But the Chancellor told me. . .

PROFESSOR. Well, he'll have another story to tell you now. They won't risk it, they have no mind to go out of office. (*With a nod.*) You know where I get my information.

(MR. PATTERSON *sits down bewildered.*)

MRS. PATTERSON. It was very good of you to come, he was just beginning to write . . . O let me introduce Matthew our nephew, you have heard us speak of him—he was giving him some help with the speech he was to have made. Matthew, this is our friend Dr. Meadows, the Professor of Moral Philosophy in Trinity College. He has done us a great service.

PROFESSOR. Well young man, you have found Nationalist politics a bad trade up to this I daresay. Not so much money coming from America?

MRS. PATTERSON (*to her husband*). Don't let it upset you Howard.

MR. PATTERSON. It is a bit of a check. I made sure I was doing the right thing. The Bar is choke full of Unionists; I may have to wait now till I'm grey for my turn.

MR. PATTERSON. Never mind, you are sure to get some good place in the end, and you are doing very well as it is. It may be all for the best; the rest of the Square mightn't have been pleasant about the change.

MR. PATTERSON. It was of you and the children I was thinking. I thought I could do so much for you.

MRS. PATTERSON. O, I am as well content, and thanks to the professor there's no harm done yet.

PROFESSOR. O yes there is; you're not out of it yet. There's a paragraph about you in the Evening mail . . .

MR. PATTERSON. A paragraph about me!

PROFESSOR (*nodding*). Yes, about your change. Wait I have it here . . . (*feels his pocket.*) No I haven't . . . but it says Mr. Howard Patterson for interested motives has determined to give his adhesion to the National side.

MR. PATTERSON. Who can have told? Louisa have you been talking?

MRS. PATTERSON. No indeed Howard, you know I have never told any secret of yours.

MR. PATTERSON. Or could the servants have overheard it?

PROFESSOR. What can you expect in a country with an eaves-dropping Press.

MR. PATTERSON. The Chancellor has told somebody. He has such a lot of relations, they are all over the place. It will be known by this in the Four Courts.

PROFESSOR. Well, it doesn't matter who told; the question is what face you can put on it.

MR. PATTERSON (*getting up*). It must be contradicted at once, I must have a letter in the next edition of the Mail. Matthew, there's a clean sheet of paper. Write this. "Sir," (*he paces up and down the room.*) "My attention has been drawn to a paragraph in your issue of this afternoon stating that I am about to change my politics. I should have thought it unnecessary to contradict a rumour of that kind, but I now do so unreservedly. I cannot imagine how it can have arisen. There is no one who can say that I have not loyally supported the Government. The division lists are there to be my witness. . ." But you haven't begun to write.

MATTHEW. Write that?

MR. PATTERSON. Yes, write that.

MATTHEW. And what about the speech?

MR. PATTERSON. Of course I won't make that speech now. Don't you understand what the professor has said? The Government has been beaten at the Manchester election, and they have given up all idea of a liberal policy.

PROFESSOR. Yes, no chance of meeting Nationalists at the Castle dinners this season.

MR. PATTERSON. Don't you see, as the Government is not going to change its policy I can't change mine. Here, I'll write the letter myself. (*Sits down.*)

MRS. PATTERSON. O Matthew you ought to have done what your uncle asked you.

MATTHEW. But what side is he on? He said a while ago he was on our side.

PROFESSOR. Well, young man, did you never change your mind about the horse you would put your money on?

MATTHEW. But I never knew anyone go against his convictions like that.

PROFESSOR. Look here, young man. There are just two sorts of people in the world, clever people who know they haven't got any convictions, and fools who have got convictions or think they have. My dear friend over there used to think he had convictions; I always knew I hadn't any. If I had I should have done my best to get rid of them as I would get rid of any other kind of swimming in the head.

MATTHEW. But . . . one's principles.

PROFESSOR (*turning his back and going to look over* MR. PATTERSON'S *shoulder*). Don't talk rhetoric.

MRS. PATTERSON. Come over here Matthew.

MATTHEW. I think it's better for me to go home again.

MRS. PATTERSON. No, no. Sit down. (*He sits down, she pulls her chair over to him.*) I don't wonder you are put out, to be brought so far, and then to find you are not wanted.

MATTHEW. But it's not that at all. (*He keeps looking indignantly at the two men.*)

MRS. PATTERSON. O yes it is; I know young people. You've had a disappointment. It's a pity you had this upset, it's a pity the Government did not know their own minds, but it can't be helped. And I daresay your uncle will find some other little job for you to do.

MATTHEW. I don't want a job, and I won't take a job. I'll go back to my own place.

MRS. PATTERSON. O you mustn't go back to idle about in that miserable dirty little town, I am sure the people there are not good companions for you.

MATTHEW. I will go back to my own place. I know men there that are beggars and schemers, and men that would cheat in a fair, and men that know the inside of a jail and that deserve to know it, and I swear to God there isn't one of them would betray Ireland the way those two men are doing it this minute.

MRS. PATTERSON. You shouldn't use such words. You will feel quite differently tomorrow, I wish you had had time to eat your lunch.

MATTHEW. I can't stand my uncle behaving like this. And as to what the professor says about convictions . . .

MRS. PATTERSON. You mustn't take too seriously what the professor said. He only means by convictions those sentimental ideas that you political young men get into your heads, and that will never help you on in life. He is a very good man, and has great influence in the College. All the young men he has had under him do well for themselves, you would hardly know they had been brought up in Ireland at all. (MATTHEW *gets up impatiently.*) I wish you had had a chance of going into the College and attending his lectures, you would feel quite differently if you had done that.

MATTHEW. I can't stand this place. (*He goes to the door and turns round.*) I can't stand this place. (*louder.*) I can't stand this place.

MR. PATTERSON. (*looking up from the letter he and the* PROFESSOR *have been absorbed in.*) What is the matter?

MATTHEW. I won't stop here after what you have done.

MR. PATTERSON. Why, what have we done?

MATTHEW. You took the side of the country for money, and now you are going to leave it again for money. What hope is there for a country where it is its educated men that sell their convictions for money and are not thought the worse of for doing it. (*He goes out.*)

MR. PATTERSON. What have you been saying to him Louisa?

MRS. PATTERSON. I don't know; nothing out of the common.

PROFESSOR (*who has been holding the decanter up to the light*). There has been nothing taken out of the decanter. I never thought a man would talk that way unless he was drunk.

Curtain.

NOTES AND MUSIC

NOTES AND MUSIC

The Poorhouse

Dr. Douglas Hyde and I wrote *The Poorhouse* together, I giving in plot what he gave back in dialogue. I would not have my name put with his then, as I thought the play would be more acceptable to Irish speakers without even the ancestry of a scenario in the "Bearla".

But now we find that players in English in their turn think we should wrong what was created in Gaelic by playing it in translation; so we have put both our names to the little play with the object rather than the hope of commending it to both sides.
May 21, 1906.

The Doctor in Spite of Himself is now played with all the "business", traditional from Molière, sent to us through the courtesy of a principal actor of the Comédie Française. We had not this "business" in time for our first production of the Play, but it does not greatly differ from that invented by Mr. William Fay. One of the Dublin papers was shocked at the roughness and simplicity of the Play, and the writer of the article, although he admitted he had never read Molière's text, accused us of putting these things into it. Now it is precisely this roughness and simplicity, as of some old humorous folk-tale, that has made it a world-famous masterpiece, for it can be translated into almost any language, or adapted into any social order that is not too complex. I saw in some paper the other day that it is popular in Persia.

A Note by W. B. Yeats in the "Abbey Theatre Programme,"
Feb. 25, 1909

When we decided to play Molière, we read, and, in some cases, tried in rehearsal, many translations, old and new, and did not find one that had vivid dramatic speech. All, except one or two that used a little Somersetshire dialect, were in ordinary classic English, which is the worst English for plays where often the most dramatic characters speak in dialect, or in bad grammar, or use many provincial words. We had to make our own translations, and we select-

353

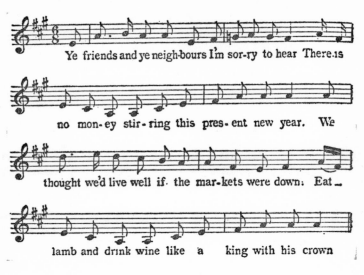

Ye friends and ye neigh-bours I'm sor-ry to hear There is

no mon-ey stir-ring this pres-ent new year. We

thought we'd live well if. the mar-kets were down. Eat _

lamb and drink wine like a king with his crown

A SONG: "WITH A LAMB IN IT"

Mal-b'rough s'en va t-en guer - re, Mi - ron

-ton, mi-ron-ton, mi-ron-tai - ne, Mal-b'rough s'en va-t-en

guer - re, Ne sait quand re - vien - dra, ___ Ne

sait quand re-vien - dra, ___ Ne sait quand re-vien-dra. ___

MALB'ROUGH S'EN VA T-EN GUERRE

ed such plays as enabled us to use always some Irish dialect, a great
deal for the servants and country men, but no more for well-to-do
men and young lovers than one could put into the mouth of an

I am go-ing out a - walk - ing

Whith - er are you walk - ing now?

Walk - ing out to meet my true love

She is not your true love now

She has giv - en me her love

It will break my heart in twain ___

Find an - oth - er lov - er now

Go and walk a - broad a - gain

WALKING

Irish country gentleman of a few years ago. This permits our players to found their characterisation more directly upon life than would otherwise be possible, and gives us something to make up for the loss of that traditional way of playing Molière which French actors inherit from his time, and can alone succeed in. This traditional way, which is at once distinguished, and, so far as the comedies we

355

Music for Dance

WOULD-BE GENTLEMAN

have chosen go, more farcical than ours, has, for all its historical and artistic interest, the disadvantage of putting the characters, so different are manners to-day, almost as far from the life of to-day as the clown and pantaloon of the circus. Even in Paris an actor has here and there advocated the abandonment of tradition, that Mascarille, let us say, might be re-made nearer to modern life;

RASCAL TIME

but, as it is impossible to modernise the words, tradition is, no doubt, essential in Paris. The word translation, however, which should be applied to scenery, acting, and the words alike, implies, or should imply, freedom. In vital translation, and I believe that our translations are vital, a work of art does not go upon its travels; it is re-born in a strange land.

The movements and business, as, unlike the words, these are as

To Bur-gun-dy I give my voice And Champagne has my e - qual choice Pommard Veuve Cli-quot in their kind To each I bring an e-qual mind Heid-sieck Mu-si - gny Vi-o-let Am - ber as may be All are wel-come un-to me If I see them flow-ing free But of all are sold The great-est I up-hold Is this that I en-fold If to Cham-pagne I give my voice Dark Pommard holds an e - qual choice To Cham-ber-tin to Veuve Cli-quot I doff my hat be-fore I go.

(drinks)

Fine

DRINKING SONG

true of one nationality as another, are sent to us by the Comedie Française.

Note on the Production of The Would-be Gentleman.

In a play like this—in a play full of colour and life and gay dresses —the setting should be as simple as possible and of some neutral

358

Gior - di - na, Gior - di - na, Ma-mouch-i of the Turks, 'Tis clear to see that he must be a ve-ry pro-per tip-top-top-per blue-blood-ed gen-tle-man. Gior-di-na, Gior-di-na, hail to the mighty Turk, Famed in feats of war, fa-mous both near and far, Hail might-y Gi-or-di-na, hail.

GIORDINA

colour. In the Abbey Theatre we used a grey curtained set with black swags, and black curtains at the back; and in the first act the only furniture was a large chair and a screen, both painted sealing-wax red. No change of scene is necessary for the second act, the large chair should be exchanged for three small ones and two small tables are needed. The table for the supper might be covered with a gold cloth, the other table—which must act as a side-table—with some duller cloth. It is well to have no properties except the absolutely essential ones, but to have all these individual and beautiful. One gold fruit-stand piled with highly-coloured fruit, some beautiful drinking-glasses, a coloured jug for wine will give an impression that a rich banquet is being prepared—an impression that fifty ill-assorted properties would never give.　　LENNOX ROBINSON.

The success of this translation owed much to Mr. Barry Fitzgerald's delicate and whimsical art, and to Miss Maureen Delany's delightful impersonation of Madame Jordain. Having seen it played many years ago (with Coquelin in the name part) with all the advantages of a large stage and a rich theatre, I had hesitated in suggesting it for the Abbey. But the skill of the producer overcame difficulties, and no change of scene was necessary or desired.

My decision that these three plays—or two, with one translation—must be my last has been made without advice save from the almanac, and rather from pride than modesty—for I do not think I have yet become, and would not willingly become, the counterpart of:—

> "some poor guest
> Who may not rudely be dismissed
> But has outstayed his welcome while
> And brings the jest without the smile!"

A. GREGORY.

Coole,
     March 1, 1928.

Mirandolina (Goldoni)

I translated Goldoni's *La Locandiera*, calling it *Mirandolina*, dolina, for the Abbey Theatre, thinking it in key with our country comedies, and it was first produced there in February, 1910. When we were putting it on again I left out two characters, the actresses, as I found the scenes into which they come delayed the action and were not needed. And I gave the whole play at that time an Irish setting, so getting a greater ease in the speaking and in the acting. And even now that it is back again in Italy, the dialogue is in places less bound to the word than to the spirit of the play.

Many years ago I had the joy of seeing Duse in the ironing scene; and the lovely movements of her hands and the beauty of the voice that called "Fabrizio!" are still clear in my memory.

A.G.

Sancho's Master (Cervantes)

For many years, I think ever since I began playwriting, I have had a desire to write one on Cervantes' great theme. Once, in *The Gold Apple* I tried to lay its ghost in the Prince seeking a fabulous cure outside the bounds of nature, and his servant groaning and grunting after him, encumbered by reason and bodily fear. But the desire was not altogether quenched, and at last the play has had to be made nearer to Cervantes' written word.

Quixote's story belongs to the world, and some of us have whispered his name, fitting it to one or another dreamer who seeks to realise the perfect in a community not ready for the Millenium, and where he is likely to meet with anger that strikes or ridicule that scorches, or to have the word flung at him that was flung by Festus at St. Paul.

In Lady Gregory's own copy she has written out a variant second paragraph.

Quixote tells his own story though each of us may cherish a newer name in our mind when his is spoken. For the world is not yet free of the dreamer seeking to realise the perfect in a community not ready for its Millenium, and where he may meet with anger or the ridicule that scorches or have the name thrown at him that Festus flung at St. Paul.

Note on the Production of Sancho's Master.

The first act of this play should be severe in tone, the scene is the room of an ascetic. In the Abbey Theatre production the walls were a dull red arras, the furniture a long blue table and two blue chairs, the decoration a pair of crossed swords and two heroic portraits. A window, a book-case, a hanging map (or almanack) and a chest are essential. In the second act it will be right to consider the well as the only essential thing, and to convey the idea of the wood as best one can with curtains or set pieces—it all depends on the size of the stage and the size of the producer's purse. The third act should be in strong contrast to the simplicity of Don Quixote's room in the first act. At the Abbey Theatre we used hangings with figures painted in dull colours and a coloured floor-cloth, but something more gorgeous might be used so long as it does not take away from the colour of the bright dresses of the Duchess and her ladies. The only furniture necessary in the first scene of this act is a couch. At the end of this scene the curtain falls for a moment, and when it rises the Duke and Duchess, the Duennas and Carasco are seen re-arranging the room to represent the Island of Barataria—placing a table and chair for Sancho's dinner, and fitting on their disguises. In plays like this and in "The Would-Be Gentleman" it seems a safe rule to have nothing on the stage which is not essential to the action of the play—the well, the table, the chairs; and no ornament which does not comment on the play—the crossed swords, the portraits. And certainly, the less ornament the better.

LENNOX ROBINSON.

The Unicorn from the Stars

I wrote in 1902, with the help of Lady Gregory and another friend, a play called *Where There Is Nothing*, but had to write at great speed to meet a sudden emergency. Five acts had to be finished in, I think, a fortnight, instead of the five years that would have been somewhat nearer my natural pace. It became hateful to me because, in desperation, I had caught up from a near table a pamphlet of Tolstoy's on the Sermon on the Mount, and made out of it a satirical scene that became the pivot of the play. The scene seemed amusing on the stage, but its crude speculative commonplaces filled me with shame and I withdrew the play from circulation. That I might free myself from what seemed a contamination, I asked Lady Gregory to help me turn my old plot into *The Unicorn from the Stars*. I began to dictate, but since I had last worked with her, her mastery of the stage and her knowledge of dialect had so increased that my imagination could not go neck to neck with hers. I found myself, too, stopped by an old difficulty, that my words never flow freely but when people speak in verse; and so after an attempt to work alone I gave up my scheme to her. The result is a play almost wholly hers in handiwork, which is so much mine in thought that she does not wish to include it in her own works. I can indeed read it after the stories of *The Secret Rose* and recognize thoughts, points of view, and artistic aims which seem a part of my world. Her greatest difficulty was that I had given her in my reshaping of the plot—swept as I hoped of dogmatism and rhetorical arrogance—for chief character, a man so plunged in trance that he could not be otherwise than all but still and silent, though perhaps with the stillness and silence of a lamp; and the movement of the play as a whole, if we were to listen, if we were to understand what he said, had to be without hurry or violence. The strange characters, her handiwork, on whom he sheds his light, delight me. She has enabled me to carry out an old thought for which my own knowledge is insufficient, and to commingle the ancient phantasies of poetry with the rough, vivid, ever-contemporaneous tumult of the roadside; to share in the creation of a form that otherwise I could but dream of, though I do that always, an art that murmured, though with worn and failing voice, of the day when Quixote and Sancho Panza, long estranged, may once again go out gaily into the bleak air. Ever since I began to write I have awaited with impatience a linking all Europe over of the hereditary knowledge of the countryside, now becoming known to us through the work of wanderers and men of learning, with our old lyricism so full of ancient frenzies and hereditary wisdom; a yoking of antiquities; a Marriage of Heaven and Hell.

W. B. YEATS.

CASTS OF THE ABBEY THEATRE
FIRST PERFORMANCES

CASTS OF THE ABBEY THEATRE
FIRST PERFORMANCES

The following plays in this Volume have been performed at the Abbey Theatre and the casts and the date of the first productions are given below:
Translations and Adaptations

16th April 1906
The Doctor in Spite of Himself—Molière

Sganarelle	W. G. Fay
Martha, his wife	Sara Allgood
Robert, his neighbour	Arthur Sinclair
Valere, servant of Geronte	A. Power
Luke, the same	U. Wright
Geronte, father of Lucy	F. J. Fay
Jacqueline, nurse at Geronte's and wife of Luke	Maire O'Neill
Lucy, daughter of Geronte . . .	Brigit O'Dempsey
Leeane, Lucy's lover	Arthur Sinclair

4th April 1908
The Rogueries of Scapin—Molière

Argante, father of Octave and Zerbinette .	Sydney Morgan
Geronte, father of Leandre and Hyacinthe .	J. A. O'Rourke
Octave, in love with Hyacinthe . . .	Fred O'Donovan
Leandre, in love with Zerbinette . . .	J. M. Kerrigan
Zerbinette	Maire O'Neill
Hyacinthe	Maire Ni Gharbhaigh
Scapin, valet of Leandre	Ambrose Power
Nerine, nurse of Hyacinthe . . .	Eileen O'Doherty
Carle	Stuart Hamilton
Two Porters	T. J. Fox, D. Robinson

CASTS OF FIRST PERFORMANCES

CHARACTERS

The Miser—Molière

Harpagon, father to Cleante, in love with Marianne	Arthur Sinclair
Cleane, Harpagon's son, lover to Marianne	Fred O'Donovan
Valere, son to Anselme and lover to Elise	J. M. Kerrigan
Anselme, father to Valere and Marianne	U. Wright
Master Simon, broker	S. J. Morgan
Master Jacques, cook and coachman to Harpagon	J. A. O'Rourke
La Fleche, valet to Cleante	Eric Gorman
Lackeys to Harpagon:	
Brindavoine	U. Wright
La Merluche	Richard Boyd
Commissionaire	S. J. Morgan
Clerk	F. J. Harford
Elise, daughter to Harpagon	Eileen O'Doherty
Marianne, daughter to Anselme	Maire O'Neill
Frosine, an intriguing woman	Sara Allgood

4th January 1926

The Would-Be Gentleman—Molière

Mr. Jordain	Barry Fitzgerald
Mrs. Jordain	Maureen Delany
Lucile, their daughter	Shelah Richards
Nicola, a maidservant	Eileen Crowe
Cleonte, in love with Lucile	Arthur Shields
Coviel, servant to Cleonte	Tony Quinn
Dorante, a Count	Michael J. Dolan
Dorimene, a Marchioness	May Craig
Music Master	P. J. Carolan
Dancing Master	M. J. Scott
Fencing Master	John S. Breen
Philosophy Master	F. J. McCormick
Master-Tailor	Gabriel J. Fallon
Journeyman Tailor	G. M. Hayes
Footmen	Tom Moran, J. Finn
Musicians	
	J. Stephenson, Walter Dillon, G. Green
Dancers	
	P. Martin, J. Sumington, F. Hodgkinson

368

CASTS OF FIRST PERFORMANCES

19th March 1908
Teja—H. Sudermann

Teja	. J. M. Kerrigan
Balthilda .	. Maire O'Neill
Amalaberga	. Sara Allgood
Bishop Agila	. Arthur Sinclair
Great Men of the old Gothic Kingdom:	
Theodemir	Sydney Morgan
Eurich	. U. Wright
Two Councillors	T. J. Fox, D. Robinson
Haribalt, a watchman	. J. A. O'Rourke
Ildebad, King's spear-bearer	Fred O'Donovan
Two Guards	A. Power, S. Hamilton

24th February 1910
Mirandolina (La Locandiera)—Goldoni

Captain Ripafratta	Fred O'Donovan
Marquis of Forlipopli	. Arthur Sinclair
Count of Albafiorita .	. J. M. Kerrigan
Mirandolina, an innkeeper .	Maire O'Neill
Strolling players:	
Ortensia	Eileen O'Doherty
Dejanira	. Eithne Magee
Cabrizio, servant at the inn	. J. A. O'Rourke
The Captain's Servant	Sydney J. Morgan

3rd April 1907
The Poorhouse
(with Douglas Hyde)

Colum	. W. G. Fay
Paudeen .	. Arthur Sinclair
The Matron	. Maire O'Neill
A Country Woman	Brigit O'Dempsey

369

21st November 1907

(with W. B. Yeats)

The Unicorn from the Stars

Father John	. . . . .	Ernest Vaughan
Thomas Hearne	. . . .	. Arthur Sinclair
Andrew Hearne	. . . .	. J. A. O'Rourke
Martin Hearne .	. . . .	. F. J. Fay
Johnny Bacach .	. . . .	. W. G. Fay
Paudeen .	. . . . .	. J. M. Kerrigan
Biddy Lally	. . . . .	. Maire O'Neill
Nanny .	. . . . .	Brigit O'Dempsey

Appendix

HEADS OR HARPS

A Comedy

PERSONS:
MR. HOWARD PATTERSON. *A barrister*
MRS. HOWARD PATTERSON.
MATTHEW DALY. *Mrs. Patterson's nephew*
DR. MEADOWS. *Professor of Moral Philosophy in Trinity*

SCENE: *A dining room in Merrion Square, with place for one laid, cold meat, decanter of sherry etc. A writing table at one side.*

MR. PATTERSON (*taking off his gloves and neckhandkerchief*). Has anyone arrived?

MRS. PATTERSON. No one, I didn't know you were expecting anybody. Won't you have some lunch, I have kept some for you.

MR. PATTERSON. No, I have had lunch. (*Sits down beside her.*) Well, Louisa, the Professor was right, everything is going well. How will you like appearing at the next drawingroom as the Solicitor General's wife?

MRS. PATTERSON. I hope the good luck is really coming, and that there is no mistake about it?

MR. PATTERSON. O yes. I mustn't tell you the particulars of all the Chancellor said but it's all right.

MRS. PATTERSON. How astonished my people at Essronan will be when they hear of this! They never expected to see me so far above them!

MR. PATTERSON (*taking her hand*). I am more glad for your sake and the children's than my own. If we have worked hard they will have the best of everything, and be able to take life easy. (*The bell rings.*) There is the door bell. He is later than I thought.

MRS. PATTERSON. Who are you expecting?

MR. PATTERSON. Would it surprise you to know that I have engaged a private secretary?

MRS. PATTERSON. A private secretary! Like the Lord Lieutenant has?

MR. PATTERSON. Well, he is not exactly like the Lord Lieutenant's secretaries.

MRS. PATTERSON. I am glad of that. There was one of them sat beside me last time we dined at the Castle, and he gave me the fidgets, looking so wise and important, and never answering the least little question without looking as if you had been setting traps for him. He put on his glasses to listen whenever I spoke, till I began to crumble my bread. I wouldn't like a secretary of that sort in the house.

MR. PATTERSON. It was the Professor who recommended me to take the secretary I have chosen.

MRS. PATTERSON. Then I am sure I shall be afraid of him. Professor Meadows is so particular, he is sure to have recommended some young man from England that will be always spick and span and open the door when I go in or out of the room and make me feel like a visitor in my own house. I have no fancy for those pompous young men.

MR. PATTERSON (*rising*). James is taking him to the drawing room. I will bring him in here. (*Goes out.*)

MRS. PATTERSON. Don't bring him in here Howard till the lunch has been cleared from the table. Let him go to the drawing room . . .

(MR. PATTERSON *comes in bringing a rough haired badly dressed awkward young man by the arm.*)

MR. PATTERSON. Here he is!

MRS. PATTERSON. O, that is only my nephew Matthew Daly. I thought it was the new secretary.

MR. PATTERSON. So it is. This is my new secretary.

MRS. PATTERSON. My nephew Matthew your Secretary!

MR. PATTERSON. Well, I thought it would be a pleasant surprise for you; you have often asked me to do something for your family. But you don't seem altogether pleased.

MR. PATTERSON. O yes, I am pleased.—But what a mess he'll make of it!

MATTHEW. That is what I think myself, aunt.

MR. PATTERSON. Well, my boy, when I described you to Professor Meadows he said you were the very man to be of use to me just now.

MATTHEW. I'm afraid I'm late in coming. I missed the first train. It was an early start; there's no one gets up very early in our house.

Mr. Patterson. You must get into punctual habits here or you won't do much good.

Matthew. It was just as well. The guard of the next train was a friend of my own and he let me pass without a ticket as far as the junction.

Mr. Patterson. That was not honest. That was cheating the company.

Matthew. We don't think much of that in our place. The company can afford it.

Mrs. Patterson. When you know your uncle better Matthew you will know he is very particular about little things of that sort.

The middle section of this other version is missing and all that remains is the following.

. . . to the country. Be a good boy now and think better of it. They will think very little of my relations if you throw away the first chance you have had.

Matthew. There's no use arguing. You call things by one name, and I call them by another. I see things from Essronan Cross, and you see them from Fitzwilliam Square. I can't stand my uncle behaving like this. And as to what the professor says about convictions——

Mrs. Patterson. You mustn't take too seriously what the professor said. He only means by convictions those sentimental ideas that you political young men get into your heads, and that will never help you on in life. He is a very good man, and has great influence in the College. All the young men he has had under him do well for themselves; you would hardly know they had been brought up in Ireland at all. I wish you had had a chance of going into the College and attending his lectures; you would feel quite differently if you had done that.

Matthew (*rising impatiently*). I will go back to my own place.

Mrs. Patterson. I will be ashamed of you, if you go back to that dirty shabby little town. The people there are no fit companions for you. I know them well, beggars and schemers, and corner boys and idlers and men that will cheat in a fair and men that know the inside of a gaol and that deserve to know it. . .

Matthew. Whatever they may be, I swear to God whatever they are, there is not one of them would betray Ireland the way those two men are doing it this minute.

Mrs. Patterson. You shouldn't use such words. You will feel

375

quite differently tomorrow. I wish you had had time to eat some lunch.

MATTHEW. I can't stand this place. (*He goes to the door and turns round.*) I can't stand this place. (*louder.*) I can't stand this place!

MR. PATTERSON (*looking up from the letter he and the PROFESSOR have been absorbed in*). What is the matter?

MATTHEW. I won't stop here after what you have done.

MR. PATTERSON. Why, what have we done?

MATTHEW. You took the side of the country for money and you are going to leave it again for money. What hope is there for a country where it is the educated men that sell their convictions for money and are not thought the worse of for doing it. (*He goes out.*)

MR. PATTERSON. What have you been saying to him Louisa?

MRS. PATTERSON. I don't know. Nothing out of the common.

PROFESSOR (*who has been holding the decanter up to the light*). There has been nothing taken out of the decanter. I never thought a man would talk that way unless he was drunk.

BRAT.